MAY 17 2016

P9-DEI-952

East Meadow Public Library
1866 Front Street, East Meadow, NY 11554
(516) 794-2570
www.eastmeadow.info

REVOLUTIONARY
DISSENT

REVOLUTIONARY
DISSENT

HOW THE FOUNDING GENERATION
CREATED THE FREEDOM OF SPEECH

STEPHEN D. SOLOMON

St. Martin's Press
New York

REVOLUTIONARY DISSENT. Copyright © 2016 by Stephen D. Solomon. All rights reserved. Printed in the United States of America. For information, address St. Martin's Press, 175 Fifth Avenue, New York, N.Y. 10010.

www.stmartins.com

Design by Letra Libre, Inc.

Library of Congress Cataloging-in-Publication Data

Names: Solomon, Stephen D., author.
Title: Revolutionary dissent : how the founding generation created the freedom of speech / Stephen D. Solomon.
Description: New York City : St. Martin's Press, 2016.
Identifiers: LCCN 2015033954 I ISBN 9780230342064 (hardback) I ISBN 9781466879393 (e-book)
Subjects: LCSH: Freedom of speech—United States—History—18th century. I United States—History—18th century—Biography. I BISAC: HISTORY / United States / Revolutionary Period (1775–1800). I POLITICAL SCIENCE / Constitutions.
Classification: LCC KF4770 .S735 2016 I DDC 342.7308/53—dc23
LC record available at http://lccn.loc.gov/2015033954

Our books may be purchased in bulk for promotional, educational, or business use. Please contact your local bookseller or the Macmillan Corporate and Premium Sales Department at 1-800-221–7945, extension 5442, or by e-mail at MacmillanSpecialMarkets@macmillan.com.

First Edition: April 2016

10 9 8 7 6 5 4 3 2 1

To Debbi Dunn Solomon,
Brian Solomon, and Sarah Solomon

CONTENTS

Eight pages of illustrations appear between pages 180 and 181.

ACKNOWLEDGMENTS

ONLY THE AUTHOR'S NAME IS ON THE COVER, BUT MANY PEOPLE SHARE THE CREDIT FOR bringing such a large project to fruition. I have many to thank.

I am tremendously grateful to New York University for its continuing encouragement of scholarly work. The university provided me with a semester sabbatical and research support during the four years it took to bring the book from idea to completion. My colleagues, especially Perri Klass, Adam Penenberg, and Mitchell Stephens, provided constant encouragement and were understanding when my mind dwelled for too long in the eighteenth century. Several student research assistants deserve my thanks. Hannah Hendler, Brian Bouton, Margaret Flavell, Rianne MacInnes, and Anna Lee helped me find information and documents that were important to my historical narratives. I appreciate all their efforts.

I am deeply indebted to several prominent scholars who provided invaluable help on this project. Ronald K.L. Collins, the Harold S. Shefelman Scholar at the University of Washington School of Law, read the proposal for the book and offered many helpful suggestions for avenues of inquiry. Once I had completed the writing, John P. Kaminski, director of the Center for the Study of the American Constitution at the University of Wisconsin and coeditor of the multi-volume *The Documentary History of the Ratification of the Constitution,* meticulously read the manuscript and marked it up with thought-provoking comments and questions. Robert M. O'Neil, emeritus professor of law at the University of Virginia School of Law and former director of the Thomas Jefferson Center for the Protection of Free Expression, also read the manuscript and, among other things, provided important observations about Jefferson's involvement in the controversy over freedom of the press. Thomas

Healy, professor of law at Seton Hall Law School and author of *The Great Dissent: How Oliver Wendell Holmes Changed His Mind—and Changed the History of Free Speech in America*, read the final two chapters and provided many helpful comments about ratification and the Sedition Act controversy.

No matter how excited a writer is about his idea for a book, nothing will happen unless a small group of people believes in it. This book would have never achieved liftoff without a few people who saw merit in my ideas and provided critical help at the outset. My special thanks go to Katherine Flynn and John Taylor "Ike" Williams, my literary agents at Kneerim & Williams. They helped shape my book proposal and then guided me with good counsel and good humor. I am very appreciative to Karen Wolny, executive editor at St. Martin's Press, who saw the potential in my project and acquired it for her list. She provided the critical editorial support and guidance to make the book a reality.

Once the manuscript was in hand, a talented production team at St. Martin's Press went to work. Thanks go to Laura Apperson for all her behind-the-scenes work, and to Donna Cherry, senior production editor, whose diligence kept the book moving smoothly through the many steps to publication. My thanks go as well to Bill Warhop, who performed his copyediting magic on my prose, Polly Kummel for her excellent proofreading, and to David Baldeosingh Rotstein, who designed a striking cover for the book. And I appreciate Christopher Cecot's work in compiling an index that makes the book easy to navigate. I am grateful to Gabrielle Gantz, associate director of publicity, and Alastair Hayes, marketing manager, for their expertise in gaining a wider audience for my work.

My research for *Revolutionary Dissent* rested largely on primary source materials. Fortunately, many of the central characters in my narratives left behind extensive writings that have been collected in books, archives, and databases. I benefitted from the extraordinary work of editors and librarians who have compiled these materials over the years into useful forms. The Massachusetts Historical Society offers an extraordinary archive of founding era material, especially on John Adams and the protests against the British. I also benefitted from collections at the New York Historical Society, the Library of Congress, the University of Wisconsin, the University of Virginia, and many other institutions.

NYU's Bobst Library was a kind of second home for me. It provided many books and collections that proved indispensable to my work, including an electronic file of eighteenth-century American newspapers. Two NYU librarians, Katy Boss and Alexa Pearce, were my expert guides through the research material. They quickly tracked down books and articles that I couldn't find myself and offered valuable advice along the way. I'm very grateful for their patient help.

I save my greatest expression of gratitude for my family—Debbi Dunn Solomon, Brian Solomon, and Sarah Solomon. They listened as I recounted stories of free speech conflicts from centuries ago, visited historical sites with me, and read and commented on some of the chapters. Most of all, they provided unwavering support and encouragement every day.

PROLOGUE

THE CHIEF JUSTICE

THOMAS HUTCHINSON THOUGHT HE HAD SUFFERED CRITICISM LONG ENOUGH. SO IN AUGUST 1767 he convened a grand jury to strike back at his critics. As lieutenant governor and chief justice of Massachusetts, Hutchinson was the second most powerful official in the colony, behind only the royal governor, Francis Bernard.

For several years, both Hutchinson and Bernard had been the targets of harsh attacks growing out of the imposition of the stamp tax that had instigated strong protests in Boston. The center of opposition was the radical *Boston Gazette*, whose publishers, Benjamin Edes and John Gill, were themselves partisans who worked closely with the opposition movement. Off their press came an unending salvo of protests—in the form of letters, articles, broadsides, and pamphlets—that attacked Bernard and Hutchinson as well as officials in London. Now the two top officials of the colony wanted some revenge to salve their wounds.

Delivering his charge to the grand jurors, Hutchinson asked them to punish Edes and Gill for their criticisms. He and others had been "treated in the most abusive Manner, and vilified beyond all Bounds," he told them.[1] Under the law of seditious libel, it was a crime to criticize the government, its policies, or officials, and thereby reduce the public esteem in which they were held. Conviction on such charges could send Edes and

Gill to a miserable jail cell for a long time. Hutchinson implored the grand jurors to act. He enjoyed what appeared to be, at least by the common meaning of the law, a surefire case against Edes and Gill.

So it was to Hutchinson's surprise that the grand jurors did not agree to his demand for an indictment. But he did not give up. The chief justice tried twice more over the next few years and failed each time.[2] (See chapter 3 for more about Hutchinson.) Now Governor Bernard himself moved to punish his critics. He went to the popular assembly with his complaint. But the lawmakers turned him away, instead approving a statement on press freedom. "The Liberty of the Press," they said, "is a great Bulwark of the Liberty of the People: It is, therefore, the incumbent Duty of those who are constituted the Guardians of the People's Rights to defend them and maintain it."[3]

Americans today would certainly agree that a free press is essential to liberty. Authoritarian regimes know that the first strategy for maintaining their power is muzzling the press and stopping the free exchange of ideas. As Americans look at the world today, they would no doubt find it hard to comprehend that the law of the colonies during the founding period made it a criminal offense for a citizen to write an article critical of government officials. Americans of the twenty-first century enjoy the right to engage in robust debate about public affairs. Every day without fail, they offer endless commentary about their elected officials and the policies they pursue, and much of the conversation is scathing. The public sphere has grown decidedly democratic. The growth of electronic media has provided everyone who has access to the Internet a platform to say what he or she pleases.

How did it happen that America moved from oppression to liberty? From a reign of royal officials asking colonial juries for indictments against their critics to a time of robust expression? That is the story I tell in *Revolutionary Dissent.* I do so not by recounting Supreme Court decisions of the modern era that expanded the right to free expression, but instead by telling stories of how the founding generation itself rebelled against the tyranny of laws punishing political dissent. The broad freedom of expression and vigorous political culture enjoyed by contemporary Americans was actually born in this country centuries ago. It began haltingly in 1687 with the tax protest of the Puritan preacher John Wise. It continued with the dissent against British taxes that started in 1765 and reached its culmination during ratification of the Constitution in the late 1780s and finally in the battles over the Sedition Act in 1800. By discovering the stories of citizens who rose in protest during that period, all the while rejecting the repressive laws designed to silence them, we can comprehend what the founding generation understood by the freedom of speech and press. Some of those citizens, like Paul Revere and James Madison and Patrick Henry, are iconic figures in American history. But many others are barely known, if at all—the minister Wise, the shoemaker Ebenezer McIntosh, the privateer and merchant Alexander McDougall, the "farmer" John Dickinson, the editors Edes and Gill, the lawyer Andrew Hamilton, and others. All of them helped to create the American concept of freedom of expression.

Before they broke from Britain, the founding generation rebelled against the imposition of taxes and standing armies in their cities, but to do so they had to rebel also against prohibitions on political dissent that were a central part of English law. Restrictions on political expression reached far back into English history, and they provided officials several ways to punish critics. Through an elaborate licensing system, the Crown for many years after invention of the Gutenberg press enjoyed the right to censor any written work and thereby prevent publication of dissent altogether. Royal agents read manuscripts, deleted portions they found offensive to the government or religion, and decided whether to issue a license to allow publication. The licensing system finally expired in 1695, freeing writers to publish their work.[4]

Though certainly welcomed, the demise of licensing still left dissenters at great risk. For the government had another weapon to control opposition speech—they could bring a criminal action for seditious libel. Parliament had made it a crime in 1275 to disseminate "any slanderous News . . . or *false* News or Tales where by discord or occasion of discord or slander may grow between the King and his people or the other great men of the Realm."[5] This crime of seditious libel made it illegal to criticize government officials or their actions, as such speech might cause a disturbance in the future. When Sir William Blackstone published his first volume of the *Commentaries on the Laws of England* in 1765, he endorsed the idea that freedom of the press meant nothing more than the right of printers to publish without prior censorship. Freedom of the press, he said, "consists in laying no *previous* restraints upon publications, and not in freedom from censure for criminal matter when published."[6]

Seditious libel came ashore in America as part of the common law adopted by the colonies. And it existed throughout the founding period as a sword poised to strike critics of the government. Hutchinson and Bernard were not the only officials to try to use the law against their enemies. Surely, then, you might think, ratification of the First Amendment in 1791 brought a swift end to this oppression, a clear rejection of speech crimes that were antithetical to its broad promise of political liberty. But history, unfortunately, is not so clear. The First Amendment, after all, contained no mention of seditious libel in its fourteen words pertaining to freedom of expression—"Congress shall make no law . . . abridging the freedom of speech or of the press"—and the drafters and ratifiers reached no consensus on its meaning. Indeed, Congress passed the Sedition Act of 1798, and the Adams administration began prosecutions that eventually landed many of its critics in jail.

Seditious libel was not eliminated easily from American law. Even in 1907, Justice Oliver Wendell Holmes wrote that the First Amendment meant nothing more than the old constrained English view expressed by Blackstone.[7] In fact, the Supreme Court did not regularly use the First Amendment to strike down state or federal laws punishing speech until well into the twentieth century, when it began to strengthen safeguards on expression.

So what did the founding generation understand to be the protections afforded by the First Amendment? Could critics of government be prosecuted and sent to jail? These questions dig deeply to the very essence of American democracy. For many years, the most prominent commentators on the freedom of expression argued that the founding generation had intended to end the harsh reign of seditious libel. By breaking away from England and creating a self-governing democracy, they had severed ties to a legal regime that punished criticism of the government. Henry Schofield, a prominent law professor at Northwestern University, concluded in an influential essay in 1914 that independence settled the question. "One of the objects of the Revolution was to get rid of the English common law on liberty of speech and of the press," he wrote.[8] And Zechariah Chafee, a Harvard Law professor, wrote a few years later that the framers of the First Amendment had "intended to wipe out the common law of sedition, and make further prosecutions for criticism of government, without any incitement to law-breaking, forever impossible in the United States of America."[9]

The Schofield-Chafee view of the demise of seditious libel dominated debate until 1960, when First Amendment historian Leonard Levy created a fault line that shook the ground under the fundamental understanding of freedom of expression. Levy challenged the prevailing view that the founding generation intended to jettison the repressive legacy of seditious libel and write into the First Amendment a broad new protection for political dissent. He wrote that "the generation which adopted the Constitution and the Bill of Rights did not believe in a broad scope for freedom of expression particularly in the realm of politics," adding: "They did not intend to give free rein to criticism of the government that might be deemed seditious libel."[10] In fact, he said, "speech and press were not free anywhere during the Revolution." During the entire colonial period up until the Bill of Rights, the people "had very little experience with freedom of speech or press as a meaningful condition of life."[11]

Levy argued that in guaranteeing the right of freedom of speech and press, the framers meant to leave intact the understanding of press freedom that existed under English common law—as Blackstone put it, merely the freedom from previous restraints on publication and nothing more. In coming to that conclusion, Levy focused on the law and theory that existed through the period. The legal structure permitted prosecution for criticism of government, and libertarian ideas to challenge these prosecutions were lacking. He examined the articles, essays, and pamphlets of the founding period and concluded that the framers had not renounced seditious libel despite numerous opportunities to do so, and for the most part they had passively accepted Blackstone's concept of press freedom. Justice Hugo Black, who was one of the strongest advocates of freedom of speech and press ever to serve on the High Court, wrote that Levy's conclusion "is probably one of the most devastating blows that has been delivered against civil liberty in America for a long time."[12]

Levy used a version of constitutional interpretation called original understanding. Championed later by Justice Antonin Scalia and others, original understanding tries to find meaning in constitutional provisions by asking what the framers and ratifiers understood them to mean when they debated the Constitution and the Bill of Rights. More broadly, it goes beyond the framers and ratifiers to ask what the reasonable public meaning was during the ratification era, or as Justice Scalia has put it, "In their full context, words mean what they conveyed to reasonable people at the time they were written."[13]

Levy's approach to originalism was unduly confining, though. He had based his conclusions on law and theory, and had not considered a broader conception of originalism, one that looked at the founding generation's daily experience with a press that was in fact free in practice. Other scholars attacked Levy's view, pointing out that newspapers—from the time of the Stamp Act protests in 1765 through the ratification of the Constitution in 1788 and the first ten amendments in 1791—had engaged in sharp and vigorous attacks against government officials on both sides of the ocean. Newspaper editors acted as if the law punishing dissent did not exist. Merrill Jensen, a leading historian of the Constitution, argued that Levy was correct about the existence of repressive law but accused him of ignoring the way newspapers actually practiced journalism. "Despite the law," he wrote, "there was freedom of expression in fact. No governmental institution, political faction, or individual was free from attacks such as few newspapers today would dare to print." Philadelphia papers, he said, published "some of the bitterest, most dishonest (and seditious) writing in American political history."[14]

The outpouring of criticism convinced Levy to read deeply into the newspapers of the founding period. When he revised his book in 1985, now calling it *Emergence of a Free Press*, he acknowledged that the newspapers "operated as if the law of seditious libel did not exist." Newspaper articles during the Revolution and afterward "raged as contemptuously and scorchingly" against the government and public officials as they had during the decade before the War of Independence, contributing to an expanded conception of the value of free expression.[15] Even so, Levy held to his claim that American libertarian theory on freedom of the press had advanced very little by the time of ratification of the First Amendment. And he held to his thesis that the Revolution and the First Amendment were not meant to wipe out seditious libel. Given that, he wondered at the vigor of the press. "That so many courageous and irresponsible editors daily risked imprisonment amazes me," he wrote.[16]

Far from being just a squabble among academics, the actions of the founding generation resonate deeply with Americans. What that generation wrote and thought during the critical period around independence helps illuminate the fundamental principles on which the new nation was born. The thoughts of the founders are important, too, because centuries later they are one of the tools used to help Americans understand the scope of the freedoms they inherited. They go a long way in assisting the US Supreme Court in interpreting the meaning of individual rights and liberties.

The Supreme Court has used various arguments to support strong First Amendment protections for speech and press. The Court's most powerful rationale recognizes that freedom of expression supports the republican form of American government. In a constitutional system where sovereign power resides in the people, freedom of expression enables citizens to fully and freely criticize officials and discuss public policy. And with a robust marketplace of ideas, the best ideas are more likely to surface. Freedom of speech and press, then, is indispensable to self-governance.

To discover the meaning of the First Amendment, the Court has also looked at America's free press experience during the founding period. In 1938, for example, the justices protected distribution of pamphlets on public streets in part by recalling the critical importance of pamphlets in the years leading up to independence—they "indeed have been historic weapons in the defense of liberty, as the pamphlets of Thomas Paine and others in our own history abundantly attest," the Court said.[17] The Court struck down prohibitions on the distribution of handbills without an author's name by citing the long history of anonymous pamphlets and broadsides—"patriots frequently had to conceal their authorship or distribution of literature that easily could have brought down on them prosecutions by English-controlled courts," the justices said.[18] The Court ruled that the press and the public enjoyed a right under the First Amendment to attend criminal trials, returning to the founding period and reasoning that an open trial "has long been recognized as an indispensable attribute of an Anglo-American trial" and that "attendance at court was a common mode of 'passing the time.'"[19] In his concurrence in another case, Justice Lewis Brandeis wrote of "those who won our independence" as believing that "public discussion is a political duty; and that this should be a fundamental principle of American government." They were committed to "the opportunity to discuss freely supposed grievances and proposed remedies."[20]

The founding period, in fact, provides rich evidence of how that generation viewed the freedom to speak and write. The evidence from colonial newspapers is powerful, but political discussion went on in many other ways as well. In *Revolutionary Dissent* I explore the outpouring of political expression that went far beyond newspapers, for it's clear that the founding generation understood their freedom to criticize on much broader grounds. The public sphere of expression expanded dramatically as the dispute with England widened in the decade before independence, with citizens airing their views in countless venues and by a multitude of means.

The stories I tell here portray Americans utilizing every form of expression imaginable to deliver their ideas and arguments. They created songs, essays, letters, cartoons, broadsides, woodcuts, appeals, petitions, resolutions, puns, poems, plays, paintings, and pamphlets. They belittled their foes with parody and satire and launched diatribes, harangues, and accusations against them. They anointed dissenters who had been jailed for their writings as martyrs to liberty. Their ministers thundered from the pulpit with political prayers and sermons. They employed powerful symbols of freedom, dedicating liberty trees and liberty poles and hanging effigies of public officials they despised. They lifted toasts, raised a chorus of huzzahs, and fired off cannon.

They also thought that they had the right to assemble with each other, for they met in taverns and coffeehouses to read newspapers and argue over the issues of the day. Outside, they paraded in the streets and parks, using pageantry and political theater to attract attention. They debated in their legislatures and town meetings while citizens filled the public galleries to watch and comment. And, again and again, they took their protests to the next step. They wrote petitions and resolutions that they submitted to the authorities in London for a redress of their grievances.

For giving meaning to the freedom of expression, no event was more important than ratification of the Constitution. Ratification moved on the tide of the most open and vigorous debate in the nation's history. America was inventing itself, and everyone felt free to voice a strong opinion without fear of punishment. Some foes of ratification even carried their opposition to its logical conclusion—they burned copies of the Constitution at public rallies. They did so with the confidence that their offensive symbolic speech was well within their rights of expression. As legal scholar Akhil Reed Amar has noted, it was significant to the meaning of freedom of expression that "the very act of constitutional ordainment occurred in and through a regime of boisterous, virtually uncensored free speech."[21] And thus a broad conception of freedom of expression was joined to the Constitution itself as an essential element of a self-governing society.

As the public sphere expanded, it became more democratic. Writers of essays and pamphlets initially aimed their works at the most educated and influential people in society—the lawyers, politicians, and merchants—by arguing in dense prose and with references to English constitutional history. Patriot leaders knew, though, that they had to draw citizens of all ranks into the discussion in order for protest to be effective. So they cultivated public opinion to support their demands of relief from officials in London and eventually for independence. The full-throated voice of the people became the foundation of the Constitution's Preamble, which enlisted "We the People" in a new compact of government.

THE EXPANDING PUBLIC SPHERE that I describe in this book leads me to several observations. First, I argue in *Revolutionary Dissent* that the founding generation defined the freedom of speech and press in large part through their rambunctious expression in newspapers and through every other means available to them. They understood freedom of expression to encompass the most vigorous and caustic criticism of public men and public measures. All of their protests against British authority were violations of seditious libel law, but that did not trouble them at all. The law criminalizing dissent was a dead letter. It fit better in a system in which the king and Parliament held sovereignty over the people, their subjects, for under such circumstances criticism of the government could threaten the authority of the state. In America, a different understanding of criticism was necessary. Popular sovereignty gave the people the power to govern themselves, and government officials served as their agents rather than their superiors. Citizens, then, required the freedom to speak freely and passionately on all the issues before them.

The rejection of seditious libel played out with Governor Bernard and Chief Justice Hutchinson in the late 1760s. Again and again they tried to punish Benjamin Edes and John Gill for their articles in the *Boston Gazette*. Again and again the entire community turned them away. Neither of the two royal officials knew quite what to make of it, for the world was changing too quickly around them. Everywhere they turned, they found rejection of the idea that citizens could be punished for criticizing government. Edes and Gill and their writers had rejected it in their continual lambasting of British policy. Grand jurors drawn from the community refused Hutchinson's demand that they indict Edes and Gill, in effect nullifying the law of seditious libel even in the face of obvious violations. And when Bernard took his complaints against Edes and Gill to the elected assembly representing the colony, he got back a resolution supporting freedom of the press. The popular rejection of seditious libel was thus complete.

How the founding generation regarded freedom of expression provides some important evidence for a liberty-enhancing view of freedom of expression. The Supreme Court, for example, has often protected symbolic speech—protest that involves flag burning and the wearing of armbands—under the First Amendment.[22] But a number of influential legal commentators and judges have rejected the conclusion that the First Amendment protects symbolic expression, calling it action and not speech or denying that there exists much if any evidence from the eighteenth century that would provide support based on the original understanding of the founding generation.[23] Given this disagreement, the Court could potentially backslide in protecting symbolic expression in the future. The Court's two major decisions protecting burning of the American flag on free-speech grounds were 5–4 decisions.[24] So in this area, and others, historical evidence from the founding period could solidify the foundation protecting symbolic and other types of expression.

Law professor Eugene Volokh, for one, has argued from historical evidence that symbolic expression should be protected under the First Amendment,[25] and I conclude the same from the history told in this book. If, as Justice Scalia says, "words mean what they conveyed to reasonable people at the time they were written," then it's clear that the founding generation regarded symbolic expression to be the equivalent of spoken or written words. Their dissent against Britain was suffused with symbolic speech that was essential to their effort. Their liberty trees, their liberty poles, their flags and effigies, and even their extensive use of the number 45—referring to the issue number of a London publication targeted for a seditious libel action—signified their resistance to British oppression. As I explain in chapter 4, symbols brimmed with meaning, providing a simple and emotional means to rally people behind the otherwise complex issues that divided America and Britain. Patriot leaders used their powerful symbols to bring out thousands to their rallies. It was the single most potent strategy to enlarge the public sphere of political expression.

The historical evidence leads me to a second observation. To the extent that the founding generation discussed the right to dissent, they focused largely on freedom of the press, a term that included any printed material coming off their presses. They said little in comparison about the separate freedom of speech, which was considered spoken words. Free speech traced its legal roots to the English Bill of Rights of 1689, providing freedom of speech and debate in Parliament without the lawmakers having to answer for it in any court. It might seem obvious to extend the parliamentary privilege of free speech in some form to citizens of a self-governing society, but in colonial America most of the declarations for freedom of thought pertained to the press. Its dominant position in circulating political views made it a target for seditious libel prosecutions. So Americans naturally focused on the press in their early efforts to protect their right to dissent. Nine of the original thirteen states protected freedom of the press in their state constitutions during the American Revolution. Only one protected the freedom of speech.[26] Did this signal that the founders regarded speech and press differently?

The founding generation made no distinction between speech and press in the way they actually engaged in their protests against the British. They used every mode of communication available to them to make their points. One means of protest merged into another. They read newspapers and gathered in taverns to argue about the articles. If they assembled under a liberty tree, they passed around broadsides and listened to speeches. For expression of their political opinions, they had almost too many arrows in their quiver to count, and they shot all of them at what they considered to be their British tormentors. In the day-to-day expression of dissent, it seems they regarded all these means of protest more or less equally. They were, it appears, practical people in this regard.

There is a third and related observation. In the latter part of the twentieth century, the Supreme Court extended the concept of freedom of speech far enough that it moved under a larger umbrella of protection that we often call the freedom of expression. The protections of the First Amendment were extended to include speech that was not spoken words in the strictest sense, and to self-expressive creative works as well.

Here, too, the experience of the founding generation that I describe in *Revolutionary Dissent* suggests that they understood speech to mean more than spoken words. They conveyed their ideas in creative ways, such as songs, plays, and poetry as well. All this expression was put to political purposes, and it expanded the idea of what speech included.

IT IS POSSIBLE, OF COURSE, for a historian to claim too much. One cannot declare with certainty the understandings of people so far in the past. As historian Jack N. Rakove has said, adoption of the Constitution itself "reflected a bewildering array of intentions and expectations, hopes and fears, genuine compromises and agreements to disagree."[27] The fact that the founding generation engaged in widespread symbolic speech, for example, does not necessarily mean that they would have approved of burning the American flag two centuries later as a legitimate form of protest. We have no way of knowing the answer for certain. But we know that the founding generation was aggressive in voicing their opinions, and they burned effigies of the people they despised and even at times copies of the Constitution to show the depth of their opposition to ratification. Others answered them by parading with the Constitution affixed to the top of a long pole—the answer to speech they disliked being more speech and more discussion, not censorship or punishment under the law.

Predictably, the story gets messy at times. The patriots did not always honor freedom of speech for others. Loyalist essays, pamphlets, and letters were vigorous in backing England in the growing dispute with the colonies, and there were instances of threats and actual violence against Loyalist printers. Although these outbursts were exceptions to the rule, the founding generation was inconsistent in other ways, too. Seven years after ratification of the First Amendment, Congress enacted a seditious libel law. It was opposed by, among others, Thomas Jefferson, who later became involved in legal actions against a few of his own critics when he became president. Jefferson may have been hypocritical. But he may also have understood the nature of political power better than most other men. He argued as a libertarian for safeguards that would protect citizens from what he saw as the inevitable lashing out of politicians against their critics—an inevitability that he himself would not escape. In any case, the founding generation displayed their weaknesses and inconsistencies as much as any generation in American history. That is part of our story as well.

OVER TIME, the founding generation developed a spirited culture of political expression, and it informed the meaning of freedom of speech and press that they wrote into the First Amendment. Alexis de Tocqueville observed that serious change starts with ideas and beliefs welling up from the people. As he wrote in another context: "Political societies are not made by their laws, but are prepared in advance by the sentiments, beliefs, ideas, the habits of the hearts and minds of the men who are part of them, and by what nature and education have made those men."[28] John Adams seemed to be in agreement. Looking back on the events of the founding period, he wrote to Thomas Jefferson that the meaning of the Revolution could be found in the vigorous political expression of the times. "What do We Mean by the Revolution?" he asked. "The War? That was no part of the Revolution. It was only an Effect and Consequence of it. The Revolution was in the Minds of the People, and this was effected, from 1760 to 1775, in the course of fifteen Years before a drop of blood was drawn at Lexington. The records of thirteen legislatures, the pamphlets, Newspapers in all the Colonies, ought to be consulted, during that period, to ascertain the Steps by which the public Opinion was enlightened and informed concerning the Authority of Parliament over the Colonies."[29]

For the founding generation, the "habits of heart and mind" involved robust debate expressed in myriad forms and in myriad places. It is that story that I tell in *Revolutionary Dissent*.

NOTE TO READERS

When utilizing quotations from primary sources, I have retained as much as possible the original spelling, punctuation, and italics. While this may occasionally make these quotations a little more difficult to read, I believe the original text helps convey meaning and emphasis. Also, I refer throughout the book to the "founding generation." The first two chapters, however, take place primarily in 1687 and 1735, before the founding generation came on the scene. The seditious libel actions against the Reverend John Wise and printer John Peter Zenger, though, provide important history and context to our understanding of the rejection of seditious libel actions after 1765.

1

THE MINISTER

JOHN WISE ARRIVED IN THE EVENING, ALONG WITH OTHER PROMINENT CITIZENS OF IPSWICH, Massachusetts. The town clerk, John Appleton Jr., had volunteered his house for the crowded meeting, which he knew was best completed before the long light of the summer day ebbed from the room, leaving only oil lamps to break the darkness. A few selectmen were there, as was the lieutenant of the town's militia, several other militia officers, and a couple of church and town officials. It was Wise, however, minister of one of the local Puritan churches, to whom everyone looked for direction. The date was August 22, 1687, and the town, located north of Boston, was gathering its strength to oppose the imposition of taxes by the British royal governor.[1] None of these men, of course, would be alive nearly eight decades later, when the colonies would erupt in protest against another tax, the hated Stamp Act, and start down the road to independence.

As the meeting began, the constable of Ipswich read the tax act and the related instructions. A heated discussion ensued, with Wise denying its legality because Governor Edmund Andros had imposed it unilaterally without action by a general assembly that was representative of the people. The group strongly agreed with Wise that the tax violated their rights as Englishmen, and then planned the town meeting that was to follow.

The citizens of Ipswich gathered on the next day to debate the tax. Although a number of people spoke, once again Wise took the lead. As he later recalled, he argued that the people "had a good God and a good King, and should do well to stand by our privileges."[2] After the citizens agreed to oppose the tax, the town clerk, Appleton, left the meeting and quickly drafted a note setting out the sentiments of the citizens. The new tax law, his draft of the note said, violated their freedom as English subjects by levying taxes without "consent of an assembly chosen by the freeholders." The meeting unanimously approved the defiant message. The town sent the note along to Andros and his General Council. Other communities, including Andover and Haverhill, also refused to cooperate.[3]

A tax revolt was under way.

WISE HAD EMERGED from humble origins. His father had been an indentured servant to a prominent deacon in Puritan society and had been given a heifer when he received his freedom around 1641. He married the same year, and then through a series of jobs made the long climb to respectable society. His son John, born in 1652, the fifth of approximately thirteen children, entered Harvard College at the age of seventeen. Since Harvard had been started some decades earlier with a mission of educating clergy to serve congregations in the colonies, it was not surprising that Wise accepted a ministry at a church in Branford, Connecticut, after his graduation in 1673. Wise was a young man of considerable intellect, but the first thing people noticed about him was his imposing physical presence—tall, broad, and strong. In fact, Wise was reputed to be one of the best wrestlers for hundreds of miles around. Challenged by another man who traveled the twenty miles from Andover for a bout, Wise put him on his back and claimed victory within a few minutes.[4]

Wise looked forward to returning to the Boston area. Residents of the Chebacco section of Ipswich, south of the town center, were weary of traveling the six or seven miles to church in bitter winter weather, so they started a new church and then called on Wise to take the pulpit in 1683.[5] Ipswich was of modest size, with a population of about fourteen hundred people.[6] Like many towns in the colony, it had expansive fields planted with corn, wheat, barley, and hay, and there was a smattering of grist mills and saw mills. But the town hugged the coastline as well, and so some residents put up wharves and others earned a living fishing. The most successful of them built timber-framed clapboard houses with steep hipped or gambrel roofs. Many residents enjoyed properties of at least a few acres and often much more.[7]

As Wise was just establishing his leadership in his new church and community, big changes and even bigger troubles were gathering over the Massachusetts Bay Colony. In London, the Royal Charter that had provided for the political governance of the colony was revoked in 1684. In its place came a new system destined to aggravate citizens who were used to running much of their own affairs.[8]

To centralize control under the Crown, James II established the Dominion of New England in 1686, unifying the Massachusetts Bay Colony with several other New England colonies. The Crown sent Edmund Andros to govern the new dominion, at the same time stripping residents of their right to local representation in an assembly. Instead, the governor would rule along with an appointed council. Andros and the council immediately tried to impose taxes without the consent of a representative body.

Each town had to appoint its own commissioner to assure local compliance with the law. It was the refusal of Ipswich, led by its local minister John Wise, to appoint a commissioner that brought the first serious tax troubles to the colonies.

WISE SURELY KNEW that speaking out against the governor and his council, whether on tax policy or on anything else, was a crime in colonial New England and indeed throughout the colonies. In fact, just nine years before the tax revolt that Wise sparked in Ipswich, a man had been prosecuted in Connecticut for complaining about taxes. After asserting that officials in New London County "sit here to pick men's pockets"—a sentiment shared widely by grudging citizens from the dawn of tax collection—he went before the Connecticut General Court and drew a fine of five pounds for his impertinence.[9] And the Maine Court of Sessions fined another man in 1685 for what the judges regarded as an insolent response to a tax collector who came to his door.[10]

There were no newspapers in Wise's time to publish accounts of trials in Massachusetts and other colonies, but the legal restrictions on speech were clear enough to everyone. The colonies had inherited from England the crime of seditious libel, whose crosshairs brought into easy range any

person who spoke out against the government, any of its officers, or public policy in general. These restrictions came from both English common
law—the accumulation of legal decisions over long periods of time—and
from statutes enacted in the colonies.

One historian who studied colonial court records found 1,244 seditious speech cases before 1700 alone.[11] Seditious speech against high
officials, including governors and magistrates, was illegal across all the
colonies and made up the majority of cases. Maryland, for example,
deemed it a crime to engage in "scandalous or contemptuous words or
writings to the dishonor of the Lord Proprietary or his Lieutenant General
[Governor] for the time being or any of the Council." Pennsylvania made
it a criminal offense for anyone to "speak slightingly or carry themselves
abusively against any magistrate or person in office."[12] Criticism did not
have to be directed against a specific official, though. Many prosecutions
were launched against people who criticized the government generally,
including criticisms of its laws and its courts, rather than an individual.
In Plymouth Colony, for example, a law in 1659 prohibited anyone who
would "speak contemptuously of the laws"—including, presumably,
against that law as well. And the legal code in Rhode Island punished people with fines, whippings, and imprisonment for merely speaking badly of
any acts of the assembly.[13]

In colonial America, the government had several venues for punishing its critics. One, of course, was the court system. But without strict
separation of powers to limit their authority, the other branches of the
government could take action as well. Royal governors and their coun-
cils had quasi-legal powers and could punish dissidents. So, too, could
the provincial assemblies, acting alone or with the executive branch. The
assemblies were the most effective at this task, since they acted directly
themselves without the need for a grand jury or petit jury—and, conveniently, sat in judgment of those who had offended them. With any criticism of an assembly or its members, or any challenge to its authority, the
legislators could summon the speaker or writer before them to answer
for a breach of privilege. They could interrogate and threaten, and finally
bring down the bludgeon of criminal sanctions.[14]

With no regular newspapers published in seventeenth-century America, most seditious libel cases involved spoken rather than printed words.
As a result, prosecutions relied on citizens who complained about words

they had heard almost anywhere—on the streets, in taverns, and other public places. And because no means of recording existed, prosecutions for seditious speech depended on testimony from people relying on recall from fallible memory. Defendants were vulnerable to witnesses who exaggerated either innocently or because they wanted to settle a score. Beyond those problems, libel was such an elastic concept that virtually any kind of complaint of unfairness or incompetence could bring on a prosecution. People risked prosecution when they lost patience and merely belittled an official. In New Hampshire, Seabank Hog was dragged to court for saying that the governor and other officials were "a parcel of pitiful beggarly curs."[15] Whether the governor was a cur was a matter on which reasonable people could disagree. But those who thought it so had to be judicious in sharing their opinion.

Many cases went beyond insults and involved serious disagreement with an official's work. In Virginia in 1653, Abraham Read was so unhappy with the governor that Read said he "would be called home into England and there they would deal well enough with him." That mild criticism cost him a fine of ten thousand pounds of tobacco.[16]

Conviction for these speech crimes against the government exposed defendants to the possibility of physical punishment. Most convictions brought fines and imprisonment, but authorities could also inflict much worse penalty if they wanted to make a larger point to the community at large. Some colonists suffered the discomfort and humiliation of confinement in the stocks, where they were exposed to the scorn of passersby who might pelt them with garbage and excrement. But that was nothing compared to what was euphemistically called "bodily correction." Most often that meant public whippings, which courts and assemblies handed out by specifying the number of lashings and sometimes also indicating the severity with which the strokes should be administered. After he criticized the Maryland legislature in 1666 as a "turdy shitten assembly," the offended lawmakers sentenced Edward Erbery to be tied to an apple tree and lashed thirty-nine times on his bare back.[17] Some punishment for seditious libel was worse still. Courts sometimes ordered that a defendant's ears be cropped or cut off entirely. Richard Barnes suffered even more. For his "base and detracting speeches concerning the governor" of Virginia in 1625, Barnes had his arms broken and then had to run a gauntlet of men beating him with their rifles. Concluding that they hadn't yet made their point, the authorities pierced his tongue with an awl.[18]

Massachusetts, the home of John Wise, had plenty of cases, too. The colony passed laws during the seventeenth century punishing anyone who criticized officials or the government.[19] Philip Radcliff denounced both the church and secular authorities at Salem in 1631, for which he was fined forty pounds and whipped. The authorities cut off both his ears and banished him from the area.[20] In 1634, John Lee insulted Governor John Winthrop by declaring that "he was but a lawyer's clerk" and doubting "what understanding had he more than himself." That comment could not be tolerated, so the court sentenced him to a whipping and a fine.[21] Peter Bussaker criticized some Massachusetts magistrates in 1636 and paid for it with twenty lashings to be "sharply inflicted."[22] And in Ipswich County Court in 1659–60, Henry Bennett insulted the judges after losing a lawsuit against another man, and was fined five pounds for his words.[23]

FOR JOHN WISE, having spoken out against taxes, it could not have been a big surprise when the warrant came for his arrest. Towns in the Bay Colony were reaching different conclusions about whether to comply with the tax. Boston, which would become the heart of colonial protest against the taxes imposed by the Stamp Act in 1765, decided to submit to the Andros tax. Some of the satellite towns around Boston rebelled. The town of Taunton refused to appoint a commissioner to collect the tax, and on August 31 the town clerk went before Andros and the council to answer for the "scandalous, factious and seditious writeing" that conveyed the town's refusal to comply. A judge was suspended from office for attending the Taunton town meeting and not acting to prevent the tax rebellion, and several constables were held for prosecution.[24]

Wise and other prominent citizens of Ipswich had also criticized the tax policy of Governor Andros and his council, and now the offended officials brought the law down against them. They seized the town records for detailed evidence of what had taken place during the Ipswich meetings of August 22 and 23, and they called Wise and others to appear for questioning before the council. After the council examined them, Wise and five other ringleaders—including John Appleton, at whose home the evening meeting of August 22 took place—were arrested and sent off to jail to await trial.[25]

Wise, according to the charge, did "maliciously and seditiously say, publish and declare" that the tax "was not legal and to obey and comply with the same were to lose the liberty of freeborn English men."[26] Hauled before the court, Wise and the other five defendants faced several hostile judges, one of whom was Joseph Dudley, who had actually ruled Massachusetts for a short time before Andros arrived as governor. Dudley was hardly a dispassionate judge. Far from that—as a member of Governor Andros's appointed council, Dudley served as a key part of the government that had imposed the tax opposed by Wise and the other five defendants. For Wise, there was no chance of getting a fair trial.

When the trial arrived on October 3, the defendants entered a plea of not guilty. Wise argued that the taxes were illegal under the Magna Carta and the laws of England that protected personal property. To that one of the judges, probably Dudley, replied, "Mr. Wise, you have no more privileges left you, than not to be sold for slaves." After the evidence was taken, Dudley gave his instructions to the twelve members of the jury, saying that he expected a "good verdict," considering that the charge "hath been so sufficiently provided."[27] As Dudley had directed them to do, the jury returned a verdict of guilty. Wise and the five others were sent to prison for twenty-one days to await sentencing. When they returned to court, the judges imposed harsh sentences. Wise, for his part, had to pay a fine of fifty pounds plus court costs and produce a bond of one thousand pounds for a year to guarantee his good behavior. The judges also suspended him from the ministry. The other defendants received similar punishment, with a ban on holding any public office.[28] Wise was permitted to return to his ministry about a month later, the same day that the town of Ipswich complied with the law by turning over the tax revenue that had instigated the protest.[29]

AS IT TURNED OUT, the Andros government would not last long. Back in England, the Glorious Revolution of 1688 deposed James II, and Boston in turn rose up in 1689 in a kind of bloodless coup to rid itself of Andros and his cronies. With his administration at an end, Andros took shelter in a fort but was taken into custody and then sent back to England. A few years later, the town of Ipswich reimbursed Wise and the other five defendants for the fines and expenses that they had incurred in their prosecution.[30]

With the tax issue finally resolved, and his foe, Governor Andros, thoroughly discredited, Wise now enjoyed the widespread respect that came with having taken on a perceived tyrant at the peak of his power. The following year, Wise served as chaplain in the colony's failed military expedition to take Quebec, held by the French.[31] And he intervened personally in the witch trials taking place in nearby Salem in 1692. John Proctor, who for many years had owned a tavern and land in Ipswich, was well known there, and he and his pregnant wife stood accused of witchcraft along with many others. Aghast at the madness, Wise wrote a petition by hand—which was also signed by thirty-one of his Ipswich neighbors—that he sent to the court in an attempt to free Proctor and his wife.[32] John Proctor was hanged, but Wise's intervention in the witchcraft trials enhanced his reputation for a steely temperament and a determination to challenge authority that he judged to be overbearing.

AT ITS CORE, John Wise's defiance of Andros's tax policy was about the power of individual citizens to govern their own affairs, rejecting autocratic rule from the top in favor of democratic consent. Wise had intervened in the political affairs in Massachusetts, but he was first a man of God. When he once again played a leading role on the public stage, it was by immersing himself in the ecclesiastical conflicts that roiled the New England churches in the early years of the new century. Though it involved church affairs, the principle for Wise was the same—the right of individuals to govern themselves, now played out in the right of the individual churches to run their own affairs free of control from church elders.

The Puritan churches throughout New England had governed themselves independently for many years. But the religious atmosphere in New England was changing. As the first generation of Puritans died away, so too did much of the religious fervor and the strict devotion to orthodoxy. The power of the church began to erode as a result, and some in the ministry moved to consolidate their authority as the best way to combat loss of faith. They tried to centralize supervisory control over the local churches, a plan that Wise opposed because his and other congregations would lose their right to self-rule.[33]

Wise had gone to jail two decades earlier by arguing in favor of self-government for towns in Massachusetts in the face of a new tax law imposed by Governor Andros. So it was no surprise that he now defended the autonomy of the congregational churches. Now in his mid-fifties, Wise was ready to explain his ideas more fully, and he did so with two pamphlets. The first, published in 1710, gave away its approach in its sub-title, "A Reply in Satire." Sensitive to how his words would be perceived in the community, Wise apologized at the start by admitting that "there may be discerned a great liberty in argument, with a mixture of satires." But he had "neither desire, nor design to hurt any man, no, not so much as a hair on his head, but I solely aim at *error*, that is the butt I level for."[34]

Hardly had the apology been off his pen when Wise drove his stake into the heart of the ministers' idea of supervisory control of the churches. "Here is mischief," he wrote, "mischief in *summo gradu*; yea, exorbitant mischief."[35] Wise then dismantled the proposals one by one, arguing that neither God nor Scripture nor the history of church governance justified the changes that were proposed. His writing often boiled with satire and sarcasm. "The very nature of an Arbitrary Government," said Wise, "is ready to put an English man's Blood into a Fermentation; but when it really comes, and shakes its whip over their Ears, and tells them [English-men] it is their Master, it makes them stark Mad." Wise charged that the plan's effect on the churches would be "to blow up its foundations."[36] Cotton Mather was incensed. In response, he preached that Wise's essay was no less than "a Satanick insult."[37]

Insult or not, Wise wasn't nearly finished. He returned even more powerfully in 1717 with another essay that historian Clinton Rossiter called "probably the outstanding piece of polemical writing of the first one hundred and fifty years of the American settlements."[38] Once again Wise challenged the church leaders in their attempt to centralize authority over individual congregations. His *A Vindication of the Government of New England Churches,* however, drew from a new well of reasoning. Rather than supporting his arguments with only God and Scripture, Wise took a new and significant course by grounding church democracy in the intellectual traditions of political democracy.

Wise drew from prior writings on natural law, especially giving credit to Samuel von Pufendorf, a German legal philosopher, arguing that man existed free in the state of nature and owed deference only to God. In forming a government, man entered into a covenant in which he voluntarily surrendered some of his rights in exchange for the benefits of society. Those rights he kept were civil rights—at their core the rights of an Englishman drawn from the Magna Carta and other English laws. Of the possible forms of government that man could devise, Wise rejected monarchy and aristocracy, arguing instead for democracy. A monarch, he said, such as England had, must not encroach on the rights and liberties of the people. "The Prince who strives to subvert the fundamental laws of the society," he wrote, "is the Traytor and the Rebel, and not the People, who endeavour to Preserve and Defend their own."[39] In favoring democracy, Wise turned his back on the dark Calvinist assessment of human weaknesses, expressing instead confidence that mankind could run its affairs most successfully through popular government.

For Wise, popular sovereignty and democracy were foundations of civil government that should be applied as well to church government. The congregational churches of New England, he had concluded, should continue to run their own affairs and resist the encroachments of a more centralized church authority.

Unsurprisingly, Cotton Mather did not like this second of Wise's pamphlets, calling it "the poison of Wise's cursed libel."[40]

"HOW HAVE MANY of our Pulpits been like Mount Aetna and Vesuvius, breathing forth flames and sulphur?" one writer asked, referring to ministers in England who were turning their attention to political concerns.[41] Another asked rhetorically whether it was not a "common Complaint" that "too few of the Clergy, especially in the Country, bend their Sermons against *Vice,* but turn themselves wholly to *Politicks?*"[42]

In the American colonies, Wise stood out in the early eighteenth century as a churchman who became a leading partisan in political affairs. In his activism he was pointing the way to the future. Half a century later, as the colonies agitated against the imposition of taxes by Parliament, John Adams would observe that "our pulpits have thundered" in opposition to the British. Indeed they had, as numerous ministers, especially in Boston, brought their fire and brimstone down against what they saw as the many injustices of British rule.

It's doubtful that Wise's writings on civil government enjoyed a large influence on the revolutionary generation. Although Wise's two essays were republished in 1772, the leading colonial essayists of the 1760s and 1770s rarely mentioned him, preferring to link themselves to Enlightenment writers like John Locke and to the Greek philosophers.[43] But in the work of John Wise, it is nonetheless true that American political expression was being born. For here was some of the first significant evidence of the bold and uninhibited speech that would define and invigorate the founding period and begin to assert an American concept of freedom of expression. Wise's legacy was clear. It was in his strong dissent against the tax policy of Governor Andros, which landed him in a Boston jail. It was in his pamphleteering against the imposition of church authority. And it was in his employment of biting satire to achieve his political ends. Democracy was at the heart of Wise's political philosophy, and he understood intuitively that robust expression lay at the heart of democracy.

2

THE ADVOCATE

ANDREW HAMILTON FACED THE JURY AS HE PAUSED TO MAKE THE FINAL POINT IN HIS SUM-
mation. He was widely regarded in 1735 as the best trial lawyer in the
colonies, and defending his client against criminal charges of libeling a
governor appointed by King George II was the greatest challenge of his
long career. Hamilton was arguing in a courtroom at City Hall in New
York, which had filled with spectators eager to see a case that people had
been talking about for months.

At fifty-nine and nearing the end of a long and brilliant legal career,
the wily Hamilton suggested to the jurors that he was not up to the challenge of such an important case defending the right of the people to air
grievances against public officials. "You see that I labor under the weight
of many years, and am borne down with great infirmities of body," he
said to the jurors. "Yet, old and weak as I am, I should think it my duty,
if required, to go to the utmost part of the land, where my services could
be of any use, in assisting to quench the flame of prosecutions . . . by the
government to deprive a people of the right of remonstrating and complaining, too, of the arbitrary attempts of men in power."[1]

Hamilton, from Philadelphia (and no relation to Alexander Hamilton), represented the defendant, John Peter Zenger, a German immigrant
and printer of the *New York Weekly Journal*. The paper was controlled by a

political faction that opposed Governor William Cosby of New York, who was so enraged by articles that criticized his policies that he ordered the newspapers to be burned. Zenger had been held in jail for eight months under an exorbitant bail that he could not pay. The law was clearly against Zenger. Under the law of seditious libel, it was a criminal offense to publish negative statements about the government or its officials. It was the job of the jury only to ascertain whether Zenger had in fact published the libel and whether it was addressed to the governor. Then the judges would determine if the published material amounted to a libel of the governor—a foregone conclusion. The possibility that the criticism of the governor was made up of truthful statements, or that it was merely the opinion held by the writers, was no defense to the charge. So, in fact, any criticism of Cosby could qualify as a punishable libel.

Hamilton was well aware that he had a losing case, so he tried an audacious move—he admitted to the jury that his client had published the material. By doing so he virtually conceded the case on the only point that the jury could decide, but Hamilton had something else in mind. Now he asked the jury to recognize the deep injustice of Zenger going to jail merely for criticizing a politician that many people in the colony disliked. Hamilton wanted them to reject the harsh law of seditious libel itself, an action now called jury nullification. Hamilton argued that the law should not permit the punishment of citizens who spoke truth, as their rights as free men depended on their freedom to challenge authority by speaking and writing.

Much was at stake, Hamilton explained. "The question before the Court and you, Gentlemen of the jury, is not of small nor private concern; it is not the cause of a poor printer, nor of New York alone, which you are now trying. No! It may, in its consequence, affect every free man that lives under a British government on the main of America. It is the best cause. It is the cause of liberty."[2]

And with that, the first major test of freedom of the press in the colonies was in the hands of the jury.

AFTER A SEVEN-WEEK SAILING from London following his appointment, William Cosby arrived in New York late on the evening of August 1, 1732, ready to serve his appointment as governor of the provinces of New York and New Jersey. He did not lose any time getting started. At about eleven the next morning, he walked the hot cobblestone streets to City Hall from his official residence at Fort George at the southern tip of the island. He did not walk alone, for the city had prepared a parade and celebration worthy of a man who carried in his hands the Crown's awesome power and authority over their growing colony. Members of the militia and many citizens lined both sides of the street. Walking ahead of Cosby was a troop of soldiers, some mounted on horses and others on foot carrying weapons. Trailing behind him were members of the governing council, leading merchants, and other assorted "gentlemen" of the city. After dealing at City Hall with the papers for his royal commission, Cosby strolled with the same crowd back to the fort, where the militia formed their company and fired three volleys of their muskets in salute.[3]

As he moved through the city, Cosby must have choked at the pungent odor cutting the air. Garbage cluttered the gutters that lined the middle of the streets, and in midsummer the stench could be overwhelming. Although sanitation was a major problem—and possibly related to the epidemics that swept New York every few years, including smallpox the year before—in other respects the city was looking better than ever. Several decades of prosperity had made it possible for an increasing number of people to construct their houses of brick or stone.

Gone now were many reminders that the city had once been New Amsterdam, under control of the Dutch. The old city wall, erected on the northern boundary of the settlement to help defend it against enemy attack, had been removed in 1699. Stones from its bastion went into the foundation for a new city hall that replaced the Dutch Stadhuis, where Peter Stuyvesant had governed the city. This grand municipal building, which symbolized the new English power, became home for the colony's assembly, the Common Council, and the Supreme Court, as well as a jail to house the city's miscreants. Removal of the stockade enabled the city to eventually expand into the farmlands and wilds to the north, but in the 1730s the town's heart beat strongly from the crowded core of the original settlement.[4]

All the pageantry and flourishes on display that summer morning overshadowed the concern that many people felt for the years ahead with Cosby ruling the colony. Much was at stake for the people of New York—who in 1731 numbered 7,045 whites and 1,577 blacks, most of them slaves.[5] For the previous twenty years, New York had seen vigorous economic growth. The increasing consumption of sugar was driving trade through the triangle composed of London, the colonies, and the British West Indies. Sugar had moved from a luxury to a staple of English society. As it did so, Britain enjoyed an enormous boost in wealth as bankers and shippers and insurers and thousands of workers who toiled in the refineries claimed their part of the treasure. Planters in the British West Indies met their need for basic foodstuffs—including flour, lumber, corn, and meat—through purchases from the colonies. Half or more of the ships entering or leaving the port in New York dealt in the West Indies trade by the 1720s.[6]

As the sugar trade developed, the New York economy grew rapidly with gains in shipping, shipbuilding, finance, and agriculture. The trade spawned a class of wealthy merchants, lawyers, and landowners, and by the time Cosby arrived, half of the city's wealth sat in the hands of about 10 percent of the population. At the same time, about one-third of white New Yorkers, and most likely almost all blacks, were essentially destitute. Catering to the affluent, many shops sold imported luxury products at prices double those in London. The wealthy built fine houses and filled them with expensive furniture and ornaments, and what could not be shipped from London was made by a growing group of artisans who crafted expensive objects with silver and gold. The local economy kept most workers busy producing vegetables and meat and making cloth, soap, candles, and other goods.[7]

The arrival of Cosby, though, came as a recession began taking its hold on the city. Increasing supplies of flour, especially from Pennsylvania, knocked down prices for New York producers, and a glut of sugar from the British West Indies hurt producers there and sharply reduced their demand for supplies from the colonies. The economic cycle was turning down. It was a time of growing uncertainty for the people of New York, who looked with some hope—and trepidation—at the new governor who walked their streets.[8]

AS JOHN WISE and the citizens of Massachusetts had found with Governor Andros, a governor appointed by the king could affect their lives in profound ways. And as they well knew, those who received appointments to these critical positions hardly came to it through rigorous screening based on past performance. With Cosby, there was reason from the very start to suspect the worst. Born in Ireland of an aristocratic British family, Cosby served as an officer in the military and showed a surpassing talent for cultivating royal connections if nothing else. He had served as equerry to the queen and had married the sister of the Earl of Halifax.[9] Cosby received an appointment as governor of the island of Minorca, in the Mediterranean Sea, but was relieved of his post for maladministration and a scandal in which he appropriated the goods of a merchant for his own gain. Cosby's bad reputation was well enough known that Cadwallader Colden, himself a future governor of New York, wondered how "such a man, after such a flagrant instance of tyranny and robbery, came to be intrusted with the government of an English colony."[10]

Political connections, of course, provide the answer, but there was hope that Cosby had matured since his days in Minorca, when he was in his late twenties. Unfortunately, it took little time for Cosby to confirm even the most extreme fears about his ability to rule the colony wisely. He immediately revealed himself as greedy, haughty, and inflammatory, interested most of all in enriching himself and in punishing anyone who dared to oppose him. He proved to be good—superb, actually—at making trouble. He lost no time doing exactly that.

Shortly after his arrival, the assembly voted to provide Cosby with a salary of 1,500 pounds per year. Cosby asked for an additional payment for work he claimed to have done to help secure defeat in Parliament of legislation that would have imposed a high tax on sugar and molasses imported from the West Indies, a measure that would have been costly for people of the colony. Despite some doubt about what influence if any that Cosby had exerted in London, the assembly agreed to pay him another 750 pounds. Cosby was incensed that the payment was smaller than he thought he deserved for the work, and badgered some members of the assembly. Finally, they appeased him by raising his supplement for the London work to 1,000 pounds.[11]

Cosby wasn't done, though, and what happened next began a cascade of events that brought about one of the most significant trials in the entire colonial period. It all started, unsurprisingly, with Cosby demanding money. Cosby had stayed in London for about a year following his appointment to fill the chair left open when the previous governor died. Rip Van Dam, president of the Provincial Council, had served as acting governor during this time and had been paid for his service. Now that Cosby was in New York, he waved before all eyes a royal order that said he was entitled to half of Van Dam's salary for the time before he arrived from London. A wiser man would have known better than to turn the heat up to boiling, as payments to royal governors were always bitter tea for American colonists under the best of circumstances. Van Dam, of course, refused the demand for half his salary, arguing that the money was rightfully his for performing the job of interim governor. Confident that he had local support for his refusal to cooperate, Van Dam then injected some theatrics into the controversy that were sure to enrage Cosby. Van Dam said he would hand over half of his salary if Cosby gave him, in return, half of all the salary and emoluments that he himself had earned in London during that same time. By Van Dam's reckoning, the exchange would mean Cosby would owe him several thousand pounds.[12]

Cosby was not amused, and he began plotting to sue Van Dam. Doing so was not easy. He couldn't sue in the Court of Chancery—Cosby himself was the chancellor and so would be hearing his own lawsuit. And a suit at common law in the Supreme Court would expose him to a local jury. He figured, and probably accurately, that jurors would be likely to favor their neighbor Van Dam against a royal governor. So Cosby took a political excursion around the jury system. He ordered the Supreme Court, whose judges were his appointees, to sit as a court of equity, enabling the case to be tried directly to the judges and so avoiding a jury. But this raised other problems. The tin-eared Cosby had not asked the assembly to assent to the new court. And no wonder, since the assembly had passed resolutions against the creation of equity courts four times in the past three decades. Such courts were often viewed as arbitrary because judges sitting without a jury relied on their conception of fairness and not on statutory and common law.[13]

Meanwhile, Cosby moved another piece on his board that would eventually expose him to a withering attack. From his first months in office, he crossed swords with James Alexander, a member of the Provincial Council. Alexander had proved himself a smart and tough politician. He had arrived in the colonies from Scotland in 1715. Only in his midtwenties at the time, Alexander immediately received an appointment as surveyor-general of New Jersey and rose quickly to a number of public offices. By the time Cosby arrived in New York, Alexander was one of the most powerful lawyers and politicians in the city and an ally of Van Dam.

Cosby saw Alexander as plotting with Van Dam against him and the Crown. In a letter just four months after he arrived in New York, Cosby wrote to his superior in London, the Duke of Newcastle, that Alexander was "very unfit" to sit in the council. Cosby said, "His known very bad character would be too long to trouble your Grace with particulars, and stuff'd with such tricks and oppressions too gross for your Grace to hear." He asked for permission to remove Alexander, which he eventually did.[14]

Cosby ran into a buzz saw at the Supreme Court, where three justices convened to hear his suit in April 1733. Lewis Morris, the chief justice, was a distinguished lawyer who had held that position for eighteen years. Morris was one of the most powerful political figures in New York and the leader of the Popular Party, which already opposed Cosby. But the other two justices were supporters of Cosby and part of the "Court" party. James De Lancey, not yet thirty years old, was the son of Stephen De Lancey, one of the wealthiest merchants in the city and head of a family that fiercely competed with the Morris clan for political control of the city. The third justice on the court was Frederick Philipse.[15]

Cosby's lawsuit renewed old animosities. On the day the proceedings opened, Van Dam's two lawyers attacked the validity of the court itself. One of the lawyers was James Alexander, whom Cosby already regarded as a political enemy. The other lawyer, William Smith, was another political ally of Van Dam. When Alexander and Smith were done arguing their point, Morris delivered an opinion that he had prepared in advance and without consulting his two colleagues on the court. He agreed with Van Dam's lawyers and declared that the court had been illegally convened because, among other reasons, the governor had not created it with the assent of the assembly. Morris published his opinion as a pamphlet for everyone in the colony to read, while De Lancey and Philipse both disagreed and voted in favor of the court's jurisdiction. In the end, the suit failed to reach a conclusion on the merits.[16]

Furious at what had transpired, and regarding it as a bald challenge to his prerogatives as royal governor, Cosby wrote a disparaging letter to Morris. The chief justice replied that he had "served the Public faithfully and honestly, according to the best of my Knowledge." Cosby had no interest in papering over the dispute and moving on. If his motive in trying to rig the courts to get Van Dam's money was transparent to all, he didn't care one bit and he obviously didn't know when to stop. On May 3, Cosby wrote again to the Duke of Newcastle, this time complaining of Morris's "excessive pride and his oppression of the people." In a long-winded defense of his lawsuit against Van Dam, Cosby also peevishly complained that Morris "never was once to pay me a visit—no, not so much as to welcome me into the province." He complained that Morris as well as his son, who sat in the assembly, presented "the utmost opposition in the King's affairs and therefore ought to be crushed in time." He told Newcastle that he would fire Morris from his position as chief justice or "be affronted, or what is still worse, see the King's authority trampled on and disrespect and irreverence to it, taught, from the Bench to the People by him."[17]

And fire him Cosby did, removing Morris from his position on August 21, 1733. Four months later he elevated his ally, De Lancey, to the position of chief justice.[18] Cosby had once again bypassed his council and made critical political decisions without consulting them. Cadwallader Colden, one of the council members, recounted how Cosby had finally informed them at a meeting of the council that he had fired Morris and appointed De Lancey as chief justice. Colden wrote that Cosby "thought this the most proper place to give the first notice of it. Upon which I said, 'Then Your Excellency only tells us what you have already done?' To which he answered, 'Yes,' I replied, 'It is not what I would have advised.' And he very briskly returned to it, 'I do not ask your advice.'"[19] Now Morris himself wrote to the Duke of Newcastle to complain about Cosby, whose conduct "has been such as fully to persuade those under his Government that he thinks himself above the restraint of any Rules but those of his own will."[20]

Cosby's imperious attitude and unilateral actions were making him enemies at every turn, and the situation was spinning out of control. Some of the most powerful men in the colony now dedicated themselves to his undoing. To better oppose the governor after losing his job as chief justice, Morris as well as his son won seats in the assembly at the end of 1733, and nearly all of their slate of candidates won election in October 1734 to the city's Common Council.[21]

Even so, Cosby was governor and representative of the king, and so he held on to political control of the province as long as he had the confidence of London. But he made sure he had another weapon working for him—his control of a newspaper that reached the people of New York with articles defending his policies. The New York Gazette was commercially viable in those early days of newspapering because it held a contract to publish documents for the government. In a practical sense, the *Gazette* was the government's paper, and so it was no surprise that it was a vigorous cheer-leader for Cosby. The governor controlled the editorial material in the paper through appointment of his close ally, Francis Harison, a member of the Governor's Council, as the editor. Harison was such a conniver and a political hatchet man that even many of his natural allies held their nose while dealing with him. De Lancey, for one, had even justified taking the job of chief justice after the dismissal of Lewis Morris because otherwise Governor Cosby might have appointed Harison. As Cadwallader Colden noted in his memoirs, "The Governor was resolved to put Mr. Harison in the office, a man nowise acceptable to anybody." Colden added that Harison "was of so bad a character, and so odious to the people, that they certainly would have pulled him from the Bench."[22]

Harison wrote many of the stories published in the *New York Gazette*. Even while Cosby was tossing Morris off the Supreme Court, Harison was fawning over the governor:

> *Cosby the mild, the happy, good and great,*
> *The strongest guard of our little state;*
> *Let malcontents in crabbed language write . . .* [23]

Control of the *Gazette* provided Cosby with a major political advantage. There were few ways to reach a mass audience in the 1730s. The world of William Cosby and Lewis Morris was almost completely barren of media to dispense news and serve as a forum for public debate and discussion. Broadsides could be printed on a sheet of paper and nailed to a tree or handed out in the center of town, and pamphlets enabled writers, once in a great while, to have discourse at great length on a vital issue. But neither was suited to reaching a large number of people on a regular basis, or for carrying on an extended dialogue on serious topics. Cosby's opponents understood very well that only a newspaper—brimming in its infancy with all kinds of possibilities—provided access to a large number of people on a regular basis.

At the same time, the growth in the number of inns, taverns, and coffeehouses was providing new venues where people could congregate and talk about Cosby and his machinations. Taverns had popped up all over the city, catering to groups ranging from hard-drinking dockworkers to prosperous merchants and officials. Coffeehouses were also becoming popular. The King's Arms in 1696 became the first coffeehouse to open in New York, a quiet place for merchants and politicians and other wealthy citizens to read newspapers and books and discuss business and political affairs over coffee or a meal. In fact, Common Council and assembly members often met in the upstairs rooms, so the King's Arms became a magnet for political discussion.[24]

With venues expanding for discussion of public affairs, it was all the more important for political factions to reach these places with printed material. Stinging from their treatment at the hands of Cosby, opponents like Morris and Alexander understood that the governor could easily outmaneuver them if he directly reached people in the city and they could not. Their only hope of circulating their views and creating an organized opposition to Cosby, and perhaps making his continuation in office untenable, would be to start a newspaper of their own. So they set about to create something without precedent in America—not simply a newspaper, but an opposition newspaper.

In doing so, they pointed a beacon to the future. As the relationship between England and the colonies worsened three decades later, the partisan press would become a vital force in colonial politics, bringing news and commentary to people up and down the coast and spreading the message of resistance to British authority. A new and vital sphere of communications was emerging in New York in the 1730s, and it would profoundly enlarge and shape public discussion and eventually help drive Americans toward independence as a self-governing people.

THAT NEWSPAPERS AND OTHER printed material could become fertile grounds for spreading ideas in opposition to the government had long troubled officials in London. In fact, their concern about criticism and active dissent predated the printing press by several centuries, back to a time when people had no way to disseminate their opinion except through the spoken word. But the invention of the printing press changed everything, making it possible to communicate to large numbers of people who could then organize their opposition more effectively.

Suppression of dissent was hardly surprising in a time when sovereign power was lodged in the government and the people enjoyed no political rights of participation in the decisions that affected them. Those who ruled without consent of the people had reason to be insecure in their power and wary of opponents eager to topple them. Whether kings or parliaments or church officials, they suppressed dissent in order to prevent the spread of ideas that could spawn disorder and even overthrow their authority. Kings feared dissenters who could gain widespread support and eventually threaten their rule. And with Catholics, Anglicans, and Puritans fighting for the souls of millions and for the establishment of their creed as the official religion of England, there was no room for the expression of opposing opinions on matters of belief. When religion and state became united under Henry VIII, with the king as the head of the Church of England, political and religious issues became intertwined and the dangers of dissent became ever more serious to those in power. In a case decided in 1704, Chief Justice John Holt explained that seditious libel had to be punished or the government would be severely at risk. "If people should not be called to account for possessing the people with an ill opinion of the government, no government can subsist. For it is very necessary for all governments that the people should have a good opinion of it."[25]

In England, the suppression of speech considered dangerous started in the thirteenth century. Over the years, the authorities used several strategies to silence people they regarded as threats. They prohibited the publication of any printed material without a license in advance, thus controlling the ideas that could circulate to the public and assuring that dissent came stillborn to the world. And if speech critical of the government did emerge despite the requirement for a license, the authorities had another weapon available to use. They could criminally prosecute those responsible under the law of seditious libel and impose severe punishment, itself a deterrent to most people who might voice disagreement with official policy. Those two weapons to curb criticism—restraints before publication and punishment for licentious writings after—served the purposes of political tyranny for centuries to come.

Parliament passed the first seditious libel law in 1275, outlawing "any slanderous News . . . or *false* News or Tales where by discord or occasion of discord or slander may grow between the King and his people." Parliament enacted another such law in 1379, but political dissent was not the only speech of interest to the censors. Dissent against religious authority was considered just as dangerous. Church authorities expanded the circle

of forbidden speech with ecclesiastical laws that punished blasphemy—
speech that they considered to be contemptuous of the accepted religious
dogma. All in all the scheme of control was comprehensive, protecting
both church and state from dissidents and doing so through the fundamental vision that power resided at the top and that the people enjoyed no
rights of participation in the decisions that affected them.[26]

If spoken words could pose a problem, the development of the printing press multiplied the dangers to authorities. The printing press made
it possible to circulate books and pamphlets and thereby spread contrary
ideas. To combat the threat of dissent spreading through print, kings and
parliaments began regulating the press and suppressing criticism. As a result, the printing and dissemination of news and opinion—what became
the newspaper—had an agonizingly slow start both in England and the
colonies. The political elite on both sides of the Atlantic understood intuitively that allowing writers to circulate their thoughts to a mass audience
carried with it the most serious of risks. These were not idle fears for the
monarchs and the established churches, for they already had experienced
the power of the presses to circulate radical ideas. The Protestant Reformation had spread throughout Europe as printed Bibles passed from
person to person. The printing of Bibles and other religious writings set
church authorities to hunting down and burning books, and sometimes
the heretics as well.[27]

The legal means of controlling the presses evolved quickly to meet the
threat. Under Henry VIII, the Crown censored religious material it considered to be heretical, and then expanded its control to political documents. Royal censors read manuscripts and deleted objectionable material
before issuing a license for its publication. Controls became even more
elaborate and crushing under Elizabeth. The Crown established control
of the presses by severely restricting ownership to only those printers it
approved. The government gave a charter to the Company of Stationers,
whose members alone had the privilege of owning a printing press. With
the monopoly came government control, as unlicensed books could be
seized and printers could lose their licenses if they failed to prove loyal.
The Court of High Commission, the supreme ecclesiastical court, performed the licensing of written material, and the Court of the Star Chamber defined the law and held trials for alleged offenders.[28]

Books and pamphlets were the typical fare, but regular printed reports—in effect, early newspapers—began in mainland Europe and
spread in the 1620s to England. Printed material such as broadsides, pamphlets, and newspapers expanded and subsided with the growth and re-
traction of licensing and censorship. In 1695, though, as licensing lapsed
for good, the latent demand for political news and the opportunity for
printers to make money drove a surge in publishing. The first newspaper
publishing on a daily basis went on sale in 1702.[29]

While the licensing system was gone, printers still worked at their
own risk. They were subject to seditious libel laws that operated like the
sword of Damocles, ready to fall on the printer who put in circulation
any criticism that would lower public esteem for the government and
might lead to a breach of the peace. The law was elastic enough to bring
any dissenter within its purview. Seditious libel became fixed in English
law—and the law governing the British colonies in America—with a case
decided in 1606, *De Libellis Famosis*. The Star Chamber said that the libel
of an official was a serious criminal act because it involved "the scandal
of government"—and "what greater scandal of government can there be
than to have corrupt or wicked Magistrates to be appointed . . . ?"[30]

All that was already accepted law, but the Star Chamber made a radical change that imperiled critics of government as never before. Until
then, the law of seditious libel had required that speech against the government be false in order to be criminal. But with *De Libellis Famosis*, the
Star Chamber ruled that a true statement could be punished as well. In
fact, the common maxim became "the greater the truth, the greater the
libel." There was a strange logic to that. After all, criticism that is true
could cause even greater scandal of government, and could pose a greater
risk to the public peace, than a statement that could easily be neutralized
because it was false. Punishment could be a fine, imprisonment, the pil-
lory, or amputation of the ears. The precedent set in *De Libellis Famosis*
lived on as part of English common law—the body of nonstatutory law
decreed over the years by the royal courts. The crime of seditious libel
was exported to the colonies along with British rule and became part of
the law governing the relationship between the king and his subjects in
America. Anyone who criticized the king or his representatives risked
spending time in a decrepit jail cell.[31]

The colonies lagged well behind London in the development of news-papers, as royal governors carried out orders from London to censor at-tempts at publication. English law forbade printing newspapers for many years in the colonies, as the authorities feared the spread of dangerous ideas. In 1671, William Berkeley, the governor of Virginia who had been appointed by the Crown, wrote to the trade commissioners in London and revealed the prevalent attitude. "I thank God," Berkeley wrote, "*there are no free schools nor printing,* and I hope we shall not have these hundred years, for *learning* has brought disobedience, and heresy, and sects into the world, and *printing* has divulged them, and libels against the best govern-ment. God keep us from both!"[32] And in the next decade, when he arrived to govern Massachusetts, Governor Edmund Andros was instructed by government ministers in London that "no person keep any printing-press for printing, nor that any book pamphlet or other matters whatsoever be printed without your especial leave and license first obtained."[33]

Finally, the first newspaper in the colonies was published in Boston in 1690. The initial issue of the paper, *Publick Occurrences Both Forreign and Domestick,* declared that it would be published once a month "or if any Glut of Occurrences happen, oftener." It took only four days from pub-lication of the first issue for one of those "occurrences" to take place—namely, the shuttering of the paper by colonial authorities. Perhaps they were not entertained by an article saying that "if reports be true," the king of France "used to lie with the Son's Wife." That was evidently a scandal best left unreported, for the government's order reminded citizens that they could not print without a license.[34]

When a newspaper started in Virginia, the cautious editor proclaimed his respect for authority. Discussing the mission of the new *Virginia Ga-zette* in 1736, the editor wrote that he did not regard the "liberty of the press" to include "any licentious Freedom, to revile our Governors and Magistrates; to traduce the established Laws and Religion of our coun-try; or any Attempts to weaken and subvert by opprobrious Writings that sacred Respect and Veneration which ought always to be maintained for authority, and persons in authority."[35] Clearly, only articles supportive of the reigning authorities would do.

FARTHER TO THE NORTH, though, in New York, another paper would begin around the same time with a far different mission—to subject Governor

Cosby to the most withering criticism and drive him from office. The opposition saw that an occasional broadside or pamphlet could not combat Cosby's abuse of power. Even then it was clear that political dissent required the most effective means of mass communication then available. Simply put, the opposition needed a newspaper.

The Morris faction approached an obscure printer in his mid-thirties named John Peter Zenger, who owned a small printing shop in the city. Zenger had sailed to the colony with his family in 1710 from Germany via England. His father had died during the passage to America, and on their arrival John, then only thirteen, was apprenticed to one of the most important printers in the colonies, William Bradford, who taught Zenger the trade for eight years. When Zenger was done, he tried his hand at printing in Maryland and then returned to work with Bradford again. Finally, he struck out on his own and opened a shop that printed a variety of books, pamphlets, and religious writings.[36] None of this modest fare, however, quite prepared him for what lay ahead. Zenger only saw the newspaper as an opportunity to make a decent living, but he would soon enough become the news himself.

The *New York Weekly Journal* began publishing on November 5, 1733, the creation of Morris and his political allies and the first opposition newspaper started in America. It wasn't just any opposition paper, though. It was dedicated—through biased reporting, biting essays, and satire—to the singular purpose of exposing Governor Cosby as an arbitrary and avaricious tyrant who was such an embarrassment to the Crown that he should be removed from office. James Alexander served behind the scenes as editor and undoubtedly wrote many of the articles, as did others from the faction that opposed Cosby. Alexander knew exactly what the mission of the paper would be. After publication of the first issue, he explained in a letter to Robert Hunter, a former governor of New York, that the *Weekly Journal* was intended "to expose him [Cosby] and those ridiculous flatteries with which Mr. Harison loads our other newspaper."[37]

True to his word, Alexander filled the pages of the *Weekly Journal* with invective against Cosby. In the first issue, the paper ran a long story recounting an election in Westchester County that returned the ousted chief justice, Lewis Morris, to the assembly. It reported an attempt by a sheriff appointed by Cosby to disenfranchise Quakers who intended to vote for Morris by requiring them to take oaths instead of affirmations.[38] The most biting material was written anonymously, as was typical of the time. Some of the criticism was heavily biased reporting of Cosby's actions, bringing out what the authors considered to be the governor's skullduggery and gross abuse of authority. It lambasted those who would go along with the governor's schemes rather than fight him head on. "A Governor turns rogue," said the paper, "does a Thousand Things for which a small Rogue would have deserved a Halter: And because it is difficult if not impracticable, to obtain Relief against him; therefore it is prudent to keep in with him, and join in the Roguery, and that on the Principle of Self Preservation."[39] The paper connected Cosby to "SCHEMES OF GENERAL OPPRESSION AND PILLAGE, SCHEMES TO DEPRECIATE OR EVADE THE LAWS, RESTRAINTS UPON LIBERTY AND PROJECTS FOR ARBITRARY WILL."[40]

The assault, though, was not always a punch to the jaw. The paper published satiric attacks that did not mention Cosby by name but that everyone knew were directed against the governor or Francis Harison, editor of the pro-Cosby *Gazette*. Although the Reverend John Wise had used satire to attack the Puritan elders of Massachusetts decades earlier, satire was relatively new as a tool of political commentary in America. London provided many models to emulate, though. With the collapse of the licensing system in England in the 1690s came an explosion of political satire. In the first half of the eighteenth century, a group of satirists including Jonathan Swift and Alexander Pope aimed their satire at the Walpole administration, and the number of satiric pamphlets rose from twelve to sixty-one in the following decade, the 1730s.[41]

Beyond its effectiveness in criticizing public figures, satire also offered a broad shield to deflect what potentially could be ruinous libel suits. "You must know, Sir, that we have several ways here of abusing one another, without incurring the danger of the law," Swift wrote. A satirist might choose not to name the subject of his attack, but instead—through description, for example—make the identity of the person clear to readers. Swift added, "We are careful never to print a man's name out at length . . . so that although everybody alive knows whom I mean, the plaintiff can have no redress in any court of justice."[42]

Because it relied on humor, satire struck at its target much more obliquely than did direct criticism, but as a form of political attack it could be even more devastating, utilizing parody, irony, and sarcasm.

A satiric work could exaggerate almost any vulnerability of a public figure—his vices, his appearance, his mannerisms, or his political policies. For a political leader who possessed too high an opinion of himself, an article that ridiculed so thoroughly that it made people laugh might be the most humbling experience of all.

The satire in the *Weekly Journal* was crude compared to the best English variety that inspired it, but it delivered the scorn and ridicule that its authors intended. One short, unsigned article compared Cosby to a monkey. "A Monkey of the larger sort . . . has lately broke his Chain, and run into the Country, where he has playd many a Monkey Trick. . . . Whosoever shall take this little mischievous Animal, and send him back to his Master, so that he may be chained up again, shall have for his Reward a Thousand thanks."[43] Then, in a subsequent issue, the paper said: "The Monkey lately Advertis'd, that has Broke his Chain, might have been easily brought back, but he is got into the Company of a little Monkey and an old Baboon."[44] Alexander attacked his opposing editor, too. Harison was "a Large Spaneil, of about Five Foot Five Inches High, has lately stray'd from his Kennel." This dog "has taken it upon him in a heathenish Manner to abuse Mankind, by imposing a great many gross Falsehoods upon them."[45]

EVERY INVECTIVE HURLED at Cosby took the *Weekly Journal* another step toward a legal showdown that Alexander certainly knew was inevitable. It was too much to believe that Cosby would resist turning the law of seditious libel against his critics. Shrewdly, then, Alexander filled the *Weekly Journal* from the beginning with articles extolling freedom of the press. Week after week, readers would see attacks on Cosby alongside other articles that justified the right of the people to speak freely and hold their political leaders and institutions accountable. Of course, any such right was theory at best, for the common law of seditious libel clearly gave the government the power to prosecute anyone who had the temerity to criticize royal officials.

To make his case for freedom of the press, Alexander borrowed from the work a decade earlier of John Trenchard and Thomas Gordon. The two British political writers had published anonymously in the London press under the name of Cato, the virtuous Roman senator who had promoted republican principles. They had written 144 essays attacking corruption

and tyranny in the British political system and arguing for liberty and
sovereignty for British citizens. They wrote that government must be responsible to the will of the people, and that the people could hold government officials accountable only if they enjoyed the right to discuss and
criticize the government free of the threat of criminal punishment for
doing so. Published in four volumes as *Cato's Letters,* excerpts would be
printed in virtually all the newspapers in the colonies and widely quoted
in political essays, making them among the most influential political essays for the American founding generation.[46]

Alexander's reprinting of some of Cato's essays on freedom of the
press was one of the early uses of Trenchard and Gordon's work in the
colonies. In fact, a Cato essay on free speech was a lead item in the *Weekly
Journal,* arguing that "where a Man cannot call his Tongue his own he
can scarce call any Thing else his own: Whoever would overthrow the
Liberty of a Nation must begin by subduing the Freeness of Speech." A
couple paragraphs later, and no doubt much to Alexander's satisfaction,
Trenchard and Gordon appeared to be writing specifically about the oppressive rule of Governor Cosby. "That Men ought to speak well of their
Governours, is true, while their Governours deserve to be well Spoken of,"
wrote Cato, "but to do public Mischief without Hearing of it is only the
Prerogative and Felicity of Tyranny."[47] Most important was the point that
Cato made in the next week's installment, that discussion of public men
and their actions was a political obligation of citizenship. "The exposing
therefore of publick wickedness, as it is a Duty which every man owes to
Truth and his Country, can never be a Libel in the Nature of Things,"
Cato argued.[48]

If Alexander was asserting the right of the *Weekly Journal* to criticize
the governor and his actions, to whom was the argument directed? It was
certainly not at Cosby. The governor was profligate in his use of power
for his own ends, and Alexander could not have expected him to be impressed in the least by political theory expounded by anonymous British
writers. Cosby held the cudgel of a potential seditious libel prosecution in
his hand, and he would certainly not hesitate to use it when the time was
right. Alexander had something else in mind.

With his argument made through *Cato's Letters,* and the continual
revelations of Cosby's dishonesty, Alexander was reaching out directly
to the people of New York, and specifically to those one thousand or so

freeholders who were qualified to sit as jurors if Cosby brought a case for seditious libel. Alexander was inviting the people to consider that they possessed political rights that were profoundly different from the common understanding—the rights of freedom of speech and freedom of the press. As James Madison would put it more than sixty years later, "a freedom in canvassing the merits and measures of public men."[49] It was an argument seeing its early light in America.

UNSURPRISINGLY, THE ACCUMULATING abuse from the *Weekly Journal* became too much for Cosby, who saw no reason to continue suffering such slings and arrows from his political enemies when he possessed weapons of his own to put an end to it. He could use seditious libel law to throw the rascals in jail. At least he thought so, since the two Supreme Court justices—De Lancey and Philipse—were allies. He had to be less certain of his prospects with a colonial jury. He had admitted as much in his lawsuit to collect money from Rip Van Dam, creating a new court in equity specifically to avoid a jury trial.

Cosby's first thrust against the *Weekly Journal* came through Chief Justice De Lancey in January 1734. De Lancey, although he knew he might later sit as a judge if a case were brought, met with a grand jury and complained that "some Men with the utmost Virulency have endeavored to asperse his Excellency and vilify his administration; they have spread abroad many seditious Libels, in order to lessen in the People's Minds the Regard which is due to a Person in his High Station." De Lancey admitted that the attacks on Cosby had been written anonymously, but said that it would be easy for the jurors to guess at the identity of the authors. The grand jurors, though, refused to return an indictment.[50]

Undaunted, the *Weekly Journal* continued its campaign against Cosby, who wrote to his superiors in London that the trio of Alexander, Morris, and Van Dam were attacking him mercilessly. In an extraordinary letter to the Lords of Trade on June 19, Cosby defended himself against the campaign to have him removed from office. After firing Morris from his position as chief justice, Cosby wrote, "His open and implacable malice against me has appeared weekly in false and scandalous libels printed in Zengers Journal." The governor went on and on about his treatment at the hands of his opponents, revealing just how obsessed he was with the opposition newspaper that was driving him not just to distraction but also to using his power to impose ever more drastic penalties. He complained of "those insolent and scandalous papers by which these vile wretches would have involved the Province in confusion." Cosby wrote that the three men "are so implacable in their malice, that I am to look for all the insolent, false and scandalous aspersions, that such bold and profligate wretches can invent."[51]

The acrimony worsened later in September 1734, following a bitter election in which Popular Party candidates defeated Cosby supporters. The next day, two ballads circulated as broadsides throughout the city with sarcastic comments about the governor and his supporters. One plunged the knife deeply with an accusation that Cosby and his election supporters were "pettifogging knaves" and "scoundrel rascals." The other ballad criticized Cosby for buying support at a political banquet the previous year by serving copious amounts of alcohol: "Stand up to save your Country dear, in Spite of usquebaugh and beer."[52]

A couple weeks later, an incensed De Lancey returned to the grand jury in a second attempt to gain indictments, this time citing the anonymously written and published songs. "Sometimes," said De Lancey, "heavy, half-witted Men get a knack of Rhyming, but it is Time to break them of it, when they grow Abusive, Insolent, and Mischievous with it." Again the grand jury, unable to identify the author or printer of the ballads, refused to indict. But this time De Lancey was ready to move in dramatic fashion. In October, he and Philipse, the second justice, ordered the ballads burned by the common hangman in front of City Hall.[53]

Now the snare was about to spring shut. A few weeks later, the Governor's Council—including Cosby, De Lancey, and Harison—met and identified four issues of Zenger's *Weekly Journal* that contained libels against Cosby's government. They voted to have the four issues burned as well. Cosby surely knew that Alexander, Morris, and Smith were writing many of the pieces that offended him so deeply, but the writings had been published anonymously and so it would be difficult to prove in a court of law who had written what. Perhaps a pile of money would motivate a witness to come forward, so Cosby issued proclamations offering a reward of fifty pounds for conviction of the author of the libelous articles in the *Weekly Journal* and another twelve pounds for conviction of the ballad writer.[54]

A couple weeks later, Cosby met with his council, including De Lancey and Francis Harison, editor of the *Gazette,* and together they began maneuvering for legal action against the *Weekly Journal*. With no authors identified, the council issued an arrest warrant against the only person whose involvement in the articles could be reliably confirmed—the printer of the newspaper, John Peter Zenger. The sheriff took Zenger into custody on November 17. For several days he was locked in a jail cell without access to pen and paper and without permission to talk with anyone. Finally, he was permitted to communicate with outsiders through the keyhole in his cell door.[55]

Zenger's arrest set the city abuzz. At a time when printing a newspaper one page at a time was a laborious process carried out by a printer and a few apprentices, removing a printer like Zenger from his shop would typically be a fatal blow to a paper. And indeed, the *Weekly Journal* fell silent, missing the first issue after Zenger's arrest. So charged was the situation that on November 23 several hundred people filled the courtroom at City Hall just to observe the hearing as De Lancey considered Zenger's request for bail. The hearing gave the crowd an opportunity to see some of the main protagonists. None other than James Alexander and William Smith appeared in the courtroom as Zenger's lawyers. Both of them would have been in jail with Zenger if not for the veil of anonymity that protected them in writing for the *Weekly Journal*.[56]

Alexander asked De Lancey to set bail so that Zenger could go home and resume work while awaiting trial. To help guide De Lancey as to what would be reasonable bail, Zenger submitted an affidavit listing his assets at only forty pounds, not including his clothes and his presses. De Lancey, though, set bail for ten times that amount, assuring that Zenger would remain locked away, far from his printing press. Zenger returned to jail, awaiting action by the grand jury. But Cosby had learned not to depend on grand juries, having failed twice to gain indictments. This time the Cosby administration bypassed the grand jury, and instead the attorney general charged Zenger by "information"—a formal accusation of crime issued by a public official.[57]

Now, finally, all the pieces were in place for a legal showdown between the factions locked in bitter conflict. In the meantime, though, as the months passed before trial, Cosby got no rest from the sharp attacks that had provoked his prosecution of Zenger. As Zenger languished in jail, the *Weekly Journal* appeared again on the streets of New York—this time printed by Zenger's wife, and aided by those shadowy literary talents who floated anonymously on and off the pages when they were not engaged in defending Zenger in court.

THE PRIMITIVE CONDITIONS in the city jail wore on Zenger, especially through the winter months. On May 1, 1735, five months after he had first been incarcerated, Zenger and another prisoner wrote a letter to city officials complaining about their cell. "With every rain," they wrote, "your petitioners are not only much discommoded, their Healths endangered, but other inconveniences may be expected. The Windows also are so much shattered that your Petitioners are not able to keep out the Winds."[58]

The case finally reached the courtroom with a show of fireworks that seemed predictable, considering the politics and the characters. Concerned that De Lancey was a partisan for Cosby, the lawyers decided once again to attack the validity of the proceedings, just as they had done when they had defended Van Dam from Cosby's lawsuit a few years earlier. On April 15, they challenged the commissions that enabled De Lancey and Philipse to sit on the court. Governor Cosby, they argued, had no power under law to appoint De Lancey and Philipse after he had fired Morris as chief justice in the Van Dam dispute. Since De Lancey could not possibly agree with them and step down, their strategy could accomplish little except plunge the case even further into a morass from which it would be difficult to recover.

De Lancey did not answer the challenge to his authority right away. He thought about what to do overnight, but his reflection did not save him from a partisan blunder that showed he could misuse his power as readily as Cosby. As the hearing resumed the next day, De Lancey struck at the two lawyers, removing Alexander and Smith not just from their representation of Zenger but also from the practice of law in New York.[59] So excessive was De Lancey's response that it brought clarity to the partisan nature of the case against Zenger, an important context for any jury called to the case. And it was a blunder that made the chief justice appear to lack the judicial wisdom to try such a sensitive case.

De Lancey appointed John Chambers to represent Zenger. Chambers was a competent lawyer, and he owed his job as recorder of the city to an appointment by Cosby. But Chambers was honest enough that he carried out one critical duty that, had he looked the other way, would have been disastrous for Zenger. Jurors were supposed to be chosen randomly on the spot from the Freeholders' Book. But when the sheriff, another Cosby appointee, presented a list of forty-eight potential jurors that he had pre-selected, Chambers recognized the irregular procedure and also that the list contained many men with conflicts of interest that tied them to the Cosby faction. Chambers objected, and De Lancey upheld the objection, as he had to do.[60]

Meanwhile, Alexander and Smith were at work behind the scenes. The case was too important for them to rely on Chambers. They needed an attorney who could aggressively argue the case and, even in a losing cause, show it to be the political trial that it surely was. So they engaged Andrew Hamilton, a leading politician in Philadelphia and perhaps the finest trial lawyer in the colonies. Born in Scotland, Hamilton rose to prominence early in his career by performing legal work for William Penn. Hamilton served as attorney general of Pennsylvania, speaker of the state assembly, and a member of the Provincial Council. By the time he had been recruited to take over Zenger's defense, he had purchased land in downtown Philadelphia for construction of a building that later became known as Independence Hall.[61]

Hamilton made his first appearance in the case—a surprise development for nearly everyone involved—as the trial began on August 4. De Lancey and Philipse presided over the session in a courtroom in City Hall with high ceilings and tall windows, every seat taken by people who anticipated a possible denouement to the intense struggle between the unpopular Cosby and those he considered his tormentors.[62]

Hamilton faced perhaps the biggest challenge of his career. The law of seditious libel gave him little room to maneuver because the role of the jury in such cases was so limited that it was almost a formality.[63] Under the common law, the jury's duty was merely to determine whether Zenger had published the words in question, and in fact intended to publish them, and whether the words referred to, in this case, the governor. These were questions of fact, and typically easy for the jury to determine. If the jury answered yes on these questions, then the trial went on to the most critical issue, a question of law that only the judges were empowered to answer—whether the words amounted to seditious libel. Thus the heart of Zenger's case was in the hands of two partisan justices, De Lancey and Philipse, and not a colonial jury drawn from the qualified freeholders. This was not a happy prospect for Zenger. But the limited role of the jury was not the only difficulty. Going back to the Star Chamber ruling in 1606, the crime of seditious libel did not permit a defense of truth. It mattered not at all that the criticisms of Cosby contained true statements or that they were matters of opinion and therefore neither true nor false.

To have any chance of winning the case, Hamilton needed to break new ground, never a strategy that provides much hope for a defendant. The jurors would have to ignore their limited role and decide the case themselves, taking it out of the hands of the justices. He had to per-suade the jury that Zenger's criticisms were true and that, contrary to seditious libel law, truth should be a defense. In other words, the jury had to return a verdict of not guilty even if they believed Zenger had published the newspaper with the criticisms. Hamilton needed an act of jury nullification—the jury acquitting Zenger because it disagreed with the fairness of the law being used against him.

Hamilton enjoyed an advantage that he could exploit. The *Weekly Journal* had enlarged the public sphere of discussion about Cosby, stimu-lating debate wherever people gathered in the city. Dissent was not a right recognized by law, but it was one that the people of New York increasingly understood was theirs if only because they had enjoyed it in practice. Since it was common for citizens to criticize Cosby wherever they met, would jurors who enjoyed that right for themselves deny it to Zenger? Hamilton decided to invite them not to.

WHEN THE TRIAL STARTED on August 4, the prosecutor, Attorney General Rich-ard Bradley, read the charges to the jury and the two justices. John Pe-ter Zenger, he said, "did falsely seditiously and scandalously print and publish . . . a certain false, malicious, seditious, scandalous libel" against Cosby.[64]

When Bradley finished reading the charge, Andrew Hamilton rose to address the judges on behalf of Zenger. He got to the point immediately, conceding that Zenger had indeed printed and published the issues of the *Weekly Journal* that were before the court and that he had a right to do so "when the matters so published can be supported with truth." Ham-ilton's statement was shocking, for he had as good as conceded the guilt of his client. Bradley pounced quickly; for him, the admission meant he would win his case. He told the chief justice that "as Mr. Hamilton has confessed the printing and publishing these libels, I think the jury must find a verdict for the King; for supposing they were true, the law says that they are not the less libelous for that; nay indeed the law says, their being true is an aggravation of the crime." Hamilton replied that his concession did not end the case; he said that Bradley must prove the words in the *Weekly Journal* articles were—as the charge stated, and emphasizing the first word—"false, scandalous, and seditious, or else they are not guilty."[65] He added that he disagreed with Bradley that "the just complaints of a number of men, who suffer under a bad administration, is libeling that administration."[66]

Hamilton had begun his assault on seditious libel. He could not have done better than to remind the jury that this legal doctrine that denied truth as a defense had been invented by the odious Star Chamber, whose "dreadful judgments" made it "the most dangerous court to the liberties of the people of England that ever was known in that kingdom."[67] Hamilton noted that in the charge filed against Zenger, Bradley himself had described the offense as "false, malicious, seditious, and scandalous libel. This word false must have some meaning, or else how came it there? I hope Mr. Attorney will not say he put it there by chance, and I am of opinion his information would not be good without it. . . . No, the falsehood makes the scandal, and both make the libel." Hamilton went on examining cases that he said supported his view. De Lancey was already growing weary of discussing what proof the law required, because it was clear to him. He was direct with Hamilton. "You cannot be admitted, Mr. Hamilton, to give the truth of a libel in evidence. A libel is not to be justified; for it is nevertheless a libel that it is true."[68]

The chief justice, Hamilton knew, would never let him prove the truth of the assertions in the articles. The law was clear on that point. But he wasn't actually arguing to the justices; he was hoping that his colloquy would influence the jury. Hamilton understood that his extended discussion would enable the jury to see the injustice of jailing a man for opposing the governor by writing the truth. If the *Weekly Journal* had indeed enlarged the public sphere of people debating Cosby's actions, wouldn't members of the jury realize that they had done the same thing as Zenger—that they had themselves engaged in criticism of the Cosby administration?

Hamilton had also judged that he didn't actually need to prove the truth in court because the jurors themselves knew what was true. After all, they had lived with Cosby for several years, and the sparring *Gazette* and *Weekly Journal* had instigated discussions throughout the city. Hamilton in fact asked the jurors to remember all that they knew about Governor Cosby and his abuse of power. He turned to the jury and said, "The law supposes you to be summoned, out of the neighborhood where the fact is alleged to be committed; and the reason of your being taken out of the neighborhood is, because you are supposed to have the best knowledge of the fact that is to be tried. . . . You are citizens of New York; you are really what the law supposes you to be, honest and lawful men; and, according to my brief, the facts which we offer to prove were not committed in a corner; they are notoriously known to be true; and therefore in your justice lies our safety." Hamilton concluded strongly. "And as we are denied the liberty of giving evidence to prove the truth of what we have published, I will beg leave to lay it down as a standing rule in such cases, that the suppressing of evidence ought always to be taken for the strongest evidence, and I hope it will have that weight with you."[69]

Hamilton had another opportunity to connect with the jurors after Bradley brought up the satire published in the *Weekly Journal*. Hamilton immediately challenged him. "Here it is plain the words are scandalous, scoffing, and ironical only as they are understood," Hamilton said. "I know no rule laid down in the books but this, I mean, as the words are understood." The chief justice intervened here, but apparently without any understanding of where Hamilton was going—that the nature of satire, which involved exaggeration, required the jury to judge the meaning of the words themselves and where truth ended and irony and sarcasm began. Thus, the jury would have to consider truth after all.

> De Lancey: Mr. Hamilton, do you think it so hard to know, when words are ironical or spoke in a scoffing manner?
>
> Hamilton: I own it may be known, but I insist the only rule to know is as I do or can understand them. I have no other rule to go by, but as I understand them.
>
> De Lancey: That is certain. All words are libelous or not, as they are understood. Those who are to judge the words, must judge whether they are scandalous or ironical, tend to the breach of the peace, or are seditious: there can be no doubt of it.
>
> Hamilton: I thank your honor; I am glad to find the court of this opinion. Then it follows that those twelve men must understand the

> words in the information to be scandalous, that is to say false; for
> I think it is not pretended they are of the ironical sort; and when
> they understand the words to be so, they will say we are guilty of
> publishing a false libel, and not otherwise.
>
> De Lancey: No, Mr. Hamilton, the jury may find that Zenger printed
> and published those papers, and leave it to the court to judge
> whether they are libelous . . .

Now Hamilton replied with a suggestion that the jury could not miss. "I know, may it please your honour, the jury may do so; but I do likewise know, they may do otherwise."[70]

Hamilton didn't let the idea drop. Now he argued to the jurors that dissent against corrupt authority was the right of a free people. The government could not "stop people's mouths when they feel themselves oppressed." He said, "When a ruler of the people brings his personal failings, but much more his vices, into his administration, and the people find themselves affected by them, either in their liberties or properties, that will alter the case mightily; and all the high things that are said in favor of rulers, and of dignities, and upon the side of power, will not be able to stop people's mouths when they feel themselves oppressed, I mean in a free government." To suppress speech through prosecutions was the work of tyrannical Star Chambers and kings, and "the practice of informations for libels is a sword in the hands of a wicked King, and an arrant coward, to cut down and destroy the innocent."[71] Hamilton continued his long soliloquy, hammering home to the jury that "they have a right publicly to remonstrate the abuses of power, in the strongest terms, to put their neighbors upon their guard, against the craft or open violence of men in authority."[72]

Hamilton began his summation to the jury, focusing on the same themes that he had advanced earlier. Referring obviously to Cosby, he argued that those "who injure and oppress the people under their administration, provoke them to cry out and complain; and then make that very complaint the foundation for new oppressions and prosecutions." He challenged the jury to lay "a noble foundation" for securing the right "both of exposing and opposing arbitrary power by speaking and writing truth."[73]

Chief Justice De Lancey gave a brief charge to the jurors, reminding them that Hamilton had conceded the only question for them to decide.

He all but told them to bring back a verdict against Zenger. With that the jurors left the courtroom to begin their deliberations. They returned in less than thirty minutes. Their foreman, Thomas Hunt, reported to the justices that John Peter Zenger was not guilty of seditious libel. The observers in the crowded courtroom shouted three huzzahs, and with that the case ended.[74]

EVEN AS ZENGER SPENT one more night in jail before his release, forty people joined Andrew Hamilton at the Black Horse Tavern for a party celebrating the verdict. The next day, as Hamilton left for Philadelphia from the harbor, he was saluted with a barrage of ceremonial cannon fire. The next month, the Common Council applauded Hamilton for "his learned and generous defense of the rights of mankind, and the liberty of the press."[75] News of the verdict spread up and down the coast and to London, with Hamilton's renown growing after Zenger himself published a book recounting the trial, which was probably the most popular book in America up to that time. As for Cosby, he lost the case and then his life a year later. Tuberculosis accomplished what several years of bitter opposition could not, the end of his unpopular reign over the colony. In leaving the world so soon after the trial, he missed the delicious irony of Zenger being appointed the following year as the official printer for the assembly.[76] It's safe to say that he would not have been happy.

What, then, was the meaning of the Zenger case? His acquittal is often noted as a landmark in the history of freedom of the press. The case, though, actually set no precedent in the law of seditious libel. In a narrow sense, it amounted to a victory for one printer, who received a unique reprieve from the application of an onerous law. But it did not change the law for those who followed. Only a written opinion handed down by a judge could potentially set the law moving in a different direction. As a verdict by a jury, the case carried no weight of precedent that a lawyer could use in the future to defend other writers and printers. Notwithstanding Hamilton's impassioned arguments and the jury's verdict, the ruling of the Star Chamber, that truth was not a defense to a libel claim, remained firmly intact.

Legal precedents, though, are not everything. The jury's resistance, coming after two failed attempts to convince grand juries to bring an indictment against Zenger, did signify a popular uprising against prosecutions intended to punish critics of government. Hamilton's arguments resonated with not just one colonial jury but also with people throughout the colonies. Seditious libel law had not changed, but public attitudes were beginning to seriously erode its foundation. The old Star Chamber rule that truth could not be used as a defense to a libel charge made no sense to people in America and seemed to emanate from a dark and repressive past. To a people aggrieved by royal officials and their overbearing policies, the idea that a man could be jailed for speaking the truth as he saw it or by expressing a critical opinion was clearly an affront to liberty. *Cato's Letters*, reprinted by James Alexander in the *Weekly Journal*, had made the central argument that criticism of government was not possible without freedom of the press. As the years passed by and relations worsened between the colonies and England, that conclusion would come to resonate all over America. More and more, people wanted to make their own decisions and run their own affairs, and for that they required the freedom to speak freely and to print and circulate their thoughts.

After the jury's verdict, popular resistance to libel charges brought by royal authorities seemed like too perilous a sea for prosecutors to navigate. In the late 1760s in Boston, as the Sons of Liberty opposed British measures infringing on the liberties of colonists, grand jurors resisted repeated attempts to indict the radical publishers of the *Boston Gazette* (see chapter 3). Indeed, from the Zenger case until independence, common law cases against dissidents all but disappeared. There appears to have been only one indictment brought for seditious libel—that of New York merchant Alexander McDougall (see chapter 5).[77] That didn't mean, though, that dissenters were free from the threat of prosecution. In colonial America, the courts were but one avenue for prosecution. Governors and provincial assemblies also held the power to suppress verbal crimes. Assemblies could summon dissenters, question them, and set penalties to punish their writings.[78]

The Zenger case enlarged public participation in politics. An entire city reverberated with debate over the conduct of government to an extent never before seen in the colonies. The *Weekly Journal* and its opposite number, the *Gazette*, provoked discussion everywhere—in homes, in taverns, in stores, in public squares. Inside a courtroom crowded with onlookers, Hamilton coaxed the jurors to reject the limited role required by the Star Chamber. Instead, they judged the value of political speech well beyond what the law allowed. They accepted Hamilton's invitation to dissent from what they had believed was an oppressive law.

With the three huzzahs that greeted the jury's verdict, America had taken a significant step toward the broader public participation and political expression that would prove essential to political liberty. It was a first tentative step, and something that the colonists would build on for the rest of the century.

3

THE EDITORS

FOR BENJAMIN EDES AND JOHN GILL, IT WAS A FEARSOME THING TO FACE THE ELDERS OF Boston. They had not been called to the town hall in 1757 for a pleasant chat or to the Green Dragon Tavern to make toasts to the king. The town leaders were in a foul mood, and it occurred to Edes and Gill that this could be the first step toward an extended stay for them in jail. After all, the two men were printers who had offended powerful figures who could prosecute them for seditious libel.

The two young men had launched the *Boston Gazette, or Country Journal* less than two years earlier, in 1755.[1] It did not take them long to begin making enemies. Trying to bring in extra revenue while building the circulation of their newspaper, Edes and Gill had been printing a wide range of material, including books, pamphlets, almanacs, and theological works. Some of the writings on religion were controversial. Boston was still a town nourished by its deep Puritan roots, and so it was no surprise that their printing of critical works on religion would bring out strong resentments.

Edes and Gill understood what was at stake. James Franklin, printer of the *New England Courant,* had gone to jail three decades earlier for offending the religious and civil authorities of the town.[2] Now it might be their turn. The selectmen spoke harshly. They told Edes and Gill that

some of their pamphlets "reflect grossly upon the receivd religious principles of this People which is verry Offensive." The selectmen held a financial threat over their heads, pointing out that Edes and Gill got official
printing business from the town of Boston, but that "if you go on printing
things of this Nature you must Expect no more favours from Us." The
loss of printing contracts with the government would be a serious financial setback that they could hardly afford, but at least they weren't going
to jail, and the town leaders had decided to give them a second chance.
Edes replied that he was sorry and that he "would take more care for the
future, & publish nothing that shall give any uneasiness to any Persons
whatever."[3]

However, Edes and Gill would disregard their promise not to cause
"uneasiness to any Persons." Less than five years later, troubles between
the colonies and England began to escalate. When the two printers once
again moved aggressively to attack those in authority, they aimed even
higher than the religious establishment of Boston. Now they launched
barbed attacks against Parliament, the British ministry, the governor of
the province, and other royal officials in America. In the next decade, the
printing shop of Edes and Gill became the center of fiery colonial opposition to British authority, especially to the Stamp Act, a tax that Parliament
imposed in 1765 requiring the colonists to use paper carrying a revenue
stamp for many of their printed documents.

The two men printed pamphlets that argued against the right of Parliament to impose taxes without the assent of the colonists themselves.
The *Boston Gazette* carried the writings, most often anonymous, of the
leading opposition leaders such as John Adams, Samuel Adams, James
Otis Jr., and James Warren. They called on Paul Revere to engrave the paper's masthead. Edes himself became a leading member of the Loyal Nine,
the radical group opposing the Stamp Act, publishing the *Boston Gazette*
by day and planning protests against the stamp distributor at night. Many
of the meetings of the Loyal Nine even took place in the newspaper's office. With Boston leading the colonial protests, reports from the *Boston
Gazette* were republished throughout the colonies and helped instigate
additional protests against the tax and the stamp distributors who were
to administer it. Francis Bernard, the royal governor caught in the mael-
strom, complained that the *Gazette* "swarmed with Libells of the most
atrocious kind."[4]

By the eve of the Revolution, it was no surprise that Edes and Gill were once again considered a target for authorities, but this time the British military. In September 1774, British troops occupied Boston (the skirmishes at Lexington and Concord were barely seven months away). An extraordinary letter was distributed that month to the British troops foretelling of "rebellion breaking out in this province" and providing the soldiers with the names of the "authors" of the rebellion—fifteen of the leading patriots of Boston, including Samuel Adams and John Hancock. These men were to be hunted down and killed if hostilities broke out. "The friends of your King and Country, and of America," the note said, "hope and expect it from you soldiers, the instant rebellion happens, that you will put the above persons immediately to the sword, destroy their houses and plunder their effects; it is just that they should be the first victims to the mischiefs they have bro't upon us."[5]

The author, though, was not finished. In an addendum to the letter, he added a few additional names of Boston citizens whom the British troops should murder, including the two printers of the *Boston Gazette:* "Don't forget those trumpeters of sedition, the printers Edes and Gill."[6]

EDES AND GILL WERE only the latest printers to cross swords with authorities. In 1735, John Peter Zenger had been put on trial for printing articles that held Governor William Cosby of New York up to withering scrutiny.

The issue of freedom of expression raised by the Zenger trial awaited a larger stage. That came with passage of the Stamp Act, a law so odious that it struck at the heart of how the colonists understood their rights as Englishmen, and so threatened the economy that many people feared a financial disaster. On both counts, many colonists saw that they had to act. By the time the protests had run their course, the colonists had exercised a far wider range of political speech than they had done before.

The protests would point the founding generation toward a much larger understanding of political expression and the power of dissent to influence public affairs. For the development of freedom of speech and press in colonial America, the Stamp Act protests would be the most important formative event. The printing press was the engine moving the protest forward, with newspapers and pamphlets enjoying wide distribution throughout the colonies. The public sphere of political expression was growing in other ways as well. The colonists opposing the Stamp Act met in taverns, town meetings, and public squares, and they sent their representatives to a congress of the colonies. They wrote letters, drafted resolutions, and sent petitions to King George III. They wrote verse and drew political cartoons. They adopted powerful symbols like liberty trees, hanged effigies of hated politicians, and assembled in demonstrations and parades. Ministers spoke from pulpits and political leaders from platforms.

After a year of wide-ranging protests, which had brought Parliament to the eve of repealing the Stamp Act, the two top officials in Massachusetts understood the power of dissent to change unpopular policy. The royal governor, Francis Bernard, wrote that the people of the colonies saw the impact of their political speech and would not submit passively in the future. "The People have felt their Strength," he wrote to Henry Seymour Conway, the British minister in charge of the American colonies, "& flatter themselves that it is much greater than it is; & will not of their own accord, submit readily to any thing they don't like; and there is no internal principle of policy which can by any Means restore the power of Government, & enforce a due subordination."[7]

For his part, Lieutenant Governor and Chief Justice Thomas Hutchinson said that "it is the universal voice of all people, that if the stamp act must take place we are absolute slaves," adding, "In the capital towns of several of the colonies and of this in particular, the authority is in the populace, no law can be carried into execution against their mind."[8]

THE STAMP ACT PROTESTS blossomed from fertile soil. Political expression had expanded in England and America for the previous hundred years and nourished colonists who opposed the tax. New venues for discussion had appeared as newspapers grew in the absence of stifling licensing laws and as people gathered and talked in public places such as taverns and coffeehouses. The threat of punishment through seditious libel prosecutions did not keep citizens from talking and complaining about the officials who governed them.

On both sides of the ocean, public houses provided a forum for discussing issues written about in the papers. London already boasted many taverns for a boisterous night out, but the first coffeehouse that appeared there in 1652 offered something very different—the perfect atmosphere for serious discussion. This new medium for social networking exploded over the next half century, with a couple thousand coffeehouses serving people in London alone by early in the eighteenth century.[9] Crowded, noisy, and reeking of tobacco smoke, the coffeehouses were known as the "penny universities" because patrons paid one pence to enter and an additional one or two pence for coffee or tea and access to the newspapers and pamphlets left out on the tables. Business was so brisk that the café owners made coffee in pots holding up to ten gallons. With licensing coming to an end, printed material in the cafés triggered discussion of every topic from literature and music to politics and commerce.[10]

In his diary of London life in the 1660s, Samuel Pepys wrote constantly of excursions to his favorite coffeehouses.[11] Historian Thomas Macaulay called the coffeehouses "a most important political institution," and "the chief organs through which the public opinion of the metropolis vented itself," a place where middle-and upper-class men went nearly every day. Some cafés like Will's were a place to be seen, said Macaulay, making it one of the most colorful places in all of London. There were "earls in stars and garters, clergymen in cassocks and bands, pert templars, sheepish lads from the universities, translators and index-makers in ragged coats of frieze," wrote Macaulay. "The great press was to get near the chair where John Dryden sate."[12]

With development of the coffeehouse culture, the political class—king, Parliament, and the aristocracy—had to share discussion of important public matters with a group of interested participants that had expanded to include the vast middle class. For Charles II, the coffeehouses suddenly looked like places where dangerous ideas might circulate and threaten the stability of the monarchy. So he issued a proclamation in 1675 to suppress the coffeehouses in London. They were places, said the king, "where the disaffected met, and spread scandalous reports concerning the conduct of his Majesty and Ministers." A few days later, petitioned by coffee and tea merchants who pointed out that he would give up substantial revenue from lost excise taxes on coffee, Charles II reluctantly rescinded his order. He could take solace in the fact that critical comment about him in the cafés at least produced good revenue to support his government and the very policies that the coffeehouse crowd complained about.[13]

The rise of the café political culture provided an important advance for public participation in government affairs. It was inside the coffeehouses, argues Jurgen Habermas, a German philosopher and sociologist, that what he calls the "bourgeois public sphere" was born—a realm in which the public could engage in vigorous discussion of contemporary affairs without the traditional subservience to authority. Habermas said that "critical debate ignited by works of literature and art was soon extended to include economic and political disputes."[14]

Where the king once imposed his will over millions of passive subjects who had little opportunity to dissent, now the public could discuss current affairs in the intimacy of a coffeehouse or through a vigorous exchange in the newspapers. The coffeehouse discussions brought a rising tide of letters to the newspapers, and together the public and the papers began to subject the king and Parliament to a much higher level of critical commentary.[15]

ACROSS THE OCEAN, in the British colonies of North America, the public sphere of political discussion was also expanding, propelled by forces as powerful as those in England. The colonists lived under English law and subject to the pronouncements of the king and Parliament. That much was clear enough. But the colonists were thousands of miles removed from the daily life and restrictions of England. It took six weeks or so for messages to go to London and even longer to return due to the Gulf Stream, and life could not stop in the meantime.

Even with royal governors living among them, the colonists enjoyed some limited self-government through their assemblies and town meetings. And because they lived in small towns and in the endless farmlands and woodlands beyond, they faced challenges that called on their ability to make decisions for themselves. They were, by nature and for their own survival, a self-reliant people. However much they felt themselves loyal subjects of the king—and the vast majority did so until shortly before the Revolution—actions by a far-off Parliament and ministry could seem out of touch with their own reality.

Another powerful force drove many colonists toward the kind of independence of thought that invigorated public discussion. For many people, the reason for coming to America was their disagreement with authorities in England, especially on matters of religion. As the Stamp Act protests unfolded in Boston, John Adams reminded everyone that the Puritans who came to Massachusetts seeking religious freedom already were protestors. Before the Protestant Reformation, Adams said, the civil and ecclesiastical authorities kept people in line "by reducing their minds to a state of sordid ignorance and staring timidity, and by infusing into them a religious horror of letters and knowledge."[16] But the Reformation brought the slow spread of knowledge that began to free men from blind loyalty to authority.

Adams wrote, in a memorable phrase, that the Puritans had "at last resolved to fly to the wilderness" to escape "plagues and scourges of their native country" and start anew. "It was this great struggle that peopled America," Adams wrote. "It was not religion alone, as is commonly supposed; but it was a love of universal liberty, and a hatred, a dread, a horror, of the infernal confederacy" of tyrannical rule that "accomplished the settlement of America."[17]

Adams was early in sounding the note of democratic self-governance, and in tying freedom of expression to the need to oversee the work of officials. The people, Adams said, have "a right, an indisputable, unalienable, indefeasible, divine right to that most dreaded and envied kind of knowledge, I mean, of the characters and conduct of their rulers." Rulers serve as agents for the people, and if they betray their trust, "the people have a right to revoke the authority that they themselves have deputed" and replace them.[18]

If rulers did indeed serve as agents of the people, vigorous discussion was required to take the measure of their performance. But legal restrictions ensnared many people who expressed themselves. Nearly all of the seditious libel cases discovered in records of seventeenth-century America came as a result of spoken words. The first printing press arrived in Massachusetts in 1638, but the output of materials was limited. The colony's authorities prosecuted some writers who circulated pamphlets challenging church or civilian authority. A theological pamphlet printed in England in 1650 was ordered burned in the Boston marketplace, and another that urged the election of rulers was suppressed in 1661 after its author acknowledged to the General Court that his writings "manifestly scandalize" the king and Parliament.[19]

The General Court passed the first censorship law in Massachusetts in 1662, and over the years various licensing requirements ebbed and flowed. Royal governors carried instructions from London to control the printing presses through licensing, even after licensing expired in England in

1695. The first newspaper in the colonies, *Publick Occurrences, both Forreign and Domestick,* was printed in Boston in 1690, but the governor and council immediately shut it down.[20]

In 1704, the *Boston News-Letter* appeared as the first regularly published paper in America, carrying "Published by Authority" directly under its title—the paper in fact was licensed by the government and approved by officials before publication.[21] A rival, the *Boston Gazette,* appeared in 1719. Until then, pamphlets had occasionally raised political issues, but now, slowly, paid advertisements voicing political opinions appeared in newspapers. By 1721, the colony was no longer under licensing, but that did not stop James Franklin from getting into trouble with his *New England Courant.* Franklin went to jail on the orders of the legislature and avoided a second arrest by hiding from the deputy sheriff.[22]

Even as Boston newspapers struggled for some semblance of freedom, many people read them either by subscription or in public places. London had its coffeehouses, but in Boston it was the taverns that served as the most vital public spaces for everyday discussion. As regulations on the sale of spirits eased, men streamed into the 162 taverns that had popped up all over town by 1752.[23] A little rum and cider had a way of freeing a man of his stiff Puritan upbringing, loosening his tongue, and getting him going in a good argument.

As in London, the newspapers and public houses enjoyed a symbiotic relationship. Many taverns made newspapers, pamphlets, and broadsides available for their customers. Even decades before the Stamp Act made the town eager for political news of any kind, James Pitson's tavern carried thirty-one pamphlets and eighty-eight books for its clientele of artisans and tradesmen, who might otherwise not have purchased the materials.[24] Later, as Boston became bitterly politicized over the Stamp Act, the taverns became hotbeds of political agitation. Many of the tavern owners were themselves men who were dedicated to defying the Stamp Act. Eighty-nine men held a license to sell spirits or run a tavern in 1765, of whom twenty were members of the radical Sons of Liberty opposed to the Stamp Act, and others were surely sympathizers, putting the town's most radical faction in close contact with thousands of Boston residents.[25]

The taverns were important as a forum for expression because they helped make political ideas popular. Through conversation in the taverns, ideas about rights and liberties from the newspapers and from learned authors of political pamphlets were made intelligible and part of the popular conversation, an element of the air that Bostonians and other colonists breathed.[26] And with that, the resistance to London's imposition of taxes could grow into a broad democratic force, providing a large group of participants for mass demonstrations and parades. One Loyalist complained in the next decade of people who "attend at taverns, where they talk politicks, get drunk, damn King, Ministers and Taxes; and *vow* they will follow any measures proposed to them by their demagogues, however repugnant to religion, reason and common sense."[27]

While taverns provided a popular forum for discussion, the political clubs of the town gave the well-connected merchants and politicians an opportunity to form political strategies. The Boston Caucus was the most exclusive, a private club that may have started as early as the 1720s in the North End.[28] Later, there was also a South End Caucus, a Middle District Caucus, and more.[29] John Adams probably referred to the South End Caucus when he noted a meeting that took place in the garret in the home of Tom Daws, the adjutant of the Boston Regiment. Adams wrote that the group would "smoke tobacco till you cannot see from one End of the Garrett to the other."[30] As with other caucuses, they argued over political affairs and agreed on candidates to promote for local offices.

The discussions in clubs and taverns birthed ideas for the Boston town meeting, where policy was made and voted on.[31] The town meeting was the iconic representation of democratic governance, where people could speak their mind on local problems and grievances. Sometimes people discussed and passed resolutions with special requests to the elected assembly and voted instructions to their delegates on the stands they ought to take on important questions.

The town meetings, though, were far from fully democratic exercises in self-governance because of the limitations they placed on suffrage. Women and free blacks could not vote. Not even all white men could vote. As was common throughout the colonies, suffrage in Massachusetts was a right restricted to white men who owned property. In the belief that only ownership of property gave people a stake in the affairs of their community, the law restricted voting to those who owned a freehold or any property of a specified value.[32] In the years before the Revolution, the percentage of men in Boston and nearby towns qualified to vote was between 56 and 70 percent.[33]

Despite limitations on suffrage, debate and criticism were becoming common whenever people met, and were often conducted at a high decibel level. "How common is it to see a Shoemaker, Taylor, or Barber, haranguing with a great deal of Warmth on the publick Affairs?" one anonymous newspaper writer observed. "He will condemn a General, Governor, or Province with as much Assurance as if he were of the Privy Council, and knew exactly wherein they had been faulty."

The writer knew where to lay the blame. "He gets his Knowledge from the News-Papers, and looks upon it undoubtedly true because it is printed."[34]

THE NEWSPAPERS, ALONG WITH editors like Edes and Gill, came into their own with passage of the Stamp Act. The imposition of a tax without consent of the people of America raised a storm of protest that greatly enlarged the public sphere, drawing in people from many walks of life and motivating them to utilize every means of expression possible to make their views known.

The developing problem between the colonies and England had its roots in the defeat of the French on the Plains of Abraham outside Quebec in 1759. The war for domination of North America was all but over, with England firmly in control, but it had been expensive in British lives and treasure. With victory, officials in London looked to the colonies as a potential source of revenue to fill depleted accounts; the national debt of England had risen from about 72 million pounds to 129 million pounds between 1755 and 1764. London also decided to station ten thousand British troops in America for defensive purposes and to stop smuggling, adding an estimated 220,000 pounds of annual expense.[35] Government ministers discussed various schemes to raise money, caring little how Americans would view taxes imposed by a Parliament sitting thousands of miles away. Their decisions would send England and America on a course of deepening conflict.

George Grenville, who had taken over from Lord Bute as prime minister in 1763, pushed enactment of the Sugar Act a year later. Although it reduced the tax on molasses by half, strict new measures to collect the tax meant that widespread evasion by colonial merchants would end.[36] Reaction in the colonies was swift and negative, with fears that the tax would reduce lucrative trade on which the colonies were dependent.[37]

Far from convincing London to reconsider, the colonies absorbed another blow in March 1765 when Parliament passed the Stamp Act. Parliament decreed that violations be adjudicated in vice admiralty courts rather than in the common law courts before a jury of peers. Vice admiralty courts, which had jurisdiction over routine maritime issues, could not remotely be justified as tribunals to hear cases involving violations of the Stamp Act. Englishmen treasured their right to be tried by a jury of their peers, and the violation of that basic civil liberty caused outrage up and down the coast.[38]

The law required that many documents—including contracts, deeds, bonds, mortgages, bills of sales, and court papers—be printed on paper with a tax stamp. Media such as newspapers, pamphlets, and almanacs also had to use stamped paper. Because the colonies did not have sufficient equipment to imprint the paper, the authorities would have to ship pre-stamped paper from Britain to America, where local stamp agents would distribute it and receive a commission of 8 percent.[39]

The stamp tax promised to raise the cost of many goods and services, threatening an economy still in the grip of a postwar recession. In Boston, the waterfront and the shipping industry, distressed by declining trade caused by the Sugar Act, faced the certainty of another falloff in business, with rising unemployment among dockworkers and ship crews, a notoriously rowdy lot to begin with. Merchants were sure to suffer, too, as well as lawyers who faced increased costs for the common legal documents that they used every day.

Printers faced a tax that they feared could make their newspapers unaffordable to many subscribers. And a tax on advertisements—in some cases effectively doubling the cost—would make ads unaffordable for many businesses.[40] As Benjamin Franklin, a printer since the 1720s and the owner of the *Pennsylvania Gazette,* wrote from London a month before passage of the Stamp Act, "I think it will affect the Printers more than anybody."[41]

The printers, though, were in a better position than anyone else to fight back. They did not wait long to do so.

BENJAMIN EDES AND JOHN GILL were friends and both only twenty-two when they decided to go into the printing business together.[42] For two young men of modest means, their opportunities in Boston were limited in 1754 to pursuing a trade. Gill had apprenticed to a printer, Samuel Kneeland. Edes, the son of a hatter and born across the river in Charlestown, may have apprenticed to Kneeland as well. After learning the trade, the two started their own printing business and launched a weekly newspaper that they called the *Country-Journal*.

Printing was the most intellectually stimulating of the trades, enabling Edes and Gill to work with authors who were among the colony's elite—well-educated lawyers, merchants, and politicians who wanted their voices to reach a broad audience. After 1760, many printers held a position of some influence, despite the fact that their trade involved heavy manual labor that put them well outside the lofty social rank of a gentleman. With the rising conflict with England, men who owned a printing press controlled to a great extent the traffic in ideas that reached the people of Boston and other towns as they debated their relationship with Britain.

The crisis with Britain drove the demand for more news and convinced patriot leaders that newspapers could be potent political weapons to sway public opinion. Each individual crisis helped birth papers at twice the rate of the growth in population between 1760 and the start of the Revolution. The number of colonial papers grew during the Sugar and Stamp Acts from twenty-two in 1763 to twenty-seven in 1765, then to forty-two as the war broke out ten years later.[43] The Stamp Act dispute helped the circulation of newspapers, too, with circulation of individual papers in the large towns averaging almost fifteen hundred.[44]

Edes and Gill faced a difficult challenge in making a financial success of their business. Most printers danced on the edge of solvency. James Parker reported that at least one-quarter of his subscribers to the *New York Gazette or Weekly Post-Boy* failed to pay their bills. The publisher of the *New-Hampshire Gazette* complained that it was "not possible to print News Papers without a Stock of Paper, Ink, Hands, and in Winters a good Fire." Some printers won contracts to print government documents to add revenue.[45] Edes and Gill struggled for subscriptions, so when the opportunity presented itself, they acquired the established *Boston Gazette*, and combined the two into the *Boston Gazette, or Country Journal*. They kept their presses busy between issues with pamphlets and almanacs, and they sold ink and paper and other goods for additional revenue, as many publishers were forced to do to pay their bills. Edes took on the job of constable to expand his contacts and bring in more printing jobs.

Like most newspapers of the founding period, the *Boston Gazette* was a weekly of four pages, although it sometimes came with a fifth "Supplement" page to accommodate periods of heavy news and advertisements. Newspapers of the time offered readers no visual allure. They had three or four columns of dense gray type on each page and articles set off by headlines only a word or two in length, simply a label of the place and date. Some mastheads added a decoration like an allegorical figure—Edes used a woodcut of a woman, Britannia, holding a liberty pole and releasing a dove of peace from a birdcage. And sometimes a rough woodcut added interest to an article or an ad deeper into the paper. Editors often printed long speeches or proclamations—sometimes as the lead item on page one—and they reprinted many articles taken from papers throughout the colonies and London. Their coverage included accounts of local events and business news such as the comings and goings of ships at the port. As the troubles deepened between the colonies and Britain, Edes and Gill and many other publishers began printing more and more letters and political articles, usually under a pseudonym, that took a strong stance on issues of the day.[46]

The troubles with Britain lifted the two young printers to prominence not only in Boston but also throughout the colonies. The pledge by Edes and Gill to the elders of Boston not to "give any uneasiness to any Persons" fell aside as the decade of the 1760s unfolded. The first person to feel uneasiness at an Edes and Gill publication was Governor Bernard. A lawyer and local government official in England, Bernard received appointment as royal governor of New Jersey in 1758 because he enjoyed the good fortune of knowing the right person—in his case, the powerful Lord Barrington, a cousin of his wife. Two years later, Bernard became governor of the province of Massachusetts. Like many other royal officials chosen for patronage reasons, he was a man who lacked critical political skills and would prove unequal to the task of governing a colony.[47]

Bernard made a serious mistake shortly after taking office. The previous governor, Thomas Pownall, had promised a seat on the Superior Court to James Otis Sr., one of the most prominent lawyers in Boston, when one opened up, but Bernard refused to honor the promise. Instead, he appointed Thomas Hutchinson to become chief justice. Hutchinson, one of the colony's wealthiest men, was already the lieutenant governor.[48] That broken promise earned both Bernard and Hutchinson the hatred of Otis's son, James Otis Jr. The younger Otis struck quickly at Governor Bernard. In 1761, the colony was embroiled in a controversy over writs of assistance, general search warrants that enabled customs officials at their discretion to search any building for goods smuggled in violation of British trade laws. Customs officers had been instructed to seek such writs from the colony's courts. Otis represented Boston merchants in opposing them. He argued before the Superior Court and before Hutchinson, whom Otis believed had stolen his father's rightful position, that the writs violated the natural rights of mankind.

Otis lost the case, but his challenge to the power of Parliament and his appeal to the basic tenets of English liberty would resound for the next decade. Otis had gained an audience in the colonies, and his challenge to British authority would become contagious.[49] "Then and there was the first scene of the first act of opposition to the arbitrary claims of Great Britain," John Adams wrote many years later. "Then and there the child Independence was born."[50]

THE CONTROVERSY OVER the writs of assistance gave way quickly to the Sugar Act and the Stamp Act. The floodgates of political speech had opened for the founding generation and there would be no closing them. Otis wrote that Parliament's passage of the Sugar Act in 1764 "set people a-thinking, in six months, more than they had done in their whole lives before."[51]

Much of the protest literature in Boston came off the Edes and Gill press. Dissent against the imposition of taxes started, not surprisingly, with some of the best-educated minds in colonial society and with material that only other well-educated people were likely to read. They began attacking Parliament with essays and pamphlets that probed deeply into the extent of Parliament's power to tax and legislate over the colonies and the limits, if any, that natural law placed on the exercise of Parliament's sovereign power.

Edes and Gill published a series of pamphlets by Otis that challenged the authority of Parliament to tax the colonies. Otis grounded his opposition in Radical Whig philosophy that the threat to liberty came from unchecked power wielded by the king and Parliament. The tyrannical James II had been overthrown in the Glorious Revolution of 1688–1689,

but Radical Whigs believed that the threat posed by overreaching authority required eternal vigilance. British imposition of taxes on the colonies
without consent was exactly the abuse of power that moved the Whigs to
action.

Just after Parliament enacted the Sugar Act in 1764, Otis wrote *The
Rights of the British Colonies Asserted and Proved*, which achieved broad
influence in the colonies and was reprinted in England. Otis acknowledged the sovereign power of Parliament—there was no legal power above
it—but declared nonetheless that even a sovereign could not do anything
it pleased. As Otis decisively wrote, "The Parliament cannot make 2 and
2, 5: omnipotency cannot do it." The imposition of the Sugar Tax without colonial representation in Parliament, he said, violated the colonists'
rights as freeborn British subjects, "depriving them of one of their most
essential rights as freemen, and if continued seems to be in effect an entire
disfranchisement of every civil right."[52]

Daniel Dulany, a lawyer and politician who had been educated at
Cambridge, wrote the most influential pamphlet. Dulany refuted the assertion by some English politicians that the colonies could be constitu-
tionally taxed by Parliament because they had "virtual" representation
in the House of Commons. The colonies, it was argued, were no different
than some important cities in England such as Manchester and Birming-
ham, which sent no representatives to Parliament and yet were considered represented there because members of Parliament represented all the
people and not just their own constituents. But Dulany argued that while
there was close interdependence and mutual interest between members of
Parliament and people in England, that was not the case in faraway America. Without a mutuality of interest, Dulany said, virtual representation
could not exist.[53] Loyalists answered with essays of their own. "The position that we are bound by no laws to which we have not consented, either
by ourselves, or our representatives, is a novel position, unsupported by
any authoritative record of the British constitution, ancient or modern,"
wrote the Anglican minister Samuel Seabury. "It is republican in its very
nature, and tends to the utter subversion of the English monarchy."[54]

Protest speech came from many of the colonial assemblies as well,
and some petitioned the king for relief. The Massachusetts House of
Representatives drafted an aggressive petition to King George III in 1764
denying the legal authority of Parliament to tax the colonies, but more

cautious politicians like Hutchinson managed to tone it down before it was sent across the water. The petition asked merely for continuation of the privilege that the colonies enjoyed of taxing themselves. Even Governor Bernard found the petition agreeable and approved it. Soon enough, New York moved well beyond Massachusetts and sent a petition of its own to London in October denying "all taxes not granted by themselves." Petitions from many other colonies followed, protesting against the tax on sugar and trying to dissuade Parliament from passing the stamp taxes that were under discussion.[55]

The argument that the colonists should enjoy the right of representation would have implications beyond the immediate issue of taxation. For the patriots were beginning their journey toward a new constitutional system in which power was exercised, and public measures taken, only with consent of the governed. Most important for freedom of speech, this system of representative democracy required broader rights of political expression than had been recognized before. If the colonies continued on this journey, it seemed that they would at some time have to rebel against the crime of seditious libel.

OVER THE NEXT DECADE, the *Boston Gazette* became the most partisan paper in America. For Edes and Gill, there was no line between publishing and political activism. They vilified Governor Bernard and the Stamp Act every Monday with a new issue of their newspaper, working as the movement's publishing arm. The editors not only published the Radical Whigs in the *Boston Gazette,* but also partnered with them in running the paper. Bernard understood the alliance all too well. Referring to Samuel Adams and James Otis Jr., two of his most prominent foes in the legislature, he wrote that "two of the chief leaders of the faction in the House are the principal managers of the *Boston Gazette.*"[56]

Bernard was not without allies of his own. Arrayed against the Boston radicals were the friends of government, a group that did not necessarily like the stamp tax but rejected expansive ideas about the rights of the colonists. They believed that Parliament was a sovereign power and as such could impose taxes, and that a conspiracy did not exist in London to violate their rights as Englishmen. They could go along with remonstrances to the king, but counseled moderation. They believed in enduring the taxes while negotiating for a better deal. Thomas Hutchinson was among the friends of government, which composed the majority of the Governor's Council in 1765.[57]

Much of the radical politics of Boston sprung initially from the Loyal Nine, the political club of nine Boston men who met regularly and directed the growing protests against the Stamp Act and the local stamp distributors. By later in 1765, amidst the growing opposition to the tax, the Loyal Nine blended into the much larger Sons of Liberty organization. From the start, Benjamin Edes was a member of the Loyal Nine. He used publishing as his base but in fact left his fingerprints all over the agitation in Boston. He did not distinguish the world of publishing from that of political activism, for to him they were one and the same.

The Loyal Nine's members came from the merchant and artisan middle class—including two distillers, two braziers, a painter, jeweler, and ship captain. Six members of the Loyal Nine, including Edes, planned the major demonstration held in Boston on August 14, hanging effigies from a giant elm early in the morning (see "The Shoemaker," chapter 4).[58] After another protest organized by the Loyal Nine at which the stamp distributor resigned, they gathered to celebrate. According to one member of the Loyal Nine, Henry Bass, they "had a very Genteel Supper provided to which we invited your very good friends Mr. S[amuel] A[dams] and E[des] & G[ill] and three or four others and spent the Evening in a very agreeable manner Drinkg Healths etc."[59] A few years later, John Adams noted in his diary that he had spent an evening with Edes, Gill, Samuel Adams, and James Otis working on editorial material for the *Boston Gazette*. "The Evening spent in preparing the Next Days Newspaper—a curious Employment. Cooking up Paragraphs, Articles, Occurrences, & c.—working the political Engine!"[60]

This "political engine" of Edes and Gill made the *Boston Gazette* into the chief organ of protest against the Stamp Act in all the colonies. They filled their pages every week with broad coverage of the developing drama—essays and articles, letters and news, resolves by colonial assemblies, and proclamations by Governor Bernard. The grease that enabled their printing press to move smoothly was political vitriol, for newspaper editors the most abundant natural resource of the time. The *Boston Gazette* often attacked all those in the colonies who supported the stamp taxes with evocative name-calling. "Let therefore all those apostate sons of venality," the paper said in a typically breathless attack, "those wretched hirelings, and execrable parricides, those first-born sons of Hell, who for a little filthy lucre, have thus as far as they were able, betray'd and murder'd their country, with the vile slander of their contagious breath and dire hissing of their forked tongues, conscious of their base perfidious lies, blush and be confounded at the light of the sun, and tremble at the countenance of the sons of honour and vertue."[61]

On December 2, 1765, a month after the Stamp Act became effective, Edes and Gill published a verse that was shocking in its portrayal of Britain. The writer compared the relationship between the colonies and their "Mother," Britain, to Britain's bloody relationship with France. Mother had given her children in America nothing less than slavery and venereal disease:

> *Spurn the Relation—She's no more a Mother,*
> *Than Lewis to George, a Most Christian Brother,*
> *In French Wars and Scotch, grown generous and rich*
> *She gives her dear Children Pox, Slavery, and Itch.*[62]

In the same issue, another anonymous writer directed calumny toward Prime Minister George Grenville, who had championed the Stamp Act, suggesting that the colonists would help him hang himself.

> *To make us all Slaves, now you've lost Sir! the Hope,*
> *You've but to go hang yourself.*
> *We'll find you the Rope.*[63]

Why waste a good hanging when it could be turned into political commentary? Another paper in town, the *Boston Evening-Post,* pointed to the execution of a man convicted of murder to score a point. "Saturday last was executed, Henry Halbert, pursuant to his sentence, for the murder of the son of Jacob Woolman—*He will never pay any of the taxes unjustly laid on these once happy lands.*"[64]

It all served the purpose of opposing the Stamp Act. "If the British Parliament have right to impose a Stamp Tax," the *Boston Gazette* said, "they have a right to lay on us a Poll Tax, a Land Tax, a Malt Tax, a Cyder Tax, a Window Tax, a Smoke Tax, and why not Tax us for the Light of the Sun, the Air we Breathe, and the Ground we are Buried in?"[65]

Not far from Boston, the *Newport Mercury* lampooned Bernard with satiric verse about his safeguarding the stamped paper in Castle William in Boston harbor:

> *Undrawn, unbroken and unpry'd,*
> *Unfelt, unsmelt, untasted, & uney'd,*
> *Unboil'd, unbak'd, unroasted, and unfry'd;*
> *Protecting them from all abuse,*
> *And keeping them unus'd, for use*[66]

At the same time in New York, Lieutenant-Governor Colden absorbed abuse from the papers. In September 1765, he complained that "virulent papers were published in the Weekly Newspapers, fill'd with every falsehood that malice could invent to serve their purpose of exciting the People to disobedience of the Laws and to Sedition."[67]

The newspapers even attacked their own, as the shelf life of colonial heroes could be perilously short if they disappointed others in the cause. After his influential defense of the rights of the colonists against taxation by Parliament, Otis responded to a pamphlet written by a Loyalist and in doing so compromised some of the arguments he had made the previous year. Now part of Boston turned viciously against him. Otis took to the *Boston Gazette* to defend himself, addressing his "once dear friends" in their "most severe and undeserved censures of a man, who has risked his life, his family, his all, in your service, more than once."[68] On the very same day, though, in a competing paper, the *Boston Evening-Post*, a writer ran Otis ("Jemmy") through with his pen, declaring,

> *And Jemmy is a silly dog, and Jemmy is a tool;*
> *And Jemmy is a stupid cur, and Jemmy is a fool;*
> *And Jemmy is a madman, and Jemmy is an ass,*
> *And Jemmy has a leaden head, and forehead spread with Brass.*[69]

Governor Bernard must have enjoyed seeing his nemesis scolded like this, but most of the time he seethed at the invective of Edes and Gill. Bernard wrote to his superiors in London that the *Boston Gazette* was the "most factious paper in America." Bernard mused that if he took a seditious libel prosecution against Edes and Gill to a jury, he would "doubt not but that they would have concurred in a severe Censure of the Authors or printers." He said that "since the factious writers of this Place have Spit their Venom against the Kings Government at home & the Legislature of Great Britain, my Patience had a severer Exercise than Usual."[70]

THE PATRIOTS OF BOSTON were not alone in opposing the taxes. At the end of May 1765, Patrick Henry stood before the Virginia House of Burgesses in Williamsburg.[71] Although he had been sworn in only nine days earlier, Henry was not a wallflower who waited his turn behind more experienced politicians. With only 39 of the 116 representatives attending the chamber at the time, Henry introduced a series of resolutions that strongly condemned the Stamp Act. The resolutions were opposed by most of the leadership of the assembly, who argued that they had sent a more conciliatory petition opposing the Stamp Act to England and were still awaiting a response.

Thomas Jefferson, who was then twenty-two and living in Williamsburg while studying law, was listening at the door to the chamber and later recalled Henry's "torrents of sublime eloquence" that carried five resolutions to passage, the fifth by just a 20–19 vote, and the others by no more than five votes. Jefferson said that the debate on that fifth measure was "most bloody." Historical accounts are fuzzy, but the fifth resolution declared that the Virginia General Assembly alone had the power to tax the inhabitants of the colony. That resolution and two others that the burgesses had either not considered or turned down outright were regarded by at least some of the representatives as treasonous. One of the resolutions that had not passed promoted resistance by stating that the colonists were not bound to obey any tax laws except those enacted by their own representatives.[72] The next day, after Henry had left town, taking his vote with him, the more conservative burgesses insisted on another vote and rescinded the fifth resolution, which had been carried by a single vote, leaving only the four most moderate ones.

With a little manipulation, though, the Virginia Resolves looked to many citizens in the colonies like a much more radical document. The Loyalist editor of the local *Virginia Gazette*, Joseph Royle, refused to publish Virginia's protest, providing an opening for critics of the Stamp Act to circulate their own version and to publish a history more to their liking. The newspapers in the North reprinted the four resolutions that had passed as well as two or three of the others that had been defeated or rescinded, as if Virginia had passed all of them. That expansion of the Resolves made them appear far more aggressive in defiance of Britain than the resolutions that were actually adopted—the expanded version called for active resistance where the enacted ones had not.[73]

The expanded version carried great weight because of the reputation enjoyed by the Virginia lawmakers. The *Newport Mercury* printed six resolutions on June 24, attributing them anonymously to "a Letter from a Gentleman in Philadelphia,"[74] and the *Boston Gazette* in turn reprinted the Newport article a week later.[75] The *Maryland Gazette* printed all seven resolutions on July 7. With protests building in the colonies, people were willing enough to believe that the influential Virginians would lead the way.

It mattered not at all to Edes and Gill that the *Virginia Gazette*'s Royle, knowing what actually happened in Virginia, published an article on August 30 expressing "no small Degree of Surprise" that newspapers in the northern colonies were printing articles about Virginia that were "destitute of Truth." Writing of the newspaper editors, he warned that "it is very certain they are often liable to be imposed upon, by designing or credulous Correspondents: In the present Instance, this is obvious to every One in the least acquainted with the late Occurrences in Virginia; for which . . . we take this Method to undeceive them, not doubting but they will instantly break off so wretched a Correspondence."[76]

In Boston, after reading the incorrect version of the Virginia Resolves in the paper, Bernard wrote in a letter to London that they raised "the Spirit of Rebellion" and "have roused up the Boston Politicians & have been the Occasion of a fresh mundation of factious & insolent pieces in the popular Newspapers." Bernard did not actually see the correct version of the Virginia Resolves until it went to London and then came back to him in Boston later in the year.[77]

With an inaccurate version serving as a model, other colonial assemblies met and passed their own resolutions. Rhode Island for the most part copied the Virginia Resolves as published in its hometown *Newport Mercury*, along with another resolution of its own that held officers of the colony harmless for acting consistent with the resolutions. In the end, most of the colonies passed resolutions of their own stating that Parliament lacked taxing power over the colonies.[78]

In Massachusetts, the *Boston Gazette* compared the Virginia Resolves to the Bay Colony's own feeble effort the previous year when conservative politicians had watered down the assembly's strong draft against the Sugar Act. As an anonymous writer put it, the Virginians' "spirited Resolves do indeed serve as a perfect contrast for a certain tame, pusillanimous, daub'd Insipid Thing, delicately touch'd up & call'd an Address; which was lately sent from this Side the Water, to please the Taste of the Tools of Corruption on the other." Just in case anyone doubted where Edes and Gill stood, the article called supporters of the Stamp Act "dirty Sycophants," "ministerial Hacks," "detestable Villains," "hungry Wolves," and "insatiable Vultures." It added "devouring Monsters," in case anyone missed the point.[79]

Politicians in Massachusetts would be "devouring Monsters" no more. Already, the Massachusetts House sent a circular letter to its sister assemblies throughout the colonies, proposing a meeting in New York to formulate a united response to the Stamp Act. Nine of the colonies participated in the meetings convened in October 1765, spending several weeks wrangling over how far to go in defining what it believed to be the extent of Parliament's power over the colonies.

In the end, the Stamp Act Congress approved petitions to the king and the House of Commons and a memorial to the House of Lords. The delegates affirmed "the warmest Sentiments of Affection and Duty to his Majesty's Person and Government." But they declared that Parliament could not impose taxes on them without their consent given by their own representatives. The delegates grounded their assertions not only in their constitutional rights as Englishmen but also more broadly in the natural rights of all mankind. The Massachusetts Assembly unanimously passed resolutions as well, declaring their rights under both the British constitution and "the law of God and nature."[80]

On November 4, three days after the Stamp Act became effective, the *Boston Gazette* published the Massachusetts resolutions. Nearly every article Edes and Gill published that day pertained to the tax. They printed the instructions voted by the towns of Plymouth, Newbury-Port, and Ipswich to their elected representatives, all passing along their displeasure with the Stamp Act.[81] From the town meetings to the local presses, the scope of political expression was growing.

AS IF THE REGULAR NEWSPAPERS were not extreme enough in their attacks on the Stamp Act, a radical new journal reached the streets of New York on September 21, 1765. The *Constitutional Courant,* which would publish only that single issue, was the work of William Goddard but mysteriously noted that it was "Printed by ANDREW MARVEL, at the Sign of *the Bribe refused,* on *Constitutional Hill, North-America.*" Printed in Woodbridge, New Jersey, it was carried by post riders to Boston and other major towns, and was reprinted several times, with a Boston edition possibly coming off the Edes and Gill press. The newspaper, Governor Bernard wrote to the Board of Trade in London, "is an infamous libel against the Government of Great Britain so outrageous & indecent, that it has been printed at a private press."[82] In New York, meanwhile, Lieutenant-Governor Colden advised against any legal action against the *Constitutional Courant,* as it would "be the occasion for raising the Mob, which it is thought proper by all means to avoid."[83]

The *Constitutional Courant* consisted largely of two essays by anonymous writers calling themselves Philoleutherus and Philopatriae. Their essays certainly ranked among the most radical writings published during the entire Stamp Act crisis. "Shall we sit down quietly, while the yoke of slavery is wreathing about our necks?" Philoleutherus asked. The colonists, he said, should "besiege the throne with petitions and humble remonstrances," and he excoriated those who "refused to cooperate in so noble an attempt." Those who took the office of stamp distributor were the "blots and stains of America" and "vipers of human kind." The other writer, Philopatriae, said that he did not endorse violence against stamp distributors, but that "the guilt of all these violence's is most justly chargeable upon the authors and abettors of the Stamp Act."[84]

The radical writing, though, was not the only significant thing about the *Constitutional Courant.* For two of its three editions also carried an image of a writhing snake across the top of the masthead on page one. It was a striking image because the snake was severed into eight pieces and labeled with the names of individual colonies or regions along with the pointed counsel "JOIN OR DIE." The serpent cartoon, first drawn by Benjamin Franklin and published in his *Pennsylvania Gazette* in 1754 and throughout the colonies, was originally directed at the disunity of

the colonies in the face of threats posed to British North America by the
French and their Indian allies.[85] The *Constitutional Courant* had appropriated Franklin's cartoon to rally the colonists in the Stamp Act crisis—
the colonists had to join together in strong opposition to the stamp tax
or, divided and impotent, watch their rights as Englishmen wither away.
Publication of the image was timed for the Stamp Act Congress, which
took place three weeks later. As the colonies moved closer to a break from
Britain, the image appeared again and again as a call for the colonies to
unify. Paul Revere altered Franklin's image for use on the masthead of the
Massachusetts Spy in 1774.[86] The *Spy*, as well as the *New York Journal* and
the *Pennsylvania Journal*, used the severed snake to protest Parliament's
passage of the Boston Port Act, which closed the port in response to the
Boston Tea Party.[87]

Franklin was not finished producing influential images. Serving as
Pennsylvania's agent in London in 1765, he was smarting from criticism
that he had not sufficiently opposed passage of the Stamp Act. Perhaps at
least in part to rescue his reputation, he produced another powerful political cartoon that he called "MAGNA Britannia: her Colonies REDUC'D."
Instead of sitting atop the world, Britain was portrayed as a woman who
had slid off the globe behind her. Now she was on the ground with four
severed limbs, which were labeled for Virginia, Pennsylvania, New York,
and New England. Her shield was on the ground near her, and her lance
had penetrated the limb of New England.[88]

Franklin's cartoon engaged a different audience than did the severed
snake, and with a different message. It was not directed at the colonies, but
rather at the members of Parliament who were debating possible repeal of
the Stamp Act in the first few months of 1766. It urged British lawmakers
to recognize that the colonies were part of Britain itself—properly subordinate as limbs but nonetheless a vital part of the body of the nation. As
Franklin himself wrote to Jane Mecom, his sister, the point was that "the
colonies might be ruined, but that Britain would thereby be maimed."[89]
Franklin handed out the image on note cards to members of Parliament.
His cartoon was also printed as a broadside and spread throughout the
colonies.[90]

Much more polite than the protests back home, Franklin's cartoon of
Britain with her severed limbs was political speech that said a lot without
saying a word.

WHETHER IT WAS A FRANKLIN CARTOON or a paper off the Edes and Gill press, political articles in the colonies went viral during the Stamp Act protests. Printers up and down the coast ran a kind of colonial version of a wire service as printed and handwritten materials moved by horseback and stagecoach and sometimes by ship.

The communications network expanded the reach of writers who opposed Britain, a critical element in spreading ideas. Articles in the Boston papers were reprinted fairly quickly in Newport, Providence, and New York, but it took three to four weeks for pieces to appear in Virginia papers and three to six weeks in Savannah. Governor William Bull of South Carolina said that newspapers from New England like the *Boston Gazette* were responsible for spreading radical ideas to his state, convincing people to physically oppose the Stamp Act. "But by the Artifices of some busy Spirits," he wrote in a letter to the Lords of Trade on November 3, 1765, "the minds of Men here were so universally poisoned with the principles, which were imbibed and propagated from Boston and Rhode Island, from which Towns, at this time of the year, Vessels very frequently arrive, that after their Example the People of this Town resolved to seize and destroy the Stamp Papers, and to take every means of deterring the Stamp Officers from executing their Duty."[91]

A close printers' fraternity aided the spread of printed material throughout the colonies. The web of connections grew as young men served as apprentices and then left to run their own press. Other connections came through families. James Franklin became a printer in Boston in 1721, publishing the *New England Courant,* and hired his teen-aged brother, Benjamin, as his apprentice. Benjamin Franklin, in turn, took his young nephew, James Jr., to Philadelphia with him, where he became a leading printer and patriot. His nephew later became a newspaper publisher in Newport. Franklin's grandson, Benjamin Franklin Bache, became publisher of the *Aurora* and a leading critic of President John Adams. The Bradford family—William, then his son Andrew, and then his grandson William—became prominent printers in the middle colonies.[92]

Political groups, too, helped spread news throughout the colonies, and they successfully recruited some printers into their membership. The Sons of Liberty boasted a number of influential printers among its members, creating a high tide of newspaper partisanship during the entire tax crisis. Like Benjamin Edes in Boston, the printers of the *Pennsylvania Journal* and the *Providence Gazette* were members of their local Sons of Liberty, and many other printers were sympathetic even if they were not members. As a result, partisan printers dominated the print media of the colonies, and saw to it that news and opinion published in one town appeared as well in many of the others.[93]

ON OCTOBER 7, 1765, Edes and Gill published, in the bottom corner of page one of their *Boston Gazette*, a box with a skull and crossbones and the words "Hereabouts will be the Place to affix the STAMPS."[94] It was a reminder to all—as if anyone would forget—that the hated tax would take effect in a little more than three weeks.

As the calendar turned to November 1, though, the protests in print and on the streets had made it impossible to enforce the law. In the colonies that would later take up arms against the British, stamp distributors had resigned, and stamped paper that had arrived on ships from England was locked away. Without stamped paper, it was illegal to conduct much of the everyday business in the colonies after November 1, including shipping, legal work, and publishing newspapers.

The potential for severe economic losses weighed heavily on the colonies. The unemployment of large numbers of people, including seamen for whom rum and idleness could be a dangerously intoxicating mixture, posed serious problems for the large coastal towns. Scores of ships lay idle in the port of Philadelphia alone. Each colony had to work out its own response, but ports in most of the colonies that had shut down in November opened again within a few months, with ships cleared for sailing in defiance of the law. All the colonies had reopened their ports by the time that the Stamp Act was repealed five months later. Without stamps, though, the civil and admiralty courts in most of the colonies stayed closed for the entire time of the Stamp Act.[95]

Printers could not legally publish their newspapers after November 1 without stamped paper, and they reacted in various ways.[96] Some, like Edes and Gill, continued publishing in defiance of the law. Some did so while veiling their identity—by omitting an imprint of the publisher's name, dropping their titles, or otherwise publishing anonymous sheets to avoid prosecution. Some printers decided to suspend their newspapers, especially in the southern colonies. The *Maryland Gazette* announced on

October 10 that it would stop publishing, using the headline "The Maryland Gazette, Expiring: In uncertain Hopes of a Resurrection to Life again." Edes and Gill couldn't resist satirizing the paper, noting the *Maryland Gazette*'s passing by saying that it had "complained of a violent cruel Kick, lingered till the 10th Instant, and then expired in great Agony, aged 21 years."[97] Death, though, proved intolerably boring for the *Maryland Gazette* publishers, so they returned with an issue in December entitled *An Apparition of the late Maryland Gazette, which is not Dead but only Sleepeth*. Two additional issues over the next few months came out as *The Maryland Gazette, Reviving* and then, finally and probably inevitably, *The Maryland Gazette, Revived*.[98]

Meanwhile, the *New-Hampshire Gazette*, with heavy black rules around all its columns of type, published a day earlier than usual on October 31 to announce its own demise before the Stamp Act took effect, saying, "*I must Die*, or submit to that which is *worse* than Death, *be Stamp'd*, and lose my Freedom." The editor continued: "FREEDOM is so natural, and SLAVERY so contrary to my Nature, that I choose a *voluntary* Death, in Hopes of escaping this Servitude.[99]

The newspaper's pulse must have continued ever so faintly in its coma. Eight days later, it awakened as the editor thought better of its demise and chose instead to defy the law by publishing a two-page issue without stamps.

GOVERNOR BERNARD HAD SAID in the waning days of the Stamp Act that there was "no internal principle of policy which can by any Means restore the power of Government, & enforce a due Subordination."[100] Even after the stamp crisis passed, he found it more and more difficult to govern a province in which Edes and Gill could publish their anti-British work with impunity. It was time to bring seditious libel law down on the two printers. A trial and conviction could cripple the paper, and maybe even shut it down.

In March 1767, the governor's ally, Lieutenant Governor and Chief Justice Thomas Hutchinson, carried his abhorrence of the *Boston Gazette* to a panel of grand jurors in Boston's Town House, the seat of government. In his charge to the jurors—a formal speech that opened the session and conveyed his priorities on potential indictments—Hutchinson told the jurors that he knew "no more dangerous Symptom in any State,

than when its Rulers are slandered, and the Authority of those who govern, is despised and trampled upon."[101]

He renewed that theme in August, motivated by new attacks made
on him in an anonymous article published in April 1767 in the *Boston
Gazette*. Hutchinson said he had been "treated in the most abusive Manner, and vilified beyond all Bounds." Hutchinson then explained to the
grand jurors his concept of freedom of the press, which conformed to the
orthodox English principle that a person could publish without a license
but could be prosecuted after the fact for criticizing a government official.
Freedom of the press, he said, "is doubtless a very great Blessing." It was
not hard for anyone to guess what was coming next. The press had to
behave itself, which meant showing a respect for authority. "Unlicensed
Printing," he said, "was never thought to mean a Liberty of reviling and
calumniating all Ranks and Degrees of Men with Impunity, all Authority
with Ignominy. To carry this absurd Notion of the Liberty of the Press
to the Length some would have it—to print every Thing that is Libellous and Slanderous—is truly astonishing, and of the most dangerous
Tendency."[102]

Nothing came of Hutchinson's complaints to the grand jury, but he
was back the following year after the *Boston Gazette* fired yet another
cannonball at Bernard. The letter that Edes and Gill had published was
short, two overheated paragraphs full of invective, and signed by "A True
Patriot." "We have had full Proof of your Cruelty to a loyal People," the
writer said. "No Age has perhaps furnished a more glaring Instance of ob-
stinate Perseverance in the Path of Malice. . . . Could you have reaped any
Advantage from injuring this People, there would have been some Excuse
for the manifold Abuses. . . . But when a diabolical Thirst for Mischief is
the alone motive of your Conduct, you must not wonder if you are treated
with open Dislike; for it is impossible, how much soever we endeavor it,
to feel any Esteem for a Man like you."[103]

It took a man of strong constitution to come forward to say that he
recognized himself in the accusations made about this unnamed person,
but Governor Bernard had Hutchinson to make his case for him. Once
again before a grand jury early in 1768, the chief justice asked for criminal
punishments. He said of the target of the libels, "It is enough if the Thing
is obvious to a common understanding"—and then provided his understanding that it was Bernard who had been "slandered with impunity in

an *infamous* Paper." Hutchinson said that "every man who prints, prints at his Peril; as every Man who speaks, speaks at his Peril." Then he tried to convince the grand jurors that it was newspapers like the *Boston Gazette,* not overreaching politicians, that most threatened the people. "This Restraint of the Press, in the Prevention of Libels, is the only Thing which will preserve your Liberty." Then he advised the jurors that the people's redress against an abusive governor was removal by the king upon a "just complaint."[104]

If the grand jurors believed in the validity of English law on seditious libel, they had all the evidence they needed to bring the indictment that the chief justice wanted. But they resisted him again.[105] Frustrated, Bernard thought that jury tampering by the *Boston Gazette* was the only way that the grand jury could have failed to charge. As Bernard wrote to London: "As soon as [the jury] came out of Court they sent for the Attorney General, and directed him to prepare a Bill against the next Morning. But in the Interval the Faction who conducts that Paper was indefatigable in tampering with the Jury; so that when the Business was resumed the next day, the Bill was opposed so effectually that it passed in the negative by a small Majority, some say of only one. Upon this occasion the Managers of the Papers were seen publickly to haunt the Grand Jury Men wherever they went; and the Arguments which were used in the Grand Jury Chamber were almost word for word the same which [James] Otis had before used in Publick."[106] Edes and Gill, of course, thought otherwise, describing a toast by the Sons of Liberty at a celebration to the "worthy and independent Grand Jurors."[107]

Governor Bernard, though, was still not giving up. Now he decided to take another route, bypassing the grand jury. He sent a message to his council saying that the *Boston Gazette* was a "libellous Paper" that "must endanger the very Being of Government." The council unanimously agreed with him on March 3, saying that the article by "A True Patriot" was "an insolent and licentious Attack on the Chief Magistrate" and that it "manifestly tends to destroy the Subordination, that is absolutely necessary to good Government, and the Well-being of Society."[108]

Bernard and his friends of government supporters on the council clearly did not grasp that an age was beginning to pass. The people of Boston had rejected subordination and saw uninhibited political speech as essential to governing themselves, at least on issues like taxation where they saw their rights infringed. The council's resolution stood no chance in the house of representatives, which was controlled by the more radical faction and speedily turned down Bernard's request for support. In a written note to the governor, the House expressed due respect for his feelings but noted that no person had actually been named in the article, and that anyway it found nothing that would affect the dignity of the government and it would "take no further Notice of it." Then the House made one of the strongest statements of any colonial body up to that time on freedom of the press. "The Liberty of the Press is a great Bulwark of the Liberty of the People: it is, therefore, the incumbent Duty of those who are constituted the Guardians of the People's Rights, to defend and maintain it."[109]

With the popular assembly coming down on their side, Edes and Gill went back on attack. "A True Patriot" confidently resumed his work. Less than two weeks later, he wrote that the province "has been most barbarously traduced; and now groans under the weight of those misfortunes which have been thereby brought upon it." He added, "We will strip the serpents of their stings, & consign to disgrace, all those guileful betrayers of their country."

And that wasn't all. In the same issue of the *Boston Gazette* in 1768, Samuel Adams wrote as "Populus." "THERE is nothing so *fretting* and *vexatious,* nothing so justly TERRIBLE to tyrants, and their tools and abettors, as a FREE press," he wrote, adding that the press is "*the bulwark of the People's Liberties.* For this reason, it is ever watched by those who are forming plans for the destruction of the People's Liberties, with an *envious and malignant eye.*" Adams added that it did not surprise him that the *Boston Gazette* had been branded as libelous. "These are the men who formed and pushed to the utmost of their power, the late *detested Stamp-Act.*" The *Boston Gazette,* he said, had "sounded the alarm."[110] Bernard was not amused, recommending that Edes and Gill be forced to identify their contributors. The two editors, he said, "are the trumpeters of Sedition, & have been made the apparent instruments of raising that flame in America," and accused them and other editors of "continually directing Daggers to the Heart of their Mother Country."[111]

To satisfy the royal governor, Hutchinson went after Edes and Gill again. He genuinely believed that the English common law crime of seditious libel obligated the grand jurors to act. So once again that fall,

Hutchinson returned to the grand jury and urged them to act firmly against the "inflammatory, seditious Libels upon Government" being published against Governor Bernard. He failed again.[112] Six months later, as the March 1769 court term began, the relentless Hutchinson finally gave up in frustration. He saw that it was pointless to continue demanding what the grand jurors would clearly never give him—authorization from the community to use the law to punish Edes and Gill, as well as some of the writers they published in the *Boston Gazette,* for criticizing royal officials of Massachusetts. Speaking to the grand jurors of their obligations to pursue certain crimes, he said, "I do not mention the Matter of Libels to you, Gentlemen—I am discouraged! My repeated Charges to Grand Juries, on this Head, both in this and other Counties, being so entirely neglected. How those Juries have got over their Oath, I tremble to think, but I have discharged my own Conscience. In short, I have no Hope of the ceasing of this atrocious Crime."[113]

Again and again, Hutchinson had tried to convince grand jurors of the province to use seditious libel law to punish critics of the government. But seditious libel had been defanged as a threat to the free expression of political views. It still existed in the legal texts, under signature of the most learned judges and commentators of the law of England. In the colonies, though, it was all but a dead letter. No jury, in Boston or elsewhere in the colonies, was likely to convict their neighbors for even the most caustic criticism of public officials.

Edes and Gill had begun as printers by apologizing to the elders of Boston for criticizing the local religious establishment. Now it seemed that not even the king himself could touch the two men as their printing press carried the attack against British authority.

4

THE SHOEMAKER

IT WAS MARKET DAY IN BOSTON, AND THE TRAFFIC OF PEOPLE ON HORSES AND IN CARTS WAS beginning to pick up at six in the morning. They rode from outlying farms over the strip of land connecting Boston to the mainland, and then down Orange Street toward the heart of town. The traffic kicked dust into the air, and the odor of horse droppings made the air pungent even before the heat of the day set in. As they reached the elm trees towering above Orange Street near the Boston Common, the travelers slowed to a stop amid a gathering of people. There, in the pale light, they could see the effigy of a man hanging from a thick branch of one of the largest trees. He was tagged with the letters "A.O."[1]

As people massed around the tree during the day—August 14, 1765—few had to be told the identity of A.O. The initials stood for Andrew Oliver, a Boston merchant whose name had been tainted by association with hated British taxes. Parliament had imposed the Stamp Act earlier in the year, and Oliver had stepped forward, as had some others in the colonies, to take the job of collecting the tax.

The protesters who raised the effigy—the so-called Loyal Nine, a group of activist merchants and artisans—had meticulously planned the demonstration and the symbolism for days. The bold effigy of Oliver stopped everyone passing by for a closer look. Dangling next to it was a riding boot, and those who had followed the incendiary articles in the *Boston Gazette* and other papers understood the boot to represent the Earl of Bute, the Scottish nobleman who until a few years earlier had been the prime minister of Great Britain. The colonists considered Bute one of the officials responsible for passage of the tax. The boot sported a green sole, green having represented freedom in British medieval folklore since Robin Hood dressed in green cloth in Nottinghamshire. And the boot itself was not empty. In case anyone still failed to understand the depth of opposition to the tax, a representation of the devil emerged from the boot holding a copy of the Stamp Act.

Several notes of verse added to the symbolism. People who got close enough to the tree could read these words pinned to the effigy's chest:

> *Fair Freedom's glorious Cause I meanly Quitted, Betrayed my Country*
> > *for the Sake of Pelf [money];*
> *But ah! at length, the Devil hath me outwitted,*
> *Instead of stamping others, I've hang'd my Self*

And these words were pinned on one of the arms of the effigy:

> *What greater Joy did ever New England see,*
> *Than a Stampman hanging on a Tree!*

As word of the spectacle spread throughout the city, hundreds of people gathered around the tree. Some wanted their papers stamped by the effigy. Early in the evening, a group of protesters led by a shoemaker named Ebenezer McIntosh cut down the effigy of Oliver, put it inside a coffin, and carried it through town. Then their demonstration took a darker course. They arrived at the building that Oliver was intending to use to administer the stamp tax. There they ripped the effigy into pieces, tore Oliver's building to the ground, and carried pieces of the effigy to Oliver's house, where they threw it into a bonfire.

It was no coincidence that Oliver resigned his commission as stamp tax distributor the next day. And a month later, the Loyal Nine returned to the massive elm tree, this time to declare it to be the "Tree of Liberty."[2]

UNLIKELY THOUGH IT WAS, Ebenezer McIntosh had been one of the key figures in the protest of August 14. McIntosh earned a modest wage as a shoe-maker, often going to the home of his customers and crafting shoes there from leather that they provided to him.[3] Many men made their living in Boston at the time as artisans—shoemakers, blacksmiths, carpenters, wheelwrights, coopers, rope makers, and stonemasons. None of these jobs would normally propel a man to a position of great influence, but McIn-tosh had achieved that status all the same. In the mid-1760s in Boston, he was well known.

McIntosh achieved his renown by moonlighting as the leader of a gang in the South End of the city. By the age of twenty-seven he could rally hundreds of men for whatever purpose he wanted. Whether to organize a big gathering or to crack open a few uncooperative heads, McIntosh was someone with whom you could do business. Through his connections in town, the lawyers and wealthy merchants who were plotting against the Stamp Act could reach out to the common man, enlarging the sphere of people involved in opposing the stamp tax.

The Boston that McIntosh knew was confined to a relatively small space, conducive to boiling over the top like a cauldron when enough political heat was applied—a situation that would soon occur. A coastal town of 15,520 people, it was perhaps more blessed in its physical advan-tages than even New York and Philadelphia.[4] Built on a peninsula about two miles long north to south, Boston grasped the mainland through a narrow strip of land called the Boston Neck. People entering the city rode their horses and carts through the Neck—at high tide the water lapped up to the road on both sides—and past a fortified gate onto Orange Street. The road proceeded past a scattering of houses and large trees, still a rural setting, and past the Boston Common toward the bustling center of town. As a growing population pushed at the natural limits of such a small space, much of the water and marshland surrounding Boston would eventually be filled in, expanding the peninsula and the Neck so much that the town evolved into part of the mainland. But in the middle of the eighteenth century there was room to grow, with large lots and open spaces outside the core of the town and even orchards along Frog Lane. Surrounding the town were rich game lands and an ocean full of cod and whale.

With its fine harbor, Boston was naturally endowed as a seafaring town, and its Puritan founders settled in to the task. The town soon teemed with waterfront activity supporting both its fishing industry and its port, the busiest in the colonies. The gem of the waterfront was the Long Wharf, lined with massive warehouses and built about a third of a mile into the deep water of the bay, enabling it to service dozens of large boats at one time from England and the British West Indies. Long Wharf connected directly to King Street and the dense commercial district of Boston with fine buildings two or three stories high. The town, with many streets leading up from the water, looked prosperous, with shops and churches and 1,676 private residences, many of which had yards around them. Church spires and cupolas dotted the skyline. One visitor from France remarked favorably on the brick and wood houses whose "form and construction . . . would surprise an European eye" because they were "not in the clumsy and melancholy taste of our ancient European towns, but regularly and well provided with windows and doors."[5] From the highest point in town, Beacon Hill, one could see across the Charles River to Charlestown. To the west of Charlestown lay Cambridge, the home of Harvard College, founded in 1636 to educate ministers to serve the colonies.

McIntosh lived in the South End of Boston, where people arrived after crossing the Neck. By the time of the Stamp Act protests, his family had lived in the city for more than a century. McIntosh was the great-grandson of a Scotsman who came to the colonies in 1652, part of a group of men who had been taken prisoner in battle by Oliver Cromwell and then deported to Boston and indentured there. Ebenezer learned to read and write and enjoyed poetry, but probably did not attend school beyond the age of fourteen, when his mother died. With his father having left town, McIntosh had to fend for himself. Most likely, he learned the shoemaker's trade from apprenticing with his uncle. In 1758, at the age of twenty-one, he enlisted as a soldier in the expedition against Canada. On his return, Ebenezer joined a local fire company, which enabled him to elevate his presence in the South End and demonstrate his leadership skills in difficult circumstances.[6]

Six years later McIntosh emerged as a leader of the South End gang. On November 5 of every year, people in Boston held their Pope Day celebration, which commemorated discovery of the Gunpowder Plot against

James I in 1605. In Boston, with its heavy bias against Catholics, people assumed there had been a Catholic plot against the king and used the day to vent their religious prejudice. They put effigies of the pope and the devil into a cart and paraded them through town, finally burning both of them.[7]

It was also a day for local doctors to pick up some extra work tending to broken bodies. The North and South Ends of town had a spirited rivalry and put on separate processions, with men from each side trying to destroy the rival's effigies. Each year it ended in a bloody fight pitting one side of town against the other, with hundreds of men using fists, rocks, clubs, staves, and whatever else was handy to bash each other as best they could. Even for such raucous events, the Pope Day procession in 1764 opened especially badly as a five-year-old boy died immediately after a cart ran him over. The idea that such a tragedy might sober the hotheads to observe a more somber day proved too radical a hope. Although town officers and magistrates tried to head off the annual confrontation, the North and South gangs met anyway at eight that evening at the Mill Bridge in the North End and fought for half an hour to settle the question of dominance for the next year. "In the Fray many were much bruis'd and wounded in their Heads and Arms, some dangerously," reported the *Boston News-Letter*.[8] As Governor Bernard himself noted, "The Captain of the North End was so near being killed, that he did not recover his senses for sevral days after."[9]

The South End won the fight, an unusual outcome in those days. With that, McIntosh's hold on the South End was solidified. At a Boston town meeting four months later, in March 1765, the shoemaker was elected as one of five sealers of leather, whose job it was to certify the quality of leather for use in various goods. He had emerged as a leader in the community, respected among the tradesmen and lower classes. And it was just in time to influence the coming events.[10]

FOR THOSE IN BOSTON plotting resistance to the Stamp Act in 1765, an alliance with McIntosh looked like a promising strategy. He wasn't going to write an essay on the rights of British subjects or craft a petition to George III. But McIntosh was capable of delivering what few men could: a crowd of several thousand to stage a peaceful protest or a select group of thugs swinging staves to make the same point in other ways. Lieutenant

Governor Thomas Hutchinson, writing after he saw months of vigorous protests in the streets, and after his own house was savaged in an ugly outburst, referred to "the rabble of the town of Boston headed by one Mackintosh" who might be called on when opponents of the tax needed a group "to hang or burn effigies or pull down houses."[11] Indeed, both peaceful demonstrations and acts of violence in Boston were well planned and were devastatingly effective.

For the Loyal Nine and other opponents of the Stamp Act, the time to plan and implement a much broader strategy of resistance came in the first half of August. Many of the Stamp Act protests involved political speech carried out by the highly educated and well connected in society— the essays written by James Otis Jr. and Daniel Dulany and others, the debates in colonial legislatures, the resolutions and petitions, and the dense letters, essays, and reports published in the newspapers. In the relatively hierarchical political society of the time, the well educated did much of their writing essentially for each other. They were gentlemen defined not only by their gender but also by their educational attainment, their sensibilities, and their social circle.

The majority of people in New England in the 1760s could read and write, but that didn't mean that they all could participate meaningfully in the discourse that was grounded in constitutional rights and natural law. The political literature of the colonial intellectual leaders, whether expressed in letters or pamphlets, was challenging to read and understand. They were filled with Latin quotations and legal and historical references that would have resonated only with those fellow citizens who shared the writers' educational background. Who else but those in their own circle would have been able to follow references to Cicero and Rousseau? As the historian Gordon Wood has observed, the leaders thought they had to appeal only to people who "were rational and enlightened, who in turn would bring the rest of the populace with them through the force of deferential respect."[12]

The less educated may not have been deeply engaged by the legal writings of the time, but they were still involved in the burgeoning protests against Britain. They eagerly consumed the colonial newspapers like the *Boston Gazette* that were obsessively focused on the stamp tax, and they discussed their grievances in the taverns and coffeehouses of the city (see chapter 3). But what was largely missing until August 1765 was the unifying power of gatherings in the public square, where people could listen to passionate speakers and show their solidarity by force of numbers in a full-throated rejection of the taxes.

The political leaders of Boston understood the power of assembly and its importance in the expression of ideas. The pageantry of demonstrations offered to bring the dissent against England off the printed page, out of the small smoky taverns, and into full public view in the streets. The assembly at the Liberty Tree was planned as political theater—a magnificent elm, an effigy, a representation of the devil, and verses of derision— so that it would attract the entire community, starting with the farmers coming to town with their produce. As word spread, the crowd expanded to include people from all over Boston and from all walks of life. Parents even brought their children.

There was nothing quite so impressive as a gathering of a couple thousand people in a town whose total population was only eight times that. For all their arguments about their rights as Englishmen, the colonial leaders understood that they faced a sovereign power that could simply choose to ignore them. If it were clear that opposition to the Stamp Act was broad and deep—that virtually all of colonial society overwhelmingly rejected it—the king and Parliament would receive a compelling message.

And so, in August, the Radical Whig leaders in Boston began a strategy of enlarging the public sphere in their protest against the Stamp Act. That meant using forms of expression much different from those they employed among themselves. The argumentative letters and essays would continue, but now they looked as well to forms of political expression that would attract and engage a broader array of people in the community who could deepen opposition to the taxes. Their goal was to make political expression more accessible to all the people, to make it more popular and democratic.

That was not their entire agenda, though. Beyond sending a powerful message to London for repeal of the Stamp Act, the colonial leaders saw an opportunity to strike hard and cripple the law at its weakest point. This was the reliance on local citizens to implement the tax. When the prime minister, George Grenville, and his men considered how to enforce the Stamp Act in the colonies, they surely realized that their options were limited. Grenville needed agents in America to store the stamped paper, distribute it, and collect the taxes, and this proved to be the Achilles heel of the system. For Grenville, the appointment of stamp distributors offered a new opportunity for patronage jobs and the political favors that would deepen loyalty to him, but giving the jobs to political appointees sent from London seemed sure to irritate the people in America. The appointment of colonists as stamp agents seemed a better choice, enabling people in the colonies to administer the tax themselves and creating some well-paying jobs for the distributors and those who helped them. Stamp distributors would receive a commission of 8 percent.[13]

The problem with American agents, though, was their vulnerability to being badly burned with the rising temperature of protests in America. As prominent people, they naturally had concerns for their reputation, the continued success of their businesses, and for the safety of their property, their family, and themselves—all of which meant that they were easily intimidated. Seeing themselves hanged in effigy by a gathering of thousands could not have been a reassuring sight for the appointed stamp distributors. It carried the condemnation of the community and damage to their reputation and business interests. Beyond that, the wanton destruction of their property by disreputable mobs went well beyond political expression into the realm of outright intimidation and insurrection.

With all this in mind, the Loyal Nine—which included Benjamin Edes, editor of the radical *Boston Gazette*—met one evening in August at the distillery owned by one of its members, Thomas Chase, and over rum punch discussed the most effective way to protest against the tax.[14] There was no faster way to engage the wider public than by calling for a town meeting or by sponsoring a demonstration outdoors. But it would require some ingenuity to attract a very large crowd. They needed something more than a rally with politicians delivering speeches, advertised by word of mouth and broadsides nailed to trees. That might attract only the most politically committed people. What they imagined instead was a bit of political theater, something so intriguing that it would create a buzz throughout the city and bring people out spontaneously to see what was going on. Their answer was to hang Andrew Oliver, the stamp distributor, by his neck from a rope tied to a limb of the most impressive tree in town.

Not Oliver himself, of course, but an effigy clearly made out as Oliver. A magnificent elm was at hand in front of Deacon Jacob Elliott's house, just across the street from the distillery where they were all drinking. And magnificent it was, with a plaque stating that it had been planted 119 years earlier, not long after Puritans founded the town. So over the next two days they constructed an effigy of Oliver and another of a devil. One of them wrote verses demonizing the Stamp Act and Oliver's role as stamp distributor. They enlisted Ebenezer McIntosh and some of his men to organize the crowd on the appointed day, August 14. Perhaps they also made it clear to McIntosh that he could further endear himself to the cause of liberty by going beyond lawful assembly and giving Oliver and others in favor of the tax a night they would not soon forget.[15]

Before dawn on August 14, McIntosh and some other men strung the effigies from Deacon Elliott's elm tree and then waited. The elm was strategically located "in the most public Part of the Town."[16] It was the South End, McIntosh's neighborhood, and not far from the Boston Neck. Everyone who came into Boston that day would lumber slowly by on carts or horses and see the effigies, and they would eventually carry the news on to the center of town. As the *Boston Gazette* described it, the event brought out "a Multitude of Spectators, who continually assembled the whole Day," and "not a Peasant was suffered to pass down to the Market, let him have what he would for Sale, 'till he had stopp'd and got his Articles stamped by the Effigy." The paper said that at dark "some Thousands" met and paraded with the effigies through the streets. It also reported—consistent with the influx of people on market day—that the gathering around the tree did not consist just of people from Boston, but also included people from Cambridge, Charlestown, and other towns.[17]

Bernard, having convened a meeting of his council that day to discuss the demonstration, reported in a letter to the Board of Trade in London that some of his advisers had characterized the protests as "a preconcerted Business in which the greatest Part of the Town was engaged."[18] The day took on something of a carnival atmosphere. John Avery, a member of the Loyal Nine, wrote to a friend that there were "two or three hundred little Boys with a Flagg marching in procession."[19] The *Massachusetts Gazette and Boston News-Letter* reported that the activities around the tree emptied workplaces all throughout the city. The people around the effigy display were "immediately inspired with a Spirit of Patriotism, which diffus'd itself through the whole Concourse: so much were they affected with a Sense of Liberty, that scarce any could attend to the Task of Day-Labour; but all seemed on the Wing for Freedom."[20]

The next evening, another gathering consisted of "a great Number of the inhabitants of this Town, of both Sexes."[21] The notation of "both sexes" was significant. Women did not have the right to vote and rarely participated in public affairs; it was a measure of the success in enlarging the public sphere of political speech that so many people were included who were not ordinarily political actors.

ON WEDNESDAY, SEPTEMBER 11, after news reached Boston that George Grenville had stepped down as prime minister, the Loyal Nine returned to the great elm and affixed a plate to the trunk declaring it to be the "Tree of Liberty." Grenville had engineered passage of the Stamp Act, and so was a constant target of patriots' ire. Then they discharged their guns in the air and drank toasts to the king.[22] They were still loyal to their king, and were confident that all would be well once he rid himself of conniving ministers like Grenville.

The colonists, of course, did not invent the use of symbols like the Liberty Tree to express ideas beyond the written and spoken word. Many others had been in use. Flags and emblems, the crown and the scepter, the cross and the crucifix—all these and more were well established as symbols that conveyed meaning in the political and ecclesiastic realms. For the colonists, though, the elm in front of Deacon Elliott's house became a symbol not of power or belief but of freedom and of opposition to arbitrary authority. It would unite patriots for the next decade. With their elm the Loyal Nine had adopted an ancient symbol of political liberty for their own purposes, one that reached back in English history. Saxon clans met under large trees, as they did before the Norman Conquest, to honor the liberty they had lost.[23] And the oak was used as an emblem of Jack Cade's Rebellion, which was brought on by grievances against Henry VI in 1450. In America, the iconography was just as meaningful. In 1652, the leaders of the Massachusetts Bay Colony had minted their own coins with images of trees in defiance of the royal prerogative over money.[24]

For the patriots of Boston and elsewhere in 1765, the Liberty Tree became an inspiring image—so majestic and so ancient, reaching for the heavens in defiance of the arbitrary forces of nature. If the power of the king and Parliament counted as only slightly less than a force of nature, the Liberty Tree fortified the patriots' resolve to oppose it when necessary. It became an important venue for political assembly, an open-air marketplace of ideas. It served as Liberty Hall, an outdoor meeting space to discuss colonial grievances and stage protests against the actions of royal authorities in the decade to come.

Dedication of the Liberty Tree and its role as centerpiece of the gathering on August 14 showed how the universe of political expression was expanding. The tree, the boot, and the effigies expressed ideas in ways very different from the essays and letters and petitions that had dominated the debate until then. Unlike other forms of expression that involved words, either spoken or printed, the tree and the effigies were symbols. But they were speech nonetheless. The Loyal Nine and others who strung the effigies of the devil and the stamp distributor did so to communicate a profound disagreement with the taxes inflicted on them by England. Their use of symbols to express opposition to the new taxes involved a completely different mode of speech, but one that was ultimately as important as the essays discussing the constitutional rights of Englishmen.

Symbolic speech, in fact, possessed some power that the written and spoken word did not. The essays and speeches against the Stamp Act used complex arguments that were foreign to many people's understanding and experience, and even vigorous opponents of the tax sometimes disagreed among themselves on many of the arguments they were putting forward. But symbols stripped away the complexity of intellectual arguments and offered immediate clarity. For the people of Boston and elsewhere, Liberty Trees and effigies of stamp distributors stood for one big idea—the right to be free of arbitrary power, exercised in a legislative body far away without participation of the colonists' own representatives.

That fundamental idea of being ruled over by an oppressive regime was easily grasped by everyone who gathered at the tree, whether they had ever read a pamphlet or listened to an oration. In that way, the symbols could drive home complex arguments in a simple, unified way. As the relationship between the colonies and England deteriorated over the issue of taxes, the patriots in Boston and throughout the colonies increasingly recognized the power of symbolic speech to excite passions and define public debate. It was an age of large political questions that challenged the colonists at every turn. In the arsenal of persuasion, a Liberty Tree or a burning effigy reflected the exceedingly complicated issues of rebellion.

Symbols possessed other vital attributes of effective political expression. Although they stood mute and passive, they brought immediate attention to themselves—the nectar that attracts the bees. Symbolic speech made protest popular, enabling active and visible opposition to the taxes to spread from the well-educated politicians and merchants to the community at large. The symbols employed by the Loyal Nine brought out thousands of people from Boston and surrounding towns, an essential element in the leaders' goal of showing the depth of opposition to the Stamp Act. The symbols also called for a response by those who looked on. Rather than inviting people to listen passively to harangues against the Stamp Act, the Loyal Nine created an intriguing scene that invited participation.

By their very nature, the symbols instigated even more speech. Everyone who came out to see the effigies of Oliver and the devil hanging silently from the tree couldn't help but talk with those around them about what they saw and what it meant for the future. It was an impromptu town meeting with vast participation. And many of the gatherings transformed themselves into marches, as the leaders cut down the effigies and carried them at the head of parades that often went from one end of Boston to the other and then back again, through King Street, the commercial center of town, with stops at meaningful places such as the Liberty Tree, the town gallows, and important public buildings.

For the founding generation, effective political protest meant employing many different forms of political expression toward the same goal. In fact, the law recognized symbolic speech as part of political expression. Symbolic expression had long been considered the equal of more common verbal speech in the law of seditious libel, and so the protesters around the Liberty Tree were engaging in seditious libel as surely as were the writers for the *Boston Gazette*. Sir Edward Coke, in his report of the case *De Libellis Famosis* in 1606, had regarded verbal and symbolic expression as legally equivalent, defining nonwritten libel crimes as pictures or signs, such as "a Gallows, or other reproachful and ignominious signs at the parties door or elsewhere."[25] And William Blackstone, in his *Commentaries on the Laws of England,* wrote that libel involved "either printing, writing, signs, or pictures."[26] With English common law exported to the colonies, legal commentators in America followed the lead of Coke and Blackstone, and in the fifty years following the Revolution lawyers and judges viewed freedom of expression as encompassing symbols as well as the printed and spoken word.[27]

After the great elm in Boston proved so effective in democratizing protest, Liberty Trees found fertile soil all over the colonies. In Newport, Rhode Island, William Read donated his buttonwood tree, and deeded a parcel of land he owned around it, to the local Sons of Liberty to use for gatherings and to stand as a "Monument of the spirited and noble Opposition made to the Stamp Act."[28] Other New England towns such as Norwich, Providence, and Cambridge dedicated trees of their own.[29] John Adams came across a buttonwood tree in his hometown of Braintree in May 1766. "The Tree is well-set, well guarded, and has on it, an Inscription 'The Tree of Liberty,' and 'cursed is he, who cutts this Tree.'" Adams added, with more than a hint that opposition to the Stamp Act was not unanimous, that he understood that "some Persons grumble and threaten to girdle it."[30] Farther south, Maryland adopted a tulip tree and Savannah an oak tree, the latter dedicated as people "drank toasts to their colleagues in Massachusetts."[31] In New York, the symbol went off in a homegrown direction as Whig leaders rejected the tree as a symbol and instead raised a tall mast to serve as a Liberty Pole, topped by a flag or vane. Everywhere people used their Liberty Trees and Liberty Poles as places to assemble to discuss politics and to hang effigies to show their displeasure.

In 1770, British General Gage wrote from New York to his superiors in London after observing the outdoor meeting places. "It is now as common here to assemble on all occasions of public concern at the Liberty Pole and Coffee House as for the ancient Romans to repair to the Forum," he said. "And orators harangue on all sides."[32]

THE HUGE GATHERING at the Liberty Tree on August 14 had been peaceful all day, but it brought understandable concern to the two highest-ranking officials in the colony.[33] The sheer size of the crowd and the effigies hanging from the tree made the gathering potentially combustible. Lieutenant Governor Thomas Hutchinson, who also served as chief justice of the Massachusetts Bay Colony, ordered the sheriff to cut down the effigies. But the sheriff's men returned without having completed the task, reporting that they feared for their lives if they dared remove the effigies. Meanwhile, Governor Bernard called a meeting of his council, which recommended that no action be taken except for assembling some peace officers to ensure that the gathering did not get out of hand.[34]

As dusk settled over Boston, a group of men cut the effigies down from the tree. Ebenezer McIntosh led a crowd carrying the effigies to the Town House, where Bernard and his council were still meeting. The crowd shouted three huzzahs in defiance of royal authority and then headed to the dock at Kilby Street, where Andrew Oliver had constructed a building for his business. Everyone presumed that Oliver would use the new office for distributing the stamped paper.

In just minutes, what had been a peaceful day turned ugly. McIntosh and a group of men tore apart the building. From there, McIntosh led them to Oliver's house on a nearby street. Outside of the house, the crowd made a scene out of beheading the effigy and tossed rocks through the windows near the street. Then they went down the street to Fort Hill, where they walked to the summit and made a bonfire out of wood from Oliver's office and burned what was left of the effigy.

Just in case anyone might still doubt their resolve, McIntosh led the mob back down the hill and to Oliver's house again. Oliver and his family had fled. The men battered in the door and entered the house, where they destroyed furniture and other possessions and stole liquor from the cellar. Lieutenant Governor Hutchinson himself arrived with the sheriff at eleven o'clock. Hutchinson and Oliver were brothers-in-law. Hutchinson ordered the mob to leave Oliver's house, but the crowd sent them retreating ahead of a barrage of stones. After another hour, McIntosh finally grew tired or bored and sent his men home. Thus ended a day that had started at dawn with a peaceful gathering at the elm tree and ended at midnight with a gang engaging in a spasm of violence.

Oliver received a visit the next day from some gentlemen who suggested that he might resign as stamp distributor. Although he had not yet received his official papers of appointment, Oliver promised to write to London and turn down the office. That night, Governor Bernard was in Castle William, the British fort in Boston Harbor, where he had fled in fear, and he composed a long letter to his superiors in London describing the events of the past two days. As he looked across the water to the city he could easily see "a Bonfire burning on Fort hill: by which I understand that the Mob is up, & probably doing mischief."[35]

A few justices and other men went up the hill and tried to disperse the crowd, telling them that Oliver had resigned. Later, the crowd went to Hutchinson's house, where they pounded on the doors of his house while

Hutchinson was hiding inside. Then they went to Bernard's house and were told that the governor was at the castle. That evening, Bernard wrote that he was "glad I was excused a Personal interview with them, as they were, as I am told, the lowest of the Mob."[36] Bernard issued a proclamation promising one hundred pounds for information leading to the conviction of the rioters.[37] A week later, on August 22, the governor wrote again that "I really fear much worse is to come than is passed," and that he could do little to head off trouble because "I am wholly without Authority."[38]

That proved to be a prophetic statement.

JUST FOUR DAYS LATER, on August 26, violence flared again in Boston. On McIntosh's menu that evening were three selections, all homes of men in government perceived to favor the Stamp Act. After making a bonfire on King Street, McIntosh split his gang into two. One group broke into the home of William Story, the deputy registrar of the Admiralty Court, and destroyed many of his possessions. The other gang went to the home of Benjamin Hallowell, the comptroller of customs, and emptied his wine cellar after ripping doors, windows, and shutters off their frames.[39]

Now they were in the mood to take the big prize. With the groups united again, McIntosh took them to Hutchinson's mansion. He had escaped with his family just minutes earlier. The men used axes to split the front door and then poured into the house. They tore off the wainscot and hacked down the partition walls. They tore the furniture to pieces and threw it out the windows and knifed the beds and let the feathers float to the street. They took all the books and papers that Hutchinson had collected over a thirty-year period and made off with nine hundred pounds sterling. Hutchinson wrote that by four o'clock in the morning "one of the best finished houses in the Province had nothing remaining but the bare walls and floors," and that "they began to take the slate and boards from the roof and were prevented only by the approaching daylight from a total demolition of the building."[40]

The next day, Bernard wrote to General Gage in a panicked tone, warning that he might not even be able to hold Castle William if the stamped paper arrived from England and was stored there. "More mischief is daily expected: Where it will end no body knows. In short, The Town of Boston is in the possession of an incensed & implacable Mob; I have no force to oppose to them."[41] He was accurate about his inability to

control a mob. He did not have British troops at hand, and Boston had
no police force. The sheriff's only option was to call on local men to help
in law enforcement, or, in extreme circumstances, call out a local militia.
But that involved getting cooperation from men whose sympathies most
likely lay with those opposing the Stamp Act.

Bernard convened a meeting of his council, which authorized a warrant for the arrest of McIntosh. The sheriff found him on King Street and
took him into custody. But he soon was back on the street. Several men
had visited the sheriff and told him that the local guards would not defend
the customhouse from any attack in the coming days if McIntosh were
not released.[42]

Once again, Bernard offered rewards for information—three hundred pounds for the discovery of the leader of the riots and another one
hundred pounds for the identities of coconspirators.[43] But no person
came forward with information to claim the substantial rewards, despite
the many witnesses to the disturbances. Two days of mob violence had
clearly shown that the risks of publicly supporting the tax, engaging in
law enforcement, or exposing the men who pillaged the homes of royal
officials carried too high a price.

Although Governor Bernard judged that the colony "is now in an
actual State of Rebellion,"[44] Boston quieted down after the second riot.
At a town meeting at Faneuil Hall the day after the second riot, citizens
voted unanimously to condemn the violence and directed the selectmen
and magistrates to do everything possible to prevent similar incidents.
Hutchinson speculated that some of the perpetrators and their sponsors
were in attendance at the meeting. "The encouragers of the first mob
never intended matters should go this length," Hutchinson wrote four
days after his house was ransacked, "and the people in general express the
utmost detestation of this unparalleled outrage."[45]

As a result of the town meeting, militiamen finally began walking
the town to assure the peace. And those who had been sponsoring McIntosh—most probably the Loyal Nine—reached out and put the brakes on
him. As Hutchinson had noted, they themselves might not have intended
the violence to go as far as it did, and at any rate they had accomplished
their goal. With Oliver's resignation, Boston had nobody in line to become stamp distributor when the law was scheduled to take effect on November 1. Anyone who considered working as a stamp distributor before

the riots knew better now. The law could not go into effect without the apparatus in place to distribute the stamped paper and collect the taxes.

Even the *Boston Gazette* criticized the violence as "horrid Scenes of Villainy." The radical Boston leaders feared that the rioting could turn the town against them. On September 2, the paper said that "pulling down Houses and robbing Persons of their Substance . . . when any suppos'ed Injuries can be redress'd by Law" was "utterly inconsistent with the first Principles of Government, and subversive of the glorious Cause."[46] Later, a writer in the paper warned that "many Men of bad Principles will take the Opportunity of publick Commotions to perpetrate their base or villanous Designs, to indulge Revenge, or prey upon private Property, by leading heated, tho' generally well meaning Multitudes into Actions that disgrace their Proceeding . . . The greatest Care therefore is necessary to keep an undisciplined irregular Multitude from running into mischievous Extravagancies."[47] The governor was not impressed. On September 21, when the stamped paper from London finally arrived in Boston, Bernard put the vessel under the protection of British warships and then stored the paper under guard at Castle William.[48]

A few weeks after the demonstrations, patriots gathered at the "Great Tree at the South End of the Town" where the effigies had been hanged and affixed a large copper plate to its trunk with the words in gold lettering: "The Tree of Liberty."[49] McIntosh, meanwhile, was given the title of "First Captain General of Liberty Tree." Most people in town understood that to be a cut at Bernard, who self-importantly inscribed his signature on proclamations as "Captain General and Governor in Chief in and over his Majesty's Province of the Massachusetts-Bay in New England and Vice Admiral of the Same."[50]

Satire was an especially delicious weapon of political speech to employ against Governor Bernard. Even if only by use of a bloated title, a mere shoemaker had been placed at the same level as the royal governor. Bernard despised McIntosh, who without elective office or royal appointment seemed at times to be in greater control of events than he.

THE POWERFUL SYMBOLS that moved political minds in Boston were not limited to the Liberty Tree and effigies of officials. The Puritan church was a powerful institution in the life of Boston, and citizens appropriated its religious symbols to their benefit. The protestors used the devil, the personification of pure evil in Puritan theology, to portray the infidels who would impose an oppressive tax on them. And some of the ministers themselves entered the controversy, using their pulpits and the iconography of the church to oppose the British in the decade leading up to the separation.

The Reverend John Wise of Ipswich had steered his pulpit into politics in 1687 by opposing taxes imposed by Governor Edmund Andros (see chapter 1). Wise set a precedent that the Reverend Jonathan Mayhew renewed in a controversial sermon that may have helped instigate the mob violence of August 26, 1765. Mayhew already was a rebel, having delivered a remarkable sermon in 1750 that provided, a quarter century before the outbreak of hostilities, legal justification for the break with Britain. Mayhew supported Whig political theory that rejected the divine right of kings and argued for the existence of a contract between rulers and the people. Although obedience to authority was normally a duty, Mayhew said, rulers "have no authority from God to do mischief" and to rule in ways contrary to their responsibility for the good of society. If they do not act to promote the public welfare, "they immediately cease to be the *ordinance* and *ministers of God* and no more deserve that glorious character than common *pirates* and *highwaymen*."[51]

Mayhew's sermon was reprinted and was well known throughout America. In his retirement, John Adams reminisced with Thomas Jefferson that as a boy he had often heard Mayhew preach. Mayhew's 1750 sermon, said Adams, "was a tolerable Chatechism for The Education of a Boy of 14 Years of Age" and that "I read it, till the Substance of it was incorporated into my Nature and indelibly engraved on my Memory."[52] Referring to the violence earlier that month in Boston—the "proceedings"—and no doubt to Mayhew, Bernard wrote on August 22, 1765, that a "congregational Minister, well known by his late Polemical writings, has, as I have been told by sevral Persons, justified this proceeding in his Sermon & prayed for its success."[53]

Just three days later, on August 25, Mayhew spoke to his congregation at the West End Church in what would become known as his most controversial speech. His sermon focused on Galatians chapter 5, verses 12 and 13, expounding on "I would they were even cut off which trouble you, for brethren ye have been called unto liberty." The next day, the riots of August 26 destroyed the homes of Hutchinson and two other officials, and word spread that Mayhew's words had instigated some to act. Henry Caner, the rector of the King's Chapel in Boston, wrote in a letter to the Archbishop of Canterbury that Mayhew "has distinguished himself in the pulpit . . . in one of the most seditious sermons ever delivered, advising the people to stand up for their rights to the last drop of their blood."[54]

Mayhew denied instigating anyone to violence but conceded that his sermon "was composed in a high strain of liberty." He did not back down from his mixing of religion and politics. He said that he had addressed the issue of the Stamp Act because the clergy in Boston had not been firm enough in opposition. The clergy had been "blamed for their silence in the cause of liberty, at a time when it was almost universally supposed, as it still is, that our common liberties and rights, as British subjects, were in the most imminent danger."[55]

AS NOVEMBER APPROACHED, Governor Bernard worried that the tense calm that had settled over Boston would quickly give way to new violence. But the violence of August was over. Mass gatherings would continue to take place, sometimes with thousands of people attending. The protests would stay peaceful, marked by speeches, effigies, marches, and other political expression. Bernard would never quite recover from the violence of McIntosh's gang, for throughout the rest of the year he wrote to his superiors in London, as he did on November 1, that "this Town is in the hands of the mob."[56]

The first of November marked the day that the Stamp Act would take effect, and five days later would be Pope's Day, always an excuse for the North and South gangs to hammer each other senseless. With no regular police force in the city, Governor Bernard and the council ordered the militia to patrol during what could be a difficult week, but the militia officers reported to him on October 31 that men had refused to serve. Embracing that as an omen that the August riots might return, Bernard left again for Castle William in the harbor.[57]

The next day started respectfully enough with bells tolling throughout the town and ships in Boston Harbor hoisting their colors to half-mast. Then the action shifted to the Liberty Tree, where the Sons of Liberty had carefully planned another event. McIntosh was once again in control, but this time the organizers told him to keep his hotheads in line. And he did. At the Liberty Tree, effigies of George Grenville, the prime minister who had pushed for the Stamp Act, and John Huske, a supporter of the Stamp Act, swung from the branches. By three o'clock, a crowd that the *Boston Gazette* estimated at several thousand people "of all ranks" had assembled at the great elm, duplicating the broad participation of the community at the August 14 gathering.

McIntosh and his men freed the effigies and placed them in a cart, and the crowd set off on a long walk through the town. They marched past the building where the assembly was in session and then continued to the North End. Then they turned back and walked to the gallows at the Boston Neck in the South End, where once again they hung the effigies. Finally, they cut them down "and in utmost Detestation" of the men that the effigies represented, ripped the effigies to shreds. The crowd gave three loud cheers and then everyone left peacefully.[58]

Governor Bernard, hiding out in Castle William, was relieved that the demonstration had remained peaceful, noting that the "innumerable people" in the demonstration included not just Bostonians but also many who had come there from "the Country." But he sounded incredulous that McIntosh had been handed the authority to direct the demonstration. "To this man it was thought proper to commit the Care of the Town on this occasion: so totally is the Town & consequently the Government in the hands of the Mob."[59] The mob, of course, was a group of men under McIntosh's control, those who pillaged the property of royal officials on two days in August. Bernard said that McIntosh "has under him 100 or 150 men trained as regular as a military Corps."[60] But Bernard never would distinguish between the real "mob" and the far larger group of citizens protesting peacefully, or acknowledge that McIntosh had led peaceful protests as well as violent ones.

On the evening of November 1, with the demonstration concluded, McIntosh met with Henry Swift, a shipwright and the leader of the North End, at the insistence of "several gentlemen"—likely from the leadership of the Loyal Nine. The two men entered into what the *Boston Gazette* called a "treaty."[61] They pledged to form a union of the North and South groups and to foreswear any violence on Pope's Day. The result, after intricate planning, was one of the most impressive political protests in colonial Boston up to that time.

McIntosh and Swift put on a street demonstration that once again utilized strong symbolism.[62] The two men dressed in military outfits.

McIntosh wore a uniform of red and blue, with a gilt gorget covering his chest, and a hat with gold lace. He carried a rattan cane on his left arm and a speaking trumpet in his right to broadcast his orders to the crowd. Several of his assistants wore laced hats and carried wands in their hands, and other men played flutes.

At noon, McIntosh and Swift each brought their groups to King Street, along with horse-drawn stages carrying effigies of the pope, the devil, and the stamp distributors. With the people that joined them there, it made for a gathering of several thousand people, according to the *Boston Gazette*. After a ceremonial union of the two groups and three resounding huzzahs, McIntosh led his South group through the North section of town, and Swift took his North group through the South section before they came together once again. The united group went to the Liberty Tree, where they enjoyed refreshments, and then began the long trek back to Copp's Hill in the northernmost part of town. They arrived at six o'clock and threw their effigies into a bonfire.

Six days later, many of the leading lights in town came together at the Royal Exchange Tavern for a "union feast"—a celebration of the fact that North and South had laid aside their differences and had demonstrated against the Stamp Act together. John Hancock was master of ceremonies at the dinner, attended by two hundred people, including Samuel Adams. McIntosh and his erstwhile nemesis, Henry Swift, sat at the head table.[63]

BETWEEN NINE AND TEN on the morning of December 16, the publisher of a Boston paper—most likely Benjamin Edes of the *Boston Gazette*—handed an anonymous letter to Andrew Oliver, the secretary of the province.[64] Oliver had suffered destruction of his office building during the riots of August 14, and the next day he had promised not to accept the position of stamp distributor. But the letter alleged that Oliver had received his official commission from London anyway, and demanded to know whether he intended to become the stamp distributor. Concerned that more mischief would occur, Oliver wrote out a reply on the spot stating that he had "taken no measures to qualify himself for the Office, nor had he any thought of doing it." Edes returned to his office and quickly inserted the original letter and Oliver's reply into the paper that went to press that very day.

Oliver had not written the complete renunciation that the Loyal Nine and larger Sons of Liberty group wanted, so they met early that Monday evening in their office on Hanover Square, across from the Liberty Tree, and wrote a short letter to him. They delivered the letter to Oliver's house, and he opened it to find that the "respectable Inhabitants of the Town of Boston" had rejected his assurance about turning down the office of stamp distributor, "which We don't think satisfactory, therefore desire that You would morrow appear under Liberty Tree at 12 o'clock to make a public Resignation—your Noncompliance will incur the displeasure of the true Sons of Liberty."

Working into the early morning, Edes and Gill set the type and printed the public notices for the event, which were posted around town early the next morning, December 17. Henry Bass, a member of the Loyal Nine and the Sons of Liberty, wrote to a friend a couple days later explaining how the group had engineered the public resignation by working all through the night. He said that "the whole affair transacted by the Loyall Nine, in writing the Letter, getting the advertisements Printed, which were all done after 12 o'Clock Monday Night, the advertisements Pasted up to the amount of a hundred was all done from 9 to 3 o'Clock." Asking his friend for confidentiality, Bass requested that he keep "a profound Secret" about the Loyal Nine's involvement, saying, "We do every thing in order to keep this and the first Affair Private: and are not a little pleas'd to hear that McIntosh has the Credit of the whole Affair."[65]

December 17 was wet, cold, and windy, a perfectly remorseless December day in Boston. A friend stopped by just before nine that morning to let Oliver know that a notice had been posted throughout the town urging people to gather at the Liberty Tree at noon to hear the resignation. Oliver also learned that effigies were being prepared in case he refused to cooperate. Wary of a public humiliation, only made worse by the dreadful weather, Oliver sent a draft of his statement to the Sons of Liberty and received it back swiftly at eleven with some alterations. He also arranged to meet several of his friends "that I might not be left entirely at the Will & Pleasure of the Populace." Oliver's request that he read the statement at the Town House instead of at the Liberty Tree was turned down.

When Oliver arrived at the Liberty Tree just before noon, about two thousand people huddled there to witness the event. He went to the second-floor window of the house overlooking the tree. With McIntosh by his right hand, Oliver signed the declaration. He read the pledge to the crowd that he would not "take any Measures for enforcing the Stamp Act in America, which is so grievous to the People."

Upon his signing, the crowd exploded with three cheers. Then Oliver looked out at the assembly and declared, "I shall always think myself very happy, when it shall lye in my power to serve this People."[66] With that, the people gave another three cheers and then scattered for shelter. Twenty minutes later, the area around the Liberty Tree was empty.

So, too, was the office of stamp distributor for Boston.

STAMP DISTRIBUTORS LIKE OLIVER completely misread the sentiments of their neighbors. They did not foresee the vigorous protests they would face. Many of them had actually competed to secure their job. A lawyer in Rhode Island wrote to Benjamin Franklin in an effort to win his support for an appointment as stamp distributor, and three Americans who were in London at the time lobbied officials there to gain a position.[67] Soon enough, they would regret having anything to do with stamps.

Boston was the hotbed of agitation against the Stamp Act, and articles in the *Boston Gazette* attacking the distributors and reporting on the demonstrations were reprinted in papers down the coast. These reports and commentary proved critical in the effort to defeat the stamp tax, for opponents throughout the colonies quickly adopted the same tactics of public demonstrations and the use of symbols—and, as well, sometimes mob action to terrorize a distributor into resigning.

The demonstration in Newport, Rhode Island, on August 27 seemed an echo of the Boston disturbance of two weeks earlier. Demonstrators gathered by six in the morning and erected a gallows near the courthouse. Then they suspended three effigies—Augustus Johnston, who had been appointed as the Rhode Island distributor of stamps, and two other men who had written in favor of the Stamp Act, along with a devil and a boot. To draw a bigger crowd, the organizers served alcohol and Cheshire cheese and sent messengers around town to spread the word. Late in the afternoon, as an exclamation point on the protest, a bonfire consumed both the effigies and the gallows. The following night, though, the situation turned ugly. A mob moved to the homes of the two writers. They smashed windows, swung axes at furniture, and carted off possessions. Then the mob moved to Johnston's house. He had fled with his family to His Majesty's ship *Cygnet,* which was at anchor in the harbor.[68] The rioters spared his house when they were assured that he was resigning his office. The next day Johnston returned to the town, and with "the Stamp-Master's Resignation being publicly read, the People announced their Joy by repeated Huzza's, etc. and the Storm ceased."[69] Chastened by the experience, Johnston now had a fresh attitude about the stamps more to the liking of the Sons of Liberty. The *Providence Gazette* wrote that he had "discovered a Zeal equal with any other American, against the Impositions from Britain."[70]

George Meserve also needed the protection that a ship provided him. Appointed stamp distributor for New Hampshire while on a trip to England, he was still on a ship in Boston Harbor on his return when he learned that he would not be safe back in Portsmouth unless he resigned his post. He finally disembarked on the Long Wharf and announced his resignation, whereupon he received three cheers and an impromptu celebration from a crowd.[71]

James McEvers in New York didn't wait to see his effigy hanging from a gallows. Appointed stamp distributor in New York, he resigned on August 26 because, as he wrote in a letter, he had "a large Store of Goods and Seldom Less than Twenty thousand Pounds Currency value in it with which the Populace would make sad Havock."[72] He wrote to Lieutenant Governor Cadwallader Colden of New York that he did not want to suffer "the same cruel fate Mr. Oliver met with at Boston."[73] In New Jersey, William Coxe resigned on September 2 although there had been no mob action.[74]

Down the coast it was the same story. In Maryland, a crowd destroyed Zachariah Hood's house. After he fled to New York, he resigned his post in a letter in which he acknowledged that he had brought out "the Hatred of the whole Continent" and that he was "unwilling to remain any longer at Enmity with Liberty and the Good of Mankind."[75] The stamp distributor for Virginia, George Mercer, went to Williamsburg on October 30 and immediately encountered an angry crowd. Shaken by his reception, he ended up in a long conversation with the governor and resigned the next day.[76]

The situation also became nasty in South Carolina. A ship from London brought stamped paper to Charleston Harbor on October 18, but the governor ordered it held in a fort to safeguard it from a mob. The next day protestors carried effigies in a funeral procession through the city,

stopping to ransack the house of one distributor before burning the effigies. The town's two stamp distributors fled to the fort and suspended
their work.[77] Less than a week later, at midnight on October 23, men
acting on the instructions of prominent individuals in the community
went to the home of Henry Laurens, a wealthy South Carolina merchant
who later became president of the Continental Congress. As Laurens recalled, many of them, "heated with Liquor & all armed with Cutlasses
and Clubbs," made "a most violent thumping & confus'd Noise" at his
chamber window and shouted "Liberty, Liberty, & Stamp'd Paper." Laurens told them he had no stamped paper in his house and accused them
of upsetting his pregnant wife. "To this they replyed in general that they
Loved & respected me," and Laurens opened the door and the men entered, most in disguise. Laurens recognized nine of them anyway, calling
them out by name even as several of them held cutlasses to his chest. After
they made a search of his house, Laurens refused to give an oath that he
didn't know where stamped paper was hidden. He assured them that he
opposed the Stamp Act "but that I could not think they pursued a right
method to obtain a repeal."[78]

When November 1, 1765, arrived, the day that the Stamp Act would
become effective, the colonies that would later engage in the War for Independence did not have anyone ready to sell the stamped paper.[79] The
widespread protests, the hanging of effigies, the pamphlets, the newspaper
articles—and, too, the mob actions and illegal destruction of property—
had persuaded stamp distributors to quit their appointments.

THE SYMBOLISM OF POLITICAL SPEECH became more creative. On the morning
of February 20, 1766, the Sons of Liberty placed notices around Boston
that they would make a public exhibition at the Liberty Tree that day of "a
Piece of Paper mark'd with America's Oppression"—a crown stamp, the
very embodiment of the hated tax.[80] The Sons of Liberty were not going
to let their neighbors pass the bitter Boston winter huddled by their fire-
places. It was time to get them outside and put the stamped paper on trial.

With as many as three thousand people present, the Sons empanelled
a jury that heard "many learned Debates" for two hours, according to the
Boston Gazette. Not surprisingly, the jurors quickly found the stamped
paper guilty of "a breach of Magna Charta and a Design to subvert the
British Constitution and alienate the Affections of His majesty's most

loyal and dutiful Subjects in *America* from his Person and Government."
Conviction in hand, the judge passed sentence on the Stamp Act.

The Sons constructed a stage with effigies of the Earl of Bute and
George Grenville. Above them on a gallows, the devil himself appeared,
holding a copy of the Stamp Act and a stamped piece of paper. With the
people roaring three cheers, the Sons cut down the effigies, placed them in
a cart, and began a parade through the town. They returned to the Liberty
Tree for another three cheers, then walked south to the town gallows on
Boston Neck to carry out the judge's sentence. The Sons built a huge bonfire and threw in the effigies and the stamped paper, the "Badge of slavery."

As the people returned to the warmth of their homes, the Loyal Nine
went to their office on Hanover Square, across from the great elm, and
drank toasts both to themselves and to George III—"our gracious, rightful and lawful Sovereign." Even the radicals were a long way from cursing
their king and moving toward separation from Britain. If only the Stamp
Act were repealed, good relations between the colonies and Britain could
be restored.

HOW DID ALL THIS political expression look to the man who represented British interests in the Massachusetts colony? Bernard chronicled the protests
in Boston through frequent and detailed correspondence with his superiors in London. He had absorbed the intense and at times vitriolic dissent, much of it aimed at him—all the essays, pamphlets, letters, poems,
satires, sermons, and demonstrations.

Through the months of protest, Bernard saw opposition to the Stamp
Act spread into a democratic outpouring that dominated all politics in the
town. Bernard argued again and again, in print and before the assembly,
that the colony should accept the stamp tax, but with the rising tide of
protest he came to realize that the people would not consent to parliamentary rule on taxes. Whigs held one-third of the seats in the House in
1765, but doubled their representation in the elections the following May.
At the same time, the friends of government group, composed of the most
moderate men, declined by half to just 19 percent of the House. And the
governor's three closest allies—Thomas Hutchinson and Andrew and Peter Oliver—lost election to the Governor's Council.[81]

Bernard's letters in 1765 described the rising opposition. On September 7, he noted "the Vehemence of the Country against the Stamp

Act." He reported that the assembly would meet "full of the passions & prejudices of the People & perhaps under some instructions from their Constituents."[82] On September 28, he reported that although Boston was relatively quiet, "the Country about it has grown more & more inflamed: Evry where have been heard loud declarations that they would not submit to the stamp Act upon any account or in Any instance."[83] By November 30, Bernard tried to explain to the Board of Trade in London why Boston "has been brought into the ungovernable state it is now in," explaining that "immense pains have been taken to poison the Minds of the people; of which the infamous Set of Newspapers which have been published here for 4 months past . . . are full proofs."[84]

Mass demonstrations were even more shocking to Bernard. Even when people took to the streets in peaceful protest, he still saw nothing more than mob rule.[85] For a man schooled on the principle that a sovereign Parliament could not be questioned, the meetings at the Liberty Tree and the marches through town were popular protests that clashed with everything he knew about governance. After witnessing months of political expression of every kind, Bernard finally understood the power of dissent. "In this Town," he wrote to the Board of Trade, "All the Power is in the hands of the people."[86]

WITH THE PEOPLE OF BOSTON and the other colonies rejecting the tax, the Stamp Act was in fact near its end.[87] London was abuzz with news of the protests and riots in America. It was becoming clear that the Stamp Act was unenforceable unless London sent stamp agents from England and approved the use of British troops, both of which would inflame passions even more.

The Rockingham ministry favored repeal, and to persuade the doubters in Parliament, it called on the large and influential community of London merchants as allies in the effort. The merchants involved in trade with the colonies had already been pinched by the Sugar Act, as many in the colonies turned away from imported goods from England in favor of items made by their neighbors. The Stamp Act promised a much more intense downturn in business. Many Americans had signed nonimportation agreements as a way of punishing the British economy and pressuring for repeal. Seeing the threat to their livelihood, many London merchants formed a lobbying group and sent petitions for repeal to

Parliament and stirred up similar opposition from merchants and factory owners in towns and cities throughout England. One observer in London wrote of the effectiveness of the colonial boycotts of English goods, which he said would bring thousands of unemployed workers into London. "The agreement of your merchants not to send for any goods from hence, until a repeal, was a clincher," he wrote. "One manufacturer who attended the parliament declared, unless that act was soon repealed, he should dismiss 1100 workmen, and it was hinted, that 100,000 manufacturers would soon be in London."[88]

After intense political wrangling, Parliament repealed the Stamp Act. But it passed another law, the Declaratory Act, that upheld its unlimited sovereignty over the colonies and its authority to pass laws affecting the colonies even without representation in Parliament. The Declaratory Act said that Parliament had "full power and authority to make laws and statutes of sufficient force and validity to bind the colonies and people of America . . . in all cases whatsoever."[89] For many in the colonies, the new law seemed to foretell more mischief in the future.

John Hancock's brig, the *Harrison*, left London with news of the repeal and arrived in Boston forty-four days later.[90] On Friday, May 16, as news spread through town, the selectmen met and set aside all day Monday for a celebration. No one was surprised that the celebration of repeal centered on the Liberty Tree. Now, symbolic speech would be used not for protest but for affirmation of their cause. At one in the morning on Monday, the church bell nearest to the Liberty Tree began ringing, followed by bells all over town. At dawn, people decorated the Liberty Tree with flags and streamers, and at noon cannon were fired at Castle William and from batteries around town. So that nobody would miss the celebration, several wealthy men paid enough money to free all the debtors from the city jail. By evening, the celebration was in full swing, peaceful but raucous, with the entire town illuminated. John Hancock lit up his house and put on his own fireworks show, entertaining "the genteel part of the town" and treating everyone to a huge barrel of Madeira wine. Meanwhile, the Sons of Liberty had built a pyramid on the Common, illuminated by 280 lamps and decorated at the top with figures of the king and fourteen patriots who had opposed the Stamp Act. About one hundred yards away they put up a stage for fireworks, and the night sky flashed with rockets.[91]

The colonists felt they had repaired a relationship gone temporarily awry. No one could yet imagine farmers facing off against redcoats at Lexington and Concord. "All was Loyalty to the King, Blessings on the Parliament of Great Britain, Honour and Gratitude to the Present Ministry, and Love and Affection to the Mother Country," said one anonymous writer in the *Boston Gazette*.[92]

A FEW DAYS AFTER the celebration in Boston, the Reverend Jonathan Mayhew stood before his congregation. With repeal of the Stamp Act, Mayhew told his parishioners that Boston and the rest of the colonies had thrown off the yoke of arbitrary power. "The snare is broken," he said, "and we are escaped."[93]

Mayhew reminded the congregation of their rights as British subjects under the Magna Carta. He addressed the outpouring of political speech that led to repeal of the law—"this diversity of humours, sentiments and opinions among the colonists." He condemned "the riotous and fellonious proceedings" of some men, but most political expression had been peaceful. The colonists' "late experience and success," he said, "will teach them how to act, in order to obtain the redress of grievances; I mean, by joint, manly and spirited, but yet respectful and loyal petitioning."[94]

All the political expression and public assemblies had, in the end, carried the day. "Had we patiently received the yoke," said Mayhew, "no one can tell when, or whether ever it would have been taken off."[95]

JOHN ADAMS HAD MISSED the revelry in Boston on repeal of the Stamp Act. He spent the morning instead in a town meeting in Braintree—which he said was "insensible to the Common Joy"—and then rode his horse south to attend the Superior Court at Plymouth the next day. "A duller Day, than last Monday, when the Province was in a Rapture for the Repeal of the Stamp Act, I do not remember to have passed," he wrote.[96]

Adams, though, fully understood how the enlargement of political speech had served the cause of opposing the Stamp Act. He wrote in his diary of the expansion of political expression beyond the upper classes. "The People, even to the lowest Ranks, have become more attentive to their Liberties, more inquisitive about them, and more determined to defend them, than they were ever before known or had occasion to be.

Innumerable have been the Monuments of Wit, Humour, Sense, Learning, Spirit, Patriotism, and Heroism, erected in the several Colonies and Provinces in the Course of this Year."

When people became "more attentive to their Liberties," Adams said, they had expressed themselves powerfully and effectively, utilizing many forms of political speech that would continue to grow in the years ahead. As Adams said, "Our Presses have groaned, our Pulpits have thundered, our Legislatures have resolved, our Towns have voted, The Crown Officers have everywhere trembled, and all their little Tools and Creatures, been afraid to Speak and ashamed to be seen."[97]

5

THE MERCHANT

IN NEW YORK ON THE EVENING OF MARCH 14, 1770, A PRISON GUARD OPENED THE DOOR OF Alexander McDougall's jail cell so that visitors could enter. There were forty-five visitors, to be exact, and all of them were women. They could not fit into the tiny cell at the same time, so most of them spilled into the hallway outside waiting their turn. For publicity's sake—and all of this was for publicity's sake—the forty-five women had been described to the public as virgins. McDougall had been jailed for criticizing the royal governor and the New York General Assembly, and his supporters aimed to draw attention to him as a martyr for the cause of liberty. If the virgins were not enough to accomplish that, the number forty-five tied McDougall symbolically to John Wilkes, a member of Parliament who had gained renown for going to jail after criticizing the king in the forty-fifth issue of the newspaper he published.

For a man confined to a damp cell in the city jail, it was an experience that was more enjoyable than any prisoner had a right to expect. McDougall proved to be a welcoming host, aided by the treats that his visitors brought with them. According to the *New York Journal*, his female callers "were introduced by a Gentleman of Note, to the Illustrious Prisoner, who entertained them with Tea, Cakes, Chocolate and Conversation adapted to the Company." Then the women proceeded to sing the

Forty-Fifth Psalm, an edited version that extolled McDougall and participatory democracy.[1]

In the coming days, as news of the virgins became the talk of the city,
McDougall's critics struck back. One of them, writing under the pseudonym Satiricus, made the mocking observation that "he that is courted in
a gloomy Prison, by Forty-Five [virgins] in one Day cannot fail of being
a MAN INDEED."[2] One wag made fun of the encounter by suggesting that
each of the forty-five virgins was forty-five years old.[3]

McDougall, a successful merchant and later a general in George
Washington's Continental Army, was a firebrand with few equals in the
colonies. He was on a level similar to that of the celebrated Samuel Adams
of Boston, cousin of President John Adams and a source of enduring pride
among Bostonians. So strong is the pull of Samuel Adams even today that
three Bostonians started a brewing company and named their beer after
him. McDougall's legacy has enjoyed no such lift. A street is named for
him in Greenwich Village in Manhattan, but it uses a different spelling
for his last name than McDougall used himself.

McDougall was well enough known in his own time, his fame growing chiefly from a broadside that—paradoxically, as it turned out—he
had authored anonymously. His supporters in the Sons of Liberty created
political theater that would consume the attention of the city for many
months. Before it was over, McDougall would be brought to the floor of
the New York Assembly itself, where the representatives whom he had
criticized in his broadside would attempt to put him on trial, with themselves as jurors—and even threaten him with a form of torture from the
Middle Ages.

Once again, a critic of government would clash with an oppressive legal system that punished dissent, in the process expanding the American
vision of freedom of speech.

IN 1738, at the age of six, Alexander McDougall arrived in New York with
his parents and four siblings after a long passage from Scotland.[4] The
family's prospects on the island of Islay had been bleak. Ranald McDougall had worked as a farmer scratching out a living on the rocky shores
of the Inner Hebrides. The family had lived in a small cottage with a dirt
floor and walls made of stone and peat. A hole in the straw-and-timber
roof allowed smoke to clear from their cooking fire.

When the family arrived in America, the elder McDougall secured a job working on a dairy farm on the island of Manhattan. He and Alexander delivered milk around town. Ranald had hopes that Alexander, who was closely schooled in the Bible, would become a minister in the Presbyterian Church. But Alexander wanted neither farming nor the ministry. He left home at fourteen to work on a small wooden ship that delivered cargo to England and Martinique. On a trip to Islay at the age of nineteen, he married a cousin and brought her back to New York, where they had three children.

By twenty-five, Alexander took command of his first ship, the *Tyger*, and began to make his fortune. The *Tyger* was a privateer whose commissioning papers said its mission was to "cruise against his Majesty's Enemies."[5] In 1757, the French and Indian War was under way and private ships aided the king by attacking French shipping in the Caribbean. Privateers like McDougall, who outfitted their vessels with heavy guns, patrolled shipping lanes and took over enemy merchant boats. They kept some of the cargo as a reward, giving them the opportunity—if they survived the venture—to gain wealth that would never have been possible for a lower-class man to accumulate on the mainland.

It was dangerous work, though, because weather and disease could bring a voyage to quick tragedy. If dealing with French naval guns was not enough, hurricane season in the Caribbean brought its own horrors for sailors in wooden boats. On September 4, 1757, McDougall's vessel was sailing in the Caribbean with several other privateers when a hurricane passed through and overwhelmed them. The wind and waves ripped at the *Tyger* and for a time seemed likely to destroy the ship, which listed onto one side. McDougall commanded his men to cut off the mast and throw four of the heavy cannon into the sea, which provided the *Tyger* with enough stability to right itself and survive the storm.[6] On the way back to New York, McDougall watched from a distance as a ship, most likely a French privateer, took over an English vessel and then turned its attention to the *Tyger*. In no condition to fight, McDougall caught the wind and escaped north. Six weeks after the storm, the *New York Mercury* noted that the *Tyger* had returned to port "in a wrack'd Condition, having felt the Effects of the late violent Gale of Wind."[7]

McDougall left for sea again a few weeks later, after the *Tyger* had been repaired, and had to endure a deadly outbreak of smallpox among his crew. His trials were rewarded the following year when, at the age of twenty-seven, he took command of a larger and more heavily armed privateer. But his time at sea was coming to an end. Under pressure to return home to his wife and children, McDougall finally settled permanently in New York after thirteen years of sailing.[8]

The hardscrabble days of McDougall's youth were far behind him. His time at sea had provided him with wealth that made him an early example of American upward mobility. He was far from the richest man in New York, but McDougall now had the capital in hand to invest in ventures that promised to multiply his wealth many fold.

McDougall immersed himself in a variety of commercial ventures. He imported sugar and molasses on consignment from growers on St. Croix and sold it as far north as Quebec, trading colonial goods such as lumber and flour back to the Caribbean and southern colonies. His financial activities as an investor were extensive as well, with fees and interest earned on money he loaned to merchants. McDougall's wealth increased quickly. He owned a cargo vessel and three thousand acres of land, and he had an account with more than four thousand pounds in London.[9] McDougall was also a slave owner. His Waste Book—a record of his daily business transactions—shows that he owned three slaves whom he valued at 190 pounds and that he had paid forty pounds "for a negro wench called Bett."[10]

McDougall soon adopted the trappings of a successful merchant. Tall for the time at five foot nine, he dressed in expensive clothes and rode a saddle horse. He acquired books and spent lavishly on furniture, especially after his wife died in 1763, and he married again four years later.[11] And he sent his sons to the College of New Jersey (later changed to Princeton University), something that his own father could only have dreamed of doing.[12] Try as he might, though, McDougall could not buy himself into the higher social ranks of the city. Behind the doors of the finest homes, where families like the Livingstons and De Lanceys entertained, his start as milk boy and privateer would not be forgotten so easily.

As one member of the Livingston family wrote, McDougall sought his fortune by going out as a privateer—"a hungry Scotchman as a robber of mankind." And after years at sea, he "returns home weighty of purse, but unpolished in manner, rough as his profession. Mean as the meanest of [his] race."[13]

IF THE LIVINGSTON CLAN looked down on McDougall, that did not prevent them from enlisting him as a political ally. The Livingstons and the De Lanceys were bitter rivals in New York politics at the time the Stamp Act conflict arose, both vying for control of the colony.

In New York, as in many other colonies, local politics and opposition to British policy in America spun a complex web. The two family parties divided on religious, economic, and political grounds. The Livingstons were Presbyterian and their wealth grew from their vast land holdings; the De Lanceys were Anglican and had built their wealth through merchant activities. Control of the assembly and the Governor's Council would provide them with power over the affairs of the colony, including an opportunity to tilt tax and other policies in their favor. So through the pre-Revolutionary period they formed coalitions to compete for control. The De Lanceys allied themselves with the Sons of Liberty during the Stamp Act crisis in 1765, and then drifted slowly toward accommodation with Britain, sending radicals over to the Livingstons by 1769.[14]

As opposition to the Stamp Act grew, radicals in New York did not have a stamp distributor to target for intimidation (chapters 3 and 4 discuss the Stamp Act protests). After hearing that a mob had destroyed valuable property belonging to Andrew Oliver, the Boston stamp distributor, James McEvers resigned from the same post in New York before a mob could destroy his goods. McEvers's judgment proved sound, for violence gripped New York for several days in November.[15]

Resistance to the stamp tax had surged in the fall. Delegates from nine colonies met in New York in the Stamp Act Congress and on October 19 passed a declaration with fourteen points of protest. The stamp taxes would be "extremely burthensome and Grievous," the delegates wrote. The colonists enjoyed all the rights of Englishmen and believed that only their own respective legislatures—not Parliament—had the constitutional power to impose taxes on them.[16]

Meanwhile, tensions were escalating on the streets. When a ship arrived from England with stamps on October 23, Lieutenant-Governor Cadwallader Colden put it under the protection of a British warship in the harbor and bolstered his defenses in the fort, where the stamps would be stored. There was growing suspicion that Colden would try to enforce the Stamp Act with military force. On October 31, more than two hundred merchants in New York took the major step of agreeing to boycott English goods until the Stamp Act was repealed. The boycott would extend even to wearing imported clothes. Robert Livingston, head of the Livingston clan and both a Supreme Court justice and member of the assembly, commented that "he that does not appear in Homespun, or at least a turned coat, is looked on with an evil eye."[17] Merchants in Philadelphia and Boston made similar pacts to boycott British goods.[18]

The next day, when the Stamp Act was scheduled to take effect, protestors led by the Sons of Liberty staged a demonstration that mirrored the protest in Boston on August 14.[19] Several thousand people met at the Commons that Friday evening. Carrying torches and candles, they marched to the walls of the fort. "The populace knocked at the gate," Robert Livingston recalled, "placed their hands on the top of the Ramparts, called out to the guards to fire, threw bricks & stones against the Fort and notwithstanding the highest provocation was given, not a word was returned to the most opprobrious language."[20]

Facing no resistance, some members of the crowd seized Colden's elegant coach from his stable and carried it back to the Commons, where effigies of both Colden and the devil swung from a gallows. According to the *New York Gazette and Weekly Mercury,* the devil was "a proper companion for the other, as 'tis supposed it was entirely at his instigation he acted." Then the crowd took the coach and the effigies back to the fort. "Under the muzzles of the Fort guns" and while Colden watched from the ramparts, they built a bonfire and burned everything. Then a group of men went to the home of Major Thomas James of the Royal Artillery, who had blustered about using soldiers to force people to accept the stamp tax. It was not a social call for a late-night toast. They dragged James's possessions into the street and made a grand bonfire while they drank the liquor they stole from his cabinets.[21]

For their part, Colden and General Thomas Gage believed that the top lawyers and merchants of the colony were responsible for the riots. Gage reported to London that "without the Influence and Instigation of these the inferior People would have been quiet." He added, "The Sailors who are the only People who may be properly Stiled Mob, are entirely at the Command of the Merchants who employ them."[22]

One of those merchants was likely McDougall. The protests against the stamp tax propelled him into the politics of the colony. McDougall's exact role during the Stamp Act crisis is not entirely clear, but his prior work as a privateer and his contacts on the waterfront would have enabled him to recruit seamen for the demonstrations. McDougall was most likely a moderate, a stance that would change in the years ahead. He was not as radical as Isaac Sears and John Lamb, the two leaders of the Sons of Liberty.[23]

McDougall enjoyed his first immersion in New York politics, and several years later campaigned for the Livingstons. But the De Lanceys won the elections of 1768 and 1769, setting the stage for a protest by McDougall that would rivet attention on him throughout the colonies.

ON MARCH 18, 1769, the Sons of Liberty in New York met at various taverns to commemorate repeal of the Stamp Act three years earlier. It was not as happy an occasion as it might have been, for the Sons themselves had been divided into rival camps since the stamp tax protests. The more radical faction, led by Sears and Lamb, thought that McDougall's moderates were not true patriots.

That night, McDougall and his men dined at Van De Water's Tavern and toasted their rivals, who were nearby at Edward Smith's. With ample rum fueling his good cheer, McDougall sent a few men to tell Sears and Lamb that he had lifted a glass to their good health. The two men rejected his overture, declaring that McDougall had not worked energetically enough for the patriot cause and did not deserve to be called a Son of Liberty. Undaunted, McDougall sent another emissary a few hours later "to try whether he could not *plead* them into a Message favorable to his Partisans," but Sears and Lamb debated whether to toss McDougall's man through the window to the street.[24]

Understandably preferring the stairs, McDougall's emissary left quickly, but this low point in the relationship between factions of the Sons of Liberty would not last much longer. McDougall himself became more radical, and he, Sears, and Lamb saw that working together promised to be a much more effective strategy.[25]

Following repeal of the Stamp Act in 1766, Parliament did not give up on taxing the colonies. The Townshend Acts quickly followed, a series of laws that included new taxes on the colonies and measures to help enforce compliance with British trade laws. Most colonists opposed these taxes, too, but the fact that they were imposed on trade, rather than on internal commerce as were the stamp taxes, helped to keep the resistance from boiling over as it had in 1765. But the Townshend Acts did instigate the most vigorous pamphleteering of the entire pre–Revolutionary War period (see chapter 7).

In New York, the most intense conflict with Parliament centered on the Quartering Act. Once the French and Indian War ended, the colonists chafed at the idea that Britain would maintain a standing army in their midst, and especially that the Quartering Act required them to pay expenses for the troops.

The issue became explosive in 1769, when the De Lancey faction took control of the assembly. Massachusetts and South Carolina had rejected the Quartering Act, rallying McDougall and the more radical Sons to lead opposition in New York. McDougall often sat in the public gallery at City Hall as the De Lancey faction in the assembly crafted a deal with Colden to support the troops in exchange for his agreement to a paper currency bill needed by merchants carrying on trade. After intense bargaining over a period of several weeks, the assembly met in closed session on December 15 and agreed by a margin of one vote to pay for the British troops, half of the money coming from the public treasury. When the public gallery opened to visitors again, McDougall heard the result of the vote.[26]

McDougall was incensed by the decision. So too were Sears and Lamb, who had previously allied themselves with the De Lancey group and now felt betrayed by them. The assembly's decision drove the three men back into each other's arms, and they would make no more threats to toss a messenger of the other out of a window.

After the assembly vote, McDougall went home and dipped his quill pen into a well of ink. He began writing an essay condemning the assembly.

ON THE NEXT DAY, December 16, a man carried a box through the streets of New York. Curled up inside the box was a youngster. Every few minutes, the man stopped as if to rest, placing the box against the wall of a building. Hidden from the view of passersby, the youngster inside the box opened a slide and attached a printed sheet of paper to the surface of the wall. Then he closed the slide. As the man moved away, a notice was left publicly posted. The man carried the box to the next place he wanted to "rest," and the youngster posted another notice. And so he went through-out town, anonymously distributing an anonymous document.[27]

The printed notice, a broadside, was addressed "To the Betrayed In-habitants of the City and Colony of New York." At the end it was signed, "A Son of Liberty." Such a simple print served as a powerful form of politi-cal expression during the controversy with Britain. Broadsides had played a major role in England for centuries, informing people of official actions by the king, Parliament, and local authorities, as well as serving as a soap-box for individuals to attack or defend a policy of the government.[28] One British nobleman complained about broadsides that circulated in London in 1763: "I can't pass along the Streets without having them crammed down my throat, by every Black guard that I meet, who is employed to dis-tribute them."[29] John Wilkes, who was expelled from Parliament for his criticism of the king, understood the power of broadsides to fire political action. He wrote approvingly to a supporter for his "printing and distrib-uting . . . incendiary papers and hand-bills. You must keep the bellows for ever in your hand to blow the coals of opposition, and be perpetually feeding the fire with fresh fuel."[30]

In America, broadsides served similar purposes and were perfectly suited for the times. If production of a colonial newspaper was ardu-ous, expensive, and time-consuming, a broadside was the opposite—the newspaper's fast and sleek cousin, a single page that was set in type and printed the same day or overnight and ready to display around town. It was the fastest form of mass communication of the age, and with the coming of the troubles with England, the protestors eagerly adopted it. With a broadside they could hit quickly and hard, keeping the public con-versation at a high pitch. Often signed only with initials or a pseudonym, broadsides provided another avenue for stinging commentary. And they were infinitely adaptable. Beyond the argumentative type like McDou-gall's, broadsides spoke in many different forms and for many purposes. Some presented ballads or poetry. Paul Revere issued his engraving of the Boston Massacre as a broadside (see chapter 6), and the Declara-tion of Independence reached many people as a broadside.[31] Some con-veyed news—during the weeks after the Stamp Act took effect, printers in some towns issued broadside versions of their own papers. Benjamin Franklin and his partner suspended their *Pennsylvania Gazette* but issued broadsides without a masthead to keep people in Philadelphia informed of the news.[32]

McDougall's broadside in the name of "A Son of Liberty" was a perfect use of the form, excoriating the assembly just days after it voted to provision the troops. But it was also significant in a way that went beyond the conflict over colonial rights. What was so remarkable about the broadside was that its author grasped the essence of political speech and its relationship with a self-governing society. McDougall opened his essay with a vigorous protest against what he saw as abuse of authority by the assembly, Colden, and the British ministry. This much was not unusual, as biting commentary filled newspapers at every turn. However, McDougall did not stop there. As he reached the end of his essay, he called for his fellow citizens to assemble in a public space and discuss their views in a free and open encounter—"assemble in the fields on Monday next, where your sense ought to be taken on this important point." And after holding their assembly, he urged the people to petition the government for a redress of grievances—"draw up a state of the whole matter, and send it to the speakers of the several houses of assembly on the continent, and to the friends of our cause in England, and publish it in the newspapers."[33] If McDougall was not the first person to tie together the ideas of protest, assembly, and petition, he did so at a critical time and on an issue of surpassing importance to his fellow colonists. Two decades later, ratifying assemblies across the new nation would enshrine in the First Amendment this progression of democratic rights—the freedom to speak and write, followed by assembly with like-minded people, and finally petition for a redress of grievances.

McDougall's attack on the authorities showed that, despite his lack of a good formal education, he understood the tenets of Whig philosophy. The government was one of limited powers, answerable to the people for the abuse of their rights. And the people possessed the right to dissent and to ultimately replace their rulers if they violated their rights. McDougall had gradually absorbed this political philosophy through his association with the Livingston faction and through his reading of colonial pamphlets and newspapers.

Going well past the constraints of seditious libel, McDougall accused the assembly of ruining the unity of the colonies against Britain. He wrote that "the minions of tyranny and despotism in the mother country and the colonies, are indefatigable in laying every snare that their malevolent and corrupt hearts can suggest, to enslave a free people." The king's ministry, he said, was waiting to see if the colonies would divide in their opposition to the British measures. "For if this should not take place," said McDougall, "the acts must be repealed."

To McDougall, the legislators were guilty of "betraying the common cause of liberty." He added: "To what other influence than the deserting the American cause, can the ministry attribute so pusillanimous a conduct" that is "so repugnant and subversive of all the means we have used" to oppose "the tyrannical conduct of the British Parliament!" He wasn't finished, asserting that the quartering payment would be financially ruinous. He accused the De Lancey faction, which controlled the assembly, of colluding with Colden to secure their continued control. Having made his case, McDougall now pointed out that the measure had passed the assembly by only one vote and so those who opposed paying for the British troops had "a respectable minority." He asked his fellow citizens to gather to discuss the matter.[34]

A crowd of about fourteen hundred assembled in the Commons, where they overwhelmingly passed a resolution opposing financial support of the troops. Then they appointed a committee—which included McDougall—to convey the resolution to the assembly. When the committee arrived at City Hall, the lawmakers turned down the resolution, saying that they believed a majority of citizens supported the expenditure. One representative, John De Noyelles, accused Lamb of proposing the resolution and thus abetting the author of the broadside. McDougall and six other members of the Sons of Liberty came to Lamb's defense, writing to De Noyelles that they had assisted Lamb at the public gathering and should be summoned as well. They argued that their use of assembly and petition was the "undoubted Right and Privilege of every *Englishman*." De Noyelles backed down.[35]

WHO HAD AUTHORED the broadside? That was something that Colden and members of the assembly wanted to know, and they were willing to pay a large bounty to find out. By adopting the pseudonym "A Son of Liberty," McDougall had followed a common practice of writers who wanted to shield their authorship of political commentary. Anonymous writings— in which the author used a pseudonym, initials, or no identification at all—had played a vital role in political debate on both sides of the Atlantic for many centuries. Parliament was so frustrated by anonymously written religious tracts that it amended the licensing law in 1637 to require identification of all authors. That didn't stop the practice, of course. Writers as prominent as Jonathan Swift, Daniel Defoe, and Samuel Johnson published anonymous essays, and the practice spread to the colonies. During the Stamp Act crisis and throughout the founding period, anonymous letters, essays, and pamphlets dominated political discourse, and the newspapers routinely published news and commentary by writers who refused to identify themselves.[36]

Anonymity proved critical to the development of freedom of the press and the spread of political ideas in eighteenth-century America. McDougall hid his identity, as did many others, to evade prosecution for seditious libel. Others did so to avoid blame for insults launched at opponents and to make it difficult for them to strike back. A well-chosen nom de plume could convey editorial benefits as well, greatly enhancing the power of the argument itself. Some writers chose multiple pseudonyms— Samuel Adams used as many as twenty-five—as a kind of sleight of hand that made it appear that their political position enjoyed the support of many knowledgeable people who were each writing on the subject.[37] This could lead to humorous exchanges, as when one writer—himself using a pseudonym, "Justice"—wanted the New York Journal "to convey a few thoughts to Poplicola, alias a [New-York] Farmer, alias Agricola, alias John Calvin . . . alias a Rhapsodist, alias a Quibbler, alias a Punster, alias a Ballad Maker, (or any other name or character he may please, for the time being, to assume)." Because Justice said that the view expressed under these names "met with the general contempt and abhorrence of every friend to the English constitution in America," the unidentified writer should make sure that "no innocent person should lie under the suspicion of being the author of writings chargeable upon himself alone."[38]

Often a writer chose a specific pseudonym because the name made a political point of its own. Some chose pseudonyms like Vox Populi, Legion, and The People to imply that a large group of citizens supported their views, while others took names such as Lover of Truth and his Country, A Friend to the Constitution, and A True Patriot to persuade readers of their high-minded purpose. Still other writers associated themselves with a popular figure from antiquity like Cato and Publius Valerius, two

Romans who advocated for a republican form of government, in order to stand in the reflected glow of their reputation.[39] Not so John Dickinson and John Adams, two lawyers who were among the most intellectually gifted in all the colonies. They chose "Farmer" and "Humphrey Plough-jogger," respectively, to use as pseudonyms to convey an impression—inaccurate though it was—that they shared with their readers a plain, unpretentious background. In the *Boston Gazette* alone, Adams also used the noms de plume "Novanglus," "Clarendon," "Governor Winthrop," and simply "U."[40]

For McDougall, "A Son of Liberty" clearly referred to the Sons of Liberty and conveyed the idea that a large and patriotic group stood with him in opposition to the assembly's decision to provision the troops. If he meant to dissuade the authorities from trying to discover his identity and prosecute him, McDougall turned out to be wrong. On December 19, a few days after the broadside circulated on the streets, the assembly voted that the paper was "a false, seditious and infamous libel." The legislators faced one small problem, however—they did not know who had written the broadside. So they told Colden to pursue the unnamed author by offering a reward of one hundred pounds to anyone who came forward to identify him.[41]

A few days later, Colden called on the people to identify the scoundrel who had criticized the assembly. His proclamation said the anonymous broadside "highly reflects on the Honour and Dignity of the House; is calculated to inflame the Minds of the good People of this Colony, against their Representatives in General Assembly; and contains scandalous Reflections on the three Branches of the Legislature." Because the broadside was "a high Misdemeanour and a daring Insult" on the assembly, the governor offered not only a reward but also a pardon from the king to any accomplice who stepped forward to identify the author.[42]

THREE WEEKS LATER, as the author of the broadside remained unidentified, a group of British soldiers from the Sixteenth Regiment made their way in the cold and darkness of a January evening to the town Commons. They carried a saw and gunpowder and various tools. They had a plan to strike at the Sons of Liberty, whom they despised as their mortal enemy.[43]

Manhattan Island put the Sons and the soldiers in close and dangerous proximity. The populated part of the city was still compact, although it had burst well beyond the early Dutch settlement. At the foot of the island was Fort George. A small park, Bowling Green, with its statue of George III, lay right outside the walls of the fort, and then Broadway moved straight up the western spine of Manhattan for about ten blocks before it reached the Commons, home for a few buildings, including the New Gaol, or public jail. Beyond the Commons lay a freshwater pond, a small grid of streets, and then an expanse of farms and forest.[44]

The Commons area was a perfect tinderbox for opposing groups. The soldiers had barracks a few steps above the Commons and performed many of their exercises there. Across Broadway from the Commons were two taverns, De La Montayne's and Bardin's, where the Sons of Liberty planned their activities and lifted toasts to liberty. And close to the Commons were a slum and a large neighborhood of middle-class artisans and other workers, rich sources of manpower for the radicals looking to raise a crowd quickly.

For the Sons and the soldiers, their conflicting visions of the world crossed at one spot on the Commons. That spot was the destination of the soldiers on this evening in January. They arrived at an odd-looking object that dominated the scene—a tall ship's mast that reached high into the air, topped by a flagpole with a banner flying. The lower part of the mast was armored with iron braces. The soldiers sawed off some of the iron and then bored a hole in the wood. They poured in the gunpowder and set it on fire, but their attempt to cause an explosion failed. Frustrated and angry, they invaded nearby Montayne's Tavern and broke windows, lamps, and bowls.[45]

The mast rising above the Commons was the town's Liberty Pole, put there by the Sons of Liberty as a symbol of resistance to what they saw as the arbitrary exercise of British power. In erecting a Liberty Pole, the Sons in New York had placed their own imprint on the symbolism of protest. Protestors in Boston and many other towns had designated a large elm or oak as a Liberty Tree, a gathering place for citizens to protest taxes imposed by Parliament (see chapter 4). But in New York, the Sons instead raised a pine mast, and it became a constant irritant to British soldiers patrolling the streets and the Commons itself.

Conflict over the Liberty Pole and the decision to supply British troops was only the latest source of tension between civilians and the soldiers in the town. Grievances by civilians against the military went back many years on a number of issues, beginning with the continual efforts of the Royal Navy to force men into service. Given manpower needs, the impressment of seamen was a widespread practice in the colonies, often accomplished by sailors who disembarked from warships in colonial ports to round up men. In November 1747, efforts to impress men in Boston Harbor brought about two days of disturbances, and impressment riots continued through the 1760s. In Newport, a group of men took over the fort in 1764 and fired cannon at the *St. John* in answer to an order for impressment. And in the same year, after the *Chaleur* seized several fishermen and the captain went ashore on Manhattan Island, a crowd dragged his landing boat to the Commons and set it ablaze.[46]

Impressment was not the only grievance. The garrison of British soldiers in New York instigated fears among many citizens of a standing army in their midst poised to snatch away their liberties. When off duty, some soldiers even competed for jobs with lower-wage laborers and mechanics, making it more difficult for colonists to support their families during a time of economic difficulties. All of this accumulating resentment made combustible tinder for a confrontation that centered on the Liberty Pole.

The Sons of Liberty raised their first Liberty Pole on June 4, 1766, to celebrate repeal of the Stamp Act. Two months later, on August 10, soldiers cut it down.[47] The next day, Sears, the Sons of Liberty leader, assembled more than two thousand people at the site of the fallen pole, hurling insults at the group of soldiers and officers nearby "till a volley of Brick Bats ensued and wounded some," according to British captain John Montresor.[48] Sears and his men lifted another Liberty Pole four days later, but it fell again to the soldiers in six weeks. It took only a day for the third Liberty Pole to go up, and six months after that for the British soldiers to take it down yet again, this time an act of vengeance on the anniversary of the repeal of the Stamp Act.[49]

It was the fourth Liberty Pole, now protected with iron, that the soldiers failed to destroy with gunpowder on that evening in January 1770. They refused to give up, though. Immediately after that failed attempt, a broadside signed by "Brutus" invited the public to the Liberty Pole to discuss the assembly's decision to pay for provisioning the troops. Three thousand people gathered there in the morning but were shocked to see that the Liberty Pole was gone. It was now across Broadway, sawed into pieces and stacked by Montayne's Tavern, having been successfully attacked the night before by the soldiers. For one writer, the actions of the troops showed "their utmost Endeavors to enslave us." The crowd passed resolutions pledging not to hire the soldiers, and agreed that soldiers out at night were to be regarded as "Enemies to the Peace of this City."[50]

Two days later—January 19—the soldiers themselves posted a broadside around the city. As if cutting down the Liberty Pole was not enough, they attacked the Sons of Liberty as "enemies to society" and charged that the earlier broadside by Brutus was a seditious libel against them.[51] That pushed some of the radicals over the edge. Sears and another man seized two soldiers posting the broadsides and took them to the mayor's office. Soon, twenty soldiers armed with cutlasses and bayonets appeared there to demand the return of their comrades. They drew their swords, but the mayor ordered them back to their barracks.

On the way there, the soldiers walked up the small rise known as Golden Hill, where other soldiers joined them. Faced by a large group of citizens, one officer said, "Soldiers, draw your bayonets and cut your way through them." A scuffle ensued, with soldiers slashing a number of people with their bayonets and some getting roughed up in return with fists and rocks. Finally, British officers arrived and took their men back to their barracks.[52] The bloodshed at the Battle of Golden Hill, as it came to be known, took place about six weeks before the Boston Massacre.

Many tensions brought about the conflict at Golden Hill, but the Liberty Pole served as the flashpoint. Up and down, up and down, up and down went the pole in a test of wills that lasted years. Both the Sons and the soldiers understood the power of symbols. Just as an elm tree had done in Boston, a tall wooden pole on the Commons in New York had become a powerful form of political speech.

And so it was no surprise that the Sons of Liberty, including Sears and McDougall, applied to the mayor for permission to erect yet another Liberty Pole on the Commons, which was public land. This time, the city council turned down their request. Permitting the actions of the soldiers to stand was unimaginable, so the Sons bought a small plot of land close by the old location. On February 6, six horses carried a pine ship's mast from the docks to Sears's land. Three thousand people accompanied the walk and gathered around as the pole was set in the ground, encased in iron bars and hoops. It stood forty-six feet high. A band played "God Save the King."[53]

EARLY ON A COLD WINTER MORNING two days later—Thursday, February 8—a sheriff knocked on the door of Alexander McDougall's home. The sheriff carried a bench warrant for McDougall's arrest. It had taken seven weeks and the promise of a large financial award, but the authorities had finally identified the man who had called himself "A Son of Liberty" on the broadside.[54]

McDougall gathered a few things, and then the sheriff escorted him through the streets and to the chambers of Chief Justice Daniel Horsmanden, who had signed the warrant charging him with authoring the broadside. "So you have brought yourself into a pretty Scrape," the chief justice told him.[55]

"May it please your Honour, that must be judged of by my Peers," McDougall replied. The chief justice told him that there was full proof that he had written and published the broadside, and that it was a false and scandalous libel. "This must also be tried by my Peers," McDougall said. After McDougall refused to post bail, the chief justice ordered him to jail.

Colden's reward of one hundred pounds had finally enticed a young printer's assistant named Cummings to come forward. Recently dismissed for bad behavior by James Parker, publisher of the *New York Gazette and Weekly Post-Boy*, Cummings now crossed his old boss by identifying Parker as the printer of McDougall's broadside. The sheriff took Parker and his apprentices into custody at the fort. Interrogated separately from Parker, the apprentices confirmed that their boss had done the work. Then Parker went before Colden and the Governor's Council. At first he refused to name the author of the broadside, but the council had prepared well. If he refused to cooperate, he would have to choose between posting bail and going to jail, and he would of course lose his position as deputy postmaster general. Parker admitted that McDougall had paid him to print his broadside.

McDougall was arrested the next day. Until a few years earlier, the island's deadbeats and criminals had been jailed in the basement and garret of City Hall. With demand for space growing, the city built its first structure dedicated entirely to incarceration on the corner of the Commons. Three stories high and built of rough stone, the New Gaol had a cupola on the roof with a bell to give fire alarms and a lantern on a pole that pointed at night toward the part of town affected by the fire.[56]

The New Gaol tested even the most hard-bitten men, especially in the winter. Conditions were so bad that one year the prisoners took an ad in one of the local papers to express their "sincere and hearty Thanks" to the public "by whose generous Donations they have been comfortably supported during the last Winter, and preserved from perishing in a dreary Prison with Hunger and Cold."[57]

Incarcerated on February 8, McDougall was spared the worst that the New Gaol had to offer, thanks to the support of his friends in the Sons of Liberty, for whom his jailing provided a singular opportunity to create political theater that would expand support for their cause.

IT'S NOT EVERY PRISONER who enjoys such a busy social schedule that he places a notice in the newspaper letting people know what time they can visit. McDougall, though, received more than two hundred visitors in his first two days of confinement in the New Gaol, so overwhelming his cell that he had to set a schedule of available times. "Many of my friends who have honoured me with their Visits since my oppressive Confinement in this Place," he wrote in the *New York Journal*, "have advised me . . . to appoint an Hour from which it will be most convenient for me to see my Friends; I do therefore hereby notify them, that I shall be glad of the Honour of their Company, from Three o-Clock in the Afternoon till Six."[58]

McDougall's confinement gave the Sons of Liberty an opportunity to rally their followers and raise opposition to the assembly's decision to pay for provisioning the troops. They immediately devised a campaign around McDougall's arrest. The Sons already knew how to make protest into pageantry. Starting with the Stamp Act protests, they had recognized that essays and pamphlets were powerful vehicles for conveying political ideas but that such writings were aimed at the most highly educated of citizens. Symbolic expression, though, opened another channel of protest. It helped make protest democratic by expressing complex ideas in a way that attracted attention and involvement by the broader community. And so the Sons raised Liberty Trees and Liberty Poles. They hanged effigies of their enemies and put them in the embrace of the devil. They marched in parades through colonial towns and held mock trials for the stamp tax before their own judges and juries.

The pageantry that the Sons devised around McDougall's confinement, though, expanded protest still more. Perhaps never before in the colonies had choreography so thoroughly been brought to the service of political expression. In McDougall, the radicals created a political martyr like a recent hero in England who had been incarcerated a few years earlier. McDougall became the "John Wilkes of America." And they attached to him a number, forty-five, that already resonated throughout the colonies as a symbol of liberty. People in the colonies could creatively use the number to express support of McDougall and bring attention to his cause.

John Wilkes was elected to Parliament in 1757 and started a publication, the *North Briton,* in 1762 largely to attack John Stuart, Earl of Bute, who had become the prime minister.[59] Although he crammed the *North Briton* with insults against Bute, Wilkes did not get into trouble until he published issue number forty-five in 1763. Criticisms of the prime minister were barely tolerable, but issue forty-five went further by attacking a speech that George III delivered to Parliament.

The government issued general warrants that led to seizure of Wilkes's personal papers and his arrest for seditious libel. Wilkes argued that general warrants, which named nobody in particular and allowed wholesale arrests at the discretion of the authorities, were a serious violation of English law. He was convicted of seditious libel in absentia after he fled to France. On his return in 1768, voters again elected him to Parliament, but the government threw him in jail for nearly two years for his previous mischiefs, precipitating widespread demonstrations. Even from prison, he was elected to Parliament and then expelled within days. Every punitive move by Parliament only made Wilkes more popular among his countrymen, and across the Atlantic as well, as a martyr for freedom of the press and civil liberties in general.

Why did many Americans identify with Wilkes? They regarded him as an ally in protesting what they saw as violations of the British constitution. Wilkes's cause was the colonists' cause, as they saw it. Wilkes had argued against general warrants in his own case, an experience that the colonists shared as they themselves fought against writs that enabled authorities to conduct searches wherever they pleased, without naming a specific location or the materials sought. His scuffles over charges of seditious libel mirrored what writers and printers in America experienced at the hands of the authorities. But it was more than identifying with the shared experience. The Sons of Liberty thought that Wilkes possessed enough influence to rally support in England for reforms that would end laws that hurt English subjects in America. As the Boston Sons of Liberty wrote hopefully to Wilkes on his return to England from exile in 1768, "You are *one* of those incorruptibly honest men reserved by heaven to bless, and perhaps save a tottering Empire."[60]

His struggles against Parliament and the king gave Wilkes an iconic stature in America. The number forty-five corresponding with the issue of *North Briton* that made him a target of prosecution took on popular significance. First in England and then in America, those who sympathized with Wilkes began engaging in an endless variety of symbolic protests with the number forty-five as the common theme. Newspapers in the colonies routinely published accounts of these activities. In London, one sympathizer sent forty-five hogsheads of tobacco as a present to Wilkes, while another shipped forty-five hogsheads of sugar and forty-five puncheons of rum. On Wilkes's birthday, supporters discharged forty-five cannon in his honor.[61] And the symbolism could get much more elaborate. A supporter sponsored a dinner in honor of Wilkes with forty-five gentlemen, and they drank forty-five gills of wine and ate forty-five eggs, followed by a five-course dinner of nine dishes each to make a total of forty-five dishes. Waiters placed forty-five pounds of beef on the table atop a display of the number forty-five inlaid with mother of pearl. As the dinner ended, forty-five ladies entered the room, and the men engaged them in forty-five dances and kissed them, naturally, exactly forty-five times. Finally, the affair ended at forty-five minutes past three o'clock.[62] The "forty-five" craze in England reached the point that a London paper ran the report, republished in the colonies, of a man who said that as he was "passing through Islington yesterday, I heard a parrot in a cage crying 'Wilkes and Liberty for ever, No. 45.'" As one passerby said, "By Jasus, that parrot is a true-born Englishman, and knows what he is about as well as the best of them."[63]

On the American side of the water, the Sons of Liberty celebrated Wilkes as well, with toasts to "Wilkes and Liberty" resounding in taverns all throughout the colonies.[64] The town of Wilkes-Barre, Pennsylvania, was named for John Wilkes when it was settled in 1769. A Boston man baptized his son with the name of John Wilkes.[65] Americans adopted the number forty-five. In 1769, the *Boston Gazette* noted that forty-five ladies engaged in spinning linen and cotton, providing cloth to replace British goods boycotted in the nonimportation agreements.[66] The Sons of Liberty in Boston made a procession of forty-five carriages, while several patriots sent a turtle to Wilkes that weighted forty-five pounds and whose voyage across the ocean, it was duly noted, took forty-five days.[67] Celebration of Wilkes reached the southern colonies as well. In an orchard outside Charleston, patriots decorated their Liberty Tree with forty-five lights and fired forty-five rockets. Then forty-five of them marched to town, where they stopped at a tavern and had forty-five bowls of punch and forty-five bottles of wine.[68]

With stories about Wilkes filling the papers, it was not much of a leap for the Sons of Liberty to see that they might create an American version of Wilkes in New York. Both had run afoul of seditious libel charges for criticizing government actions. As a successful merchant, McDougall could easily afford to pay bail and remain free awaiting trial. But he understood that sitting in a cold jail cell in the middle of winter offered an opportunity for political theater not to be missed.

The motivations of the Sons of Liberty in creating an American Wilkes were transparent to everyone. A few weeks after McDougall went to the New Gaol, Lieutenant-Governor Colden himself saw through the political theater in writing about McDougall. "He is a person of some fortune," wrote Colden, "and could easily have found the Bail required of him, but he choose to go to Jail, and lyes there imitating Mr. Wilkes in everything he can."[69] McDougall's opponents understood that his jailing could make him a martyr and inspire more dissent throughout the colonies. One anonymous writer accused the Sons of Liberty of ascribing to McDougall "a Thousand Virtues and Qualifications he never possessed" with the goal of "rendering him in some Degree *popular,* in the other Colonies; where every Thing contained in a News Paper may be implicitly believed; but in this City he is too well known to have many more Advocates."[70] News of the events in New York did spread and elicit support. As a patriot in another colony said upon hearing of McDougall's arrest, "The Gentleman's Cause imprisoned at New York, is the Cause of the whole Continent; and from this Moment, I devote my Fortune and my Life, to secure him fair Play."[71] Another promised that many supporters from other provinces would attend the trial.[72]

To transform McDougall into the American Wilkes, the Sons of Liberty needed pageantry and political theater that went beyond the effigies and demonstrations they had employed to protest the Stamp Act. The key strategy was to associate McDougall with the magical number forty-five. The effort began immediately. Within a few days of his incarceration, a "true female friend to American Liberty" visited McDougall and gave him a cut of venison marked with the number forty-five.[73] Meals provided creative opportunities to draw attention to him. On February 14, the forty-fifth day of the year and less than a week after McDougall went to jail, the *New York Journal* reported that "forty-five Gentlemen, real Enemies to internal Taxation . . . went in decent Procession to the New Gaol; and dined with him, on Forty-five Pounds of Beef Stakes, cut from a Bullock of forty-five Months old, and with a Number of other Friends, who joined them in the Afternoon, drank a Variety of Toasts, expressive not only of the most undissembled Loyalty, but of the warmest Attachment to Liberty . . . and the freedom of the Press."[74]

In March, the fourth anniversary of repeal of the Stamp Act provided an opportunity for a big event and the attention that would come with it. Three hundred members of the Sons met for dinner. Before the food was served, the group nominated ten men to dine with McDougall in his cell, "where a suitable dinner was also provided." After making forty-five toasts, including one to McDougall, the entire group walked to the New Gaol "with Music playing and Colours flying." They gave three cheers to McDougall, who answered them with cheers of his own and then delivered "a short address" through the grates of his prison window. Then the crowd moved on to the Liberty Pole nearby, taking down the flag from the top and marching with it around town.[75]

The Sons also worked in a number of their own—ninety-two—that resonated throughout the colonies. Protesting the Townshend Revenue Acts, the Massachusetts House of Representatives had sent a circular letter written by Samuel Adams to the assemblies in other colonies in 1768, arguing that the laws were unconstitutional. British authorities ordered the Massachusetts legislature to rescind the circular letter, but lawmakers refused by a 92–17 vote. By the time McDougall was arrested, the number ninety-two had become a symbol of American resistance.[76]

On March 5, forty-five mechanics met at one tavern and then marched to another, where they were met by an additional group to raise the total to ninety-two, at which time they all visited McDougall.[77] And McDougall's wife invoked it herself. She took a group of 137 "Daughters of Liberty"—forty-five plus ninety-two—to visit him at the New Gaol. "Two chambers were prepared for their Reception, where they were entertained with Tea and Cakes; and after that they sung a Number of patriotic Songs, then took their leave of him." Chapel Street was lined with "a vast number of spectators" as they went on to Mrs. McDougall's house to continue their entertainment. One newspaper noted that the women "patronized the glorious Cause, which daily gains Friends of both Sexes."[78]

For entertainment value and attention to the cause—the point of all the pageantry—none could compete with the visit of forty-five virgins to McDougall's prison cell for tea, cake, chocolates, and the singing of their own version of the Forty-Fifth Psalm. For six weeks after that, the newspapers of New York carried articles about the visit, some from writers severely criticizing McDougall. Keeping him at the center of attention was exactly what the Sons of Liberty had intended.[79]

THE BRILLIANT POLITICAL THEATER surrounding McDougall brought a strong reaction. Not all of New York was enamored with him, and the careful creation of an American Wilkes fueled strong political expression on all sides. The situation in the colony was much too complicated for a single bright line to emerge that would neatly divide those who favored compliance with the Quartering Act from those who did not. Local politics were thorny, especially with the bitter rancor between the Livingston party and the De Lancey party. Some who opposed payments for the provisioning of British troops reluctantly regarded the act as a reasonable compromise since it enabled the colony to get the bills of credit that it needed to carry on commerce. At the same time, the boycott against British goods took money out of the pockets of many merchants and seamen, creating divisions over how far people were willing to go to oppose British authority. Some were more willing than others to balance large constitutional issues with the reality of their own and the colony's economic problems. Five years before the shedding of blood at Lexington and Concord, there were multiple shades of patriotism and loyalism.

This stew of political and economic considerations played out on the anniversary of the Stamp Act repeal in 1770. With McDougall in his cell at the New Gaol, his buddies in the Sons of Liberty planned to celebrate with a dinner at Montayne's Tavern, but the owner made it clear that his tavern was closed to accommodate the "Friends to Liberty and Trade"—a group whose name alone showed their willingness to compromise on the issues that rallied the more radical Sons. Not to be outdone, Sears and other radicals quickly purchased another tavern close by their beloved Liberty Pole. They named it Hampden Hall and made it the headquarters of the Sons of Liberty. The radicals toasted McDougall at their dinner at Hampden Hall, while the Friends of Liberty and Trade ignored McDougall and instead toasted Colden, his council, and the assembly, all of whom were involved in McDougall's arrest.[80] A writer who took the name "Hampden" asked how the group that dined at Montayne's Tavern could call themselves Sons of Liberty when—at their celebration of repeal of the Stamp Act—they toasted the governor who had attempted to enforce that law.[81]

The back-and-forth attacks often employed searing language. When the *New York Journal* wrote that forty-five members of the Chamber of Commerce had visited McDougall in jail, an angry writer complained that the number had been exaggerated. Of seventy-three members of the New York Chamber of Commerce, the writer charged, "there are not above 14 or 15 of them, at most, who do not heartily despise Mr. McDougall, as an empty, insignificant, self-conceited im-p-t [impotent] body, utterly incapable of writing the scandalous Paper laid to his Charge, although he may have been the Publisher of it."[82] The De Lancey faction also tried to drive a wedge between McDougall and Sears. A writer charged that Sears had often said in public company that McDougall was not a true Son of Liberty, but instead was a "rotten-hearted villain" who was guilty of "betraying the glorious cause in which the *patriotic Sons* were engaged." Sears published a reply in which he surprisingly conceded that he had indeed called McDougall "a rotten hearted fellow" but certainly not a "villain" who betrayed the cause—evidently, in his mind, "a rotten hearted fellow" being the less serious offense of the two. He supported McDougall now because his fellow Son was acting "in the glorious Cause of Liberty."[83]

The debate in the newspapers, though, went beyond invective. McDougall sparked a cascade of commentary that dominated the newspapers in New York for the first half of 1770. One anonymous writer sustained his attack on McDougall through a series of twelve newspaper essays called "The Dougliad," striking him from every angle and often with biting sarcasm. Little escaped the author's notice, from the lessons of

English history to the political position taken by McDougall to his motivation for attacking Colden and the assembly.[84]

McDougall's supporters, often writing under pseudonyms like the Satyrist, Hoadly, and The Watchman, branded his attackers as men who had accepted tyranny. The Satyrist wrote that "these TORY AUTHORS *are undoubtedly* WRETCHED SLAVES ratling in their CHAINS."[85]

THE ANXIOUS GHOST of John Peter Zenger hovered over the legal proceedings against Alexander McDougall.

Zenger had been tried in New York for seditious libel in 1735. With the law weighted heavily against him—after all, truth was not a defense to a libel charge—Zenger won only because the jury accepted the invitation from Andrew Hamilton, Zenger's lawyer, to ignore the law and to acquit him (see chapter 2). McDougall's jailing once again raised the issue of how far a citizen could go in criticizing public officials.

If people needed any reminder, McDougall's supporters referred to Zenger again and again. They even reprinted the transcripts from Zenger's trial to refresh memories of Hamilton's arguments on his behalf.[86] In newspaper articles, the Sons of Liberty attacked seditious libel as an oppressive relic of the hated Star Chamber in England, and a violation of what they saw as their freedom to criticize overbearing officials.

Some writers admitted that they wrote to influence potential jurors. Britannicus, in an article he addressed "To a Juryman," argued in McDougall's defense that truth should be a defense to libel claims—"*truth, and all the truth,* HOWEVER DEFAMATORY, *ought always to be told;* for otherwise, how could the public ever oppose any oppression at all?" The jury, he said, must not be restricted to deciding only the question of who had written or published an alleged libel, with the judge deciding if it amounted to a scandalous reflection on government. In Zenger's case "the judges plainly showed that they sat there only during the governor's pleasure," thus making it impossible for them to fairly rule on libel.[87]

The Dougliad pushed from the opposite direction, addressing specifically "the Grand Jury for the City and County of New-York."[88] The liberty of the press, according to the Dougliad, did not protect writers "however atrocious or malignant." Dougliad's author believed that citizens must be submissive to government. Public officials deserved "*inviolable* Respect.

As our *Guardians,* they will be treated with Dignity; honoured with Submission; and sacredly defended from every Approach of Insult."

The Dougliad drew a portrait of government as a straw house always susceptible to being toppled by strong words. "If there were no Check to Malice and Falsehood," he wrote, "Government must soon sink into Contempt, and the subject be stript of protection." The very survival of society was at stake. "To traduce and vilify those in Authority, to misrepresent their Conduct, to expose them to Odium and Contempt, and to excite a general Spirit of Jealously and Distrust, must it not infallibly lead to Faction, to revolt, and open Sedition?" The author had nothing but scorn for the use of symbols like Liberty Poles, comparing their use to acts of paganism. Protestors enjoyed "the *Happiness of Assembling in the open Air,* and performing *Idolatrous* and *vociferous* Acts of Worship, *to a Stick of Wood,* called a Liberty Pole."[89]

Dougliad's author was consistent with the thinking of other writers who had defended seditious libel law. "In God's name, what business have private men to write or to speak about public matters?" wrote an anonymous pamphleteer in England who named himself Candor. Men must cede control of public matters to the king and Parliament, Candor said: "The advantage of inoffensive speech or writing, and of absolute submission to government, is so great, that I am sure every man ought to rejoice in such wholesome regulations." Prosecutions for seditious libel are "really an excellent device for keeping the scribbling race from meddling with political questions, at least from ever drawing their pens a second time upon such subjects."[90]

Candor would not have the last word, for another writer gamely calling himself Father of Candor leaped into the fray. And Father answered his "son" by rejecting Candor's views on freedom of the press. To the Father, the press had served England well through its publication of political and religious writings, deserving much of the credit for the Glorious Revolution, the Protestant Revolution, and advances in civil liberties in general. Far from passively accepting decisions made by officials, the Father argued that citizens have a right to remonstrate against official misconduct. "The liberty of exposing and opposing a bad Administration by the pen," said Father of Candor, "is among the necessary privileges of a free people, and is perhaps the greatest benefit that can be derived from the liberty of the press. But Ministers, who by their misdeeds provoke the people to cry out and complain, are very apt to make that very complaint the foundation of new oppression, by prosecuting the same as a libel on the State."[91]

Father of Candor, of course, supported the two reforms that libertarians most wanted in the common law of seditious libel.[92] The defense of truth and an expanded role for the jury were conventional arguments of advocates of freedom of the press, but the Father did not stop there. He dropped two small seeds into the ground, seeds that would lie dormant for two centuries before they found a more hospitable time to grow. First, he said that seditious libel was punished because of the possibility that the published words could later cause unrest and imperil the government or breach the peace, a concept called bad tendency. Since any critical words could potentially gain supporters and upset the established order, libel was an expansive concept that enabled officials to suppress any criticism that they did not like at its very inception, whether or not it might actually cause disorder. But the Father argued that the mere expression of words could not be criminal.[93]

The Father made his second major contribution when he went beyond the conventional libertarian idea that truth should be a complete defense to any libel claim. Now the Father leaped across intellectual time and space. He suggested that the defense of truth to a libel claim would be a critical advance but by no means enough to protect political expression. Truth was "highly commendable," he wrote, but even some *falsehood* should be protected from libel prosecution. Only writings that were "willfully false" were "certainly malicious, seditious, and damnable."[94] In other words, the Father wanted to protect not only truth but also false statements—unless the speaker knew his statement was false but published it anyway.

Why was the Father's idea so important? He grasped a critical idea about freedom of speech and press—that writing and uttering falsehoods was inevitable in the heat of debate because even well-intentioned people can make innocent mistakes. If speakers and writers who critiqued government could be jailed for falsehoods that were not made willfully, many speakers would curtail their expression and the marketplace of ideas would suffer.

Across the ocean, a writer in New York grasped the same idea, if only to protect himself from a lawsuit. Writing an open letter to the public,

Isaac Morrison apologized for criticizing a lawyer in an article he had published anonymously. The article contained false statements, he confessed, but he "was not wilful in writing *that,* or in any other Mistake there may be in that Piece," and so he hoped he "may obtain Forgiveness." Like Father of Candor, Morrison went beyond asking for a defense of truth and urged that even his false statement made in good faith be forgiven as human error.[95]

Father of Candor argued, as American libertarians would decades later, that dissent brought salutary changes to government and society. "Indeed," he wrote, referring to events in England, 'I am fully convinced, that were it not for such writings as have been prosecuted by Attorney-generals for libels, we should never have had a Revolution, nor his present Majesty a regal Crown; nor should we now enjoy a protestant religion, or one jot of civil liberty."[96]

The first glimmer of recognition was emerging that the vigor of speech and press required special protections far beyond what the law of England provided.

WITH MCDOUGALL SITTING in jail, the charge against him for seditious libel still had to go to a grand jury, which was required to vote an indictment before the case could go forward. This presented serious problems for the prosecution. The Zenger case showed that juries would not easily convict their neighbors for criticizing the government, and the popular rejection of seditious libel had only increased since then. In Boston, during the Stamp Act protests and for several years beyond, Governor Bernard and Chief Justice Hutchinson had failed again and again to convince a grand jury to indict the editors of the *Boston Gazette.*[97]

Selection of the grand jurors, then, took on great importance for any seditious libel case. And here, both sides had tried their best to influence potential jurors through their articles in the papers. They also attempted to influence the selection of the jurors themselves, as the Sons tried without success to secure appointments as jurors. Instead of assigning the jurors by regular rotation, the sheriff called a panel of men of his own choosing, the vast majority of whom were in the camp of the De Lancey party, which controlled the assembly.[98]

After the grand jury indicted McDougall, he walked from the New Gaol to City Hall on April 28 accompanied, as prosecutor Thomas Jones wrote, by "two or three hundred of the rabble of the town, headed by some of the most zealous partisans of the republican faction."[99] McDougall told them grandly that "he had cheerfully submitted to a Confinement for eleven Weeks, and was ready to continue in Goal for eleven Years, if it had been judged necessary to advance the Cause of Liberty and his country." He pled not guilty, and decided this time to pay bail and become a free man pending his trial, having spent close to three months in jail. About six hundred supporters walked with him back to his home "without Tumult or Noise," and McDougall delivered a speech to them at his door.[100]

McDougall's indictment was noteworthy in its isolation, the only indictment for seditious libel brought against a protest leader in the years leading up to the American Revolution. That Americans in general were wary of exacting criminal punishments against their fellow citizens was reflected in the extent to which the stars had to be aligned correctly for an indictment to issue. All three branches of government—the governor, chief justice, and assembly—supported the indictment, and the sheriff had to finagle the assignments in order to get a grand jury willing to do the government's bidding.[101]

Soon enough, the death of a major character changed everything. While McDougall awaited trial, James Parker died suddenly. As the printer who had worked directly with McDougall, Parker was the only person who could provide firsthand testimony that McDougall had authored the broadside. Parker's death made it pointless for the government to pursue the case. McDougall had reason to believe that he had escaped the clutches of government officials who wanted to punish him. Nothing could have prepared him for the surreal drama that was about to unfold.[102]

With a trial in the courts unlikely, now the assembly—the very body whose actions McDougall had criticized in his broadside—ordered him to appear before them for answer for his writings. Along with the courts, provincial assemblies could hear seditious libel cases. With colonial juries resisting such charges, assemblies sometimes took up the task themselves by prosecuting what they regarded as breaches of parliamentary privilege—words that they considered to be affronts to the dignity of the assembly or the defamation of its members. They did not have to bother with the uncertainties of juries; they could simply question supposed offenders and assign criminal penalties as they saw fit, a procedure that was grimly effective. That this involved an egregious conflict of interest—the offended lawmakers served as prosecutor and judge for the trial of the person whose words had aggrieved them—seemed hardly a concern to them.[103]

On December 13, 1770, nearly a year after circulation of the broadside, McDougall appeared at noon on the floor of the House.[104] Henry Cruger, the speaker, told McDougall that he stood charged with being the author of the broadside and asked him how he would plead. McDougall asked for the names of his accusers and the evidence against him, but Representative De Noyelles threatened him with contempt. Finally allowed to speak, McDougall complained that his summons for a trial had come without notice or time to prepare a defense. He said he could not plead to the charge because the assembly had already declared the writing to be a libel and so by admitting authorship he would incriminate himself on the only other matter in dispute. Not only that, but the case that the house brought against him in the common law court was still active. Trying him before the assembly while that charge was still pending, argued McDougall, violated the protection enjoyed by British citizens not to be punished twice for the same offense.

The lawmakers rebelled at his new insults. To force McDougall to plead to the charges, De Noyelles threatened him with the infliction of a medieval torture called *peine forte et dure*. Guards would force a prisoner onto his back and place heavy weights on top of him, adding more weight every day that he refused to testify. The torture might take some days, but McDougall would either cooperate or die. Appalled by the threat, Representative George Clinton noted that if the question concerned the power of the assembly to extort an answer from McDougall, they could with equal right simply throw him out of the window to the street below—"but that the Public would Judge of the Justice of it."

Finally, Cruger ordered McDougall to put his objections in writing. After Cruger read McDougall's note to the lawmakers, they approved a motion declaring that his objections were a breach of privilege and contempt of the house. And with that, the sergeant at arms took McDougall to the New Gaol. Once again, McDougall took to the newspapers and thanked "my Friends of all Ranks," assuring them that "none of their Rights shall be silently resigned."[105] He stayed in the New Gaol until March 4, close to another three months, before he finally went home. In all, he spent 162 days in jail. The charges from the common law court were dropped.[106]

At last, McDougall had played out the final act of his political theater. From the forty-five virgins visiting his jail cell to the big celebratory dinners in his honor, he had commanded not just the attention but also the participation of an enormous swath of the community. Thousands had joined in dissent or at least been drawn closer to the vortex, challenging by their actions the proscription against criticizing the government.

Successfully portrayed as the American Wilkes, McDougall had accomplished his purpose.

6

THE SILVERSMITH

A LONE BRITISH SOLDIER, HUGH WHITE, STOOD GUARD AT THE REDBRICK CUSTOM HOUSE ON King Street in downtown Boston on the evening of March 5, 1770. It was chilly with crusted snow on the street, and White stomped his feet to keep warm. With no street lamps, the only illumination came from the moon, with its muted light reflecting off the snow and ice. White's presence was an irritant to Bostonians, who deeply resented the occupation of their city by redcoats. Confrontations between the soldiers and civilians took place frequently as young rabble-rousers hurled taunts and insults at every opportunity. Boston was not alone in its conflict over British troops; two hundred miles to the south, Alexander McDougall sat in a jail cell after criticizing the New York Assembly's decision to provision soldiers in New York.[1]

Early that evening, a wig maker's apprentice, Edward Garrick, passed by White and taunted him about a fellow soldier's failure to pay his master for dressing his hair. The two exchanged insults and suddenly White stepped forward, swinging his musket at Garrick's head, bloodying him. Garrick staggered off, and as word spread of the incident, the street began filling with young men.

Church bells rang after 9 p.m., and since it was an off-hour, it brought still more men onto King Street, thinking that they were being called to fight a fire. Before long, more than a hundred men confronted the soldier, taunting him to fight. As the situation deteriorated, Captain Thomas Preston at the military headquarters down the street took a relief force of seven men out to rescue White.

Preston's men reached White and formed a curving line facing the crowd. Their muskets, on half cock and pointed low, were fitted with bayonets. Immediately, snowballs and pieces of ice and coal hit the soldiers. The crowd shouted profanities and dared the soldiers to shoot, coming close enough to shove them. A wood club flew from the rear, striking one of the soldiers and knocking him down. One man swung another club at Preston and caught him heavily on the arm, then dodged a bayonet that another soldier thrust at him. Scuffling broke out—and then a shot followed by more shots. It was over in a matter of seconds. Three men lay dead. Two wounded men would die later.

Preston and his soldiers were arrested and imprisoned in the morning as news of the tragedy spread by word of mouth throughout the city. In the days ahead, partisans seized the opportunity to define the event in the public's mind. One of them, Paul Revere, a Boston silversmith, published an engraving that depicted the incident as a brazen execution of innocent civilians by merciless redcoats firing on the command of Captain Preston, shown standing behind the soldiers with an uplifted sword. Labeled "The Bloody Massacre," the drawing circulated as a broadside throughout the city and beyond.

There was one problem, though, with Revere's drawing of the incident. Much about it was either false or exaggerated. He had intended it to be so, a stinging commentary on the overbearing nature of British authority in America. Revere had grasped the power to use political speech—in this case the art of political cartooning—to persuade people of the dangers of a standing army in their midst. Combined with an outpouring of letters, verse, town resolutions and reports, scathing sermons by Boston ministers, and critical articles in the patriot press, Revere's drawing raised the shootings into one of the defining moments of colonial opposition to Britain and an important expansion of political speech in America.

WHEN JOHN SINGLETON COPLEY painted a portrait of Paul Revere in 1768, he depicted an idealized image of one of Boston's leading artisans. Revere, then in his mid-thirties, sits behind a polished table that shows none of the scars and discolorations of an artisan's workbench. He is dressed informally in an open, full-sleeved white linen shirt with a blue-green waistcoat that he left unbuttoned. He cradles his chin in his right hand, while his left holds a round teapot whose surface is smooth and unadorned, awaiting the finishing decorations. His engraving tools lie at his elbow and ready to use.[2]

Revere was poised that year, 1768, to begin participating in the activities that would lift him into the orbit of the best-known patriots of the Revolutionary period. Still seven years ahead of him was the midnight ride to Lexington to warn of the march of British troops out of Boston—the ride immortalized by Henry Wadsworth Longfellow's now familiar line, "Listen, my children, and you shall hear, of the midnight ride of Paul Revere . . ." Important though the ride was, it was the delicate-looking engraver's tools depicted in Copley's portrait that would define Revere's most vital contribution to the patriot cause. The engraving tools look much like pens, and Revere used them to make political cartoons that circulated widely and that proved as effective as written words.

Revere's skills in copper and silver owed much to his father's influence. Apollos Rivoire had come to America in 1715 after boarding a ship in the harbor of Saint Peter Port in Guernsey, an island in the English Channel off the coast of Normandy. Dropped off by his uncle at the dock, Rivoire surely felt the profound uncertainty of what lay ahead of him. Less than a week from his thirteenth birthday, he was embarking alone on an uncertain journey across the ocean to Boston, where he would try to make a go of it without much more than his own adolescent bravado to guide him. The young Rivoire landed in Boston and took up an apprenticeship with a local silversmith. When the silversmith died seven years later, Rivoire bought freedom from his indenture and set up his own shop. He changed his name from Rivoire to Revere to make it easier for the local people to pronounce and married the daughter of a Boston merchant.[3]

Paul Revere, his son, was born in 1734 and grew up on the narrow crooked streets of the North End. The water that lapped at the docks just a few blocks away made an overpowering allure. Young boys like Paul spent much of their free time playing as the dockworkers unloaded the heavy cargo. They dove off the wharves into the cold water of the bay and climbed into the riggings of the sailing ships. More serious business called them as well. The young Revere served as an apprentice to his

father, watching him use hammers to pound silver until it took the finished shape of cups and spoons. Gradually, he learned how to work with
silver, copper, and brass. Paul went to the North Writing School, a two-
story school building where boys destined for the artisan trades received
the most basic education, learning writing on one floor and reading on
the other.[4]

Paul proved as self-reliant as his father, too. At just nineteen, he inherited the business and supported his family when Apollos died. Gradually over the years, Revere acquired the connections that would make him
familiar in colonial politics. He served in the militia during the French
and Indian War, and his growing reputation as a skilled silversmith attracted attention. Revere saw his business prosper, and he came to know
more and more of the Boston radicals, like Samuel Adams, as his customers. He made connections at the New Brick Church, where he went on
the Sabbath, and on various civic committees.[5] Gradually, Revere moved
into the ranks of the radicals themselves. He joined them for drinks at the
Salutation Inn and often retired to a private room used for meetings of
the North Caucus, a group of Whig activists whose membership counted
many artisans and seamen. Along with a few other such groups, they
discussed political affairs and put forward candidates for election at the
Boston town meetings. Samuel Adams and John Adams were members.[6]
Revere also joined the Long Room Club, whose members included the
leading radicals in Boston, who met in a room above the printing shop of
the *Boston Gazette,* whose publishers were Benjamin Edes and John Gill
(see chapter 3).[7]

Revere's immersion into politics deepened in 1765 as he joined the
Sons of Liberty in its protest against the Stamp Act. Again and again, he
contributed his special talents as a silversmith to the cause of liberty. In
1766, when it repealed the Stamp Act, Parliament passed the Declaratory
Act asserting its power to enact tax and other laws over the colonies "in
all cases whatsoever." The following year, Parliament began passing the
Townshend Acts to raise revenue by imposing duties on goods imported
to America such as tea, paper, paint, and glass. The Massachusetts House
of Representatives sent its Circular Letter, written by Samuel Adams, to
the other colonial assemblies in 1768, asking them to join Massachusetts
in opposing the new taxes. Acting on instructions from London, Massachusetts governor Francis Bernard ordered the assembly to rescind the

letter or he would dissolve the body. When the lawmakers refused to rescind by a vote of 92 to 17, Bernard carried out his threat.

The assembly's refusal to rescind the Circular Letter caused a sensation in Boston and throughout the colonies. And it motivated Revere to turn his considerable skills as an engraver and silversmith to helping the colonial cause. Commissioned by the Sons of Liberty, Revere celebrated the ninety-two lawmakers by making a silver punchbowl in their honor—the Sons of Liberty Bowl that would become an American national treasure. Revere engraved on the bowl the names of fifteen Sons as well as an inscription to John Wilkes, the British member of Parliament who was a hero in the colonies because he was jailed on charges of seditious libel for criticizing the king. Around the sides of the bowl he engraved a variety of decorative elements, including a liberty cap, flags, references to the Magna Carta and the (English) Bill of Rights, and an inscription to the lawmakers "who, undaunted by the insolent Menaces of Villains in Power . . . Voted NOT TO RESCIND."[8]

Revere was not finished. He had plenty of venom for the remainder of the lawmakers, those who had complied with Bernard's demand to rescind the Circular Letter. On a copper plate he engraved a political cartoon for printing and distribution far and wide. Calling the engraving "A Warm Place—Hell," Revere heaped scorn on the rescinders. Two devils with pitchforks prod the lawmakers into the cavernous jaws of a fearsome dragon that breathes fire and represents the Puritan idea of a forbidding Hell. A snake writhes at their feet. The engraving makes some of the rescinders, who are dressed in colonial garb, identifiable to citizens of Boston. At the bottom of the engraving is a stanza: "On brave RESCINDERS! To yon yawning Cell, SEVENTEEN such Miscreants will startle Hell."[9]

Many years later, when he had reached the age of eighty, Revere remembered that he had done the engraving when he "was a young man, zealous in the cause of liberty when he sketched it."[10]

PRINTED AND VIEWED throughout the colonies, the engraving helped promote disdain for those who backed down in the face of threats from London. But Revere's work was not original. As was common practice, he had copied the basic drawing from an existing work and adapted it to his own use. In this case, it was a volume of political cartoons published three years earlier in England. Also called "A Warm Place—Hell," the drawing commented on a political controversy at the time in England and featured six villains instead of seventeen. Revere added a winged devil to his own drawing, but all in all it was a recognizable copy, right down to the title.[11]

If Revere was going to copy a political cartoonist, England was a good place to look. It was there that cartooning began to evolve into powerful expression. In England, it started with the art of caricature, typically sketches of people, and until around 1750 many such drawings rendered their subject more or less accurately. Gradually, though, artists began exaggerating physical features in humorous and sometime cruel ways. The drawings were sold individually as prints and also incorporated into cards and books and broadsides, and they were so popular that the British Museum collection includes almost five thousand published by 1770.[12]

From drawings that focused on individuals, it was not a long leap for some artists to embrace a more expansive idea of political cartooning, moving beyond caricatures of individuals to focus instead on important contemporary issues. As their scalpel of choice, sharpened with some combination of satire, distortion, and exaggeration, the cartoon delivered commentary and scored serious political points. In fact, drawings often proved more powerful than printed or spoken words, as Britain's William Hogarth, the most important political cartoonist of the age, showed time and again with engravings that confronted the major issues of his time such as economic and political corruption, poverty, prostitution, and waste.[13]

Hogarth created one of his most famous works, *The South Sea Scheme,* in 1721, shortly after a financial collapse in Britain brought ruin to many investors. Rampant speculation in the stock of the South Sea Company drove its share price into the stratosphere, only for it to collapse suddenly amid a financial and political scandal. Hogarth had plenty to say on the subject, but his talents veered away from the familiar path of writing an editorial or an essay full of dense arguments and financial calculations. An artist and social critic, he was far more effective drawing an elaborate sketch and adding a few lines of verse, and so creating a satiric cartoon that skewered the financial speculators and the malaise of get-rich-quick schemes that devalued or destroyed honest and productive work.

Hogarth drew a tumultuous street scene, with the Wheel of Fortune at the center giving a ride to people symbolizing all walks of society, from a prostitute to a clergyman to a Scottish nobleman. A winged devil dismembers a blindfolded Fortune and tosses her body parts to the crowd, and nearby a priest reads the Bible as the figure of Honesty dies on the wheel at the hand of figures representing "Self Interest and Vilany."[14] English cartoonists following Hogarth drew satiric assaults on Lord Bute and others for inflicting the Stamp Act on the colonies. The most famous of them, *The Deplorable State of America, or Sc[otc]h Government,* depicts Liberty prostrate on the ground, saying, "It is all over with me." John Singleton Copley adapted the cartoon with Boston references and published it in the colonies.[15]

Hogarth and other cartoonists prospered in England, but their example failed, at least initially, to stimulate much similar activity across the ocean. Political cartooning began slowly in the colonies, where demonstrations around Liberty Trees employed many of the same elements utilized by Hogarth. The strategy of the political cartoonists and the street demonstrators was essentially the same—to use satire and distortion in the service of social commentary and political dissent. During the Stamp Act crisis, protestors throughout British America strung effigies of government officials from trees. There was nothing understated about these pageantries, which in many ways copied elements utilized in political cartoons. The radicals dressed up their effigies in costumes and often put them in the embrace of the devil before ripping them apart and tossing them into a bonfire. Stamp tax collectors, royal governors, and Lord Bute, whom the radicals regarded as the mastermind of the Stamp Act, were constant targets.[16]

Far from the raucous street demonstrations, political cartooning was a lonely craft of producing woodcuts or copper engravings suitable for printing. In the colonies, political cartooning made its first big splash when Benjamin Franklin published his *Join or Die* cartoon in the *Pennsylvania Gazette* in 1754, depicting a writhing snake severed into eight parts representing the colonies or regions. Franklin was trying to rally the colonies to defend themselves against the French and Indians. Two decades later, radicals revived Franklin's cartoon to rally colonial opposition to the Stamp Act, carrying the strong message that the colonies had to unite or face ruin. In 1765, Franklin drew another effective political cartoon, MAGNA *Britannia: her Colonies* REDUC'D, which showed Britain having fallen off a globe and sitting with severed limbs that were labeled Virginia, Pennsylvania, New York, and New England. Franklin's point was that Britain itself would be maimed by its policy of imposing the Stamp Act on the colonies.[17]

As Franklin and others opposed to British policy in America understood very well, political cartoons provided an effective means of influencing public opinion. Essays and letters and other written work could probe and argue an issue from many angles. But the written word was not the only weapon of persuasion, and not always the most effective. Political cartoons could move right to the heart of an issue. Franklin's severed snake spoke as powerfully about the strength that comes with unity as could an essay of any length. And Revere's drawing of two devils prodding the rescinders into the jaws of Hell resounded with the deepest Whig and Puritan fury at those who would weakly give up their rights in the face of overbearing British authority. Cartooning, too, was above all democratic. Cartoons were easy to grasp. They were another means of expression— like street demonstrations and symbolic speech—that broadened political participation to include many people who would not have read essays or editorials.

Revere surely understood all of this. As the pages on his calendar turned, the deteriorating situation in Boston between the British and the Sons of Liberty would soon call on him once again to turn his engraving tools to the cause of political persuasion.

LATE ON THE SUMMER AFTERNOON of June 10, 1768, Joseph Harrison and Benjamin Hallowell arrived at one of the wharves on the Boston waterfront. The two customs officials walked out to the *Liberty*, a sloop owned by the wealthy merchant John Hancock. They suspected Hancock of enriching himself, as many businessmen did at the time, by engaging in smuggling activities to evade the Townshend taxes. The customs officials thought that Hancock had secretly unloaded most of a shipment of Madeira wine before they had taken inventory on the ship.

Harrison and Hallowell looked across the water to the British warship *Romney* at anchor in the harbor, and waited until they saw a small boat filled with soldiers depart for the wharf. Then they boarded the *Liberty* and placed the King's Mark on the main mast, thereby seizing the sloop for the Crown. By now a crowd had gathered, and several men rushed forward and boarded the *Liberty* to prevent its seizure. The soldiers from the *Romney* arrived quickly and drove them off, and then the commanding officer took over the vessel and maneuvered it from the wharf and over the water to the *Romney*.

Their work completed, Harrison and Hallowell left the wharf and entered onto the street, where onlookers attacked them. Harrison reported that people began "by throwing Dirt at me, which was presently succeeded by Volleys of Stones, Brickbatts, Sticks or anything that came to hand." Some of the crowd went to Hallowell's house and broke windows. As an exclamation point for the evening, they stole Harrison's sailboat—"celebrated here for swift sailing"—and pulled it through the streets to the Liberty Tree. After formally condemning it, they hauled it to the Common and destroyed it in a bonfire. The customs officials bolted for the *Romney* and then to Castle William, the British redoubt in Boston Harbor.[18]

So ended another act of mob violence that had plagued Boston's protests since the Stamp Act of 1765. After local stamp distributors were intimidated into resigning their appointments, London officials understood that they needed more effective enforcement. So the new tax law created a board of customs, with five members sent from London to Boston at the end of 1767 to supervise the work of customs officials throughout the colonies.[19] Given the strong protests in Boston against the Stamp Act, placement of the customs board there was a major miscalculation.

Resentment over the new taxes and the presence of customs officials pushed Boston back into resistance. With the hooliganism that greeted the seizure of the *Liberty*, it appeared that the customs officials would not be able to perform their duties without military protection. In September, after more demonstrations at the Liberty Tree, Governor Bernard conveyed the news that soldiers would soon arrive from Halifax and others would sail to Boston from Ireland.[20]

Boston town leaders mobilized immediately. Because Bernard had dissolved the assembly for refusing to rescind its Circular Letter, the Boston town meeting invited other towns in the province to send representatives to Boston to discuss their grievances. Ninety-six towns and eight districts sent delegates, who met at the end of September. Their report, issued just as the British warships with troops aboard were sailing into Boston, complained again about taxes and the fact that the king and Parliament had ignored their petitions.[21]

Within days, British soldiers landed on Long Wharf. And Boston became a town occupied by a standing army.

FROM THE WOODEN DOCKS on the eastern side of town, Paul Revere and his friends in the Sons of Liberty could see an imposing sight in the harbor. That morning—Wednesday, September 28, 1768—a contingent of the Royal Navy came calling following a ten-day voyage from Halifax. Six warships, two armed schooners, and several transports sailed into the harbor, where other British warships already lay at anchor. The most formidable of the arriving ships were the *Launceston* with forty guns and the *Mermaid* with twenty-eight, modest size by the standards of the Royal Navy. The small armada, though, was still an imposing sight so close to a colonial town. The next evening, some soldiers aboard the ships launched fireworks and taunted passersby on boats by singing "Yankee Doodle" amid "great rejoicings." On the following day, the ships maneuvered in the harbor to the northeast side of the city "as if intended for a formal Siege," as one newspaper put it ominously.[22]

Those fears materialized at noon on Saturday as the British boats came to life. The warships sent out multiple groups of three small vessels connected by rope to each other, the lead boat with men pulling oars and the trailing two boats filled with soldiers. More than one thousand redcoats landed on Long Wharf, the most important hub of the city's sea trade; it pointed its finger a couple thousand feet into the harbor. The ships organized themselves amid the warehouses on the wharf, and then put on a show of force to make a point to the people of Boston. With colors flying and soldiers playing fifes and drums, the Fourteenth Regiment, commanded by Lieutenant Colonel William Dalrymple, marched off the wharf and up the busy commercial district of King Street to the Town House, the seat of government. They waited until the Twenty-Ninth Regiment joined them there, and then both regiments marched past shops and houses to the Common. Another detachment of soldiers followed them there with artillery.[23] The following month, two more regiments of soldiers arrived from Ireland.

General Thomas Gage promised the council that his soldiers would behave well, practicing "discipline and order."[24] After the troops had come ashore in Boston, Lord Hillsborough had written to Governor Bernard to congratulate him "on the happy and quiet landing of the troops, and the unusual approbation which his steady and able conduct had obtained."[25]

Those assurances seemed out of touch with the inevitable friction of a military garrison in a town full of people who deeply resented it as a violation of their liberties. Neither the soldiers nor the residents were likely to be happy with each other, and that is exactly the way it played out. As in New York, a deep reservoir of resentment and distrust already existed in Boston between soldiers and civilians due to impressment—the British navy's periodic sweep of colonial port cities to force men into service.

To its residents, Boston felt like an occupied town. It was no wonder, given the number of soldiers relative to the population. The British garrisoned two thousand soldiers there, plus the crews out of sight aboard British warships anchored in the harbor. That meant there was about one soldier for every adult male over sixteen years old.[26]

With so many soldiers in town, residents encountered them at every turn. Soldiers stood as sentries at residences of government officials and at other places. They manned a checkpoint at the Boston Neck, where they inspected carriages for possible deserters as people rode in and out of town. They drilled at the Common and regularly walked the streets. Despite attempts by commanders to discipline their men, the combination of young soldiers with time on their hands and plentiful rum led to disorderly behavior and increasing vice. Lewd comments and other harassment of women took place. Some soldiers engaged in theft and burglaries. And not infrequently, individual soldiers and civilians exchanged blows after some kind of instigation. Some people taunted the soldiers, especially individual sentries, calling them "lobsters" or "thieving dogs" and sometimes throwing stones or snowballs their way.[27] If that weren't enough, the British army permitted its soldiers to moonlight with civilian jobs. Many soldiers tried to supplement their meager salary, competing with civilians for jobs and often undercutting their pay.[28]

Bostonians had no way to order the army to abandon the town. But they did have their voices and their presses, and they quickly determined to use them.

ONCE THE BRITISH TROOPS settled in Boston, it did not take long before the Sons of Liberty began their onslaught in the newspapers. Their intricate planning for the coverage and dispersal of news throughout Boston and the colonies would help intensify public opinion against the standing army in their midst and make it appear that the shootings of civilians in

Boston seventeen months later was an unsurprising consequence of London's continuing violation of their rights.

Newspaper articles had been dispersed throughout the colonies during the Stamp Act crisis a few years earlier, but the plan conceived by an unidentified group of activists in Boston looked remarkably like an actual colonial news service. Creating a news service was a considerable challenge in a day when men worked heavy presses to print newspapers page by page and then sent copies by riders to the next city. With all its difficulties, the organized dissemination of news was critical to the development of political speech. It enabled political expression to ripple outward and encourage still more debate and discussion. For the Sons of Liberty, disseminating the news—at least their version of it—provided the opportunity to persuade more minds in more places with more impact.

Except for a single pseudonym used in one publication, the entire effort remained unsigned and the writers unidentified. The news service started publishing immediately on the arrival of the troops and continued for about ten months.[29] It required quick turnaround and surely some kind of agreement among printers. After the material was written in Boston, it was sent to New York, where every Thursday it appeared in the *New York Journal* and then on Saturday in the *Pennsylvania Chronicle*. From there, the same reports were published in Boston and in newspapers throughout the colonies. The material, which typically saw print ten days to two weeks after the event that it described, went under several titles such as "JOURNAL of OCCURRENCES" and "JOURNAL of the TIMES." With a longer delay, much of it cropped up in newspapers and in pamphlets in England as well.

The writers planned carefully to convey the impression that their reports were credible by taking the unusual step of separating news from commentary. Day by day, they presented a description of occurrences in the city. At the end of many of the entries, they presented their commentary on the news in italic type. By dividing news from commentary, the writers tried to create the impression that their coverage of daily happenings was strictly factual. That was important because the coverage of the military occupation of Boston was relentlessly negative, portraying the soldiers as rude, insolent, and engaging in criminal acts.

It was an ugly picture, and certainly the writers were guilty of some exaggeration and possibly even outright fabrication. Governor Bernard had absorbed criticism during the Stamp Act crisis, and he had continually tried, through Hutchinson, his chief justice, to get grand juries to indict Benjamin Edes and John Gill, publishers of the *Boston Gazette*, for seditious libel. Now he was incensed again. Writing to Lord Hillsborough, British secretary of state for the colonies, he said that "if the Devil himself was of the party, as he virtually is, there could not have been got together a greater collection of impudent, virulent, and seditious lies, perversions of the truth, and misrepresentations, than are to be found in this publication."

Bernard reached into Greek mythology to emphasize his point, referring to the nearly hopeless task given to Hercules to clean out piles of excrement from the stables of Augeas. Answering the false and seditious assertions in the "JOURNAL of OCCURRENCES," Bernard wrote, "would be a work like that of cleaning Augeas's Stable, which is to be done only by bringing in a Stream strong enough to sweep away the Dirt and the Collectors of it alltogether."[30]

ON AUGUST 1, 1769, Bernard boarded the *Rippon* for London, his term as royal governor finally up.[31] He had served for nine years during which he had become, as the highest-ranking British official in the province, a leading target for the increasing vitriol of the protestors. The *Boston Gazette* had no fond remembrances to share with its readers. Bernard had been "a Scourge to this Province, a Curse to North-America, and a Plague to the whole Empire."[32]

As Bernard's luck would have it, the *Rippon* lay in the harbor for three days awaiting a wind, within sight and sound of the city. No doubt he could observe the town's exuberant celebration of his leaving, as "the Cannon at the Castle were fired with Joy," and bells rang and cannon roared from Castle William. Celebrations took place at the Liberty Tree and around bonfires on Fort Hill and Charlestown.

Boston knew how to party, and it did so again on August 14, the fourth anniversary of the protests at the Liberty Tree that had started the long and ultimately successful campaign against the Stamp Act. The Sons of Liberty gathered that morning at their sacred elm, gave toasts to the king and others, and then 355 of them rode in carriages out to Dorchester, where they celebrated all afternoon and drank forty-five toasts at the Liberty Tree Tavern. From a relatively small band of radicals in 1765, the

Sons had expanded into a large but informal group that included on that afternoon a wide swath of Boston society—artisans and merchants, seamen and politicians. More than one hundred of them claimed a position in Boston government.[33] The public sphere was continuing to grow.

For all of these men, there was good reason to celebrate. Their relief at the departure of Bernard was matched by the withdrawal of two regiments of soldiers back to Ireland, leaving the Fourteenth and Twenty-Ninth Regiments in town. And the assembly was back after having been dissolved by Bernard for refusing to rescind its Circular Letter. If there were good feelings, though, they did not last long. The unpopular Thomas Hutchinson was now acting governor, and bitter conflict remained between the citizens and the remaining soldiers. The winter of 1770 brought more troubles. In February, tempers flared in New York after British soldiers cut down the patriots' Liberty Pole for the fourth time, leading to a free-for-all on Golden Hill between a group of redcoats and members of the Sons of Liberty. Boston, too, saw more conflict. On February 22, 1770, Ebenezer Richardson, who had been an informer to the British customs service and was despised by the Sons of Liberty, precipitated a bloody encounter that enraged the town. He tried to intervene in a demonstration at the shop of a merchant who was defying the nonimportation agreements. Chased back to his house by the crowd, Richardson fired his gun and killed an eleven-year-old boy, Christopher Seider.[34]

Four days later, as they staged a funeral for Seider, the Sons of Liberty showed once again that they understood the power of public demonstrations as a form of expression. Bringing out a big crowd made a clear point of solidarity to the other side, and it made political speech available to people in all walks of life—the coffeehouse writ large. The funeral procession started at the Liberty Tree and proceeded to the cemetery with five hundred schoolboys and another two thousand men and women trailing the coffin. The significance of the vast outpouring was not lost on Hutchinson, who said that it was intended "to strengthen the respective causes in which their leaders had engaged them."[35]

Less than two weeks later, as Boston still mourned Seider, the conflict over a standing army in the town would claim still more victims. The anger unleashed against a single British sentry on a bitter March evening would start a cascade of events that, pushed forward by robust political speech, would deepen the antagonism of the colonies toward Britain.

EARLY IN THE EVENING on March 5, John Adams had spent some hours eating and drinking in the company of friends at Henderson Inches's home in Boston's South End. Suddenly their conversation was interrupted. "We were allarmed with the ringing of Bells," Adams recalled, "and supposing it to be the Signal of fire, We snatched our Hats and Cloaks, broke up the Clubb, and went out to assist in quenching the fire or aiding our friends who might be in danger."

It was worse than he had feared. "In the Street We were informed that the British Soldiers had fired on the Inhabitants, killed some and wounded others near the Town house." Adams walked into Brattle Square, where he saw a company of redcoats with their muskets and bayonets, then went on to his house on Cold Lane. Sitting with Abigail, Adams reflected on the efforts over the previous seventeen months "to excite Quarrells, Rencounters and Combats" between citizens and soldiers. "I suspected," he said, "that this was the Explosion."[36]

The "explosion" left three civilians dead on King Street and two mortally wounded. That night, Hutchinson arrived to assure the crowd that justice would be done. Captain Preston and the soldiers under his command were arrested before dawn and held for trial. John Adams did not know in the hours after the shootings whether Boston would receive the support of its neighbors. "We knew not whether the Town would be supported by the Country: whether the Province would be supported by even our neighbouring States of New England; nor whether New England would be supported by the Continent," Adams wrote.[37]

For the Boston patriots, the battle began for the hearts and minds of fellow colonists as well as influential people in London. In the days immediately following the shooting incident, the effort began to launch a propaganda campaign to define its meaning and to influence public opinion. The goal of the Boston dissenters, led by men like Samuel Adams and John Hancock, was to show that the Townshend duties and the maintenance of a standing army in Boston were a violation of colonial rights, and that the shootings on King Street were an inevitable consequence of foolhardy British decisions. In the end, Captain Preston and most of the soldiers would be acquitted, but the fact that the shootings on King Street became the "Boston Massacre" indicated that the patriots won the larger battle to define British policy.

At a town meeting on the morning after the incident, the shootings became "the Massacre made in King Street, by the Soldiery the preceding Night" and the "horrid Massacre."[38] Not a soul at the town meeting knew that on the previous day—the day of the shootings—Parliament had started considering repeal of the Townshend duties. A month later, repeal of all but the duty on tea was complete. But on that Tuesday morning, it was the troops occupying Boston that concerned the town meeting, which demanded that Hutchinson and Colonel Dalrymple remove the two regiments of British troops from Boston. Dalrymple offered to remove one of the regiments to Castle William, but a committee of the town meeting rejected that offer, saying that "nothing less will satisfy them, than a total and immediate removal of the Troops." Within a week, both regiments left for the castle.[39]

On that Tuesday as well, a Loyalist merchant visited the law office of John Adams, asking him on behalf of Captain Preston to represent him. Preston had so far been unable to find a lawyer willing to take his case. Adams accepted the assignment, saying that legal counsel "ought to be the very last thing that an accused Person should want [lack] in a free Country." Josiah Quincy signed on as well, although his father wrote to him asking him if it were true that he had "become an advocate for those criminals who are charged with the murder of their fellow citizens." It is possible that the Sons of Liberty wanted Adams and Quincy to take the case, confident as they were of prevailing at trial and possibly concerned that a prosecution could be marred by the lack of the most effective counsel.[40] Nonetheless, the fact that the two men took the case in the midst of such an agitated town was itself a demonstration of freedom of speech at the time.

The race was on by both sides to record their own version of the incident and get it as quickly as possible into the hands of influential people. On March 12, the Boston town meeting appointed John Adams and two other men to write to the patriots' friends in London, including Benjamin Franklin, "acquainting them with the Circumstances & Facts relative to the late horred Massacre."[41] The letter summarized the incident as a conspiracy—"the soldiers have been made use of by others as Instruments in executing a settled Plot to Massacre the Inhabitants." The letter asked the friends "to prevent any ill Impressions from being made upon the Minds of his Majesty's Ministers and others against the Town by the Accounts which the Commissioners of the Customs and others our Enemies may send, until the Town shall be able to make a full Representation of it."[42] For his part, Hutchinson recognized that the quick production of the letter was intended "to secure the first impressions" on influential people in London.[43]

The town meeting appointed a committee that began to take depositions of anyone who knew what had transpired on the evening of March 5. The report with an appendix of ninety-five depositions was ready on March 19, and the town voted to hire a schooner and, three days later, empowered the town treasurer to borrow 150 pounds to carry the report to London.[44] The name that the town gave to its report—*A Short Narrative of the Horrid Massacre in Boston*—provided a good summary of the one-sided presentation inside.

The Tories were racing as well to put together their own biased version of the incident, with their own contrasting title—"A Fair Account of the Late Unhappy Disturbance at Boston in New England." And they beat the town in getting their report aboard a ship for London. On March 12, Dalrymple wrote to General Gage to tell him that he was sending a narrative of the incident to England so it "may prevent opinions being formed prejudicial to truth."[45] Four days later, one of the customs commissioners, John Robinson, sailed out of Boston Harbor with a parcel of depositions hastily put together by the military that held the town responsible for inciting the incident. As Dalrymple told Gage, "the first impression is always the strongest in such cases, an opportunity offered and I presumed to use it."[46] On April 2, the *Boston Gazette* announced that the town's version of the events left Boston.[47] On May 5, "A Short Narrative of the Horrid Massacre" was on sale in London with a frontispiece of Revere's print of the soldiers firing on civilians.[48]

Meanwhile, Captain Preston was also busy trying to manipulate public opinion from his jail cell by ingratiating himself with the town. In an unusual advertisement in the *Boston Gazette* on March 12, he praised the people of Boston for "throwing aside all Party and Prejudice" in considering the "late unhappy Affair." General Gage recoiled at what he called Preston's "Foolish Advertisement," worrying that any later unfair proceedings against him "will Justify themselves by his own Words."[49] At the same time Preston was thanking Boston, he was writing his own account of the shootings for consumption in London, excoriating the same people he had praised. They were "infusing the utmost malice and revenge into the minds of the people who are to be my jurors by false publications, votes of towns, and all other articles." Preston charged that armed militia had come to Boston on March 5 and 6, bent on a "general engagement."

His account was published in London and then found its way back to Boston. Stung by Preston's account, a committee comprising Samuel Adams and John Hancock and a few other men asked him to correct what they saw as "the most gross misrepresentations having been sent home to his Majesty and the Ministry." Preston refused to make any corrections, and so the committee itself sent a missive to London challenging Preston's account.[50]

Sentiment in Boston weighed so heavily against the British that the king's representatives were left powerless. Dalrymple wrote to Gage informing him that Hutchinson "has no earthly weight or power here." Hutchinson admitted as much to Gage, that he had no power whatsoever to run the government. In any controversy between England and Boston, "government is at an end and in the hands of the people. I am absolutely alone, no single person of my Council or any other person in authority affording me the least support and if the people are disposed to any measure nothing more is necessary than for the multitude to assemble, for nobody dares oppose them or call them to account." Street demonstrations, especially the funerals of the victims of the March 5 incident, raised emotions. "Every funeral brings thousands of people together and inflames them against the Troops."[51]

BENJAMIN EDES AND JOHN GILL had used their *Boston Gazette* as a battering ram against the Stamp Act five years earlier, and now along with the *Boston Evening Post* they went to work trying to mold public opinion.

On March 12, the *Boston Gazette* hit the streets with a report that sprawled over a page and a half of dense type with heavy black rules framing the columns. The article contained Paul Revere's first contribution on the incident—a drawing of four coffins, each with the initials of the deceased and a crude rendition of skulls and crossbones. A fifth victim would die a few days later. The first sentence of the *Gazette*'s report set the editorial tone, saying that the incident showed "the destructive Consequences of quartering Troops among Citizens in a Time of Peace, under a Pretense of supporting the Laws and aiding Civil Authority." The soldiers had been physically accosted by a large group of citizens, but to the *Boston Gazette* the shootings had been accomplished so deliberately and with such malice that it qualified as "this bloody Massacre." Captain Preston, Edes and Gill claimed, "commanded them to fire, and more snow-balls coming he again said, Damn you, Fire, be the consequence what it will!"[52]

A week later, Edes and Gill resumed their coverage of the incident with yet another grim Revere engraving of a black coffin, this one for Patrick Carr, the "fifth Life that has been sacrificed by the Rage of the Soldiery." Several pages carried reports of town meetings across the province that had passed resolutions condemning the shootings and supporting the boycott of British goods. The town of Medford condemned the "horrid & unparalleled butchery of your fellow citizens" but said that it would "serve as a specimen to show what these Colonies are to expect, if a military power shall supersede their civil authority, and their well regulated Cities and Towns are dragooned to an obedience to Laws, made, not only without but against their Consent." Cambridge protested the "late unprecedented and unconstitutional Acts of Parliament for raising a REVENUE from the Colonies without their Consent" and for quartering troops there.[53]

For the Boston resistance, circulating the news was critical to their efforts at persuasion. As with the Stamp Act protests, the largely one-sided coverage rippled outward as riders carried papers to other colonial towns. Newspapers in the closest colonies—New Hampshire, Rhode Island, and Connecticut—printed reports a week later based on the March 12 accounts published in Boston, some even copying Revere's coffins into their stories. In the lead page-one article in the *New-Hampshire Gazette*, later reprinted in other papers, a writer under the name "Consideration" decried the shedding of "the BLOOD of Innocent AMERICANS" and wrote that a standing army should never be stationed in America without the consent of the citizens. Such armies "have ever proved destructive to the Liberties of a People." He concluded: "*Where is our English Liberty?*"[54]

Condemnation of the British was not as white-hot outside of New England, and while reports in the middle colonies were comparatively restrained and factual, they still favored the patriot cause. John Holt, publisher of the *New York Journal*, first ran a factual report and hoped out loud that "nobody would be offended" by his printing of various accounts. A week later, he published a letter from a patriot in Boston, characterizing the incident as a "military execution" and accusing Preston of ordering his men to fire. He also published a broadside with copy taken from the *Boston Gazette,* including the four Revere coffins. But on April 12, he printed a letter from a Tory in Boston who blamed the shootings on the crowd that "agreed upon a general Attack upon the Troops." Two papers in Philadelphia based their stories on the broadsides and the *Boston Gazette* account, and another printed a more moderate report.[55]

Accounts took longer to reach readers in the southern colonies. On April 5 the *South Carolina Gazette* printed its report, taken from the *Boston Gazette* and the *Evening Post,* over two full pages with black borders.[56] On April 11 the editors of the *Georgia Gazette* informed readers of the Boston shootings, calling them a "massacre" and "barbarous outrages," and then devoted their page-one lead story on April 25 to a note from "Benevolus," who rejected heated rhetoric and instead lectured the king on the colonists' rights to use political speech to influence royal policy. The king's responsibility, argued Benevolus, was to "deliver his subjects from their grievances."

Addressing the value of vigorous political expression, Benevolus said that a "good King will always therefore most readily and freely hear the complaints of his people, and consider them with such attention, that his justice, kindness, and paternal care, may be conspicuous to all. To reject their petitions, to neglect the humble supplications of thousands, must be attended with the most pernicious consequences."[57]

REVERE APPARENTLY WENT to King Street shortly after the shootings occurred, for he made a diagram in pen and ink of the street scene. His drawing shows the positioning of the redcoats and fallen civilians. Revere marked two bodies closest to the soldiers with "A" and "G," presumably for the two mortally wounded men Crispus Attucks and Samuel Gray. Another victim, James Caldwell, is marked with a "C," and a boy, Samuel Maverick, with a "G" for the man who was his master. Patrick Carr, the fifth victim, who died four days later, is not represented in the drawing.[58]

Later in March, Revere came across a drawing of the shootings on King Street done by the Boston artist and engraver Henry Pelham, the half brother of artist John Copley. Revere did not leave an account of what he was thinking when he saw the Pelham drawing, but as a patriot he clearly understood the power of Pelham's sketch to define the meaning of the incident. For Pelham's interpretation of the shootings put all the blame on the British soldiers. In Revere's day, engravers typically copied drawings that they liked without permission, adapting them as they saw fit. And Revere set out to do exactly that. At his workbench, he copied Pelham's work with a few changes of his own. Across the top of the engraving he placed the inscription, "The BLOODY MASSACRE perpetrated in King Street BOSTON on March 5th 1770 by a party of the 29th REGT."

It was, according to Revere's interpretation, a massacre indeed.[59] The scene in his engraving takes place on a public square, with the Boston town hall and its clock tower looming in the background and gray buildings lining both sides of the street. All of that frames the striking drama unfolding in the foreground. On the right, a menacing line of seven soldiers in red coats and black boots point their guns fitted with bayonets at the crowd just a few feet away. In the rear, Captain Preston stands with an upraised, threatening sword, obviously commanding them to volley. The soldiers have already answered his order to fire, for clouds of smoke billow up around them. Behind the soldiers, a rifle fires from the second-floor window of the Custom House, below a sign that meaningfully reads "Butcher's Hall." Across the left foreground the crowd reels at the carnage before them. Three men lay on the street, blood streaming from chest and head wounds. Two others held in the arms of bystanders are bleeding heavily. One man reaches out toward a thrusting soldier, trying to stop his bayonet. Below the soldiers Revere added: "Engrav'd Printed & Sold by PAUL REVERE boston." Revere apparently hired Christian Remick to color the print, adding the striking red color that directly connected the soldiers' uniforms to the blood pouring out of the victims' open wounds.

In case anyone missed the point, Revere added at the bottom of the print eighteen lines of verse, which he likely wrote himself. The first of the three stanzas said:

Unhappy BOSTON! See thy Sons deplore,
Thy hallow'd Walks besmear'd with guiltless Gore:
While faithless P—n and his Savage Bands
With murd'rous Rancor stretch their bloody Hands;
Like fierce Barbarians grinning o'er their Prey,
Approve the Carnage, and enjoy the Day.

Virtually everything important about Revere's representation of the scene was inaccurate. The soldiers had not lined up and shot in execution style. Preston had not brazenly ordered them to fire. No gunfire had come from the Custom House. There was no sign on the Custom House calling it "Butcher's Hall." The civilians had not been retiring and peaceful. Many smaller details were likewise wrong. With a blue sky, only a partial moon indicated that the incident occurred at night. No snow or ice covered the ground.

But that was the point. Revere did not work as a historian trying to accurately capture the chaotic moments for posterity. He sketched instead as a patriot exercising what he understood to be his right as an Englishman—to express his view that soldiers of a standing army had murdered civilians in cold blood, a result as inevitable to him as the bitter cold of a Boston winter.

Revere advertised his print for sale in the *Boston Gazette* and the *Boston Evening Post* of March 26. Two days later, in his Day Book, Revere noted that he charged Edes and Gill, the publishers of the *Gazette,* five pounds to print two hundred impressions of his engraving. The next day, Henry Pelham wrote a letter to Revere accusing the silversmith of copying his own drawing—"as I knew you was not capable of doing it unless you coppied it from mine." He said he was "in the most ungenerous Manner deprived not only of any proposed Advantage, but even of the expence I have been at, as truly as if you had plundered me on the highway."[60]

No doubt Pelham's charge of plagiarism was true. Pelham advertised his own print in the *Boston Evening Post* on April 2, calling it "An Original Print . . . taken on the Spot," and except for some details it was similar to the Revere print that had beaten him to the market. Still a third version, this one apparently copied from Revere, was offered for sale by a Newburyport clock maker named Jonathan Mulliken.[61]

Revere's engravings quickly took on a life of their own, adorning several fiery broadsides that circulated shortly after the shootings. Edes and Gill issued a large-format broadside that reprinted the Revere engraving of the shootings, the five black coffins, and a densely packed reprinting of the *Boston Gazette*'s coverage of the incident from its issues of March 12 and 19. Additional versions of the print appeared throughout the colonies in 1770 and several editions in London.[62] A second broadside, entitled "A

Poem in Memory of the (never to be forgotten) Fifth of March, 1770," again used the black coffins—either by Revere or copied from him—to illustrate a funeral elegy to the slain young men. The final quatrain warns the colonists that they had to resist tyranny in America or forever give up their liberty:

> *If bloody men intrudes upon our land,*
> *Where shall we go? Or whither shall we stand?*
> *Then may I wander to some distant shore,*
> *Where man nor beast had never trod before.*[63]

Verse was becoming increasingly important in registering colonial protests. A broadside entitled "A Verse Occasioned by the late horrid Massacre in *King-Street*" put the patriot version of the events in verse below the five familiar black coffins. Another broadside with the five coffins, "On the Death of Five young Men who was Murthered, March 5th 1770 By the 29th Regiment," called the redcoats "cruel Soldiers" and "Murd'rers." And still another broadside showed Revere's coffins across the top with a striking headline that called the shootings "the most Barbarous and HORRID MASSACRE."[64]

During the trial of the soldiers in December, Josiah Quincy severely criticized publications like the Revere print, which he said were prejudicing the case. In considering the case against the soldiers, Quincy told the jurors to consider only "the evidence *here in Court* produced against them, and by nothing else." He implored them specifically to disregard the Revere print of the shootings, which made the soldiers look like they were executing civilians in cold blood.

"The prints exhibited in our houses," said Quincy, "have added wings to fancy, and in the fervour of our zeal, reason is in hazard of being lost."[65]

ON APRIL 16, just three weeks after his engraving of the *Bloody Massacre Perpetrated in King Street* appeared, Paul Revere was ready to release another salvo of political cartooning against the British. He bought an advertisement in the *Boston Gazette* saying that he had for sale "A Copper-Plate PRINT, containing a View of the Part of the Town of Boston in New-England, and British Ships of War landing their Troops in the Year 1768." As he had done with his print of the *Bloody Massacre,* Revere apparently copied a drawing done by another artist, this time Christian Remick.[66]

The *Landing* print provided no subtlety. Massive warships of the Royal Navy dominate Boston Harbor, their flags and streamers flying stiffly in the wind and their cannon aimed at the town. Smaller vessels filled with soldiers are making their way to Long Wharf, which extends diagonally into the harbor. Soldiers wearing bright red uniforms and resting guns on their shoulders have already taken over the lower end of the wharf, in the center of the print. Some march with colors flying past the warehouses on the wharf and toward King Street and the center of town. Revere's caption on the print said that the soldiers "landed on the Long Wharf; there Formed and Marched with insolent Parade, Drums beating, Fifes playing, and Colours flying, up King Street. Each soldier having received 16 rounds of Powder and Ball."[67]

In the corner of the print, Revere portrayed a female Native American, representing the colonies, with her foot on the throat of a soldier lying prostrate on the ground. The redcoat is wearing a military headdress with the numerals XXIX. The number twenty-nine referred to the 29th Regiment—the soldiers who had perpetrated the "bloody massacre" of his King Street print. Revere had looped together the two major engravings.

All in all, Revere conveys the image of a town living piously and peacefully amid its many church spires just at the moment that a foreign military force arrives. And "foreign" is key, for this is not a kindly England embracing its citizens in America but rather a powerful England taking possession of a defenseless foe.

For Revere, the three engravings provided a telling progression of events for his political commentary. One print portrayed the landing of British soldiers in Boston that brought a standing army to the town. A second, of the shootings, laid bare the grisly tragedy that seemed, at least to Revere and the Sons of Liberty, the inevitable outcome of London's decision to fill Boston streets with soldiers. And, last, the crude drawings of five black coffins made the tragedy of unrestrained power complete.

Released within weeks of each other, the prints contained powerful ideas about the rights of British subjects and the abuse of power—and did so without a single spoken word or a single reference to the Magna Carta, the Glorious Revolution, or for that matter the republican virtues of Cicero. Its power lay in its simplicity, its visual appeal, and its satiric exaggeration. No person in Boston or down the coast could possibly mistake the meaning that Revere intended to convey. As political cartoons, they conveyed meaning instantly and, to a large public, more powerfully than could an essay by James Otis Jr.

The political cartoon had arrived as a potent weapon in the arsenal of persuasion for colonial Americans, once again challenging the legal strictures of seditious libel.

THE REVEREND MATHER BYLES SR. stood on a Boston street corner during the funeral procession for the first four victims of the King Street shooting. Several thousand people passed him by. For some supporters of Britain like Byles, even a peaceful demonstration involving so many people evoked the prospect of mob rule. In 1770, the idea of participatory democracy was indeed foreign to those who looked to Parliament and to the royal governors to set public policy. As Byles was reported to have said to a companion with him at the time, "They call me a brainless Tory, but tell me my young friend, which is better—to be ruled by one tyrant three thousand miles away, or by three thousand tyrants not a mile away?"[68]

Other ministers lined up on the patriot side, and in their sermons they accomplished in words what Revere had done in his engraving. They described a bloody scene that displeased a wrathful God. The clergy played a major role in moving public opinion after the shootings, bringing the weight of Puritan doctrine to politics. When they preached on the King Street shootings, some of them expressed the certainty that God would approve the most extreme punishment of the accused soldiers. Hearing them thunder on politics did not surprise the people of Boston, as it was just the latest instance of ministers using their pulpits to persuade their flock on political matters.

The Reverend John Lathrop ascended his pulpit six days after the shootings to deliver a sermon of bloodthirsty revenge. The title of his sermon—"Innocent Blood Crying to God from the Streets of Boston"— promised an incendiary appeal to a higher power, and Lathrop did not disappoint. He criticized the "unparalleled barbarity of those who were lately guilty of murdering a number of our innocent fellow citizens." He continued, as if describing the Revere engraving: "How affecting, unutterably affecting, to see our fellow-citizens shot to death—their garments

rolled in blood, and corpses wallowing in gore, upon our Exchange."
Lathrop proclaimed that God's law required nothing less than that the
"cry of innocent blood cannot be allayed, but by the death of the guilty!"
He added that "if that punishment is not inflicted, innocent blood will cry
from the ground." Most of Lathrop's sermon amounted to a bloodthirsty
screed, but he paused just long enough to attribute the shootings to the
"infinite impropriety of quartering troops in a well-regulated city."[69]

A similar message came from the most radical and influential
preacher of the day, the Reverend Charles Chauncy. Fifteen years earlier,
when an earthquake shook all of Boston, Chauncy had used the event to
warn his congregants of God's awesome power in the face of human sin.
Earthquakes, he said, "of all God's judicial dispensations are the most
terrible; and the surest indication of his righteous anger."[70] Chauncy did
not confine himself to the usual themes of sin and redemption. As time
went on, he increasingly trained his fire on British policy in the colonies.
For Chauncy, God's righteous anger would punish more than just the sins
of the flesh. It might as well become an ally to the colonists in their fight
against British injustice.

So reliably radical was Chauncy that the Sons of Liberty asked him
to deliver an election-day address on May 30, nearly three months after
the shootings. In his sermon, Chauncy attacked British policy in America
on the familiar themes of Whig politics. He ascribed Boston's troubles to
the ministers of the king—"to a malignant spirit in some, who cannot
be easie without having the purses of the colonies subject to their arbitrary pleasure." Building to an emotional climax, Chauncy talked of the
soldiers and their "BLOOD GUILTINESS" and the teaching of the "supreme
legislator" who decreed "whoso sheddeth man's blood, by man shall his
blood be shed." Chauncy added, "No satisfaction shall be taken for the life
of a murderer. He shall surely be put to death."[71]

The Sons of Liberty again showed their affinity for street theater on
the day of the sermon, having arranged for the roasting of an ox on the
Common. The "Novelty of an Ox roasting whole, excited the Curiosity of
the People, and Incredible Numbers from this and the neighboring towns
resorted to the Spot, to view so unusual a spectacle," wrote the Boston Gazette. Following the service, Chauncy and many other "principal Gentlemen" went to Faneuil Hall to dine on the ox.[72]

To the chief justice, the Loyalist Peter Oliver, Chauncy was an effective advocate for the radical cause, all the more powerful because of his ability to enlist God to his point of view. "What a noble Instance this of Divinity, Zeal, Rancor & Revenge, jumbled together into one Mass!" he said, concluding that Chauncy "was always for calling down fire from heaven to destroy his political opposers."[73]

Oliver added, "*Before* the Trials, the Pulpits rung their Chimes upon blood Guiltiness, in Order to incite the People, some of whom were to be Jurors, to Revenge, in cleansing the Land of the Blood which had been shed."[74]

WISELY, THE TRIAL of the soldiers was delayed until the fall to allow the most heated passions to cool. In October, about seven months after the shootings, a jury found Captain Thomas Preston not guilty. In a separate trial a month later, six of the soldiers were acquitted and two were convicted of manslaughter. They avoided the death penalty by pleading the benefit of clergy, a legal mechanism to reduce a penalty for first offenders, and each was branded on the thumb. John Adams reflected later that his representation of the soldiers was "one of the most gallant, generous, manly, and disinterested actions of my whole life, and one of the best pieces of service I ever rendered my country." He added that "the verdict of the jury was exactly right."[75]

Samuel Adams strongly disagreed with his cousin that the jury was exactly right. Using the pseudonym "Vindex," he wrote a series of articles for the *Boston Gazette* that retried the case in print, often spicing the evidence to his own taste in order to make a point. Somebody, Adams said, simply had to be guilty. "As the lives of five of his Majesty's subjects were *unfairly* lost on the evening of the 5th of March last," he wrote, "it follows that some persons must have been in fault."[76]

In focusing so intently on the trial of the soldiers, Samuel Adams had lost sight of the larger meaning of the incident. By the time he wrote, the significance of the acquittals themselves lay in the positive impression they created that Boston could put aside its passions and judge the soldiers fairly. But the trial's significance paled next to the more critical point—that he and Revere and the Sons of Liberty had succeeded beyond any reasonable expectation in their campaign of persuasion.

Regardless of the details of the incident—and whether the soldiers or the citizens were at fault—the patriots had defined the shooting incident to their own benefit. The "horrid Massacre" was a betrayal of the rights of Englishmen, whether or not Captain Preston had given an order to fire. Indeed, as John Adams recognized, the acquittals were "no reason why the town should not call the action of that night a massacre. . . . But it is the strongest of proofs of the danger of standing armies."[77]

The Sons of Liberty had raised the shootings to the embodiment of tyranny through a broad array of political expression—articles, letters, broadsides, sermons, and reports. No expression, though, so elevated the idea of runaway British power over virtuous Americans as did Revere's three engravings. Deeply argued essays and resolutions had made the point about taxes and standing armies many times, but Revere's illustrations conveyed the same meaning simply and powerfully. In the minds of many colonial Americans, Revere had clearly laid out an inevitable and tragic narrative.

Of course, Revere's engraving of the shootings also happened to be false in many important ways. As both sides jockeyed for advantage, truth often became a casualty. The British authorities complained incessantly about lies in the colonial press. In Philadelphia, General Gage understood that the king's representatives were badly outmaneuvered in the battle of public perceptions. Gage wrote to Preston that he had "seen no accounts of that Affair, except what has been given by People possessed of the vilest Talents of Misrepresentation, and the blackest Malevolence, Malice and Falsehood, who have not done you Justice, and Compassionated your Case."[78] And he wrote to Dalrymple about the "diabolical account" in the *Boston Gazette* and other papers that is "too preposterous and absurd to gain credit with any that are not prejudiced."[79]

The Sons of Liberty saw it another way. In a report in July to friends in London, a committee of Samuel Adams and others complained that they had "observed in the English papers the most notorious falsehoods, published with an apparent design to give the world a prejudice against this town, as the aggressors in the unhappy transaction of the 5th of March."[80] And Benjamin Franklin reported on coverage in London as "so enveloped with Prejudices and Misrepresentations, that the still Voice of Truth and Candour is not heard."[81]

Much of what was written, spoken, and drawn about the shootings on King Street amounted to distortions and misrepresentations. Much of it on both sides was propaganda. But vigorous political speech, as colonial protestors understood, was often not polite, often not completely truthful, and often not presented in the same mannerly and deferential way that courtiers addressed the king.

It was, instead, robust and uninhibited—and, in some cases, as sharp as the point of an engraver's tool.

Andrew Hamilton, the attorney for John Peter Zenger, convinced a jury in New York in 1735 to rebel against the oppressive law of seditious libel and free the printer from jail. Their decision contributed to a broad recognition decades later that new safeguards were needed to protect press freedom.

Samuel Adams helped organize resistance in Boston to onerous British regulations. He wrote patriotic letters and essays, some in the radical Boston Gazette, *under numerous pseudonyms. (Charles Goodman, engraver, from a portrait by John Singleton Copley / Courtesy of the Library of Congress)*

LIBERTY TREE, 1774,

CORNER OF ESSEX AND ORANGE STREETS.

The world should never forget the spot where once stood Liberty Tree, so famous in your annals.—*La Fayette in Boston.*

The Liberty Tree on the main road into Boston became the rallying point for loud demonstrations—often including effigies hanging from branches—against British regulations imposed on the colonies. The use of liberty trees and liberty poles spread throughout the colonies, part of an outpouring of symbolic speech that enlarged the public sphere of political expression. (Houghton Library, Harvard University)

St—p!   St—p!   St—p!   No:

Tuesday-Morning, December 17, 1765.

THE True-born Sons of Li-
berty, are defired to meet under LIBERTY-
TREE, at XII o'Clock, THIS DAY, to hear the
the public Refignation, under Oath, of ANDREW
OLIVER, Efq; Diftributor of Stamps for the Province
of the *Maffachufetts-Bay.*

A Refignation ? YES.

*Distributed throughout Boston, this broadside called people to
the Liberty Tree on December 17, 1765, to hear the besieged stamp
distributor renounce his appointment. (Massachusetts Historical
Society)*

*Alexander McDougall,
a New York merchant,
was jailed on seditious
libel charges. The Sons
of Liberty orchestrated
a campaign that
made him famous
throughout the
colonies as a martyr
for press freedom.
(Engraved by H.
P. Hall and Sons /
Courtesy of Miriam
and Ira D. Wallach
Division of Art, Prints
and Photographs:
Print Collection, New
York Public Library)*

Paul Revere lent his skills as an engraver to the patriot cause and produced illustrations that were more powerful as political commentary than many written works. They reached the public through newspapers and broadsides. (Portrait by John Singleton Copley / Courtesy of the Museum of Fine Arts, Boston)

Paul Revere's three engravings expressed his narrative of British oppression—military occupation (above) leading inevitably to a bloody confrontation and the deaths of civilians (following pages). Here, Revere depicted powerful British warships in 1768 overwhelming Boston, portrayed as a sleepy, innocent town dominated by church steeples. British soldiers are shown landing in the town to begin an occupation that culminated in the Boston Massacre. (American Antiquarian Society)

Paul Revere's engraving defined the shootings of March 5, 1770, as the "Bloody Massacre" and was potent propaganda in turning the colonies against Britain. (Library of Congress)

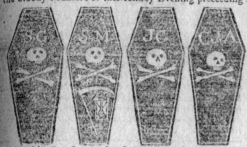

Diftreffes, and to whom we are greatly obliged on this Occafion—No one knows where this would have ended, and what important Confequences even to the whole Britifh Empire might have followed, which our Modera-tion & Loyalty upon fo trying anOccafion, and ourFaith in the Commander'sAffurances have happily prevented.

Laft Thurfday, agreeable to a general Requeft of the Inhabitants, and by the Confent of Parents and Friends, were carried to their *Grave* in Succeffion, the Bodies of *Samuel Gray, Samuel Maverick, James Caldwell,* and *Crifpus Attucks,* the unhappy Victims who fell in the bloody Maffacre of theMonday Evening preceeding !

On this Occafion moft of the Shops in Town were fhut, all the Bells were ordered to toll a folemn Peal, as were alfo thofe in the neighboring Towns of Charleftown Roxbury, &c. The Proceffion began to move between the Hours of 4 and 5 in the Afternoon ; two of the un-fortunate Sufferers, viz. Meff. *James Caldwell* and *Crifpus Attucks,* who were Strangers, borne from Faneuil-Hall, attended by a numerous Train of Perfons of all Ranks ; and the other two, viz. Mr. *Samuel Gray,* from the Houfe of Mr. Benjamin Gray, (his Brother) on the North-fide the Exchange, and Mr. *Maverick,* from the Houfe of his diftreffed Mother Mrs. *Mary Maverick,* in Union-Street, each followed by their refpective Relations

Paul Revere's drawings of coffins representing citizens killed in the Boston Massacre resounded throughout the colonies, driving home the consequences of a standing British army in their midst. (American Antiquarian Society)

John Dickinson energized the patriot cause by writing some of the most influential essays on the rights of the colonists. But in the end he could not bring himself to sign the Declaration of Independence. (Portrait by Charles Wilson Peale / Courtesy of Independence National Historical Park)

Patrick Henry brought forceful oratory to his opposition to the Constitution. The Virginia ratifying convention, though, narrowly approved the Constitution despite his strenuous arguments against it. Vigorous political speech during the ratification period signaled the founding generation's embrace of robust expression. (George Bagby Matthews after portrait by Thomas Sully / Courtesy of the United States Senate)

John Adams wrote approvingly of vigorous dissent during the troubles with Britain, but as president he signed the odious Sedition Act to punish his political opponents. (Pendleton lithograph of portrait by Gilbert Stuart / Courtesy of the Library of Congress)

As vice president, Thomas Jefferson worked in secret alliance with James Madison to oppose the Sedition Act of 1798, the cudgel that the Adams administration used against dissidents. He had earlier helped convince Madison to support a constitutional amendment protecting the freedom of speech and press. (Portrait by Charles Wilson Peale / Courtesy of the U.S. Department of State)

James Madison, the primary author of the First Amendment, wrote a resounding defense of the freedom of speech and press in 1800 in response to the Sedition Act. He tied freedom of speech and press to the needs of a self-governing society. (Portrait by John Vanderlyn / Courtesy of the White House Historical Association)

7

THE FARMER

ALL OF THE DELEGATES TO THE CONTINENTAL CONGRESS WHO GATHERED AT THE PENNSYLVA-
nia State House on the morning of July 1, 1776, knew that this would be
a special day. The resolution for independence that Richard Henry Lee of
Virginia had introduced three weeks earlier would finally come to a vote.
It was a sweltering summer morning, already almost 82 degrees by nine
o'clock, making their meeting room, with its windows shut to ensure secrecy, especially uncomfortable.[1]

The delegates understood the long path that the colonies had traveled
to reach this day, from the protests over the Stamp Act more than a decade
earlier to the bloody clashes at Lexington and Concord. Now the ominous
shadow of British military power lay over all of the colonies. A few days
earlier, General George Washington had reported that about fifty British
warships were closing in on New York Harbor. In the South, more than
fifty warships had appeared near Charleston.[2] And recently, the *Roebuck*
and *Liverpool* had been uncomfortably close by, blockading the Delaware
River below Philadelphia. When the warships ventured up the river, a flo-
tilla of small boats from Pennsylvania exchanged fire with them.[3]

John Adams, one of the strongest advocates of independence, was ex-
ultant that the vote was at hand. "This morning is assigned for the greatest debate of all," he had written before going to the statehouse that day,

adding his confidence that the vote would go in favor of independence. "May Heaven prosper the new-born republic, and make it more glorious than any former republics have been!"[4]

When the session began, the delegates heard a reading of three letters from Washington and one each from conventions held in the previous two weeks in New Jersey and New Hampshire.[5] Then came a resolution from Maryland that empowered its delegates to vote in favor of independence. Finally, the time for debate had arrived, and all attention focused on John Dickinson of Pennsylvania.

Dickinson was one of the most famous men in all the colonies, revered for his intellectual leadership in aggressively opposing the revenue acts passed by Parliament. His *Letters from a Farmer in Pennsylvania* had been celebrated all over the colonies in 1768, and since then he had composed endless essays, letters, and pamphlets that laid out careful legal arguments defending the rights of the colonists. Other essayists had made their contributions, but Dickinson's pen had done more than any other to embed the protests of the colonists in the history of English constitutionalism. If any man could lay claim to this day, it was Dickinson.

Dickinson, though, could not lead the colonies to their final destination as an independent country. For the past year, bloodshed in New England had further radicalized most leaders of the patriot cause, and they had moved past Dickinson to embrace independence. Dickinson was one of the few men in the room who was prepared to vote against it. John Adams had derided him as weak and tentative. The two men were barely on speaking terms.

As Dickinson rose to address the delegates, he knew he would persuade none of them—and in the process, unwind much of his hard-earned reputation. But he felt compelled to speak as a matter of principle. "The Consequences involved in the Motion now lying before You," he said at the start, "are of such Magnitude, that I tremble under the oppressive Honor of sharing in its Determination."

He continued, with resignation. "My Conduct, this Day, I expect will give the finishing Blow to my once too great, and my Integrity considered, now too diminish'd Popularity."[6]

IN JANUARY 1741, when Dickinson was eight years old, his family loaded their possessions into horse-drawn wagons and climbed aboard to begin their journey to their new home. The Dickinsons were not a family moving west to build their future on the dangerous frontier beyond the colonial settlements. In fact, John's father, Samuel, represented the third generation of Dickinsons to live in America after coming from England. He was one of the wealthiest planters in Maryland, with more than nine thousand acres devoted largely to tobacco and worked by slave labor. Now he was settling his family in Kent County, Delaware, where he owned more than three thousand acres and had built a handsome mansion for his family called Poplar Hall. The house was easily accessible by horse or by boat from Philadelphia, a growing center of commercial activity.

Dickinson was raised in the Quaker tradition and schooled at home by his parents and tutors. He was a bright, serious young man, and by his teenage years he was more attracted to the life of the mind than to the running of a large plantation. At the age of eighteen, he went to Philadelphia to work as a law clerk for John Moland, one of the leading attorneys in the city. In the absence of a formal system of learning and certification, an apprenticeship was the avenue to practicing law, a system that produced few learned men comparable to those who practiced in London. For Dickinson, practical training offered little challenge. With his intellectual drive, he decided to pursue law studies in London, where Moland had studied. England was the wellspring of the law adopted in the colonies and the place to learn about the commercial agreements that bound trade with the colonies.[7]

Dickinson's considerable gifts were of the mind, while his physical frailty put him constantly at risk of illness. His letters home to his "Honoured Mother" and "Honoured Father" are full of references to illness as well as assurances that he is well and taking good care of himself. So, too, he let his parents know that he had no interest in filling his hours with carousing on the town. "As to the vicious pleasures of London," he wrote to his mother, "I know not what they are; I never hear of them, & never think of them." He reported that he arose at five in the morning to read for eight hours and was in bed by ten.[8] Given his nature, those assurances may have actually been true.

Dickinson's three years in London absorbed him in the common law, which in turn required a close study of history because common law decisions find their justification in old precedents. Dickinson read heavily in legal commentators and works of English history, focusing intensely on the writings of Sir Edward Coke, the great English jurist. Coke's writings led Dickinson into the source material, and he plunged into leading historians and classical writers. From Tacitus he learned about the forefathers of the ancient Saxons who came from Germany to settle England. The Saxons had established some of the earliest practices of representative government, but had surrendered their liberties to the conquering Normans in 1066. Ever since, Englishmen had struggled mightily to recapture their rights from overbearing kings, beginning with King John signing the Magna Carta in 1215.[9]

Coke himself fought to preserve English liberties against the incursions of royal authority, leading Parliament in 1628 in writing and enacting the Petition of Right, which protected some liberties of the people from infringement by the king and his ministers. The Petition of Right became one of the three central documents of the English Constitution, including the Magna Carta and the Bill of Rights of 1689.

Dickinson absorbed the lesson that individual rights had to be secured in documents, but that documents themselves were but paper protections. English history told him that the people could protect themselves from tyranny only by constant vigilance and by resistance to a ruler's assertion of illegal power. The people, he said, needed wise leaders who would enforce the law and respect its limits. "Laws in themselves certainly do not make men happy," he wrote from London. "They derive all their force & worth from a vigorous & just execution of them."[10] To achieve greatness, a nation required leaders who practiced public virtue, a dedication to the common good over selfish gain. That was a quality sorely missing in London, where he saw "the most unbounded licentiousness & utter disregard of virtue which is the unfailing cause of the destruction of all empires."[11]

Dickinson returned to America in 1757 with his natural conservatism enhanced—a conservatism based on his deep respect for past struggles for liberty and for the principles of English constitutionalism. He settled in Philadelphia and began practicing law. In 1759, he was elected to the Delaware Assembly and a year later became speaker. He lost his seat in 1761 but became a member of the Pennsylvania Assembly two years later.[12]

In 1762, Dickinson wrote to his good friend and fellow lawyer George Read, whom he had known since the days they had apprenticed together in Moland's law office. Dickinson included a personal aside at the end of his note. Just shy of his thirtieth birthday, he revealed so much of himself in so few words—a statement of his personal ambition tempered by the virtue he esteemed from his study of the ancients. "I confess," he wrote to Read, "I should like to make an immense bustle in the world, if it could be made by virtuous actions."[13]

As the threads that bound Britain and America began to unravel, Dickinson would indeed "make an immense bustle in the world," and do it with notable virtue.

FOR DICKINSON, all the serious strands of his life—his piercing intellect, his extended education in London, his fascination with English constitutional history—brought him inevitably to the one form of political expression that provided a vessel deep enough to carry his ideas. Dickinson became an essayist, a pamphleteer.

Pamphlets held a special place in the world of colonial speech. Political writers utilized the printing press in many ways to circulate their material, and each medium provided its own advantages and sometimes engaged different audiences. Writers published letters and short essays in the newspapers, which were read not only in private homes but also in the inns, taverns, and coffeehouses of the major towns. They wrote broadsides to react quickly to events and distributed them from hand to hand and nailed them up in public places. Pamphlets offered something different. They were the perfect medium for extended development of complex ideas and arguments, and adaptable enough to easily carry essays, sermons, state papers, and much more. Sometimes writers combined media, first publishing a series of letters in the papers and then collecting them in a pamphlet. With contentious issues engaging the colonists at every turn, American writers produced as many as fifteen hundred pamphlets in the years between 1763 and 1783.[14]

Pamphlets as a medium were easily adaptable. They were far easier and cheaper to produce than books. They could be written at any length, could be serious or scurrilous, and were fast enough off the press that they could burst into the middle of developing events. One pamphlet, in fact, could beget another pamphlet delivering a sharp response, which in turn begat still another and another until it might finally end in a flurry of scolding abuse. When the Welsh clergyman Richard Price wrote a pamphlet, *Observations on the Nature of Civil Liberty,* in support of the rebellious Americans in 1776, thirteen writers wrote pamphlet rebuttals.[15]

Like so many other forms of political expression taken up in the colonies, pamphlets traced their ancestry to the other side of the ocean. Queen Elizabeth recommended to the Court of High Commission in 1559 that because many pamphlets contained writings that were "heretical, sedicious, or unsemely for Christian eares," no person should publish them without a license.[16] In 1588, a Puritan writer using the pseudonym Martin Marprelate began a pamphlet war against the Anglican episcopacy, calling the bishops "profane, proud, paltry, popish, pestilent, pernicious, presumptious prelates." Church authorities commissioned pamphlets to attack Marprelate in return before they finally silenced him by confiscating his presses.[17]

Far from being high-minded publications, pamphlets suffered from a reputation for carrying material that was rude, deceitful, and ephemeral. They mushroomed in the seventeenth century, with the imagined Popish Plot to kill King Charles II in 1678 generating hundreds of dueling pamphlets and the lapsing of the Licensing Act in 1679 feeding the frenzy still more. By the Glorious Revolution ten years later, pamphlets had become an important vehicle of political writing.[18]

In the colonies, too, pamphlets provided a medium well suited to the needs of serious commentary. If the king and Parliament were violating the rights of Americans, it would take an extended argument to explain the reasons why this was so. Colonial writers used a broad array of literary devices. Sarcasm, parody, ridicule, metaphor, and allegory were frequent weapons of choice, and so was satire. One writer, Richard Bland, attacked an opponent by taking on his persona and writing in his voice so convincingly that the other man had to explain to his followers who was writing which pamphlet.[19]

Thoughtful writers like Dickinson drew deeply from Western intellectual history and traditions. Well-educated colonists were generally familiar with classical authors, and writers of serious commentary often called for the assistance of friends like Homer, Sophocles, Thucydides, Aristotle, Cicero, Tacitus, and Pliny. But it was the Enlightenment figures who spoke most directly to the needs of colonial writers. Pamphleteers cited a broad array of thinkers, including Locke for discussions of natural rights, Montesquieu for British liberty and the separation of powers in government, and Grotius and Pufendorf on natural law. And there were other sources as well. New England Puritanism contributed the idea that

God's hand had shaped the colonies, and that the king was restrained by the divine intent that he govern his subjects justly. Then, too, pamphleteers of the founding generation put talismanic weight on the writings of the English critics John Trenchard and Thomas Gordon, whose *Cato's Letters* from the 1720s dissected political liberty and freedom of the press.[20]

When the troubles began with British taxation of the colonies, pamphlets became the most vital medium for arguing deeply about colonial rights. In 1764, James Otis Jr. wrote a pamphlet that attacked the Sugar Act because the colonists had no seats in Parliament. "The very act of taxing exercised over those who are not represented," Otis wrote, "appears to me to be depriving them of one of their most essential rights as freemen, and if continued seems to be in effect an entire disfranchisement of every civil right."[21] Other pamphlets followed as colonial writers made the case that even a sovereign power like Parliament could go too far in imposing its will.

The next year, passage of the Stamp Act inflamed the colonies all over again. (See chapters 3 and 4.) The controversy enabled Dickinson to emerge as a major political figure who would begin writing many of the most important documents of the founding period. As one of the delegates that Pennsylvania sent to the Stamp Act Congress in New York in October 1765, he drafted the Declaration of Rights and Grievances, arguing that the new tax violated the historic rights of the colonists and that taxes could not be imposed without their consent.[22]

The launching of Dickinson's star, though, took place a few years later. After repealing the Stamp Act, Parliament replaced it with the Townshend Acts, taxing imported products such as glass, paper, and tea. Dickinson took up his pen and wrote a series of twelve essays to protest. Three days after the *Pennsylvania Chronicle* published the first essay on December 2, 1767, he sent a note to James Otis Jr. in Boston. He enclosed a copy of the article and some of the other writings in the series yet to be published, so that Otis "can determine its True worth."

Mindful of the close ties that Otis maintained with Boston's radical press, Dickinson told Otis that his writings could "be dispos'd of as you think proper."[23]

"I AM A FARMER, settled, after a variety of fortunes, near the banks of the river *Delaware*, in the province of *Pennsylvania*."

And so began, in the most soothing of tones, the essay that Otis began reading. The first of a twelve-part series, it would become perhaps the most intellectually powerful and influential writing of the decade before the Revolution. As was typical of political writers at the time, the author chose a pseudonym, identifying himself only by his work tilling the land. But John Dickinson was certainly no farmer.

Dickinson understood that his symbolism and his construction of the essay could enhance the power of his political message and broaden the public sphere of people reading a serious political tract of this kind. He wanted to engage the tavern crowd, which was not the usual target for serious pamphleteers, and give them the legal and political language for opposing the Townshend Acts. Although he wrote the essay all at once as a single composition, he rejected the conventional form of a long pamphlet—his letters were later collected in a pamphlet—in favor of more informal and inviting letters that newspapers could easily serialize. Publication in newspapers put his work into the hands of many more people than a traditional pamphlet would reach, and provided shorter pieces that people could more easily consume. As people talked about his letters, his audience would grow for each later one in the series.

The letters were an intricate production. The series format enabled Dickinson to better control the impact of his work by repeating critical points to drive home his message. In his third letter he even fabricated an assessment that the first two letters had been "received with so much favour." He went on to address objections to his arguments that he said people had raised in past weeks—again, he had invented all of the objections in advance so that he could go back and hammer critical points yet again.[24]

The presentation of the essays as letters dovetailed with the persona that Dickinson adopted. The Farmer created a personal connection with his readers. He portrayed himself as a man offering reflections on current events to his friends, an invitation to sit in a comfortable chair with him. The opening words of his essay echoed with a pastoral voice that spoke to the understanding of an eighteenth-century colonial audience. After introducing himself as "a Farmer," Dickinson went on in an equally serene manner:

> I received a liberal education and have been engaged in the busy scenes
> of life; but am now convinced, that a man may be as happy without

bustle, as with it. My farm is small; my servants are few, and good; I have a little money at interest; I wish for no more; my employment in my own affairs is easy . . .

Being generally master of my time, I spend a good deal of it in a library, which I think the most valuable part of my small estate; and being acquainted with two or three gentlemen of abilities and learning, who honor me with their friendship, I have acquired, I believe, a greater knowledge in history, and the laws and constitution of my country, than is generally attained by men of my class.[25]

Dickinson's adoption of the pastoral voice of the "Farmer from Pennsylvania" was carefully calculated, and a brilliant stroke.[26] The choice of pseudonym in protest writings was serious business in colonial America, designed to align the writer with certain positive associations related to politics or personal integrity. The adopted names Cicero and Publius, for instance, would enable a writer to wear the togas of republicanism.

Even more so than a name from classical antiquity, though, the persona of a farmer spoke to mythical qualities that deeply resonated with colonial Americans. Theirs was largely an agrarian community, steeped in a timeless reverence for the land. A farmer in their eyes enjoyed a special patina of virtue and honesty. Withdrawn from the hubbub of the city and partisan politics, a farmer could view great conflicts from the quiet of his fields, providing him a kind of detached and selfless wisdom. But Dickinson was not satisfied with such a generalized character. His farmer would be special even among his peers. He "has enjoyed a variety of fortunes" and he has "a little money at interest," which suggested to readers that Dickinson's Farmer had achieved success with his horse-drawn plow against all the storms and pestilence that nature could throw against him. Such a man was worthy of respect. As for money, "I wish for no more"— so not only was he a successful man, but a modest one as well. He had achieved, from his family and the land, all that life offered of importance.

Dickinson would not leave it even there. The Farmer had put aside his well-worn boots and was now retired to his library, where he could spend time among his many books, reflecting on the condition of his beloved country and talking with his friends, "gentlemen of abilities and learning." The Farmer was carefully humble. He had hesitated in stepping forward out of deference to others more knowledgeable than he. "Conscious of my own defects," he wrote, "I have waited some time in expectation of seeing the subject treated by persons much better qualified for the task; but being therein disappointed, and apprehensive that longer delays will be injurious," he must himself address the issues dividing the colonies and England.

Dickinson's construction of the persona for his essay was now complete. His Farmer was a man of considerable accomplishment, modest disposition, and quiet wisdom. He was a man worth listening to. The contrast could not have been more sharply drawn in the minds of the colonists for whom Dickinson wrote. They compared the plain-speaking humility of their own Farmer, retired on the banks of the Delaware, to what they regarded as corrupt, overreaching, and self-aggrandizing officials thousands of miles away in London.

As Dickinson demonstrated even before beginning his legal arguments, all political expression is not born equal.

EVEN FOR THOSE WHO READ the Farmer closely in 1768, it would have been difficult to comprehend the full impact of his *Letters*. He argued against the Townshend Acts, but implicit in his writing was a larger idea of enormous impact. For in opposing the law, the Farmer challenged Parliament on the most basic level of authority. He argued that Parliament lacked the sovereign power to pass laws that bound the colonies on internal matters, an argument that would conclude in 1776 with the Continental Congress declaring that Parliament had no power over the colonies whatsoever, and that the colonies would govern themselves. And with popular sovereignty came a powerful imperative—the need for freedom of expression so that citizens could effectively govern themselves.[27]

As the Farmer penned his essay, it was clear enough that Parliament held the sole sovereign power over all of Britain. The Glorious Revolution of 1688–89 had created a constitutional monarchy, wresting much of the power from the king and placing sovereignty in a Parliament consisting of King, Lords, and Commons. Parliament held the supreme, undivided legal authority in the land, and all persons were subject to its rule. In 1765, William Blackstone wrote in his *Commentaries on the Laws of England* that in every state there must be "a supreme, irresistible, absolute, uncontrolled authority, in which . . . the rights of sovereignty reside."[28] Legal commentators and British politicians could envision no state of affairs in which another independent legislative body could coexist with Parliament in the same geographic area.

In practice, though, Parliament's undivided sovereignty always worked somewhat tentatively in the colonies, owing to the reality that thousands of miles separated England and America and that it took months for messages to move back and forth across the Atlantic. The colonies, under their status as royal colonies, enjoyed considerable self-rule. London appointed governors and other high officials, but colonists elected local assemblies that passed laws that stood unless the king rejected them. Parliament cared little about how the colonies went about their business, at least until the protests of the 1760s, and as a result the assemblies, town meetings, and local courts controlled much of daily life. The assemblies even set taxes with the blessing of London. So the colonists, by and large, ran their own affairs, an unofficial kind of popular sovereignty on their own shores even though the supreme power lay across the ocean with Parliament.

From the perspective of the colonists, then, Parliament's passage of the Stamp Act upset what they saw as the natural order of things. Their protests focused on what they believed to be a violation of individual rights: the imposition of taxes without their consent. But they began arguing as well that the Stamp Act imposed taxes on internal commercial activity, something that their own colonial assemblies had traditionally controlled. So they contended in early essays that Parliament had the right to exact external taxes on trade, but not internal taxes.

When Parliament repealed the Stamp Act and replaced it with the Townshend Acts, the duties that were imposed on certain imported goods looked to British lawmakers like the external taxes that the colonies would tolerate. That's when Dickinson, with his *Letters*, shifted the debate. He examined the basic relationship between Britain and the colonies. Britain, said the Farmer, had no right at all to tax the colonies to raise revenue, whether it was an internal or an external tax. Only the colonies could impose a tax to raise revenue to run their own affairs. Parliament, said the Farmer, was limited to imposing duties related to the regulation of trade in the empire. It depended on the intention of Parliament in passing a law.

In Dickinson's view, then, Parliament's authority over the colonies was not supreme and all encompassing, as Blackstone had written of English law. Instead, it was divisible into spheres, with Parliament supreme only when it acted in ways related to its position as the head of the whole empire. It could regulate, wrote the Farmer, "in such a manner as she [England] thought most conducive to their mutual advantage and her own welfare." Britain must honor the "indisputable, the acknowledged exclusive right of the colonies to tax themselves."[29]

All at once, the Farmer had elevated the disagreement between the colonies and Britain to a different orbit. According to the Farmer, Parliament did not, as it had said in the Declaratory Act, enjoy the "full power and authority to make laws and statutes of sufficient force and validity to bind the colonies and people of America . . . in all cases whatsoever." No more important local power existed than taxation. A free people must control the purse strings. "Where this is the case," the Farmer wrote, "*they have a constitutional check* upon the administration, which may thereby be brought into order *without violence:* But where such a power is not lodged in the *people,* oppression proceeds uncontrolled in its career, till the governed, transported into rage, seek redress in the midst of blood and confusion."[30]

The Farmer's challenge to undivided parliamentary sovereignty was taken up throughout the colonies. In November, Governor William Franklin of New Jersey wrote to Lord Hillsborough that there "is scarce an Assembly man in America, but what either believes that the Parliament has not a Right to impose Taxes for the Purposes of Revenue in America, or thinks that it is contrary to Justice, Equity and Sound Policy to exercise that Right, under the present Circumstances of the Colonies."[31] But serious opposition to the Farmer's ideas came from many in England as well as Loyalists in America. William Knox answered the Farmer in a pamphlet a year later. Soon to be appointed British undersecretary of state for the colonies, Knox argued that the supremacy of Parliament could brook no compromise. Its power was in no way divisible. "All distinctions," he said, "destroy this union; and if it can be shown in any particular to be dissolved, it must be so in all instances whatever."[32]

After the Farmer's *Letters,* colonial thinkers would continue to develop the idea of shared sovereignty, a concept that would be, as historian Gordon S. Wood has described it, "the most important abstraction of politics in the entire Revolutionary era."[33] On the day of independence, the Continental Congress finally concluded that Americans must be free of all British authority and run their affairs themselves. Later, the founding generation would carry its ideas about shared sovereignty to the creation of their own government. When they wrote the Constitution, they designed a system of federalism based on the division of power between national and state governments.

The debate over the division of power between Parliament and the colonies would also have a momentous impact on freedom of expression. The patriots rejected Blackstone's view of Parliament as the supreme power and elevated popular sovereignty in its place. In doing so, they changed the fundamental relationship between ruler and citizen. In a system in which the ruler held all power over a subservient population, seditious libel law was seen as helping to protect his legitimate authority. But with popular sovereignty, the relationship was reversed—citizens held the power to govern themselves and employed officials to represent them. If the people, not Parliament, held sovereign power in America and ran their own affairs, they required freedom of speech and press to criticize public policy and public officials, complain about what they considered the abuse of authority, and participate in elections. Seditious libel law, then, conflicted with the requirements of a self-governing society.

In so many ways, the Farmer, retired to his library on the banks of the Delaware, had posed the central political question of his time.

THE AUTHORSHIP OF *Letters from a Farmer* remained unknown except to a handful of friends and acquaintances. Dickinson's law clerk, John MacPherson Jr., had copied the manuscript for him but denied in a letter any knowledge of the Farmer's identity. "This however is certain," wrote MacPherson, "he is a friend to his country, & has contributed . . . towards the delivery of America from Slavery."[34]

The *Boston Gazette* began the series on December 21, almost three weeks after the first essay appeared in the *Pennsylvania Chronicle*. Governor Bernard did not know the identity of the Farmer when he sent copies of his writings to Lord Barrington, the secretary at war, in London at the end of January.[35] In March, Benjamin Franklin reported to his son William that Lord Hillsborough, secretary of state for the colonies, had told him that "he believed he could guess who was the author, looking at my face at the same time, as if he thought it was me."[36]

It was not until May 16, 1768, that the *Pennsylvania Chronicle* revealed Dickinson as the author,[37] and by then his *Letters* were a sensation in the colonies. Once again, as in the Stamp Act crisis three years before, the network of printers from Boston to Savannah had gone to work setting type. Within a few months, nineteen out of twenty-three English-language papers in the colonies had published Dickinson's work. Beyond that, printers issued seven pamphlet editions, making the *Letters* the most widely circulated writing in the colonial period until that time. A reference to the Farmer was published in a colonial paper every week during the eleven months following the beginning of publication of the *Letters*. Historian Carl F. Kaestle estimated that the *Letters* reached about eighty thousand of the two hundred thousand free adult literate males in the colonies, an extraordinary circulation.[38]

The *Letters* circulated even as the situation in the colonies continued to deteriorate. In February 1768, the Massachusetts House had passed its Circular Letter opposing the Townshend Acts and sent it out to the other colonies. Lord Hillsborough had responded by instructing Governor Bernard to dissolve the assembly if it did not revoke the letter—something he did after the assembly refused to rescind it in a vote on June 30. Meanwhile, customs agents in Boston had seized John Hancock's sloop, the *Liberty,* for evading the tax on wine.

All over the colonies, people celebrated the Farmer even before they knew his identity. These local tributes, too, were printed in papers up and down the coast, encouraging an echo of the applause everywhere. Towns voted tributes to his fierce defense of colonial rights in the face of British power. In March, the Boston town meeting voted that thanks be given to "the ingenious Author" of letters in which "the Rights of the American subjects are clearly stated and fully vindicated," and appointed a committee of Samuel Adams, John Hancock, and others to prepare a letter of appreciation.[39] A town meeting in Lebanon, Connecticut, even embraced the Farmer's persona by asking if they might "penetrate the Veil of your modest Retirement" to offer thanks for having "vindicated the Rights of America."[40] On the second anniversary of the repeal of the Stamp Act, patriots drank toasts to the Farmer all over the colonies, including at taverns in Boston and New York and at the Liberty Trees in Boston and Petersham.[41] So revered was the Farmer that a paper reported the rumor that a Virginia man had left in his will "a handsome Fortune to the patriotic Author of the FARMER's Letters."[42]

Even a ship out of Philadelphia was named the *Farmer*. Although his name commanded respect far and wide, the Farmer's fame was not powerful enough to tame the forces of nature at sea—alas, the ship was listed as "entirely lost off Cadiz."[43]

LOYALISTS DID NOT JOIN in the celebrations, and soon enough some of their most able writers struck back. Some writers launched scorching attacks on the Farmer. A Tory using the name Machiavel wrote that the *Letters* contained "the basest misrepresentations, the blackest ingratitude, the most groundless predictions of vassalage and slavery, the warmest incitements to opposition and violences, and no great affection to the King and Parliament."[44] Another, named Country Farmer, wrote a scathing satire of the Farmer's retirement to a life of books, saying he was skilled in "logic, mathematics, natural and moral philosophy, rhetoric, geography, chronology, history, law, physic, divinity, politics and magic" and that he had been applauded by "*great men* and *little men,* by things *animate* and things *inanimate,* by the *fowls* of the *air,* and the *fish* in *Schuylkill.*"[45]

Sarcastic attacks might erode the Farmer's persona, but the Loyalists knew they could exact no serious damage without squarely challenging the Farmer's legal arguments. For that, a Loyalist writer published a ten-part series in the *Boston Evening-Post,* attacking the idea of Parliament surrendering some of its sovereign lawmaking power to the colonies. A colonial assembly could not exercise concurrent or superior power to Parliament, which would be the case if Parliament were excluded from taxing the colonies. In that case, "the people would become the sovereign judges of the extent of parliamentary authority, and a rude insulting mob exercise the power of legislators," he wrote, adding: "Subordinate legislatures would be gravely set to work to limit the authority of a superior one, and every species of confusion that is to be feared from the despotism of democracy, would be attendant upon a display of so profound a piece of casuistry."[46] The king himself would lose his supreme position. "In the one *instance,* each American governor would display all the authority of a British King; and in the *other,* drop gently into the character of a King's representative only."[47]

The writer drew a bright line in the sand—the sovereign enjoyed indivisible power. "We are subjects to the British King; as such we are bound to obey him," he wrote. "This obedience, being the essence of our allegiance, is *absolute*."[48]

DICKINSON REMAINED A STEP ahead of the Loyalists. Having called upon James Otis in December for his help in publishing the *Letters* in Boston, Dickinson came back to him in July with a second piece of writing. This time it was not an essay. "I inclose you," he told Otis, "a song for American freedom."[49]

The celebrated Farmer who had expounded on Lord Coke and English constitutional rights had indeed written a song. He had composed it in eight stanzas of rhyming verse plus a chorus, crediting Arthur Lee, "a worthy friend," with two of the verses. For the melody Dickinson adopted "Heart of Oaks," a song by the composer William Boyce that celebrated British military victories. Dickinson's song found a receptive ear in Otis. A few weeks later, the Farmer's "Liberty Song" appeared in the *Boston Gazette*.[50] It spread quickly to papers and broadsides all throughout the colonies, with a reach as extensive as his *Letters*.

> Come join Hand in Hand, brave AMERICANS all, And rouse your bold
>   Hearts at fair LIBERTY's call;
> No tyrannous Acts shall suppress your just Claim
> Or stain with Dishonor AMERICA's Name.
> Then join Hand in Hand brave AMERICANS all,
> By uniting we stand, by dividing we fall;
> IN SO RIGHTEOUS A CAUSE let us hope to succeed,
> For Heaven approves of each generous Deed.[51]

Dickinson reduced the arguments in his *Letters* to a simplistic and rousing call to unity, forcefully stating at the outset that all "brave Americans" would heed the call of liberty to resist "tyrannous acts" that threatened their "just claim" to the constitutional rights of Englishmen. The Townshend Acts, he said, were a scheme to violate those freedoms by lifting the colonists' money without their consent. He wrote of liberty as a patrimony that the colonists enjoyed from their legal history—"their *Birthrights* they priz'd." And his appeal—"by uniting we stand, by dividing we fall"—would become as memorable in the American lexicon as

Benjamin Franklin's cut-up snake for advocating unity in the face of an outside threat.

With his "Liberty Song," Dickinson built on a tradition that reached far back to sixteenth-century England. Writers composed crude ballad verse on any subject they thought would interest the public—accounts of public events, political and religious commentary, and fantastical stories of various kinds—and suggested a popular melody rather than composing a new one. They printed the lyrics on broadsides, often with a woodcut at the top of the page for decoration, and sold it everywhere people gathered in the cities and carried it by horseback to rural areas. Even licensing laws failed to stop a medium that offered a cheap and easy way to reach the public and the opportunity to make money. With the birth of newspapers, songs found yet another outlet to spread political commentary.[52]

Songs and music became an important part of colonial culture as well, and the latest English ballads found their way over on ships. Soon enough, writers in America began publishing their own songs set to familiar melodies from England. As songs became more politicized with the increasing strains with London, colonial writers could easily adapt the tunes with new lyrics.

In the colonies, songs of dissent had long bedeviled the authorities. Back in 1734, as he pursued seditious libel charges against the printer John Peter Zenger, James De Lancey of New York told a grand jury of two songs that he considered seditious against the government. "Sometimes heavy-witted men get a knack of rhyming," he said, "but it is time to break them of it when they grow abusive, insolent, and mischievous." The hangman burned the two songs—a symbolic act, since they were circulating by broadside—and a reward issued for the identification of the writer.[53] Twenty years later, a printer was ordered arrested for circulating a ballad that satirized debates in the Massachusetts House of Representatives and that, in the eyes of the lawmakers, "contained many Expressions horribly prophane & impious."[54]

Political songs grew ever more popular in the ten years before independence. One song circulated during the Townshend Acts to encourage women to support the boycott of British goods by spinning their own yarn instead of buying it from England. Among those who responded was

a group that met at the home of a Boston minister and spun more than
two hundred skeins of yarn.

> *First, then, throw aside your topknots of pride;*
> *Wear none but your own country linen;*
> *Of economy boast, let your pride be the most,*
> *To show clothes of your own make and spinning.*[55]

That songs received such an enthusiastic reception was hardly surprising.
They represented an important expansion of the public sphere of political expression. As Dickinson himself understood, his *Letters* were challenging to read. But he was certain of one thing—everyone could sing.
And that enabled him to leverage his newfound fame by reaching a much
broader audience.

Songs existed as a universal currency that could readily bring patriotic enthusiasm. People could read the lyrics on paper or easily learn
them in a group, and because songs were so often set to a popular melody,
they quickly spread. A song invited participation by all ages and made no
distinction based on literacy or social class. Songs could be a rousing addition to gatherings in the streets, at Liberty Trees, or in taverns, lifting
emotions and enabling people to unite in their disdain for what they saw
as British overreaching.

Political leaders understood the influence of songs. As Dickinson
wrote to Otis when he sent him the "Liberty Song," it was because songs
"are frequently very powerful on certain occasions, I venture to invoke
the deserted muses."[56] John Adams dined in Dorchester in August 1769
with 350 members of the Sons of Liberty, and after drinking toasts they
sang the "Liberty Song." "This," wrote Adams, "is cultivating the Sensa-
tions of Freedom."[57] Joel Barlow, who wrote many songs for the patriot
cause, said that he had "great faith in the influence of songs," adding:
"One good song is worth a dozen addresses or proclamations."[58]

All throughout the colonies, the "Liberty Song" gave people another
reason to lift a toast to the Farmer. In Charleston, a group of mechanics dedicated a Liberty Tree and sang the verses. In Boston, the Sons of
Liberty assembled at the Liberty Tree—"a concourse of people of all
Ranks"—to celebrate the anniversary of the demonstrations that had
started the Stamp Act protests three years earlier. "The Music began at

high Noon," according to one report, and ended with "the universally admired *American* Song of Liberty. The Grandeur of its Sentiment, and the easy Flow of its Numbers, together with an exquisite Harmony of Sound, afforded sublime Entertainment to a numerous audience, fraught with a noble Ardour in the cause of Freedom." The crowd toasted both King George and the Farmer and heard both French horns and the roar of cannon.[59]

Loyalists could no more ignore the "Liberty Song" than they could *Letters from a Farmer*. One writer took up the cause with a clever parody two months later that humorously attacked the Sons of Liberty for protests that led to attacks on property.[60] It went on for ten stanzas plus a chorus, painting the dissenters as "banditti" and urged them to "Gulp down your last dram, for the gallows now groans":

> All Ages shall speak with Contempt and Amaze,
> Of the vilest Banditti that swarm'd in those days,
> In Defiance of Halters, of Whips and of Chains,
> The Rogues would run Riot,—dam'd Fools for their Pains.

As often happened, one political writing spawned another and another, and so a patriot writer threw it all back at the Loyalists with the "Parody Parodiz'd" or the "Massachusetts Liberty Song."[61] Starting with "Come swallow your Bumpers, ye Tories! & roar," the writer admonished people to stand together and "join hand in hand, brave *Americans* all, to be Free is to live; to be Slaves is to fall."

> All Ages shall speak, with Amaze and Applause,
> Of the prudence we show, in support of our Cause!
> Assur'd of our safety, a Brunswick still reigns,
> Whose free loyal Subjects are strangers to Chains.

BEST-SELLING SONGWRITER and pamphleteer might be an odd combination of achievements, but it made Dickinson very much in demand. He drove through the streets in his finely appointed coach pulled by four horses. Delegates were gathering from all the colonies this last week of August 1774 to attend the First Continental Congress, filling the town with a buzz of important things about to happen. Although Dickinson was not a delegate—he would become one in October—he was still the Farmer, and a man from whom people wanted advice.

Dickinson, one of the wealthiest men in Philadelphia, had good reason to be proud of his adopted town. With a population nearing thirty thousand, Philadelphia was the largest colonial city and one of the most prosperous, with a long row of wharves along the Delaware River teeming with ships that moved cargo to and from England and the West Indies. Wheat and lumber were the primary exports from the port, but the economy also counted many artisans and manufacturers. Dickinson passed through the town's precisely planned grid of streets, many planted with trees, and past numerous shops offering a variety of fine goods.

Philadelphia was a logical place to hold the First Continental Congress, not just because of its convenient location in the middle colonies, but also because it had developed a public sphere that supported vigorous political discussion. The town boasted seven newspapers, not all of them faithful to the patriot cause, and twenty-three printing shops turning out papers, pamphlets, broadsides, and other materials that sold in almost thirty bookstores. As in Boston and New York, people converged on the taverns and coffeehouses to read the papers, exchange news, and argue about the conflict with Britain over colonial rights. William Bradford, a member of the Sons of Liberty, had a hand in much of the public sphere—he was a powerful printer as well as the proprietor of both a bookshop and the London Coffee House, one of the most popular places for merchants and politicians to gather and talk about the issues of the day.[62]

Dickinson that morning stopped to see John Adams, who had arrived in town a few days earlier to serve as a delegate from Massachusetts. The men exchanged pleasantries, with Dickinson explaining that he had been ill and suffering with the gout, and that this visit was his first excursion for some time. Like all patriots, Adams admired the Farmer for his powerful defense of American rights. So it was a surprise for Adams to see that the Farmer's physical bearing was so fragile, as if he had been exhausted by the outpouring of his own strong pen. "He is a Shadow—tall, but slender as a Reed—pale as ashes," Adams wrote in his diary. "One would think at first Sight that he could not live a Month. Yet upon a more attentive Inspection, he looks as if the Springs of Life were strong enough to last many years."[63]

As the weeks went on, the two men met again many times both socially and politically, and the respect that Adams held for the Farmer

only increased. Soon after the Congress began its sessions, Adams accepted an invitation to dine with Dickinson at his Fairhill mansion.
"Mr. Dickinson is a very modest Man and very ingenious, as well as
agreeable," Adams wrote of their dinner. "He has an excellent Heart,
and the Cause of his Country lies near it."[64] Adams wrote again about
a dinner with Dickinson in mid-September. "A most delightful Afternoon we had. Sweet Communion indeed we had—Mr. Dickinson gave
us his Thoughts and his Correspondence very freely."[65] And on October 3, Adams noted enthusiastically that Dickinson was allied with two
other Pennsylvania politicians in strongly opposing British incursions
on the rights of the colonists. "Mr. Dickinson and Mr. Thompson, now
joined to Mr. Mifflin, will make a great Weight in favour of the American Cause," he wrote.[66]

The positive remarks were not surprising. Celebrated throughout
America as no other man of the time, the Farmer had only added to
his reputation since his *Letters from a Farmer* and his "Liberty Song" in
1768. He had gone back into print to urge that Philadelphia merchants
sign a nonimportation agreement, the same weapon that the colonies had
wielded successfully to help gain repeal of the Stamp Act a few years earlier. Dickinson had spoken at public meetings and written articles to urge
unity. The Philadelphia merchants eventually agreed to join Boston and
New York in the boycott, and most other port cities joined as well. Unsurprisingly, shipments of goods from Britain to the colonies plummeted.
Faced with severe economic losses, Parliament repealed the hated Townshend Acts early in 1770, retaining the duty on tea.[67]

Tea, then, became a central issue of contention, with the question of
the Parliament's right to tax the colonies continuing to consume public discussion. In Boston, Samuel Adams had already concluded that the
colonies had to be independent from Britain, something that Dickinson
and most of the colonists did not yet accept. Adams now called on him to
write still more on a subject on which they did agree—that the taxing of
Americans without their consent was a violation of their rights. "Could
your health or leisure admit of it, a publication of your sentiments on this
and other matters of the most interesting importance would be of substantial advantage to our country," Samuel Adams wrote in March 1773,
adding that the Farmer was one of America's "ablest advocates."[68]

A few months later, Parliament passed the Tea Act to save the failing
East India Company by granting it a monopoly in the colonies. Dickinson

wrote a broadside this time as "Rusticus," urging on November 27 that "no Man will receive the Tea, no Man will let his Stores, nor suffer the Vessel, that brings it, to moor at his Wharf." But the Farmer carefully couched his words in reconciliation—a stance he would clutch tightly in the years ahead as those around him became more radicalized. He said that "when any Difference arises, as on the present unhappy Occasion, let us act so as to leave Room for a return of the old good Humour, Confidence and Affection, which has subsisted between Great-Britain and this Country, since the first settlement of the Colonies."[69]

Within a month, the chances for "a return to the old good Humour" plunged when members of the Sons of Liberty boarded cargo ships in Boston Harbor, dumping the East India Company's tea into the water. The Boston Tea Party so enraged Parliament that it enacted the Coercive Acts—known in the colonies as the Intolerable Acts—that closed the port of Boston and put British authorities firmly in control of the government of Massachusetts. General Gates took over as governor and Boston once again became an occupied town.

It was outrage over the Coercive Acts that brought delegates from most of the colonies to Philadelphia for the First Continental Congress. Meanwhile, Dickinson had written yet another pamphlet, stating once again that Parliament's power over the colonies was limited—that "by the laws of God and by the laws of the constitution a line there must be beyond which her authority cannot extend."[70] By the middle of October, the delegates to the Congress had officially made the Farmer's position their own, adopting resolves that proposed to cut off the power of Parliament at American shores. The colonies wanted to tax themselves and otherwise run their own affairs, submitting to Parliament only for regulation of external commerce that worked for the benefit of the entire empire.

If the Resolves represented the pinnacle of the Farmer's popularity, his steadfast dedication to accommodation with England began soon to wear on the more radical delegates like John Adams. Congress decided to petition the king with colonial grievances, and appointed a committee that included John Adams and Patrick Henry to draft a petition. Congress debated the draft and then recommitted it for additional work, adding Dickinson—who had recently joined the Congress as a delegate—as a member of the committee. Dickinson set about rewriting the petition, making it more conciliatory, explaining later that "the draft brought in by the original committee was written in language of asperity very little according to the conciliatory disposition of Congress."[71]

The committee introduced the new draft on October 24, and Congress approved it the next day. Although he signed the petition, John Adams was unhappy with its more moderate tone. Massachusetts was suffering. The port of Boston, after all, had been closed and the town was once again occupied by a standing army, and to Adams the situation was deteriorating beyond the point where the delicate scratchings of a pen would win anything. Now Adams was having second thoughts about the Farmer and his soft glove in the face of British provocation, telling his diary that there "is no greater Mortification than to sit with half a dozen Witts, deliberating upon a Petition, Address or Memorial."

"Mr. Dickinson," he added in a change of heart about his Pennsylvania colleague, "is very modest, delicate, and timid."[72] John Adams and the Farmer were now heading in different directions.

WITH ADAMS MOVING AWAY from the Farmer and toward a stance favoring a break from Britain, his group of Boston friends provided him with some unusual support—unusual because it came in a form that stretched the typical boundaries of political expression.

The first support came a few months later, on January 15, 1775, with a letter from James Warren. "Inclosed are for your Amusement two Acts of A dramatic performance," Warren wrote.[73] He was passing along to his good friend a play called The Group, written by his wife, Mercy Otis Warren.

As the conflict between Britain and the colonies intensified, Americans used every possible medium to express their views. The Warren and Adams families were close, and John had encouraged Mercy Warren to use her writing gifts to contribute to the patriot cause. Women did not typically participate in public affairs, and in fact could not vote, but for Mercy politics seemed ingrained in her genetic code and she knew and corresponded with many of the patriot leaders. Her father was James Otis, the politician and lawyer, and brother James Jr. was the prominent politician and pamphleteer against British taxes to whom Dickinson had sent his Letters and his "Liberty Song," seeking his help in publishing them in Boston. Her husband, James Warren, served in the Massachusetts House of Representatives.

The Group was not her first literary work firing lead balls at British targets. She had already anonymously published two plays in Boston newspapers—*The Adulateur* and *The Defeat*—that aimed withering satire at Thomas Hutchinson and other apologists for the British. With live theater banned in Boston, the plays were meant only for reading. In 1774, her poem on the Boston Tea Party, solicited by Adams himself, appeared in the *Boston Gazette*.[74] Finally, with *The Group*, she had once again scornfully criticized Loyalists who she thought had abandoned the patriot cause for their own personal gain. Adams turned the play over to the *Boston Gazette*, which printed it eight days later.[75]

A week after publication, an uncertain Mercy Warren wrote to Adams asking how appropriate it was for her to criticize public officials. "Personal Reflections and sarcastic Reproaches have Generally been decry'd by the wise and the worthy, both in their Conversation and Writings. And though a man may be greatly criminal in his Conduct toward the society in which he Lives. How far, sir, do you think it justifiable for any individual to hold him up the Object of public Derision." Sensitive about her own image as a woman, she also asked even if "personal Acrimony might be justifiable in your Sex, must not the female Character suffer."[76]

In his answer, Adams said that it is the role of political speech to take the measure of public men. In a moment of reflection, he passed along what he had learned about the power of free speech during the protests against Britain. "The faithfull Historian delineates Characters truly, let the Censure fall where it will," he wrote. "The public is so interested in public Characters, that they have a Right to know them and it becomes the Duty of every good Citizen who happens to be acquainted with them to communicate his Knowledge. There is no other Way of preventing the Mischief which may be done by ill Men; no other Method of administering the Antidote to the Poison."

As to Mercy's concern about the propriety of a woman engaging in political speech, Adams had assurances. "Nature, which does nothing in vain, bestows no mental Faculties which are not designed to be cultivated and improved," he wrote.[77]

The group around Adams also included John Trumbull, a young Connecticut lawyer who had studied in his office in Boston in 1774. Trumbull returned to his home when Adams left for the Continental Congress in

August. Early the next year, Silas Deane, a Connecticut member of the Congress, asked Trumbull to write a satire on contemporary events. Trumbull had already published a poem attacking the British over the Boston Port Bill, which punished the city after the Tea Party.[78]

Since the Stamp Act protests, newspapers routinely carried short poems, many of them satiric, that made biting attacks on the opposition. In papers crammed with heavy prose, a protest delivered in a dozen lines of verse attracted a lot of eyes, and they were reprinted up and down the coast. But some writers were far more ambitious and produced poetry the length of a pamphlet, telling a story of British oppression. From 1765 through 1783, seventy-seven long political poems appeared that were in the Hudibrastic tradition of the mock-heroic narrative. Fifty-five put their stinger in the king, royal governors, British generals, and Loyalists, with others ridiculing speeches and official proclamations. Many used biting satire. One writer described an officer moving his men meticulously at night to overwhelm nothing more than a children's fort, and another mocked the inalienable right to happiness in the Declaration of Independence by proclaiming, "Tho' your chief happiness in life, / Should be to kiss your neighbour's wife."[79]

Trumbull's satire, *M'Fingal*, first appeared in 1775 and unfolded leisurely at thousands of lines of rhyming couplets. It starred a fictional Loyalist named Squire M'Fingal, who at a town meeting ineptly debated Honorious—probably modeled after Trumbull's old boss, Adams—in an attempt to discredit arguments for independence. At the end of the debate, patriots took M'Fingal to the Liberty Pole, where they tarred and feathered him.

ROUGH TREATMENT OF LOYALISTS in a literary work was one thing, but persecution played out on the streets of colonial America as well. As the colonies moved ever closer to a rupture with Britain, and as they became incensed by British measures such as the Intolerable Acts, some of the more radical patriots struck at the Loyalists with acts of violence and intimidation. Freedom of the press, unfortunately, did not always mean equal freedom for both patriots and Loyalists.

The Loyalist press published widely in the decade before independence, dueling the patriots with articles and pamphlets. As politics became more partisan, though, Loyalist printers faced increasing problems.

Even some printers striving for neutrality suffered for not fully joining the patriot cause. The publishers of the *Boston Evening Press* angered both patriots and Loyalists with their articles, resulting in evaporating subscriptions that forced the paper to cease publication.[80] Much worse were vigilante actions. John Mein, the Loyalist publisher of the *Boston Chronicle*, published ship manifests in 1769 that he claimed showed prominent merchants importing boycotted goods. He was attacked by a mob and fled Boston for England.

The situation may have been even worse in New York, where John Sears fomented attacks on the offices of Loyalist printers.[81] Sears was a rough character who began as a privateer and then led a mob in New York that engaged in violent acts for the patriot cause. Sears engaged in a running battle of invective with James Rivington, printer of the Loyalist *New York Gazetteer.* After news reached the city of bloodshed at Lexington and Concord in 1775, Sears and his men broke into Rivington's shop and destroyed printing plates and copies of a Loyalist pamphlet. Rivington fled to a British ship in New York Harbor. He declared in a petition to the Continental Congress that "he would be cautious, for the future, of giving any further offense."[82] Finally, the New York Provincial Congress issued a resolution permitting him to return to his business.[83]

Sears struck again. In the fall, he led his mob on a destructive foray in which he kidnapped several Loyalists, including the Reverend Samuel Seabury, a Loyalist pamphleteer. Then about seventy-five men rode their horses into New York "with bayonets fixed" and destroyed Rivington's press.[84] Early the next year, he led another mob of forty men to the home of another printer, Samuel Loudon, and destroyed copies of a Loyalist pamphlet.

MORE TYPICAL THAN VIOLENCE, though, was the endless dueling of opposing writers. John Adams was engaging in an intense debate with an anonymous writer who called himself "Massachusettensis." Unknown to Adams, Massachusettensis was a good friend, Daniel Leonard, a lawyer who had been a Whig partisan before leaning Loyalist after the Boston Tea Party.

Men like Adams and Dickinson frequently had to put their business aside to write hundreds or even thousands of words in response to some provocation. So it was with Massachusettensis, who began on December

12 publishing the first of seventeen letters in the *Massachusetts Gazette* that defended royal authority. Massachusettensis argued that colonists should submit to the supreme power of Parliament, warned that the radicals were engaging in treason to win separation, and predicted that Britain would make war rather than lose America. Concerned about the impact of the series, Adams quickly put his own pen to the task of answering Massachusettensis. He began a thirteen-part series of letters six weeks later, writing under the name Novanglus with a dense analysis of English history. He concluded that the colonies were independent of Parliament and that the king's power itself was not absolute.[85]

With that skirmish finished, the delegates returned to Philadelphia in May for the Second Continental Congress. By then, their problems had intensified a thousandfold. The king had turned down their petition of grievances, and on April 19, British troops had fought with colonial militia at Lexington and Concord. Now Dickinson himself despaired that the ocean was widening between the colonies and England. "But what topics of reconciliation are now left for men who think as I do, to address our countrymen?" he asked in a letter on April 29. "To recommend reverence for the monarch, or affection for the mother country? . . . No. While we revere and love our mother country, her sword is opening our veins."[86]

His own words deeply pained Dickinson. As he well knew, few "topics of reconciliation" remained. In fact, John Adams had gone to Lexington a few days after the battle and talked with citizens along the route of the British march. He had concluded that "the Die was cast, the Rubicon passed," and that "if We did not defend ourselves they would kill Us."[87] For Dickinson, though, the fire inside did not burn as hot. He remained a profoundly conservative man for whom rupture from Britain remained something to be avoided until no other possibility remained. Having studied law in England and developed a deep admiration for its legal history, he still believed the answers lay in the constitutional past. He vowed not to give up, a stance that increasingly put him at serious odds with Adams.

The New England colonies had suffered the most in the conflict with Britain, and so their delegates were generally among the most radical in Congress. But through much of 1775, most delegates still thought of themselves as loyal British subjects. They preferred to stay part of Britain but under a new set of rules, sharing sovereignty with Britain in such a way that they could avoid taxation by Parliament and run their own

day-to-day affairs. With hostilities already under way, Congress established the Continental Army and appointed George Washington as its
commanding general, but drafting petitions became contentious.

The delegates appointed a committee to write a declaration laying out
the "causes and necessity of their taking up arms" against Britain. The
declaration was "to make known the justice of our cause," and it enumerated in detail the violations of colonial rights that Parliament had exacted
on the colonies. After a draft was debated and sent back to the committee,
Dickinson and Thomas Jefferson joined the group. Jefferson produced
several drafts, and recalled later that Dickinson thought that his draft was
too harsh and set about softening the language. On balance, some scholars have concluded that Dickinson actually strengthened the language of
the Declaration.[88] But Jefferson's recollection decades later, though probably inaccurate on the specifics of the rewriting, surely struck the target
in portraying in a larger sense how delegates viewed the 1775 version of
the Farmer. "It was too strong for Mr. Dickinson," Jefferson wrote. "He
still retained the hope of reconciliation with the mother country, and was
unwilling it should be lessened by offensive statements. He was so honest
a man, & so able a one that he was greatly indulged even by those who
could not feel his scruples."[89]

Dickinson also insisted that the delegates draft yet another formal
appeal to the king, what aptly became known as the Olive Branch Petition. Once again he took up his pen and produced a document that was
indeed an olive branch. Addressing the king himself—"Most Gracious
Sovereign"—Dickinson blamed the king's ministers, not the king himself,
for "persevering in their measures, and proceeding to open hostilities for
enforcing them," putting the colonists in a position "so peculiarly abhor-
rent to the affections of your still faithful Colonists." Finally, he beseeched
the king to guide them to "a happy and permanent reconciliation."[90]

Many delegates thought such a petition pointless—Adams called
it "this Measure of Imbecility"[91]—but the Farmer's reputation still carried enough weight among the delegates. "Congress gave a signal proof of
their indulgence to Mr. Dickinson," wrote Jefferson, "and of their great
desire not to go too fast for any respectable part of our body, in permitting him to draw their second petition to the King according to his own
ideas, and passing it with scarcely any amendment. The disgust against

this humility was general; and Mr. Dickinson's delight at its passage was the only circumstance which reconciled them to it."[92]

Although Adams signed the petition, his relationship with Dickinson had finally broken. At one point in the proceedings, Adams stepped out of the room. Dickinson followed Adams from the statehouse and confronted him outside. Adams recalled in his diary that Dickinson had harsh words for him. "What is the reason, Mr. Adams, that you New Englandmen oppose our Measures of Reconciliation?" Adams remembered Dickinson as saying, adding that if he did not agree with attempts at reconciliation, "I, and a Number of Us, will break off, from you in New England, and We will carry on the Opposition by ourselves in our own Way."[93]

Adams thought Dickinson weak and increasingly an obstacle to preparations for independence. He expressed that criticism in a letter to Abigail Adams, strongly praising Benjamin Franklin and giving Dickinson low marks in comparison. "I wish his [Franklin's] colleagues from this City were All like him, particularly one, whose Abilities and Virtues, formerly trumpeted so much in America, have been found wanting."[94]

ADAMS WAS ABOUT to encounter the trouble that could ensue from a communications network in which correspondence was not secure from prying eyes. Letters were critically important to public debate and discussion, enabling people to express ideas to political friends and to plot strategy to move their agenda forward.

Most letters were intended to be private. However, in terms of seditious libel, the risks could be as great as with public speech because the system of moving letters from place to place exposed them to theft. On July 24, Adams held nothing back when he wrote letters to Abigail and to his close friend James Warren in Boston. To Warren, Adams complained about Dickinson that a "certain great Fortune and piddling Genius, whose Fame has been trumpeted so loudly, has given a silly Cast to our whole Doings." He also wrote that the Continental Congress should have already "moddelled a Constitution" and "raised a Naval Power." To Abigail he wrote in a similar way about a confrontation with Britain. Adams entrusted his two sensitive letters to a messenger who, as fortune would have it, was captured by British troops near Newport, Rhode Island. To Adams's embarrassment, his letters were published in the *Massachusetts*

Gazette and sent by General Gage to London, where some newspapers printed them.[95]

Not only was his "piddling genius" comment about the Farmer now out in public, but so too were his complaints to Warren that the Continental Congress should by then have written a constitution and raised a navy—public evidence that he wanted separation. His sentiments for independence and military preparation were certainly seditious libel and probably treason as well. General John Burgoyne called Adams "as great a conspirator as ever subverted a state."[96]

Adams's comments about Dickinson only made relations between the men worse. When they passed each other on Chestnut Street a few months later, Adams reported that he bowed and took off his hat, but that Dickinson passed by. "We are not to be upon speaking Terms, nor bowing Terms, for the time to come," wrote Adams.[97] Samuel Adams had turned against Dickinson now as well, saying that he had urged "the Necessity of making Terms of Accommodation with Great Britain. With this he has poisnd the Minds of the People, the Effect of which is a total Stagnation of the Power of Resentment, the utter Loss of every manly Sentiment of Liberty and Virtue."[98]

It was no surprise that the Olive Branch Petition was a dead letter when it arrived across the ocean. London officials would not, in the end, accept the idea that colonial assemblies could work independently of Parliament, that there could be two independent lawmaking bodies operating in the same state. Either the colonies submitted to the indivisible supremacy of Parliament, or they were in revolt. The king refused even to receive the Olive Branch, for he had already told the colonists what he thought of their actions. On August 23, after news of the battle at Bunker Hill reached London, the king had issued a proclamation declaring that the colonies were in "an open and avowed rebellion" and "traitorously preparing, ordering, and levying War against Us." He ordered that the government "suppress such rebellion." Then, at the end of October, he delivered an address to Parliament in which he said that the colonies were carrying on a war "for the purpose of establishing an independent Empire."[99] With the king's tough stand, Parliament passed the Prohibitory Act, one of its most punishing laws yet. It outlawed trade with the colonies and treated American ships as enemy vessels subject to capture and forfeiture to the Crown.

In Philadelphia, the last hopes of avoiding separation had rested on the king demanding a more conciliatory colonial policy from his ministers and Parliament. Most of the patriot leaders saw their problems as emanating from Parliament and the king's scheming ministers, not with the king himself. Throughout the Stamp Act and the Townshend Acts protests, the Sons of Liberty had marched and hanged effigies and then repaired to local taverns to drink toasts to the king, whom they thought would eventually set things right. Now it seemed increasingly clear that the king had chosen warships and grenadiers over compromise.

As patriot leaders considered the king's tough stance, the weight of sentiment moved past Dickinson toward independence. The Farmer, who had carried the cause of American rights since his *Letters* of 1768, had been left behind.

WITH THE FARMER'S STAR now dimming, another writer in Philadelphia suddenly took his place as the most influential of the colonial pamphleteers. Thomas Paine could not have been more different than Dickinson, the patrician lawyer. Born in Thetford in 1737, Paine had dropped out of school at thirteen and apprenticed himself to his father, a corset maker, then went to sea for a few years on a privateer. Paine carried the distinction of having failed at almost everything he did in England. He was twice dismissed from the Excise Commission. His tobacco shop in Lewes went out of business. His marriage ended.[100]

Paine, though, managed to do one thing right—he got an introduction to Benjamin Franklin in London. And he impressed him. Paine wanted a fresh start in America, and Franklin wrote a letter of introduction for Paine to his son, William, the governor of New Jersey. In his letter, Franklin judged Paine fit for a modest job as a clerk, assistant tutor, or assistant surveyor. He made no mention that Paine had the potential to help lead the colonies into a revolution against Britain.

Paine almost didn't survive the trip to Philadelphia. When he landed there late in 1774, sick almost to death with typhus, he needed a stretcher to make it off the boat. Once he recovered, he got a job as managing editor of the new *Pennsylvania Magazine,* and quickly took to journalism. He wrote articles under Atlanticus, Vox Populi, and other pseudonyms,[101] and showed a hint of his antiestablishment sentiments by criticizing the hypocrisy of colonists who complained of British tyranny while enslaving human beings brought from Africa.[102]

All these writings provided the foundation for a project that would profoundly affect thinking in the colonies about independence. Paine met Benjamin Rush, a young physician and friend of John Adams and other delegates to Congress. Rush himself had been drafting thoughts about independence, but "shuttered at the prospect of the consequence of its not being well received." But Paine, he said, had "nothing to fear from the popular odium" because he, unlike Rush, "could live anywhere."[103] Rush urged him in the fall of 1775 to write a pamphlet laying out his ideas. When Paine's *Common Sense* came out in January, it set off fireworks up and down the coast. It immediately became the most important political pamphlet since Dickinson's *Letters from a Farmer,* with twenty-five editions coming off the presses. Paine himself figured that 150,000 copies were sold.[104]

Paine's writing style expanded the public sphere of discussion as no other pamphleteer had done since Dickinson. Eight years earlier, Dickinson had successfully enlarged the audience for his *Letters* by adopting the persona of a farmer retired to his library, and before its appearance as a pamphlet he had divided it into twelve shorter and more palatable newspaper pieces. But readers of his essay still encountered dense legal arguments that invoked classical authors and constitutional history.

Common Sense burst forth all at once in language for anyone who could read and so made political discourse more accessible. Paine, according to historian Eric Foner, "forged a new political language" to enlarge his readership.[105] Unlike other pamphleteers, Paine himself came from the middle class and wrote for the middle class. As a magazine writer and editor, his daily craft aimed at a broad audience. "As it is my design to make those that can scarcely read understand, I shall therefore avoid every literary ornament, and put it in language as plain as the alphabet," Paine explained of his approach to public writing a few years later.[106] *Common Sense* was unique in its authorial voice, with language chosen for its accessibility and forcefulness, with fewer long words and shorter sentences than other pamphlets of the time.[107] Paine avoided difficult legal concepts and sidestepped the usual pantheon of authorities, and instead made the arguments through his own forceful reasoning. Edmund Randolph, later governor of Virginia and a delegate to the Constitutional

Convention, said that Paine had "poured forth a style hitherto unknown on this side of the Atlantic" and that it was "pregnant with the most captivating figures of speech."[108]

Paine's political stance also set him apart from Dickinson.[109] Paine declared himself for independence, and there could be no more olive branches because the monarchy itself was a hopeless corruption. He wrote invective, lashing the king as the "Royal Brute" and attacking the very legitimacy of kingly power and with it the English constitutional system. Looking back into antiquity, he said of kings that "we should find the first of them nothing better than the principal ruffian of some restless gang, whose savage manners or pre-eminence in subtility obtained him the title of chief among plunderers." William the Conqueror's taking of the throne in 1066 proved the utter corruption of the system. "A French bastard landing with an armed banditti and establishing himself king of England against the consent of the natives, is in plain terms a very paltry rascally original," Paine wrote.

Paine rejected reconciliation, arguing that the colonies gained no advantage from staying part of Great Britain. America could gain strength from separation, as "there is something very absurd, in supposing a continent to be perpetually governed by an island." In stirring words Paine painted the significance of independence for the colonies and the powerful vision of an American future. "We have it in our power," he wrote, "to begin the world over again."[110]

Paine's work struck a powerful chord in the colonies. With armies already maneuvering in the field, and the king having declared the colonies in rebellion, *Common Sense* pushed people to a final rejection of Britain. Randolph of Virginia said *Common Sense* contained "abuse of the British government not before seen in America in so gross and palpable forms." He added that "the public sentiment which a few weeks before had shuddered at the tremendous obstacles, with which independence was environed, overleaped every barrier."[111]

With *Common Sense* packing the energy of a coastal nor'easter, Loyalists couldn't let it pass without making an answer. But no writer on the continent could possibly compete with Paine's robust prose and stylistic innovations. Two months after Paine's writing hit the streets, James Chalmers released a pamphlet under the pseudonym Candidus, hoping upon hope that a pamphlet with the name *Plain Truth* could trump one named *Common Sense*. It was no contest. Chalmers's prose was plodding in comparison, and for all practical purposes he conceded access to the larger public sphere that Paine had so successfully reached. Chalmers argued, as so many others had done, from close interpretations of history and enlisted Hume and Montesquieu for assistance, which meant that few people in the taverns would pay much attention.[112]

Another Loyalist, the Reverend Charles Inglis, an Anglican minister in New York, called his pamphlet *Deceiver Unmasked* and accused Paine of targeting "the passions of the populace." Instead, Inglis appealed to "cool reason and judgment." It was getting a bit late for that. A group of Sons of Liberty radicals looted the shop of the printer, Samuel Loudon, and burned up to two thousand copies of Inglis's pamphlet. "It has met with its Demerit," wrote one Sons of Liberty stalwart.[113]

THE TIME HAD COME for the delegates to the Continental Congress to vote on independence.[114] On June 7, Richard Henry Lee of Virginia introduced a resolution that the colonies "are, and of right ought to be, free and independent States, that they are absolved from all allegiance to the British Crown, and that all political connection between them and the State of Great Britain is, and ought to be, totally dissolved."[115]

The declaration required the votes of nine colonies for passage, but unanimity was critical for the future of a new nation facing the greatest military power on earth. Five colonies had not yet authorized their delegates to vote for independence, but some state conventions and assemblies were meeting in the next days to consider the question anew. Dickinson and several other influential congressmen—James Wilson of Pennsylvania, Edward Rutledge of South Carolina, and Robert R. Livingston of New York—said they were sympathetic with the resolution but were not yet ready to declare for separation. So the delegates postponed further consideration of the resolution for three weeks, until July 1. In the meantime, they appointed a committee, including John Adams, Franklin, and Jefferson, to draft a declaration of independence to have ready should the resolution pass. As the calendar turned to a new month, the Continental Congress took up the question again. By then, several more of the colonies were on board with separation, freeing their delegates to vote in favor. Only New York, which was reviewing its stance, still forbade its delegation from voting for independence.

Dickinson had spent the last month preparing for one last speech urging that the colonies wait longer. He had his opportunity on the morning of July 1. The provocations by Parliament were serious, but as he had said seven months earlier, "Procrastination is Preservation. States acting on the Defensive, should study for Delays." He had added that "the best Causes have been ruin'd by an Excess of virtuous Zeal, too hastily to promote them."[116] Dickinson knew that nothing he could say would stop the inevitable approval of the resolution, but he wanted to make his objections again. The colonies had applied for assistance from France and should wait for its reply. Many domestic issues should be resolved, including the formation of state governments, a compact between the states, and a settlement of land disputes. "We should know," Dickinson told his fellow delegates, "on what Grounds We are to stand with Regard to one another." Failure to adequately prepare for independence, he said, would be to "brave the Storm in a Skiff made of Paper." The colonies needed more time. "When our Enemies," he said, "are pressing Us so vigorously, When We are in so wretched a State of Preparation, When the Sentiments & Designs of our expected Friends are so unknown to Us, I am alarm'd at this Declaration on being so vehemently presented."[117]

Listening to Dickinson, John Adams credited his adversary with the able argument of a good lawyer. "He had prepared himself apparently with great labour and ardent Zeal," Adams wrote, "and in a Speech of great Length, and with all his Eloquence, he combined together all that had been written in Pamphlets and News paper and all that had from time to time been said in Congress by himself and others."[118] When it came time for a delegate to answer Dickinson, Adams himself spoke extemporaneously, using the arguments he had been making for at least a year.

It was time to count votes, but Adams still had only nine of the thirteen colonies on his side. Four colonies were still not ready to vote in favor of independence. Pennsylvania's delegation, with Dickinson voting no, was four to three against the resolution. South Carolina also opposed it. Delaware's delegates were split one to one. And New York's delegates still had no authority to vote for independence. Rather than record a final vote, the delegates agreed to put it off for one more day, hoping that some persuasion could take place overnight.

The delegates assembled again the next morning. Once again they were ready to vote on the resolution for independence. Summoned by a messenger moving quickly on horseback, a delegate from Delaware had arrived to cast his vote in favor of independence, resolving that colony's one-to-one split of the day before. South Carolina changed its position and now voted in favor. New York, following its instructions from home, again abstained. And what of Pennsylvania? Would it still vote four to three against independence?

In his "Liberty Song," written eight years earlier, Dickinson had memorably captured the critical need for unity of purpose—that "by *uniting* we stand, by *dividing* we fall." Now, as they looked over to the Pennsylvania group, the delegates noticed that two of the seven members had not taken their seats for the vote. Robert Morris, who had voted no the previous day, was absent. So was Dickinson. With their abstentions, Pennsylvania moved from a one-vote rejection of independence to a one-vote approval.

The Farmer had stepped aside. Twelve colonies had voted for independence, and a week later New York joined them, achieving unanimity.

SIX WEEKS AFTER DELEGATES voted on the resolution, Charles Thomson, secretary of Congress, reached out to address the dismay that Dickinson felt that the patriots had abandoned him after he had led them for so long. Thomson's note was graced with the honesty and gentleness of a good friend. "There are some expressions in your letter," Thomson wrote, "which I am sorry for, because they seem to flow from a wounded spirit. Consider, I beseech you and do justice to your 'unkind countrymen.' They did not desert you. You left them."[119]

One of those "unkind countrymen," John Adams, had grown weary over the endless talk, the essay upon essay, the letter upon letter, what he expressed in frustration to Abigail Adams as "worn out with scribbling, for my Bread and my Liberty."[120] But as much as anyone, Adams should have appreciated the importance of all the resolutions and petitions. Having been a leader among the patriots since the Stamp Act crisis of a decade before, he understood the critical role of political speech of all kinds to win support. Until late June, a number of the colonies had not provided their delegation with the authority to vote for independence. Persuasion was still important, and the passage of time and the continued discussion had helped convince people, especially in middle and southern colonies, that separation was the best course to pursue.

On July 3, once the delegates had agreed to independence, Adams reflected in a letter to Abigail that all the talk and writing had served a vital purpose. "Time has been given for the whole People," he wrote, "maturely to consider the great Question of Independence and to ripen their Judgments, dissipate their Fears, and allure their hopes, by discussing it in News Papers and Pamphletts, by debating it, in Assemblies, Conventions, Committees of Safety and Inspection, in Town and County Meetings, as well as in private Conversations, so that the whole People in every Colony of the 13, have now adopted it, as their own Act.—This will cement the Union, and avoid those Heats and perhaps convulsions which might have been occasioned, by such a Declaration Six Months ago."[121] Adams expressed similar sentiments nearly four decades later, in his retirement correspondence with Jefferson. In the time before independence, he said, he was "not aware of the importance of those compositions. They all appeared to me, in the circumstances of the Country like childrens play at marbles or push pin."

But he could see more clearly now the value of the freewheeling political discussion of the final year before independence, and he was ready in effect to make a concession to the Farmer. "I was in great Error, no doubt, and am ashamed to confess it," he wrote to Jefferson, "for those things were necessary to give Popularity to our Cause, both at home and abroad."[122]

8

THE PLANTER

AFTER SPENDING THE SUMMER OF 1787 IN PHILADELPHIA, WHERE HE HAD PRESIDED OVER THE drafting of the new Constitution, George Washington left for his estate at Mount Vernon.[1] The bad roads made for an eventful trip home, for three days short of Mount Vernon his carriage and two horses fell into the Elk River as the bridge he was crossing collapsed. Befitting a man who had bested the most formidable military power on Earth, Washington was unhurt and unfazed by the rotten timbers, having dismounted from his carriage and walked ahead of it just before the bridge came down.[2]

Washington attended once again to the business of running his plantation and enjoyed his majestic views of the Potomac. But he was thinking about the challenge of steering his home state of Virginia to ratification of the Constitution, no easy matter given political divisions within the state. Two days after his arrival, Washington wrote a note to another distinguished Virginian, Patrick Henry, and enclosed a copy of the Constitution. He knew that Henry would be a key actor in the ratification convention in the state, and he feared for the worst.

Henry was an immensely popular politician who had served three consecutive one-year terms as the first governor of Virginia after independence, followed by another series of terms from 1784 to 1786. Henry had turned down an opportunity to serve in the Constitutional Convention.

A strong advocate of states' rights, he might have vehemently opposed the plan in Philadelphia to enhance the power of the national government.

Anticipating resistance from Henry, Washington suggested in his letter that the Constitution could be amended later. "I wish the Constitution which is offered had been made more perfect," he wrote, "but I sincerely believe it is the best that could be obtained at this time—and as a constitutional door is opned for amendment hereafter—the adoption of it under present circumstances of the Union is in my opinion desirable." Washington also expressed concern for the divisions in the country. "From a variety of concurring accounts it appears to me that the political concerns of this Country are, in a manner, suspended by a thread."[3]

With its wealth, population, and respected leadership, Virginia was a key to ratification. Although ratification by nine states would put the Constitution into effect for them, the new nation would be severely weakened if it went forward missing any of the bigger states. Virginia looked to be a toss-up. Washington wrote to James Madison, who had played a leading role in drafting the Constitution, expressing some hope that Henry would prove to be supportive. Madison, serving in the Confederation Congress in New York, wrote back fully aware that Henry would exert enormous influence in the Virginia convention. "Much will depend on Mr. Henry, and I am glad to find by your letter that his favorable decision on the subject may yet be hoped for," Madison wrote to Washington on October 18.[4]

The very next day, though, Henry replied to Washington that he would oppose ratification by Virginia. "I have to lament," Henry wrote, "that I cannot bring my Mind to accord with the proposed Constitution. The Concern I feel on this account, is really greater than I am able to express."[5] With Henry certain to lead the opposition, Washington and other supporters of the Constitution—the Federalists—began to rally their forces.

Madison did not wish to serve in Virginia's ratifying convention, but with the outcome looking very much in doubt, he felt the intense pressure of his friends to participate. To blunt Henry's anticipated assault on the Constitution, Washington and other Federalists urged Madison to run for election as a delegate to the Virginia convention. "Many have asked me with anxious sollicitude," Washington wrote to Madison, "if you did not mean to get into the Convention; conceiving it of indispensable necessity."[6] Madison could not match Henry's fire as an orator—no man could—but his knowledge of government and his deep involvement in the debate that took place in Philadelphia made him the best hope to answer Henry and carry Virginia to ratification.

"Mr. Henry," Madison wrote to Thomas Jefferson, "is the great adversary who will render the event precarious."[7]

A DEBATE BETWEEN Madison and Henry promised to sway minds on the floor of the Virginia convention, part of a larger dialogue that resounded all over America. The ratification debates were critical to the evolving understanding of freedom of speech and press, but not because political expression of those years pushed against the confining limits placed on it by the law of seditious libel, as it had during the protest against Britain. In fact, the people could say what they pleased during the ratification process, and not concern themselves for even a moment that they might be prosecuted for their criticism.

During ratification, Americans provided by their own actions a clear picture of what they understood to encompass their freedom of political expression.[8] Their proposed Constitution was a compact that established popular sovereignty, a government whose authority was derived and continually maintained by consent of the people. In the very act of considering their new Constitution, Americans engaged in exactly the vigorous debate that popular sovereignty required. The theory of their new government made political discussion a civic duty, and the people embraced it in every medium, including the streets, the newspapers, and the convention halls. If the meaning of the freedom of speech and press is derived from the understanding that the founding generation had before and during ratification, then it was clear that free and open debate of the most vigorous kind was not only acceptable—it was also the expectation.

After they enlarged the public sphere of expression during their troubles with Britain, the ratification process represented the final destination of their journey, the full-throated voice of an entire people engaged in deciding the powers and limitations of their own government. It was a government in which sovereignty, the ultimate power, lay with them and not with public officials. The founding generation understood that popular sovereignty required self-governance, that self-governance required broad freedoms of political expression, and that political expression subject to harsh penalties would only impoverish them all. During the ratification period, they operated in a world in which political speech was sometimes smart and oftentimes scathing. If the process was messy, it was still better to take their own measure of public men than to live under the crushing weight of rulers whose decisions could suffer no challenge.

Participation in public affairs had moved from the core of social and political elites outward to embrace many segments of society. While essays and pamphlets provided a heavy crossfire about legal rights, colonial leaders enlisted masses of people with more inherently democratic forms of expression. Cheap newspapers spread all kinds of writings, taverns became havens for impromptu debates, and Liberty Trees and public streets became meeting places for speeches and political theater. Meanwhile, there was an unending stream of poems, songs, and satire.

The people's voice became critical to the protests against Britain and brought the colonies to support separation. There was no turning back, for public participation and public opinion became central to the legitimacy of republican institutions, a requirement for elected representatives to push their ideas forward. Some men in America's political elite mistrusted democratic urges. But they competed at every opportunity to turn opinion to their side.[9] Nothing emphasized that fact of political life with more clarity than the process of ratification of the Constitution. When John Adams circulated a volume defending a strong central government in 1787, Madison commented to Jefferson that it would "become a powerful engine in forming the public opinion."[10] Archibald Stuart, who would become a delegate to the Virginia convention, noted of those who debated the Constitution that "We are all contending for popular applause."[11]

The following year, at the New York ratifying convention, Alexander Hamilton argued that public opinion exerted a major influence over government, especially republican ones. "All governments, even the most despotic, depend, in a great degree, on opinion," said Hamilton. "In free republics, it is most peculiarly the case: In these, the will of the people makes the essential principle of the government; and the laws which control the community, receive their tone and spirit from the public wishes."[12]

Political leaders and common citizens produced a vast trove of writings, speeches, articles, and letters during the ratification period in a massive effort to move public opinion. After the ratification process was nearly done, Francis Hopkinson wrote to Thomas Jefferson with an assessment of the debate throughout the country. "Since the world began, I believe no Question has ever been more repeatedly & strictly scrutenized or more fairly & freely argued, than this proposed Constitution," Hopkinson wrote.[13]

A burgeoning newspaper business carried much of the discussion. On the eve of independence, forty-two newspapers were published in the colonies.[14] By ratification eleven years later, the industry had swelled to about ninety-five papers, and they devoted much of their space to everything from news to letters to long essays. In the first two months after the Philadelphia convention ended, at least seventy-five papers printed the text of the Constitution.[15] In fact, when the Pennsylvania Assembly agreed to pay for printing the Constitution in English and German for distribution throughout the state, one legislator objected to the public expense because it had already been printed in so many handbills and almanacs.[16]

As the country turned to ratification, newspaper editors filled their pages with a broad array of writings. "The Newspapers in the middle & Northern States begin to teem with controversial publications," Madison wrote just a month after the Constitutional Convention ended.[17] Some articles were reprinted in as many as fifty papers.[18] Most of the eighty-five essays in the series that became *The Federalist,* written in support of the Constitution by "Publius"—Madison, Hamilton, and John Jay—were first printed in New York papers between October 27, 1787, and May 28, 1788. They were aimed at influencing New Yorkers to support the Constitution and elect Federalists to the state ratifying convention. The essays proved so powerful that they were quickly collected in book form and distributed far and wide.[19]

The public debate on the Constitution took many forms. Broadsides and pamphlets papered the land. Multitudes of private letters laid out the views of their authors, many of them delegates to the conventions and others in quiet private life. People gathered to hear speeches, voted for the delegates to represent them at the conventions, and took seats in the galleries to watch the debate. It was a nation consumed in a discussion of its future.

It was also a nation confident that it could carry on its discussion without fear of prosecutions for seditious libel. No matter what political faction controlled a state or its convention, the opposition understood that it was free to engage in raucous debate with whatever dose of emotion or erudition it pleased. Some opponents of the Constitution burned copies in protest, while others burned the effigies of prominent leaders like James Wilson, Thomas McKean, and Elbridge Gerry.[20] As for the newspapers, an ongoing "paper war" included "virulence, ferocity, and scurrility," but many people viewed it "as a reflection of the freedom that Americans enjoyed."[21]

The deluge of political material rained coins on printers throughout the country. One of them exulted over his good fortune by publishing "The News-Mongers' Song" in an Albany paper.[22] It struck a chord among fellow publishers who were likewise enjoying all the additional business, for it was reprinted fourteen times in seven weeks and even instigated a parody.[23] One verse of the song rejoiced in the profits.

> *Much joy, brother printers! The day is our own, A time like the present*
> *sure never was known:*
> *Predictions are making—predictions fulfil,*
> *All nature seems proud to bring grist to our mill.*

In this dreamy state of affairs for printers, they created a virtuous cycle in which more commentary led to more responses and ultimately to more readers for the news and opinion of the day.

FOR PATRICK HENRY, the new Constitution was no dreamy state of affairs. He strongly opposed it. But unlike other leaders in the ratification debate, he wrote very little in opposition to ratification, relying instead on his oratorical gifts.

In Henry's youth, there was little to suggest that he would make a significant contribution to political life. Born in 1736 the son of a planter, Henry had little formal schooling for a boy of his station, and far less than other first-rank contemporaries like Dickinson, Madison, and Jefferson. He left common school at the age of ten and then took lessons from his father in math, Latin, and Greek. Henry never attended college, but he read on his own and absorbed British and Western history and the tenets of Christian faith. He formed a worldview that government required virtuous men to act selflessly and in the best interest of society. But man was fallible, and public officials would naturally attempt to use their power to subjugate others. Henry deeply distrusted the concentration of power.[24]

His father saw a future for Patrick as a merchant. While other sons of planters went off to a prestigious college, Patrick clerked in a local store when he was fifteen. A few years later, his father set up Patrick and his brother William in a country store of their own, even buying the inventory of goods for them to sell. In those days, store owners built their businesses by extending generous credit to farmers who were awaiting the next big tobacco crop, a strategy that could cripple a store owner if many farmers defaulted. That is exactly what happened with the Henry brothers, who lasted just a year in business.[25]

A failed businessman at eighteen, Patrick enjoyed a quick boost in his fortunes when he married sixteen-year-old Sarah Shelton, who came from a wealthy landowning family a few miles from his home. He immediately took possession of a three-hundred-acre farm as a dowry, and with it six slaves. Henry joined the wealthy Virginia planters in growing tobacco largely for markets in Europe. He and Sarah had their first of six children within a year—a brood that grew with eleven additional children after Sarah died and Henry married again. But his farmhouse burned a few years after his wedding, and he moved his family to the overseer's cabin. Attempting to diversify his income, he opened another country store, but once again his shop failed. At twenty-three, needing to support his family, he began work in the tavern owned by his father-in-law across from the courthouse in Hanover, serving drinks and providing entertainment by playing his violin. He wore work clothes and often went barefoot. It was there that he met Jefferson, who was beginning to take classes at the College of William and Mary in Williamsburg.[26] "His manners had something of coarseness in them; his passion was music, dancing, and pleasantry," Jefferson later recalled. "He excelled in the latter, and it attached everyone to him."[27]

After a winter of bar keeping, Henry set out with yet another plan— to combine farming and law, as so many wealthy planters had done in Virginia. Instead of going to school, though, Henry set out to study law on his own, a challenge he completed in as little as six weeks. According to Jefferson, who spoke sometime afterward with the examiners, one of them refused to sign Henry's license and two others did so while "acknowledging he was very ignorant of the law, but that they perceived him to be a young man of genius, and did not doubt that he would soon qualify himself." Henry had his license to practice law, although he lacked even the basic knowledge of how to file a plea or make a motion.[28]

Through his mid-twenties, Henry looked to the world like an amiable enough character who was unlikely to flourish in life. If he had failed at running a country store, if he had failed at farming, if he had failed a second time at running a store and then had barely passed his law examination, it seemed doubtful that success would ever creep up from behind and catch him by surprise. That finally happened in 1763, though, when he took on a case called the "Parson's Cause." The Anglican Church was the established church in Virginia, and the colony paid the clergy in tobacco that they then sold to support themselves. When poor harvests crimped the supply of tobacco and sent its price soaring, the clergy still received the same amount of tobacco, which was worth much more. Meanwhile, farmers suffered with a much smaller crop. So the House of Burgesses passed two laws that changed the payment from tobacco to cash. After the clergy complained about the law, the King's Privy Council in London struck it down, and the Reverend James Maury followed with a lawsuit against the colony to recover back pay for the difference between the cash salary and the actual price of tobacco. Henry represented the county in its attempt to reduce the amount of back pay owed to Maury.

The case was a coming-out party for the young Henry, who discovered the combination of theme and delivery that would quickly elevate him from obscurity to the top rank of colonial patriots. His argument to the jury brought to the fore his exceptional speaking skills, marked by a strong and modulating voice and an ability to make his case with passion. Perhaps influenced by some of the evangelical preachers of the time, Henry grafted some of their methods of direct emotional appeals into speeches about law and politics. And, just as important, he married his oratorical skill to a theme that would resonate all over the colonies for decades. He attacked the clergy for elevating their own interests over those of the people they served, and he attacked the king himself for overturning a law passed by the popular assembly—the king "degenerates into a tyrant, and forfeits all right to his subjects' obedience." Even as Maury's lawyer complained that Henry had "spoken treason," his message convinced the jury, which returned just one penny in damages to Maury.[29]

Two years before the Stamp Act roiled the colonies, Henry had developed a narrative about overbearing power that he hammered again and again as the relationship deteriorated between England and the colonies. Soon enough, he would carry that narrative to a national stage.

VOTERS WHO WERE PLEASED by Henry's defense of their tax money voted him to the House of Burgesses in 1765. His triumphs at the polls and in the dispute over ministers' pay erased his early failures and launched him into the realm of the leading Virginia politicians. Henry never lacked for confidence, nor did he believe in quietly marking time behind more senior leaders.

No sooner had Henry reached Williamsburg for the start of his service than word came that Parliament had passed the Stamp Act. The burgesses were surely unhappy but finished their business quickly, and then most of them left town for the summer. Henry saw his opening. The king's overturning of the assembly's laws on clergy pay and the passage of the Stamp Act were woven of the same cloth, he thought, a violation of the rights of the colonists as Englishmen. He already had a winning argument, and now he pressed it to his new colleagues in the House of Burgesses with a series of resolutions that directly challenged the king and Parliament. Only the people's representatives could decide the taxes they would pay, a right that was "the Distinguishing Characteristic of British FREEDOM."[30]

With the Virginia Resolves, Henry began to secure his reputation as a leading provocateur against the British. He went to the First Continental Congress in 1774, and John Adams remembered that Henry understood even then that the colonies and Britain were close to the breaking point. Adams said that "there was not one member, except Patrick Henry, who appeared to me sensible of the Precipice, or rather the Pinnacle on which he stood, and had candour and courage enough to acknowledge it."[31]

In the House of Burgesses in March 1775, less than a month before the clash at Lexington and Concord, Henry proposed that Virginia arm itself for what he saw as an inevitable clash with Britain. What Henry actually said is shrouded in mystery, for his first biographer reconstructed his speech decades later. Henry supposedly ended his speech—and it did sound like Henry in all his oratorical passion—with the famous words, "I know not what course others may take; but as for me, give me liberty or give me death!" His reputation as a patriot greatly enhanced, Henry became the first postcolonial governor of Virginia.

BOTH PATRIOTS AND BOTH VIRGINIANS, Patrick Henry and James Madison were in most other ways polar opposites. Where Henry was a brilliant orator, Madison was shy and spoke in so low a voice that people could barely hear him. Where Henry satisfied himself with a thin veneer of learning, Madison bore ceaselessly into the core of things, making himself the most learned man on politics of his time. Where Henry wrote little, Madison filled many volumes with his letters and essays.

Born in 1751 on a plantation that would become known as Montpelier, Madison found a strong mentor at college who helped steer his intellectual development. Although brought up in the Anglican Church, the established church of Virginia, the young Madison enrolled at the College of New Jersey (now Princeton University), a hotbed of dissenting Protestantism. John Witherspoon, a leading Presbyterian minister from Scotland, had recently arrived as the new president of the college. Witherspoon strongly opposed church establishments as well as British attempts to set up an Anglican bishop in the colonies. Witherspoon joined the patriot cause in America, becoming a delegate to the Continental Congress from New Jersey and a signatory of the Declaration of Independence.[32]

Madison graduated in two years instead of the usual three, but he stayed on to continue studying with Witherspoon. He immersed himself in the study of English history, especially the conflict between Parliament and the king that culminated in the English Bill of Rights of 1689.[33] Madison impressed Witherspoon not only with his intelligence but also with his piercing focus on academics. "His only relaxation from study," said Witherspoon, "consisted in walking and conversation."[34]

Madison was a young man best suited to a quiet life, and on his homecoming to Montpelier, he wrote to William Bradford, a close college friend in Philadelphia, that he had returned "into my Native land and into the possession of my customary enjoyments Solitude and Contemplation."[35] But the world was changing in a way that summoned him from the comforts of reflection to use his intellectual gifts for a larger purpose. Awakening to the idea of public engagement, Madison wrote to Bradford in January 1774 congratulating him on "your heroic proceedings in Philada. with regard to the Tea." Philadelphia had passed resolutions against the tea duty, and an assembly of six thousand people had turned away a ship filled with tea. "Political Contests are necessary some-times as well as military to . . . instruct in the Art of defending Liberty and property," Madison wrote to Bradford.[36]

Closer to home, Madison had been troubled by the persecution of religious minorities in neighboring Culpeper County, Virginia. Some Baptist ministers had been jailed for preaching and for publishing reli-gious material without prior approval of the Anglican elders. With With-erspoon's teachings about religious liberty echoing in his mind, Madison told Bradford that he had protested the arrests. "I have squabbled and scolded abused and ridiculed so long about it, to so little purpose that I am without common patience," he wrote, asking his friend to "pray for Liberty of Conscience to revive among us." Madison ruminated with Bradford about the benefits of religious liberty over a system in which one faith was favored. As he wrote to Bradford, "Ecclesiastical Establishments tend to great ignorance and Corruption all of which facilitate the Execu-tion of mischievous Projects."[37]

At the age of twenty-five, Madison was elected to the Virginia con-vention in 1776 and immediately made a lasting impact on religious lib-erty. The convention was drafting a declaration of rights, and one article used the word "toleration" to describe the protection of religious practice. Madison thought "toleration" was a term that patronized minority believ-ers and did not convey the idea of equality. Instead, he drafted and suc-cessfully substituted the more egalitarian phrase that "all men are equally entitled to the full and free exercise of religion, according to the dictates of conscience." Free exercise became a model for protecting religious liberty in the Bill of Rights more than a decade later.[38] In the next decade, Madi-son guided Jefferson's Bill for Religious Freedom into law, disestablishing the Anglican Church as the church of Virginia and guaranteeing religious freedom for all Virginians.[39]

When Madison went to the Continental Congress in 1779, he began to see the critical weaknesses of the Articles of Confederation, which would shape his thinking about a new form of government for America. The Articles had created a league of sovereign states under a confedera-tion government, an arrangement so weak that the country struggled to accomplish basic functions. Having suffered from the concentration of British power, Americans had given their central government little power under the Articles. Among other deficiencies, there was no power to tax, no legitimate currency, and no effective way to respond to foreign aggression.

Ever the student, Madison set out on a deep study of the history of confederacies. He enlisted Jefferson in Paris to send him every treatise he could find on the government of confederacies. In his library at Montpelier, looking out at the Blue Ridge Mountains in the distance, Madison made many pages of detailed notes early in 1786 that he called *Notes on Ancient and Modern Confederacies,* listing their characteristics and "vices," or defects. A year later, he went at it again, this time with extended notes on the *Vices of the Political System of the United States,* reflecting both the weakness of the Articles as well as the vices of the various state governments. Madison used his notes during the debates at the Constitutional Convention and the Virginia ratifying convention, and for his *Federalist* essays. Ultimately, Madison's central conclusion was that the American system suffered from the lack of a strong central government.[40] "The want of some such provision seems to have been mortal to the antient Confederacies, and to be the disease of the modern," Madison wrote to Jefferson.[41]

Madison's careful study prepared him for the convention in Philadelphia in the summer of 1787. The mission of the delegates was to amend the Articles of Confederation. Madison and some others, though, immediately put into place a more ambitious agenda—scrapping the Articles entirely and writing a new constitution. Madison's Virginia Plan, a new outline of government submitted at the start of the convention, set the convention on its course. What emerged at the end was a strong national government with three branches, the power to tax, raise an army, and legislate on a wide variety of issues of national concern. Edmund Randolph and George Mason of Virginia and Elbridge Gerry of Massachusetts refused to sign, concerned about the concentration of power in a new federal government and the absence of a bill of rights.

Henry had not attended the convention in Philadelphia. Trying to recruit him, Governor Edmund Randolph had written to Henry that "every day dawns with perils to the United States. To whom, then, can they resort for assistance with firmer expectation, than to those who first kindled the Revolution?" Henry fervently believed in the principles of the Revolution—did the colonies not rebel against a powerful central government and the abuses of liberty that inevitably flowed from it? He supported a structure in which most of the power was held by the individual states, not a central government. And Henry feared that the powerful northern states would control a new federal government to the detriment of states like Virginia. Henry, though, retired to his plantation and declined the offer to go to Philadelphia, without giving a reason.[42]

Madison feared the worst when he heard of Henry's refusal to serve at the Constitutional Convention. As he wrote to Governor Randolph, Henry's refusal "to join in the task of revising the Confederation is ominous."[43]

WITH THE PROPOSED CONSTITUTION laying out a stronger central government that he thought dangerous, Henry was not going to miss the Virginia ratifying convention. Both Madison and Henry girded for a major fight. As they took the reins of the two factions in Virginia, there was one thing that neither had to worry about—prosecutions for seditious libel, even though the crime still existed in the common law. Twelve of the thirteen original states, including Virginia, had adopted the English common law system.[44] But by 1787 seditious libel was all but a dead letter in practice, a relic that had met with overwhelming popular rejection.

Freedom of expression had taken a step backward during the years of the most intense crisis with Britain. In the years right before independence, acts of intimidation and outright violence against some Loyalist writers and printers had chilled some of the voices criticizing the patriot cause (see chapter 7). And after the bloody conflict between the colonies and Britain commenced, the Continental Congress recommended in 1776 that states pass laws to prevent people from being "deceived and drawn into erroneous opinions respecting the American cause." All of the states enacted laws punishing anti-patriot speech or requiring loyalty oaths, some focusing on derogatory comments about Congress, state legislatures, or the Continental currency. Virginia in 1776 passed a law punishing speech by making it illegal to utter "any word" defending the king or Parliament or to talk to people to "persuade them to return to a dependence upon the crown of Great Britain."[45] These repressive laws served as a brake on the broader movement toward freedom of thought, but they were understandable given the circumstances. Those who passed such laws were engaged in a revolt that amounted to an act of treason against Britain, they had only a meager military force to throw against the greatest army in the world, and they faced the likelihood of severe

punishment if Britain prevailed in the conflict. Under those circumstances, they could think that clamping down on dissent was a reasonable
act of self-preservation.

In other ways, though, the foundation was strengthening for freedom
of expression. Oddly, in light of the laws restricting anti-patriot speech,
the states simultaneously protected the press in their most fundamental
law. Their concern focused on the press most of all because it was printed
material, rather than spoken words, that had been the target of British
repression in decades past. Nine of the eleven states that adopted constitutions during the Revolutionary War included a clause protecting freedom
of the press. Only Pennsylvania protected freedom of speech.[46] Virginia
enacted the first press clause in 1776 in the Virginia Declaration of Rights,
drafted by George Mason—"That the freedom of the Press is one of the
greatest bulwarks of liberty, and can never be restrained but by despotick
Governments." Since so many states enshrined it as a protected right,
freedom of the press represented a preeminent value in America. These
declarations, though, were terse and vague, and the wording typically fell
some degrees short of a ringing prohibition. If the clauses were meant to
do away with seditious libel, the lawmakers did not explicitly say so.[47]

For a number of years, too, the intellectual foundation supporting freedom of expression had been growing stronger through the ac-
cumulated writings of libertarian political thinkers. Their arguments
relentlessly chipped away at seditious libel. In 1770, the Reverend Philip
Furneaux attacked the common law restrictions on speech about religious
matters. Blasphemous libel was a cousin to seditious libel, protecting the
good name of religion. Furneaux rejected the idea that a speaker could
be punished simply because of the bad tendency of words to cause a disturbance. Only overt acts—bad deeds—should be subject to punishment.
Opinions alone did not disturb the public peace, and should be left alone.[48]

Most significantly, libertarian writers began linking the freedom of
speech and press to democratic self-governance. An anonymous writer
going by the name Centinel wrote a series of essays in the *Massachusetts
Spy* in 1771 defending the freedom of the press. Referring to an unnamed
lawyer who had passed along his views to him, Centinel said that long ago
only libels of private persons were recognized and that criminal libel was
"unknown to the principles of a free constitution." The reason, he said,
"seems to be founded on the maxims of a free government. It supposes

that rulers are servants to the people, and that that people, for whom they were *created*, had a right to thus call them to account." In those few lines, Centinel had anchored the freedom of political expression to budding ideas in America about popular sovereignty—that citizens govern themselves and enjoy the right to criticize those who serve them in office.[49]

In 1775, James Burgh, a British politician, wrote in his influential *Political Disquisitions* of the function of free speech in checking the bad conduct of officials. He argued that "all history shews the necessity, in order to the preservation of liberty, of every subject's having a watchful eye on the conduct of Kings, Ministers, and Parliament, and of every subject's being not only secured, but encouraged in alarming his fellow-subjects on occasion of every attempt upon public liberty." He added that if an official "is falsely accused, he has only to clear his character, and he appears in a fairer light than before."[50] A year later, Jeremy Bentham extended the argument. He argued for a broad immunity for political speech, noting that political freedom could be measured in large part by how far "malcontents may communicate their sentiments, concert their plans, and practice every mode of opposition short of actual revolt, before the executive power can be legally justified in disturbing them."[51]

MANY DELEGATES TO THE Constitutional Convention were still riding their horses or coaches home from Philadelphia as robust debate began over their handiwork. A writer named Tar and Feathers, as nasty as he could be, confirmed that the arguments over the Constitution would engage sharp elbows as well as sharp minds. Nine days after the convention adjourned in September 1787, an anonymous writer in the *Freeman's Journal* in Philadelphia criticized some provisions of the Constitution. It took only two days for another writer to post a sharp reply in the *Independent Gazetteer* proclaiming the Constitution to be "a masterpiece in politics." Ominously, he warned that the critic should find another subject to write about "if he wishes to escape the just resentment of an incensed people, who perhaps may honor him with a coat of TAR and FEATHERS." The next day brought a writer in the *Gazetteer* calling himself "Fair Play," criticizing the previous author for his threats—"Tar and feathers, I believe, never made a convert to any system whatever."[52]

Fair Play failed to dissuade writers from an outpouring of caustic words. The debate over ratification was sometimes malicious, hardly a surprise for a founding generation whose political expression traced its genetic code to the raucous press attacks against Britain during the 1760s. There could hardly be surprise at "the 'paper war' that developed and the virulence, ferocity, and scurrility with which it was fought."[53]

Both sides used their political muscle to get the upper hand, and the Federalists enjoyed a considerable advantage in the newspapers that supported their position. Of the ninety-five or so newspapers publishing at the time, historian Jürgen Heideking found that only twenty-one were impartial, publishing on both sides of the debate. Fifty-three papers were either strongly or moderately Federalist in their selection of articles, compared to just eight that were Anti-Federalist—that is, opposing ratification of the Constitution.[54]

Eleazer Oswald was perhaps the most effective Anti-Federalist printer, and off his press came some of the most important writings attacking the Constitution. He started on October 2 in auspicious fashion, printing as a broadside and then in his paper an address against the Constitution signed by many members of the Pennsylvania General Assembly. Within five weeks, the address appeared twelve times in Pennsylvania and sixteen times outside the state. Oswald wasn't finished. In December, after Pennsylvania ratified the Constitution, he printed the *Dissent of the Minority,* whose importance lay in its call for amendments to the Constitution. Anti-Federalists saw the *Dissent* as an opportunity to influence other ratifying conventions that would soon debate the Constitution. It was reprinted in thirteen papers, with the *Pennsylvania Gazette* remarking that "zealous opposers of the constitution" had distributed the report "even into the western country of Georgia" in search of citizens to persuade.[55]

Next off Oswald's press was a series of eighteen essays by an Anti-Federalist writer named Centinel. His fierce attack on the Constitution, full of personal invective against the framers, portrayed a strong national government that stole away power held by the states. A "despotic aristocracy," he said, would run the government. The essays enjoyed a long life in many newspaper reprints, as well as in broadside and pamphlet form, with the first essay alone reprinted in nineteen papers.[56]

The essays kept coming. Cato wrote seven articles against the Constitution in the *New York Journal.* Then came Brutus with his sixteen essays against the Constitution, in turn bringing out a battalion of Federalist writers in response as Madison worried that Brutus "strikes at the foundation [of the Constitution]."[57] And then came *Letters from the Federal Farmer,* an Anti-Federalist pamphlet of forty pages distributed in Pennsylvania, New York, Connecticut, and elsewhere.[58]

Countless letters and essays in favor of ratification flew around the states as well, none so influential as *The Federalist.* Trying to counter Henry and the Anti-Federalist surge in Virginia, Madison sent many of the essays to George Washington and requested that he circulate them there. Madison coyly hinted that he was one of three authors. "You will recognize one of the pens concerned in the task," he wrote. Washington had the essays printed in Richmond, as the battle for the hearts and minds of the people of Virginia pointed forward to the state's ratifying convention.[59]

VIRGINIA PROMISED TO BE a major battleground for ratification. In another letter to George Washington in December, Madison explained how he saw the various factions in Virginia. He thought there were three groups; the first being those who favored adoption of the Constitution as proposed. The second faction, he thought, also favored the Constitution but only with the inclusion of certain amendments—"a few additional Guards in favor of the Rights of the States and of the people." And in the third group were those, led by Henry, who might also approve of the Constitution with amendments but whose changes would "strike at the essence of the System" in a way that would in effect keep the existing Confederation or result in "a partition of the Union into several Confederacies."[60]

Henry expected to have several major figures in Virginia politics on his side. As governor of Virginia and a framer at the convention in Philadelphia, Edmund Randolph had views that would tip the scales more heavily than most delegates. Randolph had favored creation of a strong federal government, but he had grown increasingly concerned about protecting the vital concerns of Virginia, an agrarian state compared to the relatively more urban northern states. Randolph wanted the state ratifying conventions to do more than vote the Constitution up or down as a whole; he made a motion to permit the conventions to suggest amendments to the Constitution and then convene a second constitutional convention to consider them. When his proposal was defeated, Randolph refused to sign the Constitution, but he left his options open to support the Constitution during the ratification process.[61]

On his return to Virginia, Randolph remained silent on his views until December, when he finally circulated a pamphlet that was reprinted in newspapers throughout Virginia. Randolph favored a second convention to consider amendments, but in his next-to-last paragraph he said that if he lost that fight he would nonetheless "accept the constitution."[62] A relieved Madison wrote to Randolph that he had read his essay "with pleasure" because in Virginia those in opposition "notoriously meditate either a dissolution of the Union, or protracting it by patching up the Articles of Confederation." Patrick Henry, he said, was "driving at a Southern Confederacy." He argued that a second constitutional convention would be "infinitely precarious" as factions would fight for their specific agendas and overwhelm the forces binding them together—the "local sacrifices necessary to keep the States together, can never be expected to co-incide again."[63]

George Mason, on the other hand, did not appear to be as accommodating as Randolph. He demanded that the delegates in Philadelphia draft a bill of rights to protect the people from abuses of power.[64] Mason wrote out his objections to the Constitution and sent them to Washington on October 7. He noted that his complaints were relatively few but that "some of them are capital ones." Worried that Mason's statement would turn many Virginia voters against the Constitution, Washington responded by circulating to newspapers the strongly pro-Constitution speech of October 6 by James Wilson, one of the most influential delegates to the Constitutional Convention.[65] Wilson addressed the absence of a bill of rights by arguing that congressional authority came solely from "the positive grant expressed in the instrument of union," and that all other power was reserved to the people. Because the Constitution gave to Congress no enumerated power over the press, for example, it was devoid of any authority to legislate on matters affecting press freedom. In fact, said Wilson, a bill of rights declaring freedom of the press "might have been construed to imply that some degree of power was given, since we undertook to define its extent."[66]

Opponents of the Constitution held the absence of a bill of rights as a weapon to defeat the Constitution. Even Jefferson, Madison's ideological friend, wrote from France to decry the failure to protect the liberties of the people, including freedom of religion and the press. As Jefferson argued, "A bill of rights is what the people are entitled to against every government on earth, general or particular, & what no just government should refuse, or rest on inference."[67]

The notes between Madison and Jefferson were part of a deluge of letters written throughout America during ratification, comprising one of the most important means of political speech used to influence the conventions. Madison authored about 160 letters in a little over two years to December 1789. Washington wrote more than 137 letters in the period between September 1787 and March 1789 as he tried to orchestrate ratification.[68]

The writing of letters crossed political spheres and social class, and included the rough compositions of people living far from the cities. Some writers were prolific with their correspondence. Many letters, both signed and anonymous, were sent to newspapers for publication in an attempt to set out the case for or against the Constitution. Private correspondence, though usually hidden from public view, proved as vital in the battle to win public opinion. But writers could not assume that their thoughts would remain private. Some correspondence, meant to be confidential, ended up printed in newspapers, and given the lack of security of the mail service, some letters were stolen or opened to satisfy curious eyes.[69]

Outside of speaking in person, letters served as the best way for political leaders to communicate with each other. Those who wrote most frequently and to a broad array of people were the nerve centers for exchanging intelligence among a much larger community, a critical function for spreading ideas and strategy. Madison and Henry Knox, both in New York, received intelligence from informants in Boston on developments in the Massachusetts convention, and in turn passed the information on to others. They helped prepare both sides for the ratification battle about to begin in Virginia.[70]

JOHN MARSHALL PROPOSED in October 1787 that the General Assembly call a convention so that the people would have the Constitution "for their free and ample discussion." Marshall understood that only with robust political speech could the people fully examine the new compact.[71]

Henry began campaigning hard with a strong message—that the Constitution concentrated too much power in the national government, and abuses of individual rights would follow. Letters flew back and forth as partisans passed on their sightings of Henry and as each side tried to assess the strength of the other. Edward Carrington, for one, campaigned in favor of the Constitution in three counties just south of the James River in the worst of February weather—"the state of the ice is such as renders the passage of the River unsafe." Carrington wrote to Madison that he had traveled through "the Neighbourhood of Mr. Henry, and I find his politics to have been so industriously propagated, that the people are much disposed to be his blind followers."[72] On the same day, Carrington also wrote to Henry Knox, saying he was traveling "in the Midst of Mr. Henries influence, and I find he has pretty well prepared the people for being his blind followers—his demagogues are loud in their clamours against the Constitution, professing a determination to reject unless amendments can be had even at the hazard of [Virginia's] standing alone."[73] Madison heard from John Blair Smith that Henry's speeches to his constituents were "gross & scandalous misrepresentations of the New-Constitution," and that he had written letters to influential people in Kentucky. "It grieves me to see such great natural talents abused to guilty purposes," Smith wrote.[74]

With Henry gaining strength, supporters of the Constitution in Virginia urged Madison to run for a seat at the convention from Orange County. His neighbors were divided in their sentiments and Madison's election was certainly not guaranteed, so friends pressed him to return from New York to campaign.[75] "You must come in," Governor Randolph wrote to him on January 3. "Some people in Orange are opposed to your politicks."[76] James Gordon Jr. wrote that "it is incumbent on you with out delay, to repair to this state; as the loss of the constitution in this state may involve consequences the most alarming to every citizen of America."[77] Even Madison's father implored his presence, saying that "there are some who suspends their opinion till they see you, & wish for an explanation, others wish you not to come, & will endeavor to shut you out of the Convention, the better to carry their point."[78]

Madison left New York around March 4, but the "badness of the roads & some other delays retarded the completion of my journey" until March 23. The next day, which was set for the elections, Madison appeared at the county courthouse and "for the first time in my life" delivered a "harangue of some length in the open air on a very windy day." Madison and James Gordon were elected to represent the county at the ratifying convention. "It is very probable that a very different event would have taken place as to myself if the efforts of my friends had not been seconded by my presence," Madison wrote.[79]

AS MADISON LEFT FOR VIRGINIA, loud public celebrations in states that had already approved the Constitution injected another expressive element into the politics of ratification. Once again, supporters of the Constitution showed that they had learned the lessons of a few decades earlier, when the Sons of Liberty had expanded the public sphere and energized political speech by making a spectacle out of street demonstrations.

As states ratified the Constitution, public festivals swept huge numbers of people into the political arena and whipped up enthusiasm among supporters. The impact of the festivals rippled far beyond the cities in which they were held, for they were reported in letters and newspapers around the country and most likely impressed many uncommitted citizens that support was swelling for ratification. As one writer described the celebration in Boston in February, "It will tend to convince the country people more, than the most elegant reasoning."[80]

In Maryland, supporters of the Constitution held daylong festivities after the state ratified the Constitution. It was a colorful spectacle meant not just for them but also for people in other states. At nine in the morning on May 1, a cannon blast signaled the start of a long procession of three thousand people through the streets of Baltimore. People marched by occupation, in many cases dressed in their work clothes and carrying the tools of their trade. First came farmers with a plow, followed by millers, inspectors of flour, and millstone makers. Behind them were the butchers, bakers, brewers, distillers, blacksmiths, nailers, carpenters, painters, glaziers, glassmakers, masons, stonecutters, cabinetmakers, carriage makers, coppers, tanners, shoemakers, saddlers, harness makers, hatters, stay makers, comb makers, barbers, silversmiths, watchmakers, coppersmiths, plumbers, tallow handlers, printers, physicians, ministers, judges, and, finally, lawyers. When the marchers arrived at Federal Hill overlooking Baltimore harbor, a feast was awaiting them.[81] It included 1,025 pounds of beef, 560 pounds of ham, 22 ox tongues, and 800 loaves of bread, along with 240 gallons of cider plus beer and peach schnapps.[82]

The organizers understood the meaning of symbols. One display was a tower constructed of wood with the number thirteen carried through to every detail as a theme to represent the number of states in the nation—thirteen floors, spires, arches, and so on. They also constructed a ship, the *Federalist,* "completely officered and manned, rigged and sailed

& borne on a carriage drawn by horses." To celebrate Maryland becoming the seventh state to ratify, the ship showed its seven sails on the top of Federal Hill.[83]

Supporters of the Constitution did not keep such a spectacle to themselves, not when it promised to persuade others. Twenty-two newspapers around the country reprinted the *Maryland Journal*'s description of the event.[84]

BY HORSE AND BY STAGECOACH, delegates to the ratifying convention made the arduous trek to Richmond. With the convention called for Monday, June 2, and hundreds of delegates and onlookers due to attend, the city buzzed over the weekend with political talk as people arrived and filled the taverns and inns.

Designated the state capital during the war nine years earlier, Richmond had none of the charm of Williamsburg, the former seat of government, which was near the coast and considered vulnerable to British attack. Richmond, with a population of about four thousand, including slaves, had about four hundred modest wood houses, often with an outside kitchen and smokehouse. The town was a busy inland port just below the falls of the James River, the farthest point that boats could navigate inland. Its role as state capital and regional commercial center attracted wealthy planters as well as rough sailors and frontiersmen. The town offered a rural ambience, with dirt roads that turned to thick mud and hogs and goats roaming the streets. The taverns entertained men whose gambling and drinking often brought on fights that continued out in the street.[85]

To that combustible mix the ratifying convention attracted many spectators who came to Richmond to watch the debate from the public gallery. "Richmond is exceedingly crowded, & many of no principle & desperate Fortunes are attending there," wrote one spectator, who added that there were a "prodigious number of People from all parts of the Country, a great proportion of them Anti Federalists, & clamorous in their opposition out of Doors, ready to pursue any desperate step countenanced by their party within the House."[86]

In Richmond and elsewhere, attendance overflowed the available seats, more evidence of the expanding public sphere of political speech. When daily sessions ended people spilled out into the streets to debate among themselves. In Boston, "the gallerys are so crowded, that in order to get in you must be there an hour before the seting of the Convention," wrote one observer.[87] Ezra Stiles wrote of the Connecticut convention that there was "a great conflux of gentlemen from all parts of the state to attend and hear the deliberations."[88]

The delegates in Richmond convened that Monday at the statehouse, but to accommodate the delegates and spectators, they decided to hold their sessions the following days at a larger building. The Virginia convention promised a formidable meeting of political minds, one with few equals in the founding period or after. Henry was there arguing against the Constitution, as was George Mason, principal author of the Virginia Constitution and the Virginia Declaration of Rights. Edmund Randolph, the governor, had also opposed the Constitution in Philadelphia. Madison was there, and Edmund Pendleton, the president of the state's high court of chancery and supreme court of appeals. So, too, were James Monroe, the future president, and John Marshall, the future chief justice of the United States.[89]

With all the intellectual firepower assembled in Richmond, the Virginians had arrived at their convention with the potential to exert a strong influence on the other states. Nine states were required for ratification. By the start of the convention on June 2, eight were already aboard, with South Carolina the latest to approve on May 23. Rhode Island, which had been alone in refusing to participate in the Constitutional Convention, had rejected the Constitution in a referendum on March 24. So Virginia or any one of the other three states that had yet to vote—New Hampshire, New York, and North Carolina—could vault the Constitution to ratification for the states that had approved it.[90]

The new nation, though, faced a tough road if the largest and wealthiest states did not join. Massachusetts and Pennsylvania were already in assent, so the Virginia and New York conventions were of overriding importance. With Virginia's convention beginning in early June, the debates in Richmond were sure to affect decisions elsewhere. The remaining states, said Anti-Federalist Richard Henry Lee, "will depend much upon Virginia for their determination on the Convention project of a new constitution."[91]

For supporters of the Constitution, a win in Richmond could help bring the other states into the fold. The debate in the remaining states might then focus less on the contentious issues raised by the document than it would on the hard question of whether to join the Union or be left out. Opposition could fade if the consequence of refusing to ratify was the uncertain future of going it alone, outside the Union.

ALL EYES TURNED to Patrick Henry on June 4 as he rose to speak for the first time in the Virginia convention. Everyone had anticipated this moment for many months. "The public mind, as well as my own," he began, "is extremely uneasy at the proposed change of Government."[92]

Henry took a few minutes to warm up to the task of defining his opposition to the Constitution, using "uneasy" and "disquieted" to describe the feelings of the people of Virginia before moving to more forceful words. Why did the delegates to the Philadelphia Convention abandon the existing Confederation, he wanted to know. The convention's charge was to amend the Articles of Confederation, and "for this purpose they were solely delegated." Yet the delegates engaged in an "utter annihilation" of the Articles. "Was the real existence of the country threatened—or was this preceded by a mournful progression of events?" he asked. Instead, the convention produced "this perilous innovation" that consolidated so much power in the national government that, as for the people, "their liberty will be lost, and tyranny must and will arise."[93]

When Henry was finished, Randolph began a speech of several hours. Any hope that he would join Henry vanished immediately. Randolph lifted his arm to draw attention to it. "I will assent to the lopping of this limb," he said, "before I assent to the dissolution of the Union." He had refused to sign the Constitution, he explained, because he opposed a decision to require the state conventions to vote on the new Constitution without consideration of amendments that they might propose to address their concerns. But now amendments would have to wait until after ratification and follow the process that the Constitution set out. Too many states, Randolph explained, had ratified the Constitution without insisting on prior amendments, and so continuing to insist on them would bring "inevitable ruin to the Union."[94]

George Mason, Henry's primary ally in opposing ratification, spoke to the delegates after Randolph finished. Unlike Henry, Mason conceded the "inefficacy of the confederation." The Constitution, however, created one consolidated government, which "is one of the worst curses that can possibly befal a nation." Among other things, Mason objected to the federal government directly collecting taxes, which "is calculated to annihilate totally the State Governments." An "indispensible amendment," he said, would empower the states to levy their share of federal taxes, and only if they failed to do so would the federal government be able to act. Mason, though, finished by vowing to "most gladly put my hand to it [the Constitution]" if amendments took care of his concerns.[95]

Madison felt good about the opening day, especially with Randolph's declaration of support. Randolph, he wrote that evening to Washington, had "thrown himself fully into the federal scale. Henry & Mason made a lame figure & appeared to take different and awkward ground. The federalists are a good deal elated by the existing prospect."[96]

HENRY'S LONG SPEECHES often dominated the convention. One letter writer reported that Henry on the fourth day of the convention, June 5, "spoke all that day (Thursday) all Friday, Saturday, Monday, Tuesday, and Wednesday, and was still speaking on Thursday, the date of our information." Henry had not spoken all that time, but it must have seemed to many people that his talks, stretching for hours, would not conclude until the tobacco harvest called him back home.[97]

In the realm of political expression, great oratory such as Henry's went hand in hand with all the many forms of printed material in moving men's minds.[98] Evangelical preachers had raised emotional oratory to a kind of art form in the early part of the eighteenth century, and politicians like James Otis Jr. during the Stamp Act crisis and then Henry had adopted it to their own advantage. A speech could be printed afterward, but the fact that oratory itself could not be replicated meant that its impact was greatest in the assembly in which a speech was delivered. Even so, as John Adams had noted in 1758, powerful rhetoric "may be used to rouse in the Breasts of the Audience a gallant Spirit of Liberty."[99]

Unlike many leaders of the founding generation, Henry wrote very little and enjoyed minimal respect for his knowledge of law or of history. Jefferson remembered Henry as "the greatest orator that ever lived," and a man who understood people well enough to use his oratory to attain great popularity. But his "judgment in other matters was inaccurate, in matters of law it was not worth a copper." Poorly read, Henry "drew all natural rights from a purer source, the feelings of his own breast. He never, in conversation or debate, mentioned a hero, a worthy, or a fact in Greek or

Roman history, but so vaguely & loosely as to leave room to back out, if he found he had blundered."[100] As Edmund Randolph said, Henry spoke "from the recesses of the human heart."[101]

Whatever the source of Henry's inspiration, his oratory at the Virginia convention moved many people. One man in the gallery, on hearing Henry describe the loss of rights that would be brought on by a powerful government, "felt his wrists to assure himself that the fetters were not already pressing his flesh; and that the gallery on which he was sitting seemed to become as dark as a dungeon."[102] James Breckinridge, a supporter of the Constitution, said that Henry's "eloquence and oratory far exceeded my conception: In such an Assembly he must to be sure better adapted to carry his point & lead the ignorant people astray than any other person upon earth; Madisons plain, ingenious, & elegant reasoning is entirely thrown away and lost among such men."[103]

On June 5, Henry stood before the delegates for many hours, beginning his first major assault on the Constitution. In doing so, he certainly had no fears that what he said would cross any boundaries of speech deemed unacceptable under the law. That battle had been won by all those dissenters who had spoken out in the decades before, including Henry himself in his frequent words in defense of liberty.

As he did throughout the convention, Henry attacked again and again the creation of a strong national government. The trouble with the Constitution, he said, began with its very first words. "We the people" was a compact that made a "pernicious" change in the nature of American government. The Articles of Confederation had been a compact among the states, and should have been continued in the Constitution by making it an agreement of "the states of America." Instead, a compact of the people created a powerful consolidated government and reduced the power of the states. "Here," declared Henry, "is a revolution as radical as that which separated us from Great Britain."[104]

The Constitution showed nothing but deformities, said Henry. Hammering on the theme of centralized power, he charged that the Constitution "squints towards monarchy." It lacked adequate checks on the authority of national leaders. "Your president may easily become King," he said. Henry demanded to know "that age and country where the rights and liberties of the people were placed on the sole chance of their rulers being good men, without a consequent loss of liberty?" The president would command an army, and would certainly use it "to make one bold push for the American throne." And then it would be, "Away with your President, we shall have a King. . . . And what have you to oppose this force? What will then become of you and your rights? Will not absolute despotism ensue?"[105]

With so many evident defects, Henry argued two days later, on June 7, the Constitution needed serious revision and it had to be done before ratification. It would be foolish to adopt this new form of government without first correcting the problems. As he said, "A previous ratification of a system notoriously and confessedly defective will endanger our riches—our liberty—our all." The fact that other states had ratified earlier without a call for amendments did not preclude Virginia from demanding them, and if the amendments were reasonable, "they will receive us. Union is as necessary for them as for us."[106]

Madison replied to Henry on many occasions. Other speakers had engaged Henry and his supporters, but none of the other lights of Virginia politics burned as bright as Madison. Nobody else had his knowledge of the Constitution and political systems. Madison spoke so quietly that other delegates could barely hear—the transcriber of the debates had noted that he "spoke so low that his exordium could not be heard distinctly."[107] Madison met Henry's many censures of the Constitution with detailed responses. Two brilliant men bestowed with dissimilar but equally compelling gifts were at work—Henry with his commanding oratory and Madison with his commanding intellectual depth.

Madison wondered how Henry could deny that the Articles of Confederation had failed and that a new plan of government was needed. "Why have complaints of national and individual distresses been echoed and re-echoed throughout the Continent?" he asked, as he catalogued the complaints.[108] Madison addressed Henry's criticism of a compact of "we the people." A compact of the people rather than the states placed sovereignty where it belonged, and it was a design that would safeguard individual rights. Power was "in the hands of the people—delegated to their Representatives chosen for short terms. To Representatives responsible to the people, and whose situation is perfectly similar to their own:—As long as this is the case we have no danger to apprehend."[109]

Madison, as resident scholar, took out the voluminous notes he had prepared the previous spring on the failure of confederacies. He talked about the inadequacies of the Amphyctionic league and the Achaean league, the Germanic and Swiss systems, and the experience of the confederate government of Holland. The "uniform conclusion," he said, "is, that instead of promoting the public happiness, or securing public tranquillity, they have, in every instance, been productive of anarchy and confusion; ineffectual for the preservation of harmony, and a prey to their own dissention and foreign invasions." And, he added, "does not the history of these confederacies coincide with the lesson drawn from our own experience?"[110]

Madison went on. The power to tax and raise an army was critical to defense. Without that, a foreign power could attack the states that were weakest or most remote, picking them off one by one while the confederation struggled to raise men and supplies to fight back. "The General Government," said Madison, "having no resources beyond what are adequate to its existing necessities, will not be able to afford any effectual succour to those parts which may be invaded."[111]

In the days after the initial clash of swords, both sides agreed that the outcome was too close to call. William Grayson, an Anti-Federalist, wrote that "our affairs in the Convention are suspended by a hair: I really cannot tell you on which side the scale will turn: the difference I am satisfied on the main question will be exceedingly small indeed." James Madison agreed. "The majority on either side will be small & at present the event is as ticklish as can be conceived," he wrote.[112]

ON THE SAME DAY, June 7, newspaper editor Eleazer Oswald rode into Richmond from Philadelphia. Oswald, who printed the Anti-Federalist *Independent Gazetteer,* carried letters from a group of New York opponents of the Constitution to like-minded delegates in Richmond, including Henry and Mason. He stayed two days there, long enough for the Virginians to give him letters to carry back to New York containing the news that they had already drafted amendments to the Constitution. Oswald returned to the road, and after a seven-day ride, he arrived in New York City with his trove of letters.[113]

Oswald's grueling days on horseback were emblematic of the challenge of disseminating printed words throughout the country. In order for political expression to thrive, it had to be mobile. Whatever the thoughts committed to paper, their impact was heavily dependent on the distribution network. Letters, pamphlets, and newspapers had to move from city to city in order to engage people.

A system to transmit news and ideas, then, comprised the nervous system of political speech. During the debate, the *Pennsylvania Herald* called the postal system "that great channel which serves at once to gratify the curiosity, and to collect the voice of the people."[114] In eighteenth-century America, though, writers could not take distribution for granted when the movement of ideas was prone to the trauma of both nature and human failing. Ships delivered some written materials up and down the coast, taking about ten days between Philadelphia and Savannah, but storms put everything at risk. On land, critical information moved only as fast as a horse could gallop over a rudimentary system of dirt roads cut through the expanses of forest and meadow. Even with an ambitious ride, the trip from the Virginia to the New York ratifying convention—Richmond to Poughkeepsie—took a full week with a relay of three riders handing off papers to one another at prearranged spots. A rider carrying news from New York to Boston needed two and a half days at top speed.[115]

Riders often dealt with wretched conditions, moving over paths strewn with rocks and splashing through thick mud when it rained. Edward Carrington complained to Madison of ice on the falls at Richmond and "a Canoe with difficulty makes its way through the Falls and by that means my letters from the post office have today got to me."[116] John Adams described his ride from Braintree to Baltimore during bitter January weather in 1777 as "a march like that of Hannibal over the Alps."[117] And Abigail Adams, on a trip through New Jersey, complained of "the worst Roads I ever travelld the soil is all clay. the heavey rains & the constant run of Six stages daily, had so cut them up, that the whole was like a ploughd feild, in furroughs of 2 feet in deepth, and was very dangerous."[118]

Just when it was needed most, the post office system fell short. In 1788, the post office tried to save money by giving its mail contracts to riders rather than stagecoaches, which were more expensive but relatively reliable. The postmaster also ended the practice of allowing printers to exchange their newspapers through the mail without charge. Now each printer had to negotiate his own deal with the riders, some of who refused to carry newspapers and some others who tossed the papers away or sold them. Anti-Federalists complained that newspapers containing their own essays by such writers as Brutus and Cato never made it through for reprinting in the convention towns, something they charged to partisan activities by Federalists.[119] In a letter to John Jay, Washington said that the "friends of the constitution" wanted citizens "to be possessed of every thing, that might be printed on both sides of the question," and that the failed deliveries gave Anti-Federalists an excuse for arguing that "the suppression of intelligence, at that critical juncture, was a wicked trick of policy, contrived by an aristocratic junto."[120]

In such an uncertain atmosphere, both sides cobbled together their own alternative systems, at least between critical cities holding the ratifying conventions. On May 19, Alexander Hamilton in New York wrote to James Madison with an important request. It was essential, he said, for the Federalists trying to ratify the Constitution to set up a communications network to quickly get news to and from some of the state conventions. To make it work, riders had to be signed up in advance, ready to saddle their horses and take to the roads at a moment's notice.

Hamilton and other Federalists who would push for ratification at the New York convention in Poughkeepsie needed to know immediately of any positive news from other states. Ratification by the Virginians would help convince delegates up north to ratify as well. With Anti-Federalists in control of the New York convention by a margin of twenty-seven votes (forty-six for the Anti-Federalists and nineteen for the Federalists), Hamilton and the minority would wield more leverage if nine states—and especially Virginia—approved. Then the Anti-Federalist delegates would have to decide whether New York would join the new union or go it alone. "We think here that the situation of your state is critical," wrote Hamilton, adding that "the moment any *decisive question* is taken, if favourable, I request you to dispatch an express to me with pointed orders to make all possible diligence, by changing horses &c." He added, for emphasis, "All expenses shall be thankfully and liberally paid."[121]

Hamilton organized a rider system for the Federalists. In addition to enlisting riders to carry news between Richmond and Poughkeepsie, he set up an express from Concord, New Hampshire, to Poughkeepsie. Writing to the president of the convention in New Hampshire, he said that the rider should "take the *shortest route* to that place, change horses on the road, and use all possible diligence. I shall with pleasure defray all expenses, and give a liberal reward to the person." At the same time, another Federalist set up a duplicate rider express to Poughkeepsie through Springfield, Massachusetts.[122]

The Anti-Federalists, too, set up their own network. Their most important line of communication was between New York City, Poughkeepsie, and Richmond as the opponents of the Constitution tried to coordinate their proposal for amendments before ratification. That is what brought Eleazer Oswald to Richmond on June 7 as a courier of letters from the New York Federal Republican Committee.[123] Madison worried about Oswald's presence, reporting to Hamilton on June 9 that Oswald "has closet interviews with the leaders of the Opposition."[124] A week later, Madison wrote again to Hamilton, saying that the Anti-Federalists were most likely trying to delay a vote on ratification or even to adjourn without a vote, "which is preferable game" for them.[125]

Oswald carried letters back to New York, including one from Henry observing that four-fifths of Virginians opposed the Constitution. "And yet strange as it may seem," Henry wrote, "the Numbers in Convention appear equal on both Sides; so that the Majority which way soever it goes will be small."[126]

IF HENRY HAD A winning argument in such a close convention, it was the failure of the delegates in Philadelphia to protect individual rights in the new Constitution. The colonists had suffered serious British violations of their rights in the pre-Revolutionary years, and when they wrote their own constitutions at the beginning of the war, protection of their liberties was often of paramount importance. Seven states attached declarations of rights to their constitutions and two others enacted laws that were similar to bills of rights.[127]

No state was more attached than Virginia to the importance of a bill of rights. The Virginia Declaration of Rights of 1776 guaranteed trial by jury, free exercise of religion, and freedom of the press, among other things. Mason, the principal author of the declaration, had refused to sign the Constitution in Philadelphia and said then that a declaration of rights "would give great quiet to the people."[128] Jefferson favored a bill of rights. And another leading Virginian, Richard Henry Lee, had highlighted the omission of a bill of rights when the Confederation Congress received the Constitution in September 1787 for transmittal to the states for ratification. Lee had introduced a series of amendments, the first of which called for a bill of rights, but his proposal was defeated.[129]

The issue of a bill of rights had been discussed earlier in the Virginia convention, and Henry came back to it again on June 16. This time, Henry and Mason argued for a bill of rights by attacking another clause in the proposed Constitution. It gave Congress the power to "make all laws which shall be necessary and proper for carrying into execution" the specific powers granted. Congress, for example, had been given the power to regulate commerce among the states and to borrow and coin money, and the clause provided it with the authority to pass various laws necessary to put those powers into effect. The Federalists argued that the clause did not expand the authority of Congress since it limited such lawmaking only to the powers already enumerated. Congress could not violate freedom of the press because it had no enumerated power over the press. But opponents feared that, in the hands of an aggressive federal government, "necessary and proper" provided sweeping and undefined powers that could be used to violate individual rights such as press freedom.[130]

Henry hammered on this theme. "The necessity of a Bill of Rights," he said, "appear(s) to me to be greater in this Government, than ever it was in any Government before." Assurances by the Federalists that Americans retained all rights not specifically given away to the federal government were simply not good enough. Henry wanted to explicitly spell out the rights of the people. "Why not say so?" he asked. "Is it because it will consume too much paper?" Without protections for the press, he said, he was left to hope that Congress would "take care as little as possible, to infringe the rights of human nature." But he added, "They are not however expressly restrained."[131]

The next day, Henry came back once again to a bill of rights. Now he told the delegates that he found a kind of bill of rights in Article 1, Section 9, which protected several rights of the people—it limited Congress on suspensions of habeas corpus and forbade it from passing bills of attainder and ex post facto laws. These provisions, said Henry, "are express restrictions which are in the shape of a Bill of Rights." Compared to the Virginia Declaration of Rights, the protections of Article 1, Section 9, "are so feeble and few, that it would have been infinitely better to have said nothing about it." Obviously, Henry said, those who framed the Constitution found it necessary to protect some rights after all, despite the assertion that the people retained those rights that were not explicitly given up to the government. "The fair implication is," he said, "that they [the federal government] can do every thing they are not forbidden to do." And so, he concluded, Americans needed a bill of rights to fill out the list in Section 9. Randolph replied that Congress had been given no power to punish the press. "If it be," he asked, "I again ask for the particular clause which gives liberty to destroy the freedom of the press."[132]

The following day, Madison wrote that the upcoming vote on ratification balanced on a thread. "There is not a majority of more than three or four on either side," he wrote. "Both sides claim it. I think however it rather lies as yet in favor of the Constitution. But it is so small as to justify apprehensions from accidents as well as change of opinion."[133]

ON JUNE 24, with the convention coming to a conclusion, George Wythe offered a motion that the delegates ratify the Constitution, and along with it propose amendments for the first federal Congress to consider. His motion included a preamble that protected the liberty of the press, the rights of conscience, and trial by jury.[134]

Henry immediately attacked. Why protect only three rights? "Will not all the world pronounce, that we intended to give up all the rest?" Henry still could not fathom the idea of ratifying the Constitution and only later considering amendments to fix the problems he thought it posed. "Do you enter into a compact of Government first, and afterwards settle the terms of the Government?" he asked.[135]

Unsurprisingly, Henry pulled out a motion of his own to supplant the ratification vote. Before adopting a new Constitution, he said, Virginia should draft and circulate a declaration of rights. He presented forty amendments to the delegates, half of which comprised a bill of rights.[136] Once again, Madison replied that it was not practical to demand amendments before ratification. If nine states ratified, putting the Constitution into effect, those states might say "with a great deal of propriety—'It is not proper, decent, or right in you, to demand that we should reverse what we have done.'" Their stance, Madison went on, would be that "it is more reasonable that you should yield to us, than we to you.—You cannot exist without us—You must be a member of the Union."[137]

When Henry took the floor again a little while later, he knew he had just this final opportunity to capture a few delegates who might turn the convention in his favor. He moved beyond the proposed Constitution and called on higher authorities. "I see *beings* of a higher order, anxious concerning our decision," he said. When he looked "beyond the horrison that binds human eyes" to "see those intelligent beings which inhabit the aetherial mansions, reviewing the political decisions and revolutions which in the progress of time will happen in America," he believed that everything depended "on what we now decide." The consequences were not for Virginia alone, Henry said. "We have it in our power to secure the happiness of one half of the human race."[138]

And just then, as he concluded perhaps his most emotional speech at the convention by reaching out to those "aetherial mansions," a ferocious thunderstorm struck Richmond and shook the building full of delegates. "So remarkable a coincidence was never before witnessed, and it seemed as if he had indeed the faculty of calling the spirits from the vasty deep," wrote Spencer Roane, a state senator and son-in-law of Henry.[139]

WHEN THE CONVENTION MET the next day, June 25, the "spirits from the vasty deep" that had electrified Henry's speech were quiet once more, abandoning him to the cold reality of an up or down vote on the Constitution. The galleries filled, with one spectator estimating that more than one thousand people attended the session, "with minds agitated by contending and opposite opinions." As he described it, "Awful and solemn was the pause which preceded the question."[140]

Henry offered a resolution to send amendments to the states for their consideration. The delegates voted it down by a vote of eighty-eight to eighty. Then came George Wythe's resolution to ratify the Constitution now and amend it later through recommendations to the first Congress. The resolution passed by eighty-nine to seventy-nine. Virginia had finally ratified, but barely.[141]

Henry already had a list of amendments, so it took only two days for a committee that also included Mason, Madison, and others to complete its work. The delegates approved a bill of rights and twenty additional amendments proposed by the committee. The list of rights was similar to the Virginia Declaration of Rights, including an article that proclaimed the freedom of speech and press.[142]

Richard Henry Lee, a signer of the Declaration of Independence and now a staunch Anti-Federalist, remained profoundly worried that in the Constitution the framers had laid aside their old revolutionary principles of restrained government as the best guarantee of individual liberty. "It will be considered, I believe, as a most extraordinary Epoch in the history of mankind, that in a few years there should be so essential a change in the minds of men," Lee wrote on June 27. "'Tis realy astonishing that the same people who have just emerged from a long & cruel war in defence of liberty, should now agree to fix an elective despotism upon themselves & their posterity!"[143]

IF THE FEDERALISTS in Richmond thought that their vote made Virginia the critical ninth state to agree to the Constitution, they were soon disappointed. New Hampshire had ratified on June 21, four days before Virginia, by another close vote of fifty-seven to forty-seven. As Virginia had done, the New Hampshire delegates proposed amendments to the Constitution. By the end of the ratification process, seven states had ratified with recommendatory amendments.[144]

Express riders took many days to deliver the news. Immediately after New Hampshire's vote, a rider carrying a note to Alexander Hamilton set out for the New York convention in Poughkeepsie, galloping first to Springfield, Massachusetts. He handed off the note to another rider, who delivered it to Hamilton on June 24, for an elapsed time of seventy-one hours. Then a rider left Poughkeepsie with a note for Madison in Richmond, reaching Alexandria four days later and handing it off to another rider, who arrived in Richmond on June 29, a few days after the Virginia convention had adjourned. Meanwhile, riders carrying news of Virginia's ratification raced north in a relay, with one arriving in Poughkeepsie seven days later, on July 2. The rider dismounted from his horse and walked into the convention to tell the delegates.[145]

The news of Virginia's ratification reached Albany the next day, and supporters of the Constitution began to celebrate. Bells rang all over the city and ten cannon shook the air. Not everyone was happy at the news, though. At nine the next morning, before the July 4 celebrations began, a group of about fifty Anti-Federalists met at Hilton's tavern. They attached a copy of the Constitution to a pole, hoisted it aloft, and then walked to

Fort Frederick. There, they put a flame to the Constitution and watched it burn to ashes.

Supporters of the Constitution answered them. At five that afternoon, hundreds of people marched with a pine tree more than thirty feet high to the place where the Constitution had been burned. They stood the tree on the ground with the Constitution fixed to the top. Then they fired cannon and gave three cheers. Later, the two groups scuffled, with about two dozen suffering injuries.[146]

Ratification by New Hampshire and especially Virginia put enormous pressure on the delegates. Would they want New York left out of the Union? New York ratified on July 26 as Virginia had done, with proposed amendments.[147] The ratification period was coming to a close, and Americans across the political spectrum had been free to express themselves. The Constitution printed on paper became a symbol to be hoisted up a pole and either reviled or celebrated. Americans felt free to do both, a testament to the robust debate that had enlarged the public sphere in the decades since the protests had started against British authority. "We the people," as the Constitution began, spoke in many different voices.

9

THE FRAMER

ON JULY 2, 1798, THOMAS JEFFERSON PULLED UP TO THE MAIN HOUSE AT MONTPELIER. THE vice president of the United States was riding from Philadelphia to his own plantation at Monticello, but he had decided to spend the night with his friend and close political ally James Madison.[1]

Jefferson had good reason for the dark mood he brought with him to Montpelier. Feverish talk of a possible war with France had taken over Congress, dominated by the Federalist Party (unrelated to the Federalists of the ratification battles) of President Adams. The immediate provocation was the seizing of American merchant ships by the French and their shabby treatment of American diplomats sent to Paris. The Adams administration was preparing for war, while the opposition Democratic-Republican Party—including Jefferson and Madison—vigorously criticized what they regarded as war hysteria.

More immediately on Jefferson's mind was the Federalists' work on passage of the Alien and Sedition Acts, as he had apprised Madison in a series of letters from Philadelphia. The Alien Friends Act, which had passed just a few weeks earlier, enabled the government to deport aliens thought to be "dangerous to the peace and safety of the United States." A second Alien Act, aimed at male citizens of hostile nations, was close to passage, as was a Sedition Act designed to punish the opposition for criticism of President Adams and Congress. To Madison and Jefferson, all of these acts violated the Constitution. The Sedition Act in particular, they believed, violated the First Amendment's guarantee of freedom of speech and press, ratified only seven years earlier.

On his way to Montpelier, Jefferson had stopped for a dinner in Fredericksburg, where his allies had lifted toasts to him. That was a welcome respite for a man in such a tough spot. Jefferson was a political opponent of Adams yet served as his vice president, a complication made possible by the way elections were held at the time. Jefferson had to be especially circumspect in opposing the president whom he served.

Madison and Jefferson spent hours in discussion about how to deal with the Federalist policies that they felt threatened the country. Most likely they sat out on the large Tuscan portico of the brick mansion, looking beyond the fields of tobacco to the Blue Ridge Mountains on the horizon and enjoying some relief from the heat as the sun fell below the hills. On the following day, July 3, Jefferson left for Monticello, a one-day ride.[2] Eleven days later, Congress passed the Sedition Act and prosecutors began bringing charges against editors and politicians who had criticized Adams or his administration.

Jefferson and Madison feared being caught up in the prosecutions themselves, as the Sedition Act prohibited conspiring "with intent to oppose . . . measures of the government." The mail was notoriously unreliable, with postmen often pilfering letters and handing them over to the opposition. It was a wise decision to proceed with such care, considering the course of action that the two men had just plotted at Montpelier. Unable to block the Federalists from their political mischief in Congress, they had decided instead to enlist the help of state legislatures to protest the Alien and Sedition Acts. Not long after they parted, the two men penned anonymous resolutions of protest for the legislatures of Virginia and Kentucky.

For Madison, and for the young republic, the most important outcome of the meeting at Montpelier on July 2 would come two years later. Madison, the father of the Constitution and the First Amendment, would write about the relationship between political speech and American democracy in such elegant and powerful terms that it would stand for the next two centuries as the nation's most important statement about the freedom of expression.

THE VIEW FROM MONTPELIER of the gentle slopes of the Blue Ridge Mountains, often shrouded in haze, provided sustenance to James Madison his entire life. The family had owned land in the Tidewater region of Virginia since the mid-seventeenth century, but James's paternal grandfather received a land patent in the fertile piedmont lands of what is now Orange County in the 1720s. He sent an overseer and slaves ahead to erect buildings and clear the land to raise tobacco, then moved the family there in 1732. Twenty-five years later, James's father had expanded the plantation to more than four thousand acres of wooded hills and arable pasture and farmland. Known as Mount Pleasant, the plantation had a distillery and ironworks. James Sr. quickly became one of the wealthiest planters in the area, at the same time carrying out civic responsibilities by serving in positions such as sheriff, coroner, and colonel in the militia. He built a new plantation house from 1763 to 1765, a two-story brick dwelling he called Montpelier, one of the finest houses at the time in Orange County.[3]

James Jr., or Jemmy, as he was often called to distinguish him from his father, loved the green rolling hills and forests of Montpelier and drew strength from his quiet reflection there. But like so many wealthy men of Virginia who served in politics—including Jefferson, George Washington, James Monroe, Patrick Henry, and Edmund Randolph—Madison spent long stretches of time away from home. The political centers of Richmond, Philadelphia, and New York were long rides by horse or coach, and so a trip often consumed weeks or months. Even so, Madison's second-floor study was where he completed some of his most important work. It was there in 1786 and 1787 that he spent months reading and making notes from books that Jefferson had sent to him from Paris on the history of confederations, convincing him that America's own Articles of Confederation would doom the new nation to second-class status. He went to the Philadelphia convention determined to cast aside the Articles and write a new constitution with a much stronger central government.[4]

Madison and Jefferson enjoyed a warm personal relationship. Jefferson was eight years older than Madison and mentored him in the politics of the founding period. They met in 1776 when both were delegates in the first Virginia House of Delegates. Madison lost his bid for reelection the following year. But he had already impressed those around him with his work on a declaration of rights, and he returned the same year with an appointment to serve as one of eight advisers on the Governor's Council, which shared power with the governor, then Patrick Henry. When Jefferson succeeded Henry as governor in 1779, Madison continued as a member of the council and was elected by the House of Delegates to the Continental Congress.

Still in his late twenties, Madison's star was growing brighter in Virginia politics. His work with Jefferson brought them together in a collaboration that would profoundly affect the country. "Our acquaintance there became intimate; and a friendship was formed, which was for life, and which was never interrupted in the slightest degree for a single moment," Madison wrote many years later.[5] When Madison became president at the expiration of Jefferson's two terms, one observer who knew them both wrote of Jefferson that a "father never loved son more than he loves Mr. Madison, and I believe too that every demonstration of respect to Mr. M. gave Mr. J. more pleasure than if paid to himself."[6]

The connection between the two men deepened after both suffered losses in love that greatly affected them. Jefferson's wife, Martha, died in September 1782, leaving him "a gloom unbrightened with one cheerful expectation."[7] A short time later, Madison fell in love with Catherine (Kitty) Floyd, the fifteen-year-old daughter of a congressman from New York. Madison was then thirty-two years old, so shy and cerebral that he was far more confident in the warm embrace of political conflicts than he was in wooing a young lady. The grieving Jefferson had been with Madison and Kitty in Philadelphia early in 1783, and after leaving them he wrote to his friend. Remembering his fulfilling life with Martha, he told Madison that a marriage to Kitty "will render you happier than you can possibly be in a single state." Madison was touched by Jefferson's sentiments, replying awkwardly that he "had sufficiently ascertained her sentiments. Since your departure the affair has been pursued." He added, "The interest which your friendship takes on this occasion in my happiness is a pleasing proof that the dispositions which I feel are reciprocal."[8]

By the summer, James and Kitty had ended their relationship. She had fallen for a medical student much closer to her own age. Madison told Jefferson of their breakup in a letter in August in which he referred vaguely to "one of those incidents to which such affairs are liable." Jefferson wrote back counseling an attitude of hope that he himself had struggled to achieve. "I sincerely lament the misadventure which has happened from whatever cause it may have happened," wrote Jefferson. "Should it be final however, the world still presents the same and many other resources of happiness, and you possess many within yourself. Firmness of mind and unintermitting occupations will not long leave you in pain."[9] In fact, eleven years later, Madison married the widow Dolley Payne Todd.

Letters flew back and forth between the two men as the world of books and ideas knit them into a common cloth. Jefferson offered Madison the use of his library at Monticello during the winter of 1784—"I beg you to make free use of it"—but Madison wrote a month later that the winter weather "has been so severe that I have never renewed my call on the library of Monticello."[10] Jefferson tried to entice Madison to join his friends James Monroe and William Short in buying a property that would make them neighbors. "Monroe is buying land almost adjoining me," he wrote. "Short will do the same. What would I not give you could fall into the circle." He added that a 140-acre property was on sale only two miles from Monticello, "all of good land, tho' old, with a small indifferent house on it." He asked Madison to "think of it." Madison gently turned down Jefferson's invitation. "I know not my dear Sir what to reply to the affectionate invitation. . . . I feel the attractions of the particular situation you point out to me; I can not altogether renounce the prospect; still less can I as yet embrace it."[11]

By the time the Sedition Act came before Congress, the two men also pursued commercial dealings with each other. Both were engaged in major home construction projects. Having temporarily retired from public life, Madison was building a two-story addition to Montpelier. His family would live on one side of the house, and his parents on the other. On Christmas Day 1797, Madison wrote to Jefferson ordering thousands of nails to be made at the Monticello nailery. Jefferson replied in the first week of January that "all the nails you desire can be furnished from Monticello," adding that "I presume you will not want them till your walls are done."[12] In the fall, the two men shared a carpenter, with Jefferson informing Madison that one particular craftsman laying floors at Monticello "has been detained by several jobs indispensable to the progress of the carpenters, & to the securing what is done against the winter."[13] In reply, Madison asked his friend to forebear sharing another craftsman who "has been under the spur to keep the way prepared for the Plasterers."

Expecting to see Jefferson soon, Madison added: "Be so good as to bring a memorandum from your nailery of the amount of my debt to it."[14]

Making nails was a sideline for Jefferson, for both he and Madison were largely dependent for their income on slaves raising wheat and tobacco. For years they wrote to each other about serious affairs of state and at the same time often reported on the prospects for their crops and the prices they might fetch in the markets. "We apprehend our wheat is almost entirely killed: and many people are expecting to put something else in the ground," Jefferson reported in January 1797. "I have so little expectations from mine, that as much as I am an enemy to tobacco, I shall endeavor to make some for taxes and clothes."[15] It was Madison's turn a year later. "The wheat fields in general retain their sickly countenance," he reported, and as a result "the ensuing crop will be very short, whatever change for the better may happen in the residue of the season."[16]

By the time the Sedition Act became law in 1798, Madison and Jefferson were close political allies and the best and most trusting of friends. They needed to be so, for the secret scheme they launched to fight the Sedition Act could, by the terms of the law itself, have landed them in jail for a long time.

THE SEDITION ACT POSED the latest and most significant obstacle to freedom of expression. Americans had long fought against seditious libel, beginning with the trial of the Reverend John Wise in 1687 (see chapter 1) and continuing through the founding period. Juries had largely neutralized the crime by refusing to jail those who were accused of violating it. If by consensus of the community the crime was all but dead, the First Amendment appeared to have erected a formidable constitutional barrier after its ratification in 1791. Or did it?

In the fall of 1788, with Jefferson in Paris as minister to France, Madison had led ratification forces in the Virginia convention to a narrow victory over Patrick Henry's Anti-Federalists (see chapter 8). But Madison and his political allies had made a critical decision. To prevent previous amendments or the calling of a second constitutional convention, either of which could have doomed the Constitution, Madison had agreed to a demand that commanded support not only in Virginia but in many other ratifying conventions—amendments to the Constitution to be drawn up by the first federal Congress and submitted to the states.

Madison and his allies had thought a bill of rights was superfluous. At the Constitutional Convention, Charles Cotesworth Pinckney of South Carolina had proposed a clause that press freedom should be protected, but Roger Sherman of Connecticut replied: "It is unnecessary. The power of Congress does not extend to the press."[17] And so, as James Wilson said at Pennsylvania's ratifying convention, "no law, in pursuance of the Constitution, can possibly be enacted to destroy that liberty."[18] Patrick Henry and his allies, though, deeply distrusted centralized national power, and they had discharged much of their fire in Richmond on the failure to explicitly protect rights.

Madison and Jefferson, ideological allies on so many issues, had disagreed on the question themselves. Madison had written to Jefferson a few months after the Richmond convention to express lukewarm support for a bill of rights. He had been skeptical in part, he wrote, because limitations on paper—"parchment barriers," he called them—often did not work. As he noted, "Experience proves the inefficacy of a bill of rights on those occasions when its controul is most needed. Repeated violations of these parchment barriers have been committed by overbearing majorities in every state."[19] Jefferson's response from Paris in March 1789 conceded that a bill of rights was no guarantee that the government would stay within bounds, but "it is of great potency always, and rarely inefficacious." And Jefferson emphasized that it would provide standards that judges could enforce—"which has great weight with me, the legal check which it puts into the hands of the judiciary."[20]

Jefferson's letter carried great weight with Madison, and Virginia politics pushed him to a full endorsement of a bill of rights. Madison stood on shaky political grounds in his own state. Henry and his allies controlled the Virginia legislature. Henry flexed every political muscle to keep his nemesis Madison out of national politics. The legislature of each state elected its two US senators. Henry lobbied hard against Madison, arguing on the floor of the state legislature that Madison was so despised that his election would send "rivulets of blood throughout the land." Henry's efforts helped win the vote for Richard Henry Lee and William Grayson, two Anti-Federalists, with Madison finishing third. Madison turned his focus to running for the House of Representatives, and Henry once again went to work, this time using his majority to draw Madison's congressional district. They aligned the new congressional map to put Montpelier in a district comprising counties that had mostly opposed ratification of the Constitution. The five weeks of campaigning in winter weather—diary entries of the time noted brutal conditions including three inches of hail on one day—took its toll on the delicate Madison, who suffered frostbite one day while riding home after delivering a speech.[21]

In the end, Madison countered Henry's false charge that he viewed the Constitution as perfect and in no need of amendments. Madison did that in speeches as well as in letters. His most influential letter, which was reprinted in a Virginia newspaper five days before the election, endorsed amendments "for all those essential rights, which have been thought in danger, such as the rights of conscience, the freedom of the press, trials by jury, exemption from general warrants, & c."[22] Madison won and took his seat in the first Congress in New York City.[23]

Four months later, on June 8, Madison made good on his promise. On the House floor he introduced amendments that had been suggested by state ratifying conventions or were already contained in state constitutions. Among the rights to be protected, he said, was expression: "The people shall not be deprived or abridged of their right to speak, to write, or to publish their sentiments; and the freedom of the press, as one of the great bulwarks of liberty, shall be inviolable." Madison said that it was time to "expressly declare the great rights of mankind secured under this Constitution." Even though many states protected rights in their constitutions, some had no bill of rights and others had "very defective ones." And to those who thought a listing of rights amounted to mere parchment protections—he had thought so himself—Madison echoed Jefferson in arguing that independent courts would act as the "guardians of those rights."[24]

Madison's initiative on a bill of rights met a subdued reaction in Congress and the country. His proposals went to committee, where they were revised before consideration on the House floor. It was a process that Madison referred to as "the nauseous project of amendments," yet he felt personally committed because, he said, the Constitution "would have been *certainly* rejected" by his own state of Virginia without assurances of amendments to follow.[25] Madison actually had proposed two amendments protecting expression. One prohibited the federal government from infringing on freedom of speech and press. The second prevented state governments from doing so—in addition to restricting them from infringing on religion and the right to trial by jury in criminal cases. The House passed both amendments, but the Senate, sensitive to states' rights, rejected the proposed amendment that limited the states despite Madison's insistence that it was "the most valuable amendment in the whole list."[26]

The House and Senate voted approval of twelve amendments in September and they were sent to the states for ratification. The amendment safeguarding the freedom of speech and press—"Congress shall make no law . . ."—was originally numbered as the third, but when the states ratified all but the first two amendments, the third amendment became the first in the Bill of Rights.[27]

WHAT EXACTLY DID the founding generation understand the freedom of speech and press to mean after ratification of the First Amendment? Perhaps surprisingly, it was hard to say for sure. The words in the amendment protecting freedom of expression were only fourteen—"Congress shall make no law . . . abridging the freedom of speech, or of the press . . ." The phrasing of so profound an idea in so brief a manner gave it great energy, shattering many years of restrictions on political expression. Or so it seemed at first glance. But how far did the protection reach? The amendment's few words said nothing specifically about the issues that had bedeviled libertarians for so many years. The amendment said nothing of seditious libel at all. Looking closely at the exact words of the amendment, what was *the* freedom of speech and press that Congress was forbidden to abridge? Was it just the freedom existing at the time under the common law—the freedom to publish without prior censorship, but subject to prosecutions afterward—or much more than that? Either way, with the restriction against abridging speech and press resting only against Congress, states were still free to punish political expression subject only to their own constitutions.

The restless ghost of seditious libel was never far from any discussion of press freedom. Even Jefferson, who made many abstract declarations in favor of a free press, had not deeply thought out exactly how far he would go in protecting freedom of the speech and press. In January of 1787, he seemed ready to move beyond the defense of truth and protect even erroneous statements. "The people are the only censors of their governors; and even their errors will tend to keep these to the true principle of their institution," Jefferson wrote. "To punish these errors too severely would be to suppress the only safeguard of the public liberty."[28]

The following year, though, Jefferson appeared to pull back on whether erroneous statements should be protected. In a letter to Madison from Paris in 1788, he declared that an amendment protecting the press "will not take away the liability of the printers for false facts printed." A year later, after Madison sent him the amendments he had drafted, Jefferson said that "I like it as far as it goes." But he said again that he would not protect "false facts affecting injuriously the life, liberty, property, or reputation of others or affecting the peace of the confederacy with foreign nations."[29] Jefferson's removal of "false facts" from protection—if that is what he intended—would confer little protection on writers and printers engaged in vigorous dissent because factual mistakes are routine.

The ratification process provided no clear consensus on what the freedom of expression meant in law. At the ratifying conventions for the Constitution, numerous opponents argued for a bill of rights that would include protection for freedom of the press, but they did not definitively define the extent of the freedom they understood to be theirs. James Wilson, though, who was one of the leading political theorists of the time, said at Pennsylvania's ratifying convention in December 1787 that freedom of the press meant what it meant to Blackstone, that a writer could be prosecuted afterward "when he attacks the security or welfare of the government or the safety, character, and property of the individual."[30]

Nor did the deliberations of the First Congress that voted for the amendments offer evidence of exactly what the framers understood freedom of expression to mean. Congress considered five versions of what became the First Amendment. Madison's draft went to a House committee that rewrote the language but left behind little to explain its work, and debate in the House was brief and focused largely on the right of assembly and redress of grievances. The Senate took up the amendments, but records add little. Lawmakers rejected a motion that would have qualified the amendment by saying that press freedom would be protected "in as ample a manner as hath at any time been secured by the common law." Passage of this limitation would have been catastrophic to any hopes of expanding press freedom beyond the common law recognition of seditious libel as a crime.[31]

Once the amendment limiting just the federal government from infringing on freedom of speech and press arrived at the states, the ratifying legislatures left a meager record of what they understood those freedoms to mean.[32] Outside of the ratifying process, prominent members of the founding generation held conflicting views. Despite his revolutionary credentials, John Adams appeared to hold a limited view of press freedom in 1789. He wrote that the Massachusetts constitution protected the press from seditious libel prosecutions only if the defendant could prove truth—and only then if the writings were "published for the Public good."[33]

A group of libertarians, though, most of them writing under pseudonyms, were breaking through the orthodoxy and making their most significant argument—that freedom of expression played a central role in supporting a political system in which the people governed themselves.[34] Popular sovereignty required continual assent by citizens through regular elections. And assent in turn required that the people have the right through vigorous speech and a free press to critically examine public officials and public measures.

As early as 1774, the Continental Congress itself had alluded to this role for the press. In the first of a series of three letters addressed to the inhabitants of the province of Quebec, designed to draw sympathy for the Americans in their dispute with Britain, the delegates wrote that a free press was critical "in its diffusion of liberal sentiments on the administration of Government" and in providing a forum "whereby repressive officers are shamed or intimidated, into more honourable and just modes of conducting affairs."[35] The idea became more widespread in the next decade. Candid argued in 1782 that since public officials are elected, "therefore it highly behoves the people in general to be well acquainted with the characters of each other individually." He added that the press was the best vehicle "to apprize the people of their danger from the choice of unworthy persons to act in public stations." Candid insisted as well that falsehoods about public officials should be punishable only if malicious.[36]

Junius Wilkes, an anonymous writer, wrote the most remarkable essay of the entire period. He went beyond Candid in arguing that even "false and groundless" claims must be protected, as society "must not expect perfection in this life"—an early recognition, to be developed later, that false statements are inevitable in the heat of political debate. Wilkes opposed any prosecutions for seditious libel, saying that those who hold office "are merely public servants and stewards, and, as such, accountable at all times to the people." He also argued that press freedom drew meaning out of the actual practices of the founding generation in rebelling against the British. Political expression, he wrote, "produced the *American* struggle for liberty, and gave birth to our glorious independence! Had those illustrious worthies who maintained our cause been intimidated from publishing their sentiments under an idea of 'transgressing the law,' and involving the Printer with prosecutions as a libeller, there is no doubt we should have sunk to the lowest class of slaves. Injured as we were, there could be no redress."[37]

The Federal Farmer wrote in 1788 that a free press is "formidable to those rulers who adopt improper measures." Newspapers could be "the vehicles of abuse, and of many things not true; but these are but small inconveniences, in my mind, among many advantages."[38] Another anonymous writer, Centinel, argued that with a free press, "it is next to impossible to enslave a free nation." He added that officials of "tyrannical disposition . . . have ever been inimical to the press, and have considered the shackling of it, as the first step towards the accomplishment of their hateful domination, and the entire suppression of all liberty of public discussion."[39] George Hay, who sat in the Virginia House of Delegates, also rejected seditious libel. Writing under the name Hortensius, Hay said that a citizen has protection to "say every thing which his passion can suggest; he may employ all his time, and all his talents, if he is wicked enough to do so, in *speaking* against the government matters that are false, scandalous, and malicious."[40]

Among the framers, it was James Madison who joined the ideas of popular sovereignty and freedom of the press, doing so when he introduced the amendments to the House on June 8. Madison argued that freedom of expression had to have a different meaning in America because of the major difference in the form of government between the two countries. In England, the Magna Carta protected the people only against the king, with Parliament guarding the rights of all Englishmen against actions of the Crown. Across the ocean, though, Americans had placed power in the people themselves. Both the executive and legislative departments were elected by the people and responsible to them. "The people of many states have thought it necessary to raise barriers against power in all forms and departments of government," Madison said.[41] The most powerful such barrier was a people free to speak and write without fear of punishment.

Madison and the first federal Congress put these ideas to work in the structure of the First Amendment itself.[42] In its final form, the amendment laid out a progression of six rights required by a self-governing people. The first two rights—forbidding the "establishment of religion" and guaranteeing the "free exercise" of religion—protected an individual's freedom of thought. The government could neither coerce belief nor forbid a citizen from putting belief into practice. Having protected the freedom of thought in the realm of conscience, the amendment then secured the freedom of speech, the right to form ideas and to express them to fellow citizens. Some ideas need circulation to a much larger audience beyond a conversation or speech, so the amendment next protected freedom of the press, the institutional means for reaching the multitudes that might be persuaded to the speaker's point of view. The fifth right allowed citizens to put those ideas to collective action, protecting the right of assembly to bring people together in the streets and parks. And, finally, the sixth right embraced the final step in this democratic process—safeguarding the freedom to petition elected officials for a redress of grievances. The progression of freedom of speech through petitioning was Madison's democratic ideal of Americans running their own affairs—"in all these ways they may communicate their will"[43]—and there was no room in its conception of popular sovereignty for the government to make criticism of officials a criminal act.

Madison returned to this idea five years later. During a congressional debate in 1794, he argued that citizens enjoyed the right to criticize the government. "Opinions are not the objects of legislation," Madison said, adding that "the censorial power is in the people over the Government, and not in the Government over the people."[44]

And with all that, finally, there arrived the glimmering of a powerful libertarian theory supporting freedom of speech and press in America.

THE CENSORIAL POWER referred to by Madison was in the air that people breathed. The founding generation's understanding of freedom of expression takes special significance from the period surrounding ratification of the Constitution and the First Amendment. Freewheeling debate was the norm as they approved the documents establishing their government and their rights as citizens, a strong indication that they understood the First Amendment to incorporate the freedom that they themselves enjoyed. They would be unlikely to approve guarantees for freedom of speech but understand its meaning so narrowly that it would allow prosecution for the very speech they were engaging in at the time.

The period during and immediately after ratification of the First Amendment also becomes noteworthy as one of the most venomous in American history. The venom was aimed at the first president, George Washington, and at partisans of the two political parties that were beginning to form in America.

Washington had commanded the colonial army to victory, chaired the Constitutional Convention, and been elected the first president, but reverence for him dissipated after he took office. Partisan battles began over the meaning of the Constitution. Perhaps this should not be surprising, for many provisions of the Constitution had been written in general terms and so left major decisions for the future. Would policies tilt toward the interests of an agrarian economy or toward one served largely by manufacturing and finance? How would the balance fall between respect for states' rights and the need for enhanced federal power? Other questions were more immediately connected to conflicts in the world— would America favor France or England as the two great powers fought for dominance?

These basic political divisions played out fiercely in Washington's own cabinet. Opposing political parties formed around Treasury Secretary Hamilton and Secretary of State Jefferson. During ratification, supporters of the Constitution had been called Federalists (and those opposed, Anti-Federalists), but the Federalist Party that formed in the next decade was different. Hamilton's Federalists expanded the power of the government through creation of a central bank and other financial measures, and generally supported manufacturing interests in the North. The opposition, which took the name Democratic-Republicans, or Republicans, were led by Jefferson and then-Representative Madison. They opposed Hamilton's programs, and favored traditional agrarian interests. They feared a drift toward the very monarchy against which the colonies had rebelled.[45]

The divisions inside Washington's cabinet played out in bitter scheming, often done in anonymous writings that criticized and often demon-
ized opponents. Jefferson was behind many of the machinations against
Washington, often calling on his friend Madison to take up his pen.
Madison published a series of eighteen anonymous essays in the *National
Gazette* against the Washington administration beginning in late 1791.
Hamilton, for his part, attacked his cabinet colleague Jefferson in an
anonymous essay.[46] Alarmed by Hamilton's defense of extensive executive
power over foreign affairs at the expense of Congress, Jefferson implored
Madison to defend the prerogatives of Congress. Targeting Hamilton, Jefferson advised Madison, "For god's sake, my dear Sir, take up your pen,
select the most striking heresies, and cut him to peices in the face of the
public."[47] The result was an extended duel of essays by Hamilton and
Madison writing as Pacificus and Helvidius, respectively, debating the
power of the legislative and executive branches to forge foreign policy.[48]

If the backbiting in his own cabinet was severe, Washington suffered
just as much from the venom aimed at him by the press. Jefferson and
Madison even conspired to recruit Madison's old college friend Philip
Freneau to start a newspaper opposing Washington. By the end of his
first term, Freneau's *National Gazette* and Benjamin Franklin Bache's
Aurora led the attacks on Washington.[49] Again and again, the press accused Washington of employing the trappings of royalty. "We have given
[Washington] the powers and prerogatives of a king," Freneau wrote in
1795, during Washington's second term. Soon, America would have a "hereditary monarchy and a house of lords—provided Great Britain does not
chuse to take us once more under her protection as COLONIES."[50]

The floodgates opened fully in Washington's second term. America's
relationship with Britain had eroded badly. With Britain and France at
war, British warships in the Caribbean were stopping American merchant
ships to prevent trade with France. Washington sent John Jay, the chief
justice, to London to work out a treaty. When he did so, Republicans lambasted the administration for what they considered unfavorable terms for
the United States. As the Senate approved the treaty, loud protests broke
out. The use of effigies, which had became so popular with the Stamp Act
protests, now flared anew. According to Jay, he was so unpopular that he
could have seen his way after dark in much of the country by the light cast

from his effigy being consumed in flames.[51] Bache accused Washington of having been a British spy and having accepted a bribe from the British early in the conflict. Washington replied that Bache's "calumnies are to be exceeded only by his impudence, and both stand unrivaled."[52] In 1796, near the end of his administration, Washington complained to Jefferson that he had no idea that reports would be made "in such exagerated, and indecent terms as could scarcely be applied to a Nero; a notorious defaulter, or even to a common pickpocket."[53]

Washington's retirement to Mount Vernon after two terms in office brought no moratorium on the political scrum of the previous half-dozen years. If anything, the political fault lines sheared even more. John Adams, the nation's second president, faced a deepening crisis that threatened to immerse America in the intractable conflicts in Europe. Just a few years after the French Revolution began, France had defeated many of the major countries on the continent and was at war with Britain. Jay's Treaty had resolved American troubles with Great Britain, but French leaders were unhappy that America had chosen sides. They withdrew the French minister from the United States and declined to accept the American minister. French warships seized American merchant vessels.[54]

What made the situation even more explosive, though, was the rude treatment given to an American delegation sent to Paris—an incident that became known as the XYZ Affair. To resolve the problems between the two nations, Adams sent three emissaries to Paris to meet with the French foreign minister, the Marquis de Talleyrand. But Talleyrand refused to receive them. Instead, he sent three intermediaries—identified in dispatches to America as X, Y, and Z—who said that Talleyrand would negotiate only if America met certain conditions. Talleyrand demanded a bribe and a large, low-interest loan to bolster French coffers for its military adventures against Britain.[55] Hamilton was appalled. "Money, money, is the burden of the discordant song of these foul birds of prey," he wrote.[56]

With French corsairs feasting on American merchant ships, the nation began to prepare for war, building ships and enlisting thousands of volunteers to fight.[57] Americans feared the worst, anxious about taking on the world's greatest military power. Their own nation was barely two decades into its own nationhood and lacking a large and effective military force, and compared to France looked weak and vulnerable. As

Hamilton wrote, "We may have to contend at our very doors for our independence and liberty."[58] The drumbeat of fear became irrational, fed by Federalist-leaning newspapers warning against a crazed and merciless enemy. Every man, said one writer, should remove his loved ones from the line of fire—otherwise, they would watch their wives in their "violation and expiring agonies" and their daughters "being deflowered by the lusty Othellos." As for the men, they would be "devoured alive by bloodthirsty cannibals."[59]

Despite the bloody excesses of the French Revolution, many Republicans like Jefferson admired the Republic of France and its democratic principles. They disagreed with Hamilton and the Federalists and criticized the slide to war. Amid the contagion of fear, the Federalists began a politically expedient campaign to paint their Republican political opponents as American Jacobins who cared more for France than they did for their own country.[60] America had a French population of about thirty thousand. Many Federalists saw them as an immigrant faction that would carry out the bidding of France and destroy the nation from within.[61] Hamilton made some of the most egregious smears against the opposition, pointing to the "indefatigable and malignant exertions which they are making to propagate disaffection to our own government." What he called "the French faction in America" will "join the standard of France if once erected in this country."[62]

A large majority of the newspapers supported the Federalists, but one that did not was so scurrilous that it drove its targets to apoplexy. Benjamin Franklin Bache, publisher of the *Aurora*, had conspicuously failed to inherit his grandfather's genes for even-tempered intelligence, instead making his mark every week with incendiary prose. He tore into Washington and then later into "the blind, bald, crippled, toothless, querulous ADAMS."[63] And then there was the radical journalist James T. Callender, a transplant from Scotland who turned his invective against Adams. Jefferson provided Callender with financial support as he discharged his pen against the Federalists.[64]

For the Federalists, the remedy was a law that would finally shut down the criticism and deal with what they regarded as a traitorous column within the country. Even one of the leading Federalist writers, William Cobbett, called for a law to deal with the dissent. "Surely," wrote Cobbett, evidently in denial that he might ever be prosecuted under different political circumstances, "we need a sedition law to keep our own rogues from cutting our throats, and an alien law to prevent the invasion by a host of foreign rogues to assist them."[65]

Perhaps nobody expressed the Federalist view more effectively than Alexander Addison, a judge who delivered a charge to a grand jury in Pennsylvania. "Speech, writing, and printing are the great directors of public opinion, and the public opinion is the great director of human action," Addison said. And it was the press that controlled public opinion. "Give to any set of men the command of the press, and you give them the command of the country."[66]

As the crisis grew around the conflict with France, the press in America was as caustic and uninhibited as it had been during the colonial protests against the British. But many dissenters were about to pay a steep price. A time had arrived that Jefferson would call "the reign of witches."[67]

ALL THE CALUMNY, all the name-calling, all the criticism both high and low—to the Federalists, the unceasing attacks in the press and the pamphlets were putting the nation at great risk.

During the deepening conflict with Britain that started in the mid-1760s with the imposition of taxes on the colonies, John Adams had made numerous statements supporting freedom of expression. He had approved the broadening public sphere that had included essays and pamphlets and fiery sermons from the pulpit. A broad-based dissent was critical to the cause to which Adams had given his support. Even as late as 1797, Adams still viewed sharp criticism of his own writings as helping to circulate his views. "The more they write and the more they lie about those volumes," Adams wrote about one of his circulating books, "the more good they do. They have caused them to be read in the last six months by more persons than would have read them in an hundred years."[68]

As he moved into his presidency, though, the verbal assaults by Republicans set him on a course of repressing his opponents. Leading men in his party began calling for a law to punish the Republican writers. Although Adams may not have specifically asked for a seditious libel law, his own public pronouncements included complaints about his critics. In April 1798, he wrote about "a spirit of party, which scruples not to go all lengths of profligacy, falsehood, and malignity, in defaming our government."[69] In June, he wrote to the citizens of Braintree, Massachusetts, that he was concerned about the "tongues and pens of slander, instruments with which our enemies expect to subdue our country."[70]

Abigail Adams had no reluctance about calling for punitive measures against her husband's critics as well as measures to check immigrants. Her political judgments were valued by John, and may have influenced him to sign the bill. Complaining about the "vile incendiaries" spewing "caluminiating abuse" against John in Bache's *Aurora*, she told her sister Mary Cranch on April 26 that "nothing will have an Effect until congress pass a Sedition Bill." A month later, she added: "I wish the laws of our Country were competent to punish the stirer up of sedition, the writer and Printer of base and unfounded calumny. This would contribute as much to the Peace and harmony of our Country as any measure, and in times like the present, a more carefull and attentive watch ought to be kept over foreigners."[71]

Republican leaders voiced deep fears about the likely crackdown on aliens and on the opposition press. In May, Madison wrote to Jefferson that the bill on aliens under consideration in the Senate "is a monster that must for ever disgrace its parents."[72] The next month, Jefferson wrote to Madison that the alien and sedition bills "are so palpably in the teeth of the constitution as to shew they mean to pay no respect to it."[73]

At the end of June, Henry Tazewell, a US senator from Virginia, sent Madison a copy of the bill on seditious libel. Capturing the mood of the times with a bit of dark humor that referred to the excesses of the French Revolution, Tazewell promised to send Madison "an account of whatever may occur that can be interesting, if I am not Guilotined."[74]

TAZEWELL WAS NOT GUILLOTINED, fortunately. The Federalists meant to cut off political expression that opposed their policies, but they generously planned to spare the heads of the writers themselves. Nonetheless, they did write into law severe penalties for dissent against the Adams administration, intending not only to punish writers after printing their work but also to scare them into keeping their inkwells firmly capped in the first place.

From mid-June to mid-July of 1798, Congress approved four laws that became known as the Alien and Sedition Acts. Fearing that French residents would take up arms against the nation, the Alien Act gave the government the power to imprison or expel residents from any country at war with the United States. The Sedition Act made it illegal to write, print, or utter "any false, scandalous and malicious writing or writings" against the government, either house of the Congress, or the president with intent to defame them or to bring them "into contempt or disrepute," or to "excite against them . . . the hatred of the good people of the United States."[75]

The word "scandalous" was an infinitely elastic concept, one that could stretch enough to ensnare any opponent. A writer could bring about a "scandal" that brought an official into "contempt or disrepute" simply by firing off criticism and convincing citizens that the official was a man of especially poor judgment. Such writings, appraising the conduct and wisdom of public officials, comprised the essence of self-governance. But under the law it could bring criminal charges.

It was a classic seditious libel law, but the Federalists grafted onto it the two most important safeguards that libertarians had wanted going back to the trial of printer John Peter Zenger in New York in 1735 (see chapter 2). Finally, the law granted the defense of truth for people accused of defaming the government, rejecting the oppressive common law rule that punished criticism of government whether it was true or not. And following in the footsteps of Fox's Act, which had been enacted in England in 1792, the Sedition Act expanded the power of the jury, giving it the right in libel cases to decide, subject to the judge's instructions, all questions of law and fact and to reach a general verdict. It reduced the power of judges with ties to entrenched political factions to determine the fate of a critic of government.[76]

These concessions were certainly advances in the law, but they amounted to putting mascara on a dragon. For the Sedition Act of 1798 was indeed a fearsome law. By definition, it protected the Federalist politicians that controlled the federal government. The law punished only criticism aimed at offices then in the hands of the Federalists—both houses of Congress and the president—and conspicuously omitted the office of vice president, held by Jefferson, a Republican. And it had its own sunset provision, conveniently expiring on the last full day of Adams's first term. It would be in effect during the election campaign of 1800 to weight the scale in favor of Adams and the Federalist incumbents in Congress, who would be shielded by the law from the worst criticism while enabling them to fire away freely against their opponents.

The Federalists, of course, argued that the First Amendment did not prevent prosecutions for writings critical of the government. Robert Goodloe Harper, a representative from South Carolina, argued that the First Amendment added nothing to the old Blackstonian common law view of freedom of the press—that is, it protected nothing more than the right to publish without prior restraints and "not that no law shall be passed to regulate this liberty of the press."[77] Representative Harrison Otis of Massachusetts even read on the House floor an extract from Blackstone's *Commentaries* and added, "Where lies the injury in attempting to check the progress of calumny and falsehood? Or how is society aided by the gross and monstrous outrages upon truth and honor, and public character and private peace which inundate the country?"[78]

The shock brought by the Sedition Act—that the Adams administration clearly intended to use it to prosecute its critics and shut down opposition speech—forced a fast and broad rethinking of the safeguards needed for political expression. Republicans were fighting for their political lives, and they realized that the defense of truth offered no real protection for their political commentary. So they articulated a new idea of freedom of expression that built on the ideas of past libertarians who had emphasized its connection to popular sovereignty. As Madison had said on introducing the amendment nine years earlier, the American conception of self-governance required citizens able to oversee their own affairs. If government officials were safe from criticism, said Albert Gallatin of Pennsylvania, "you thus deprive the people of the means of obtaining information of their conduct, you in fact render their right of electing nugatory."[79] John Nicholas of Virginia argued that "the people have no other means of examining their conduct but by means of the press, and an unrestrained investigation through them of the conduct of the Government." Loss of press freedom, he said, "would be to destroy the elective principle, by taking away the information necessary to election."[80]

For Gallatin, the Constitution and amendments had locked this understanding into the fundamental law of the land. Returning to the arguments surrounding ratification, Gallatin argued that the federal government held no enumerated power to legislate over the press. With the First Amendment added to expressly deny that such power existed, it seemed clear, he said, "that Congress could not pass any law to punish any real or supposed abuse of the press."[81]

Grafting the defense of truth onto the crime of seditious libel was an illusory protection, essentially worthless for the kind of dissent that animated politics in America. Gallatin said the legislation "was intended to punish solely writings of a political nature," which "almost always contained not only facts but opinions. And how could the truth of opinions be proven by evidence?"[82] In fact, much of the heated expression amounted to name-calling and rhetorical hyperbole, expression that was intentionally exaggerated to make a point.

What was the purpose of the legislation? Most obviously, he said, it was repression of the political opposition. Gallatin declared that the Federalists supposed that anyone who opposed the administration by speaking or writing "is seditious, is an enemy, not of administration, but of the Constitution, and is liable to punishment."[83] He added later, "Is it not their object to frighten and suppress all presses which they consider as contrary to their views; to prevent a free circulation of opinion; to suffer the people at large to hear only partial accounts, and but one side of the question; to delude and deceive them by partial information, and, through those means, to perpetuate themselves in power?"[84]

It was clear, Gallatin said, that the "true object of the law is to enable one party to oppress the other."[85] And Nicholas added, "This bill would, therefore, go to the suppression of every printing press in the country, which is not obsequious to the will of Government."[86]

WHILE CONGRESS DEBATED the Sedition Act, Jefferson left Philadelphia on his horse for a long journey back to Monticello in the midsummer heat.[87] He was happy to return to the home he loved so much, but he felt somber about the menacing clouds gathering over Congress. Over the last few months, he had exchanged letters with friends expressing his grave concern that political repression was on its way—repression in the form of "an Alien bill worthy of the 8th or 9th century" and a sedition bill whose object was "the suppression of the whig presses."[88]

On his stop at Montpelier on July 2, Jefferson and Madison made plans to oppose what they saw as an unconstitutional assertion of power over the free exchange of ideas. Their options, though, were limited. The Federalists controlled the federal government and held the majority in the legislatures of most of the states. So they decided to write resolutions protesting the new laws and submit them to a few friendly assemblies in the southern states. They dared not commit their plans to writing. For Madison and Jefferson, scheming as they were against the Adams administration, secrecy was critical in all that they did. Jefferson was the vice president opposing a policy of his own president, and both men's strong opposition to the Sedition Act was itself an illegal act under the law they were fighting. So they would entrust their plans and ideas only with each other and with a handful of their closest political friends.

Although Madison and Jefferson frequently wrote to each other, they apparently exchanged no letters between July 21 and October 26. The two men understood that posting letters to the mail posed a serious risk. They worried that some of their letters were intercepted and opened by their political opponents, with contents ending up in newspapers sympathetic to the Federalists. Because of that, they often avoided the mail and entrusted correspondence to friends and servants. Sometimes they wrote in code to each other.[89] As Jefferson wrote to Monroe during the middle of the Sedition Act prosecutions, "I shall seldom write to you, on account of the strong suspicions of infidelity in the post offices. always examine the seal before you open my letters, and note whether the impression is distinct."[90]

After their meeting on July 2, Madison and Jefferson began writing resolutions against the laws. Jefferson gave his completed draft to a trusted friend, Wilson Cary Nicholas, asking him to have the resolutions submitted to the North Carolina legislature. But Federalists were gaining strength in the North Carolina assembly, so Nicholas wrote to Jefferson that he had passed along the document to John Breckinridge, a representative in the Kentucky legislature, who was certain that Kentucky would approve the resolutions. Nicholas wrote that he had told Breckinridge of Jefferson's authorship because "I knew him to be worthy of confidence," and "he has given me the most Solemn assurances upon the subject."[91] Jefferson replied with approval of the new plan, and added that he had "no secrets" from Madison. "I wish him therefore to be consulted as to these resolutions," Jefferson wrote.[92]

In early November, Breckinridge himself headed a committee that introduced the resolutions, although with no identification of Jefferson as author, and in short order both houses of the legislature overwhelmingly approved. But Breckinridge had significantly softened Jefferson's most controversial proposal, the method suggested for redress of the grievance.

The Kentucky Resolutions characterized the nation as a compact among states, with each state free to judge on its own infractions of the compact as well as "the mode and measure of redress." Jefferson's draft had put forward the radical idea that each state had the power "to nullify of their own authority" any act of the federal government that it judged to be beyond the power delegated to it by the Constitution. The states, he said, could "concur in declaring these acts void, & of no force," and could take steps to assure that they were not put into effect within their own jurisdiction. But Jefferson's extreme remedy of nullifying a federal law had been removed by Breckinridge and replaced with a much more temperate recommendation that other states merely help repeal the laws.[93]

Meanwhile, in November, Jefferson turned his attention to influencing Madison, who was home at Montpelier writing a separate set of resolutions for introduction into the Virginia legislature. He sent Madison a copy of his draft of the Kentucky Resolutions as well as the version approved by the Kentucky legislature, urging him that "we should distinctly affirm all the important principles they contain."[94] In the next few weeks, when Madison finished his own resolutions, he gave them to Nicholas, who once again was serving as intermediary. Jefferson read Madison's completed draft of the Virginia Resolutions and wrote to Nicholas suggesting that he make some changes to add a sharper edge. Madison's writing had been couched in language too moderate for Jefferson's taste.

Madison's resolutions discussed abuses of power by the Federalists. Where there was "a deliberate, palpable, and dangerous exercise of other powers not granted by the said compact," the states "have the right, and are in duty bound to interpose for arresting the progress of the evil." Madison discussed the exercise of powers that he considered dangerous, including the Sedition Act that Congress had enacted in violation of the First Amendment. Finally, Virginia asked other states to agree in finding the laws a violation of the Constitution.[95]

Madison had written that the Alien and Sedition laws were unconstitutional, but Jefferson suggested that Nicholas alter the remedy. Instead of merely inviting other states to cooperate in dissolving the laws, he wanted to ask the states to join Virginia in the radical declaration that "the said acts are, and were ab initio—null, void, and of no force, or effect"—the recommendation that states themselves could overrule a federal law. Nicholas obliged with almost those exact words, and then John Taylor introduced them in the Virginia House of Delegates on December 10. However, just before the delegates voted on December 21, Taylor made a successful motion to delete the more aggressive words of Jefferson and restore the more moderate ones of Madison that the states could "concur with this commonwealth in declaring as it does hereby declare, that the aforesaid acts are unconstitutional." Without the word "null" in the final resolutions, the legislators hoped that the state would not be understood as taking upon itself the power to invalidate the laws.[96]

For Madison and Jefferson, the behind-the-scenes editing revealed a deep difference of approach. Jefferson believed that states could themselves declare laws enacted by Congress to be null and void. Madison, on the other hand, believed that the states could mobilize protests but lacked the power themselves to invalidate laws. The suggestion, though, that the states had the power to judge the constitutionality of federal laws brought waves of opposition from legislatures in other states, all but overshadowing the substantive arguments against the Alien and Sedition Acts.

AS MADISON AND JEFFERSON PREPARED their resolutions attacking the legal basis for the Sedition Act, their Republican friends around the country pushed back against the restrictions on speech. Repression failed to either silence the Republican dissidents or to send them scurrying into the shadows. Instead, it brought a defiant reaction, a result that should not have surprised anyone with a memory of colonial history. As the administration adopted suppression as its official policy, Republicans reacted with the same disdain for seditious libel as the patriots had shown in the years before separation. Criticism not only continued unabated, but actually intensified. Public meetings in a number of states brought out large numbers of people who wrote resolutions against the laws, including four thousand citizens in two Pennsylvania counties who signed petitions.[97]

The Federalists could have ignored the rowdy Republican press, for the Adams years began with a lopsided dominance of newspapers favoring their own party. In part, that was because the Federalists were tied to moneyed merchant and banking interests that had cash to spend on advertisements, making many editors reluctant to oppose them. The media historian Jeffrey L. Pasley has estimated that three-quarters of the papers were neutral or leaned toward the Federalist Party.[98]

The Federalists enjoyed a battalion of editors who could cajole and curse with the most vitriolic printers of the colonial period, and none more effectively than William Cobbett. For pure theatrics, nobody could match his nickname, Peter Porcupine, or the name of his newspaper, *Porcupine's Gazette,* whose quills regularly impaled the opponents of Adams. Cobbett and the leading Republican editor, Benjamin Franklin Bache of the *Aurora,* skirmished on a regular basis, with Cobbett calling Bache "a liar; a fallen wretch; a vessel formed for reprobation; and, therefore, we should always treat him as we would a TURK, a JEW, a JACOBIN or a DOG."[99]

Repression had the opposite of its intended effect. Rather than shut down and scare off the opposition press, it sent more Republicans scrambling to start their own papers. For every dandelion that prosecutors slashed off at its stem, the seeds blown into the air alighted in new places and quickly emerged as new opposition papers. In reaction to the Sedition Act, some of the new editors saw their partisanship as a virtuous response to official repression. Alexander Martin, the editor of the Baltimore *American,* praised any editor who "is capable of soaring above the flattery of villainy, and the adulation of power."[100]

Republican leaders encouraged the founding of new partisan papers, and editors found an increasing number of willing writers and readers. "The engine is the press," Jefferson wrote to Madison. "Every man must lay his purse & his pen under contribution," and he urged his friend "to set apart a certain part of every post-day to write what may be proper for the public."[101] At passage of the Sedition Act, about thirty-seven Republican or Republican-leaning newspapers were publishing. In the first year and a half after passage of the law, nineteen more were founded. In 1800, twenty-five Republican papers started up, compared to sixteen that leaned toward the Federalists. In all, then, the number of Republican papers more than doubled during the two and a half years after passage of the law. For many Republican papers, repression was great for business, lifting circulation as people flocked to read the condemnations of the Federalist politicians. By the time the presidential elections of 1800 came around, a newly vibrant Republican press scorched Adams and other Federalist politicians in an outpouring of criticism that was oblivious to the Sedition Act.[102]

For the most combative paper, the *Aurora*, Bache reported to his subscribers at the end of August that a prosecution against him for seditious libel had increased his business. "The encrease in the circulation of this paper has been beyond the editor's most sanguine expectations," he wrote, and so "the daring hand of persecution already counteracts its own designs." He added that many subscribers had settled old debts and provided advances on their subscriptions, although the paper still retained thousands of dollars of receivables on its books from subscribers, a common problem for printers of the time.[103] Jefferson himself wrote in retirement many years later of the key role played by the Republican press, especially the *Aurora*. These papers energized the Republicans, he said, "when our cause was laboring, and all but lost, under the overwhelming weight of it's powerful adversaries," and it accomplished an "unquestionable effect . . . in the public mind, which arrested the rapid march of our government towards monarchy."[104]

While newspapers carried the burden of the attack against the Adams administration, Republicans did not forget the other forms of political expression that had been so effective since the mid-1760s. Once again, symbolic imagery provided a unifying rallying point. Partisans on both sides used colorful cockades in their hats to show allegiance to their cause. In Philadelphia, more than one thousand young men paraded to President Adams's house in May 1798 with black cockades to show their support of his stance against France. On the next day, Republicans marched with tricolor cockades to make their own statement. In other demonstrations during the period, protestors ridiculed their opponents by putting cow dung in their cockades, while others scripted political theater that involved mock funerals for the cockades they did not like.[105]

The symbolic imagery of effigies returned as well. In 1777, two decades earlier, Adams had said that he would like to see the likenesses of General William Howe and his officers swinging from a gallows. "It would give me no pain to see them burned or hanged in effigy in every town and village," he confided to Abigail Adams.[106] Now, though, Adams as president surely felt pain on hearing about protestors hanging his own effigy at the College of William and Mary. An angry *Porcupine's Gazette* responded by saying that the college must be headed by a "bitter, seditious, envious wretch," and that it would be preferable to educate a child "under tuition of a common thief, than send him amongst this rascally seditious crew." And in

Stamford, Connecticut, protestors strung Adams's effigy from gallows in front of the meetinghouse and then set it afire. A notice posted near the effigy proclaimed that people "who venerate this intended Despot, may here pay their last homage to his remaining ashes."[107]

Liberty Poles mushroomed throughout the country. In Newburgh, New York, Republicans raised a pole with an inscription that included "NO SEDITION BILL."[108] In a town in the Maine district of Massachusetts, more than one hundred Republicans lifted their Liberty Pole with a chorus of huzzahs, then made toasts to "Freedom of speech, trial by jury, and liberty of the press." That did not end the matter, for a group of Federalists cut the pole down—just as British troops had done to Liberty Poles erected by the Sons of Liberty before independence—then raised their own toasts.

Understanding the power of symbols, one man had a different idea for the name of the Liberty Poles. "May all Sedition Poles fall like Lucifer, never to rise again," he said.[109]

TO THE FEDERALISTS, the very emblems of protest—the Liberty Trees and Poles that had carried the patriots to the Revolution—had now become symbols of sedition. The Federalists would, sorrowfully enough, use their most vindictive prosecution under the Sedition Act to jail David Brown, who had shown the temerity to lift a Liberty Pole in Dedham, Massachusetts.

Immediately upon passage of the law, Adams put his secretary of state, Timothy Pickering, in charge of hunting down violators. Pickering was a severe and strident Federalist, a man "whose manners are forbidding, whose temper is sour and whose resentments are implacable," according to Abigail Adams.[110] So single-minded was Pickering that he scoured newspapers each morning and called on informers to prospect for writings that might become the basis for a prosecution. Safe from prosecution himself, Cobbett of *Porcupine's Gazette* even went so far as making a list of papers whose editors seemed like a good target for Pickering.[111]

Pickering's prosecution of Brown was peculiar because he was entirely harmless, and it showed the extent of Federalist persecution.[112] Brown exercised no power, held no office, owned no newspaper. He had fought in Washington's army and now, in his forties, had spent some years in manual labor while traveling through Massachusetts talking on politics, much like an evangelical preacher except without the thousands of swooning listeners. Brown argued that an oligarchy ruled the country for its own benefit, holding the common man subservient by "every means that the Devil has put in their hands." In October 1798, Brown arrived in Dedham, a town that boasted a strong core of committed Republicans who applauded his words and raised a Liberty Pole that month to show their revulsion at Federalist policies. They attached a sign to the pole with the mild complaint, "No Stamp Act, No Sedition, No Alien Bills, No Land Tax; downfall to the Tyrants of America, peace and retirement to the President." A Boston paper, though, complained that the Dedham Liberty Pole was the "Jacobin Pole" and a "rallying point of insurrection and civil war."[113]

Brown argued that if the people were denied their right to criticize public officials, they would erupt "like the burning mountain of Etna, and will have an unconditional redress of their grievances." As it turned out, it was the Federalists who erupted. A judge ordered a federal marshal to destroy the Liberty Pole, but a group of Federalists beat him to it, felling the pole amid a melee with some Republicans who tried to stop them. The prosecutor filed a warrant for Brown's arrest. Fisher Ames, a prominent Federalist who lived in Dedham, characterized Brown as "a wandering apostle of sedition," an accusation that proved partly correct because the marshal could not find Brown, who had in fact wandered out of town.

Meanwhile, the authorities arrested Benjamin Fairbanks, a well-heeled Dedham farmer, for his part in raising the Liberty Pole. After Brown was finally arrested, the two men decided to plead guilty and throw themselves on the mercy of the court. What mercy there was went to Fairbanks, however. Samuel Chase, a justice on the US Supreme Court, presided over the proceedings while riding the circuit. Chase had been a member of the Sons of Liberty protesting against the Stamp Act in Maryland, and had gone on to serve in the Continental Congress and sign the Declaration of Independence.[114] Now, after a plea for clemency from none other than the Federalist Fisher Ames, Chase gave Fairbanks six hours in prison and a fine of five dollars. For Brown, who had no political connections, Chase imposed a severe punishment—eighteen months in jail and a fine of more than four hundred dollars. In 1800, nearing the end of his sentence, Brown petitioned Adams for a pardon because he could not pay the fine, a condition for being released. Adams refused, then refused a second time.

Due to poor records at the time, the number of cases brought against Republicans is uncertain. The Federalists, though, appear to have brought at least fifteen cases against their opponents, including nine under the Sedition Act, three under federal common law, and three under state law. There were ten convictions. Five Republican papers either shut down or suspended publication during their time of trouble.[115]

Few public servants of the time—or of any time, for that matter—proved as grimly effective at their appointed task as Pickering. Pickering's first target was Matthew Lyon, editor of the *Vermont Journal,* who also happened to be a Republican congressman from Vermont. Lyon's offense was having written that the president had allowed "every consideration of the public welfare [to have been] swallowed up in a continuous grasp for power, in an unbounded thirst for ridiculous pomp, foolish adulation, and a selfish avarice." Only five days elapsed from indictment to conviction and a penalty of four months in jail and a fine of $1,000 plus court costs. As Jefferson observed in a letter to Madison, "The words called seditious were only general censures of the proceedings of Congress & of the President." A group of Republicans, including Jefferson, Madison, and Monroe, helped pay the fine.[116]

James Callender, the long-standing critic of the Federalists who at times received financial support from Jefferson, quickly became another victim of the law. Callender had, among other writings, called the administration "a tempest of malignant passions" and Adams a "hoary headed incendiary." Callender had to reckon with Justice Chase. Although the Sedition Act expanded the role of juries to decide a case, in reality federal judges sided with the government so often and so stridently that many times they seemed like prosecutors themselves. They often severely limited the ability of defendants to introduce evidence and arguments, and delivered one-sided instructions to juries.[117]

Justice Chase started the prosecution of Callender after seeing his writings while traveling to Richmond. Chase presided over the trial, ruling out much of the most effective defense testimony. Callender got nine months behind bars and a fine of two hundred dollars. Five years later, when Chase was impeached and tried by the Senate—a move that failed to garner the required two-thirds vote—he was accused of "rude, contemptuous, and indecent conduct" during the Callender trial.[118]

And so it went, trial after trial. One editor whom the Federalists dearly wanted to jail was Benjamin Franklin Bache. The scurrilous editor of the *Aurora* was so high on the Federalists' list that they did not even wait for passage of the Sedition Act to pursue him. Just as the bill was introduced in the US Senate in June, the Federalists charged him under the common law. Bache, however, was one editor who escaped the Federalists' grasp. Yellow fever struck Philadelphia that summer and claimed his life.[119]

EVEN AS REPUBLICAN WRITERS heard the doors to their prison cells lock behind them, Madison and Jefferson suffered a complete rejection of their efforts to oppose the Alien and Sedition Acts. Their sense of national politics had betrayed them. A strong argument against the statutes as a violation of the Constitution would have provided them the best opportunity to rally support for possible repeal. But they had gone considerably beyond that with their proposed remedy, creating an easy target for the Federalists, who charged that the Republicans meant to dissolve the nation and were prepared to rebel.[120]

The Virginia and Kentucky Resolutions received unanimous rejection by the ten states that considered them. All of the rejections came from states north of the Potomac, where Federalists controlled every legislature. These states, predictably, said that the Alien and Sedition Acts were consistent with the Constitution, and opposed the idea that state legislatures could reject an act of Congress. Only the Supreme Court, Federalists said, held the power of review.[121] No replies came from the states in the South, where Republicans enjoyed enough strength to create a standoff.[122]

In the face of rejection, Jefferson pressed the case. In a letter to Madison on August 23, he asked his friend to meet him at Monticello, at the same time proposing that they draft new resolutions for Virginia and Kentucky that answered the states that had rejected the earlier protest— "the principles already advanced by Virginia & Kentucky are not to be yielded in silence." Jefferson said that they should express "in affectionate & conciliatory language our warm attachment to union with our sister-states," but added an aggressive threat should other states continue their abuse of the Constitution—that they were ready "to sever ourselves from that union we so much value, rather than give up the rights of self government" protected by the Constitution.[123]

Always careful and conservative, Madison softened Jefferson's tough stance when he visited him at Monticello. After the meeting, Jefferson wrote to Wilson Cary Nicholas again on September 5 and this time failed to include the "sever ourselves" wording. Now he would act "in deference to his [Madison's] judgment" and "should never think of separation but for repeated and enormous violations." Nonetheless, the Kentucky Resolutions of 1799 asserted that the states could judge whether a federal law violated the Constitution, and declared state "nullification" a justifiable remedy for obnoxious laws. In the years ahead, the suggestion that states could nullify federal laws that they opposed—or "interpose" to stop a federal action seen as dangerous, as the Virginia Resolutions put it—would be invoked again and again without success in various crises, making it an unfortunate legacy of the Sedition Act controversy.[124]

With the second version of the Kentucky Resolutions passed, attention focused on Virginia. Madison, now a member of the Virginia Assembly, began writing a strong defense of the Virginia Resolutions.[125] The prosecutions that struck hard at Republican editors motivated him to do more than protest. He would undertake a major rethinking of the meaning of freedom of speech and press in America.

A NEW LIBERTARIAN THEORY was of necessity finally emerging from what had been scattered writings in the past. All through the pre-Revolutionary period, and through the fiery debate over the Constitution, Americans had acted in every way like the common law crime of seditious libel did not exist. They had shown through their own uninhibited speech a new understanding of freedom of expression. All the while, though, the legal structure supporting attempts at repression had remained intact—aside from a handful of libertarian writers, there had been no frontal attack on seditious libel itself that would finally rid the country of archaic understandings.

The Sedition Act, though, changed all that. The defense of free speech that began with opposition to the enactment of the law in 1798 continued the next February as Republicans in Congress moved aggressively to attempt to repeal it. Although they lost on a straight party-line vote, they effectively undermined the foundation on which the crime of seditious libel stood. John Nicholas of Virginia said that the doctrine of seditious libel was derived from Britain, where the king is hereditary and is regarded as incapable of doing wrong. Public officers, in turn, also cloaked themselves with inviolability as the king's representatives. "It was, therefore, of course, that they should receive a different sort of respect from that which is proper in our Government, where the officers of Government are the servants of the people, are amenable to them, and liable to be turned out of office at periodical elections."[126]

It was Madison, though, who finally brought the libertarian arguments together in one compelling essay. He had started this task when he had introduced what would become the First Amendment in 1789. Now Madison fully developed his defense of freedom of expression. His "Report of 1800," approved by the Virginia House of Delegates that January, defended the Virginia Resolutions against the charge that the state had gone too far in asserting a power to reject laws enacted by Congress. He softened the argument significantly by saying that states opposing the constitutionality of a federal law were merely offering an opinion, and that only the federal courts held the power to make rulings on the Constitution. Protests by the states, he said, should regard only a "*deliberate, palpable* and *dangerous* breach of the constitution."[127]

Madison turned to the question of whether the Sedition Act violated the First Amendment and did so with the special credibility of having been the primary author of the Bill of Rights ten years earlier. This was Madison looking back at the First Amendment and explaining the meaning he thought that the framers intended. Although his account would have carried even more weight had he written it when it was proposed and ratified, he wove together many themes that he had written about in years past. No American could match him for both his deep immersion in the events surrounding the Bill of Rights and his knowledge of political structure.

In the kind of carefully reasoned argument for which he had become famous, Madison explained why freedom of political expression was indispensable to the American conception of government. The British system, said Madison, echoing Nicholas a year earlier, embraced leaders who were not answerable to the people. The king, who inherited his power, was considered to do no wrong, and Parliament was also largely hereditary and a sovereign power. In America, though, sovereignty resided with citizens who elected public officials to represent them, and these officials were considered neither omnipotent nor infallible. "Is it not natural and necessary," Madison asked, "under such different circumstances, that a different degree of freedom, in the use of the press, should be contemplated?"[128]

To exercise self-governance, Americans needed to scrutinize public officials and their actions. Criticisms of public officials would by their very nature tend to bring them into contempt or disrepute, which is what the Sedition Act made the focus of punishment. When public officials violated their trust, wrote Madison, then "it is natural and proper, that, according to the cause and degree of their faults, they should be brought into contempt or disrepute, and incur the hatred of the people." Punishment of criticism would slash at the heart of self-governance. "The value and efficacy of this right, depends on the knowledge of the comparative merits and demerits of the candidates for public trust; and on the equal freedom, consequently, of examining and discussing these merits and demerits of the candidates respectively." In addition, in an election, the law shielded public officials from harsh criticism but not the candidates who opposed them. Because of that, incumbents would "derive an undue advantage."[129]

Madison returned to the ratification battles in Virginia and other states over whether a bill of rights was necessary. Once again, he argued that the Constitution gave the government no enumerated power over the press. To satisfy opponents who insisted on more explicit protections, many states recommended amendments to make the protection of individual rights more explicit, and the first federal Congress and the states approved the amendment that guaranteed freedom of speech and press. So the Constitution gave the federal government no power over the press, and, in addition, the First Amendment provided an express denial of any such power. As a result, said Madison, "the Federal Government is destitute of all such authority."[130]

The Sedition Act had finally made truth a defense to a charge of seditious libel, but Madison recognized that such a defense in political speech was illusory. Truth was difficult to prove in a court of law, and in any case most political writings involved opinions, inferences, and conjecture not subject to verification.[131] With the sword poised to fall on writers who offended officeholders, Madison worried that seditious libel would chill speech. Some nasty expression was inevitable, and should not be an excuse for repression. "Some degree of abuse is inseparable from the proper use of every thing; and in no instance is this more true, than in that of the press," Madison wrote, adding that "it is better to leave a few of its noxious branches to their luxuriant growth, than, by pruning them away, to injure the vigor of those yielding the proper fruits."[132]

Madison's fierce attack on seditious libel called again on a powerful lesson from history, this time the understanding that Americans themselves had of freedom of speech and press. To Madison, freedom of expression meant the actual speech that the American people had engaged in. "In every State, probably, in the Union," he wrote, "the press has exerted a freedom in canvassing the merits and measures of public men, of every description, which has not been confined to the strict limits of the common law. On this footing the freedom of the press has stood; on this footing it yet stands."[133]

Uninhibited freedom of expression, he said, was in large part responsible for the separation from Britain as well as a kind of second revolution that took the country from its weak Articles of Confederation to the new Constitution. "Had 'Sedition acts,'" he argued, "forbidding every publication that might bring the constituted agents into contempt or disrepute, or that might excite the hatred of the people against the authors of unjust or pernicious measures, been uniformly enforced against the press; might not the United States have been languishing at this day, under the infirmities of a sickly Confederation? Might they not, possibly, be miserable colonies, groaning under a foreign yoke?"[134]

It was, Madison argued, "to the press alone, chequered as it is with abuses, the world is indebted for all the triumphs which have been gained by reason and humanity, over error and oppression; who reflect that to the same beneficent source, the United States owe much of the lights which conducted them to the rank of a free and independent nation; and which have improved their political system, into a shape so auspicious to their happiness."[135]

Ultimately, then, the legacy of the Sedition Act is that it pushed many of the best minds in America to construct a new foundation for freedom of expression by coupling it with the needs of a self-governing society.

IF AMERICANS WERE DEDICATED to the freedom of speech, how do we account for the repressive Sedition Act, which Congress passed just seven years after ratification of the First Amendment? What does this say for the meaning of political expression?

The narrow common law definition of freedom of expression had been embedded in law for many centuries, and it is perhaps too much to expect that it would be completely rejected overnight. Americans had clearly repudiated it in practice, from the early 1760s onward, as they dissented by every means. But changes in the legal structure took time to catch up with what the founding generation did in actual practice. With constitutional protections for political expression so new, there was no body of legal precedent to keep it from sinking into the quicksand represented by centuries of the repressive common law. Even in the second half of the twentieth century, much more extensive protections for freedom of speech did not keep the government from punishing critics during times of national peril.[136]

Although it was a powerful anti-speech law, the Sedition Act provides little traction for discovering what the founding generation meant by freedom of expression. Congress passed the law during what appeared to be an almost certain war with France, the world's premier military power. The Federalists used it solely as a spear to impale their Republican critics. A crackdown on dissident speech was not particularly surprising under such circumstances.

The Federalist who controlled Congress in 1798 bore little resemblance to the group that had drafted the First Amendment just nine years earlier. Membership in Congress had almost completely turned over in that short period of time—only eighteen representatives and senators remained of the ninety-five framers of the First Amendment who sat in the First Congress. And of those eighteen who remained in Congress, only ten voted in favor of the Sedition Act. Not one of the four Federalist lawmakers who guided the Sedition Act to passage had been a member of the First Congress.[137]

Ultimately, the Sedition Act was a complete political failure. Americans rejected the repressive tactics. Republicans continued their vigorous criticism of Adams, and their newspapers exploded in number during the years that the prosecutions took place. Voters showed their displeasure. Representative Matthew Lyon gained reelection from his jail cell as his constituents rebelled against his prosecution. The excessive partisanship of the anti-speech law contributed to the defeat of John Adams in his bid for a second term.

THOMAS JEFFERSON EMERGED from his boardinghouse on New Jersey Avenue at around noon on March 4, 1801. A group of riflemen and artillerymen paraded on the street as the president-elect walked up Capitol Hill, accompanied by a group of congressmen as well as militia officers with their swords drawn. Artillery fire shook the air as Jefferson entered the Capitol, where he quickly made his way to the Senate Chamber. More than one thousand people—members of Congress and the public—crowded the room as he took the chair of the presiding officer.[138]

Only a few weeks earlier, Jefferson had won the presidency on the thirty-sixth ballot taken in the House of Representatives. He and his running mate, Aaron Burr, had tied in the Electoral College, their Republican ticket having turned Adams out of office after one term. The Sedition Act had expired just the day before, and Jefferson grasped the opportunity to talk about the intolerance of dissent that had marked the last few years.

Although the majority would always prevail in a democracy, even so "the minority possess their equal rights," he said. "And let us reflect that having banished from our land that religious intolerance under which mankind so long bled and suffered, we have yet gained little if we countenance a political intolerance, as despotic, as wicked, and capable of as bitter and bloody persecutions." He went on, counseling the unity of Americans despite differences of opinion. "We are all Republicans, we are all Federalists. If there be any among us who would wish to dissolve this Union or to change its republican form, let them stand undisturbed as monuments of the safety with which error of opinion may be tolerated, where reason is left free to combat it."[139]

The Sedition Act had caused a backlash of disgust at the Federalists that was in part responsible for their losing their congressional majority as well as the presidency. The nation had not gone to war, and the law had been a total failure, for dissent had flourished and opposition newspapers had proliferated. John Quincy Adams, son of John and later a president himself, wrote that the Sedition Act was "an ineffectual attempt to extinguish the fire of defamation, but it operated like oil upon the flames."[140] Jefferson pardoned those who fell to the Sedition Act, and Congress later agreed to repay their fines. As he wrote in a letter to Abigail Adams a few years later, he regarded the law "to be a nullity as absolute and as palpable as if Congress had ordered us to fall down and worship a golden image."[141]

Not long after his presidential term ended, Adams had regrets about the wisdom of his party's enactment of the Sedition Act. He did his best to distance himself from the law, claiming that he never really wanted it but went along. He thought that it was a product of a crisis that imperiled the nation's security. Adams tried to put the blame for the Sedition Act on Hamilton, who, he said, had provided instructions to Federalist leaders in Congress. "I recommended no such thing in my speech," Adams wrote. "Congress, however, adopted both of these measures." However, he added: "I knew there was need enough of both, and therefore I consented to them." But, he said, "as they were then considered as war measures, and intended altogether against the advocates of the French and peace with France, I was apprehensive that a hurricane of clamor would be raised against them, as in truth there was, even more fierce and violent than I had anticipated."[142]

That fierce "hurricane of clamor" began to swirl from the portico of Montpelier on July 2, 1798. It did not subside until Madison, the father of the First Amendment, defined the American meaning of freedom of speech and press.

AFTERWORD

THE SEDITION ACT EXPIRED ON THE LAST DAY OF THE ADAMS ADMINISTRATION, BUT THE embers from that partisan fire continued to glow for years. The Federalists and Republicans could not resist wielding seditious libel actions against each other to settle old scores.

For a brief time, it looked like this speech crime might be put aside. After freeing those still in jail for violating the Sedition Act, Jefferson early in his first term expressed optimism that libel prosecutions would end. He wrote to Levi Lincoln, his attorney general, that he "would wish much to see the experiment tried of getting along without public prosecutions for *libels*. I believe we can do it."[1]

As it turned out, they could not do it. Even Jefferson himself could not resist. Like Adams before him, Jefferson quickly grew agitated by the calumny directed at him. Leading the way was James Callender, a journalist who had been convicted under the Sedition Act and now returned with a personal vendetta against Jefferson. Callender expected a political reward for his support of the Republican cause, but his fiery writing made him too radical for Jefferson, who refused his request to be appointed postmaster of Richmond. Callender lashed out vindictively at the president with a torrent of invective that included allegations that Jefferson had fathered children with one of his slaves, Sally Hemings.[2] By his Second Inaugural Address, on March 4, 1805, Jefferson bitterly complained that "the artillery of the press has been levelled against us, charged with whatsoever its licentiousness could devise or dare."[3]

Despite his broad pronouncements about the importance of a free press, Jefferson had always had a somewhat formalistic idea of how far that freedom should extend. He expressed his aversion to protecting newspapers that published false facts, and he expressed little reluctance about libel prosecutions initiated by the states rather than by the federal government. Rather than condemn all seditious libel actions as destructive to a self-governing society, as Madison had done, Jefferson argued that by its terms—"Congress shall make no law . . ."—the First Amendment expressly forbade only action by the federal government to restrict the press but left the states free to do as they pleased. He said as much to Abigail Adams in defending himself from her criticism for pardoning writers convicted under the Sedition Act for vilifying her husband. Jefferson said that he had acted because the Constitution was clear on the matter. "While we deny that Congress have a right to controul the freedom of the press, we have ever asserted the right of the states, and their exclusive right, to do so," he wrote in 1804.[4] At his Second Inaugural Address the following March, he complained about the vicious criticism of his own administration and again refused to rule out seditious libel actions by the states. Scandalous writings, he said, "might, indeed, have been corrected by the wholesome punishments reserved and provided by the laws of the several States against falsehood and defamation; but public duties more urgent press on the time of public servants, and the offenders have therefore been left to find their punishment in the public indignation."[5]

Some public servants, though, did push for prosecutions. In all, about thirty prosecutions for libel took place over the fifteen years after expiration of the Sedition Act, the vast majority of them brought under state law and instigated by whichever political party held the upper hand in any one state.[6] In New York, Republicans prosecuted the Federalist editor of *The Wasp*, aptly named for the burning stingers it put into Jefferson. The case against Harry Croswell proceeded under New York common law, which followed the Blackstonian definition of seditious libel that did not even permit the defense of truth.

After Croswell's conviction, Alexander Hamilton, who had supported the Sedition Act of 1798, defended Croswell on his appeal. Hamilton's six-hour oration in favor of allowing the defense of truth as long as it was published for "good motives" and for "justifiable ends," as well as for an expanded role for the jury, impressed New York legislators. The next year, they passed a libel statute conforming to Hamilton's view of the defense of truth, and many other states copied those provisions into their own law and constitution. But Hamilton's version of the defense of truth was qualified—it applied only if the writer had published for good motives and for justifiable ends—and so was even more restrictive than the infamous Sedition Act, which allowed the defense of truth without qualification.[7]

Jefferson had his fingerprints on a few prosecutions. But unlike Federalists during the Adams administration, he saw seditious libel actions as a dose of bitter medicine rather than a weapon to use in an extensive campaign to silence his foes. Pennsylvania governor Thomas McKean wrote to Jefferson in 1803 complaining about the press and asking whether the president agreed that "infamous & seditious libels . . . may be greatly checked by a few prosecutions." Jefferson agreed with that strategy, grousing that the Federalist press had practiced "it's licentiousness and it's lying to such a degree of prostitution as to deprive it of all credit." He added that he had "long thought that a few prosecutions of the most eminent offenders would have a wholsome effect in restoring the integrity of the presses. not a general prosecution, for that would look like persecution: but a selected one." He even sent a copy of a paper that might provide a handy target for McKean.[8]

A few years later, Jefferson became intertwined with one of the rare federal seditious libel prosecutions. A Republican prosecutor in Connecticut got an indictment against six Federalists in 1806, including four writers and two ministers for their sermons attacking Jefferson. Although the Sedition Act had long expired, the Republicans used what they said was a federal common law version of the crime. Jefferson found out about the prosecutions about six months later, but did not intervene to recommend that the prosecution be dropped until a defendant threatened to disclose a personal scandal involving Jefferson's alleged attempt to seduce a young married woman decades earlier.[9]

WHAT DID THE FOUNDING GENERATION understand by the freedom of speech and press? The founding generation appeared to see freedom of expression in the broadest possible terms, at least in regard to the way they actually practiced it. As I have discussed in *Revolutionary Dissent*, Americans all through the founding period expanded the public sphere of political speech, engaging in every possible means of dissent available to them, from newspapers and pamphlets to songs, sermons, speeches, poems, plays, letters, petitions, liberty trees, and much more. Political expression could be erudite and even scholarly, but scurrilous often seemed more the norm.

Vigorous speech did not stop once the colonies separated from Britain. The ratification process involved what is still the most extensive political debate in the nation's history, and the fact that the Constitution itself came into being amid full and free discussion is itself significant. Such was the case, too, in the years after ratification, with commentators flailing at politicians and each other during the two terms of George Washington as the two political parties came into existence. And the First Amendment guarantees of freedom of expression came into being amid raucous speech throughout the country. Americans debated and protested as if the crime of seditious libel did not exist. They could hardly have understood that the First Amendment would allow prosecutions for the kind of freewheeling debate that they had engaged in even as they ratified the Constitution and Bill of Rights.

Over time, the founding generation began to reconsider the legal underpinnings of freedom of expression as well. From the early 1760s onward they established the freedom of expression in practice, and then they began to do so in law as they reacted to the repression of the Sedition Act. First in the articles of lonely libertarians, and then in the writings and speeches of Madison, Gallatin, Nicholas, and others, Americans began to tie freedom of expression to the requirements of a self-governing society. In America, citizens had the duty to continually assess the performance of those chosen to represent them. As Madison wrote in his Virginia Resolutions, it is the "right of freely examining public characters and measures, and of free communication among the people thereon, which has ever been justly deemed the only effectual guardian of every other right."[10]

More than any others of his peers, Madison understood and articulated the practical and legal underpinnings for freedom of expression in America. For some others, the story is messy as they grappled both with the needs of a self-governing society and the excesses of an exuberant press. Adams had made frequent statements during the founding period about the power of free speech to change minds—"our presses have groaned, our Pulpits have thundered." And Jefferson had asserted that if he were to decide "whether we should have a government without newspapers or newspapers without a government, I should not hesitate a moment to prefer the latter." The reputation of both men suffered for their involvement with seditious libel prosecutions. Historian Leonard Levy considered Jefferson's inconsistency on civil liberties to be his "darker side."[11]

Looked at another way, their vision was remarkably prescient as to their own behavior once in office. Speaking as libertarians from the Enlightenment tradition before they became president, Adams and Jefferson understood the lesson that history offered about politics and power—that public officials could not be blindly trusted to act in the best interest of citizens, and that officials tended to punish their strongest and most effective critics. Alas, that applied to Adams and Jefferson themselves. Even they could not resist the feelings to which all human beings are prone, the emotional wounds produced by persistent and often mean-spirited criticism and the urge to strike back. Once elected president, they acted consistent with their own vision of how government officials act, confirming the necessity for constitutional protections for critics of official conduct.

Adams and Jefferson indeed suffered vicious attacks during their time in office. Jefferson so soured on newspapers that he wrote during his presidency in 1807 that they were nothing but vessels overflowing with lies. "Nothing can now be believed which is seen in a newspaper," he wrote. "Truth itself becomes suspicious by being put into that polluted vehicle." He suggested that papers be divided into four sections. The first section, truths, "would be very short." The second section, probabilities, "should rather contain too little than too much." The third and fourth sections, possibilities and lies, "should be professedly for those readers who would rather have lies for their money than the blank paper they would occupy."[12] Seven years later, now out of office, his mood had not brightened. "I deplore, with you, the putrid state into which our newspapers have passed, and the malignity, the vulgarity, & mendacious spirit of those who write for them."[13]

In their retirement, though, with the heat of partisan politics securely behind them, both Adams and Jefferson took a more expansive view of freedom of expression. Adams regretted having signed the Sedition Act, calling it and the Alien Act "war measures" and thus implying that seditious libel would be justified only in the context of national security.[14] And he told Jefferson that for him the meaning of the Revolution "was in the minds of the people" and required a close reading of colonial literature to "ascertain the Steps by which the public Opinion was enlightened and informed."[15]

Jefferson, too, seemed once again to embrace the importance of the press and expressed views that put him back in the forefront of libertarians. In a letter to a French citizen in 1823, three years before his death, Jefferson wrote of the critical role that the press played in a democracy and said that publications should be protected unless they caused "personal injuries." Presumably, mere criticism and scurrilous language would not be enough to justify punishment of speakers and writers. "This formidable censor of the public functionaries, by arraigning them at the tribunal of public opinion, produces reform peaceably, which must otherwise be done by revolution," he wrote. "It is also the best instrument for enlightening the mind of man, and improving him as a rational, moral, and social being."[16]

IN THE END, it was Madison's vision that won the day in America. In his "Report of 1800," he had constructed a new legal theory that married popular sovereignty to the freedom of speech and press. And, he said, Americans expected the uninhibited freedom of thought that they had enjoyed during the founding period—"On this footing the freedom of the press has stood; on this footing it yet stands."[17]

It took a very long time, though, for the legal structure to catch up with the actual freedom they enjoyed during years of freewheeling debate. The Supreme Court had little opportunity to expound on the meaning of freedom of speech in the nineteenth century. The First Amendment on its face limited actions by only the federal government and there were few free speech controversies involving the national government during that time. If a state used its libel law to punish dissent, the defendant could test the law's validity only under a state constitution, and not the First Amendment. All that changed in 1925, when the Court said that the freedom of speech and press were protected from abridgement by the states through the due process clause of the Fourteenth Amendment, ratified in 1868.[18]

Even as late as 1907, though, the Court held a miserly view of the freedom of speech, with Justice Oliver Wendell Holmes declaring that the First Amendment embraced Blackstone's old common law concept of freedom of the press—that it prevented only previous restraints on publications and not punishment after the fact.[19] During the First World War, Congress enacted espionage and sedition laws and, along with some states, began prosecuting opponents of the war and assorted other radicals. Led initially by Justice Holmes's opinion in *Schenck v. United States,* the Court's "clear and present danger" test led to numerous convictions of people who were merely protesting government policy but assumed by the justices to be provoking illegal action.[20]

Later in 1919, Justice Holmes changed his mind about the freedom of speech and set the Court moving toward the much more expansive conception of freedom of speech articulated by Madison.[21] In a case upholding the conviction of a group of Russian immigrants for their pamphlets opposing America's deployment of troops to Russia, Holmes wrote a dissenting opinion that rejected the idea that seditious libel was compatible with the First Amendment. "History seems to me against the notion," he said, pointing out that the country "had shown its repentance for the Sedition Act of 1798, by repaying fines that it imposed."[22]

To Holmes, as to Madison, freedom of speech provided a self-governing people the power to respond in a democratic way to the issues before them. Even ideas that challenged the most fundamental beliefs in society must have their chance to gain the support of citizens. "Congress certainly cannot forbid all effort to change the mind of the country," he wrote. Although the majority in society may believe strongly in a particular policy, he added, history had shown that "time has upset many fighting faiths." Rather than suppress dissent, he extolled the value of the marketplace of ideas—that "the ultimate good desired is better reached by free trade in ideas—that the best test of truth is the power of the thought to get itself accepted in the competition of the market." And that, he added, "is the theory of our Constitution."[23]

Holmes used strong language to describe the ideas that deserved protection. He said that "we should be eternally vigilant against attempts to check the expression of opinions that we loathe and believe to be fraught with death, unless they so imminently threaten immediate interference with the lawful and pressing purposes of the law that an immediate check is required to save the country." And so, Holmes had concluded, even ideas that shook the foundations of society—those "fraught with death"—should be protected unless they came very close to fomenting immediate illegal action.[24]

In 1927, in a case involving prosecution of a woman who had helped organize the Communist Labor Party of California, Justice Louis Brandeis wrote the most eloquent and powerful defense of free speech rights since Madison's "Report of 1800."[25] Brandeis recalled in a memorable way the original understanding of the founding generation, referring to the people "who won our independence" and once adding "by revolution." His reference to the founding generation, and specifically to the people who won independence, clearly separated the American understanding of freedom of expression from the narrow definition inherited from England.[26] To Brandeis, the primary value of freedom of speech and press was its contribution to self-governance in a democratic society. "They believed," wrote Brandeis, "that freedom to think as you will and to speak as you think are means indispensable to the discovery and spread of political truth; that without free speech and assembly discussion would be futile."[27]

Brandeis clearly disagreed with the Federalists who passed the Sedition Act of 1798 in the belief that dissent could undermine government. Instead, Brandeis argued that "the greatest menace to freedom is an inert people; that public discussion is a political duty; and that this should be a fundamental principle of the American government." The founders understood that it is "hazardous to discourage thought, hope and imagination; that fear breeds repression; that repression breeds hate; that hate menaces stable government; that the path of safety lies in the opportunity to discuss freely supposed grievances and proposed remedies, and that the fitting remedy for evil counsels is good ones. Believing in the power of reason as applied through public discussion, they eschewed silence coerced by law—the argument of force in its worst form. Recognizing the occasional tyrannies of governing majorities, they amended the Constitution so that free speech and assembly should be guaranteed." He went on: "Those who won our independence by revolution were not cowards. They did not fear political change. They did not exalt order at the cost of liberty." The founding generation, he wrote, had "confidence in the power of free and fearless reasoning applied through the processes of popular government."[28]

Holmes and Brandeis had thus entered the same room where Madison was sitting, but it remained a lonely place for almost another four decades. In 1964, a seditious libel case rose to the Supreme Court out of the turmoil of the civil rights movement. Finally, more than a century and a half after ratification of the First Amendment and the bitter skirmish over the Sedition Act, the Supreme Court rejected seditious libel in America. The occasion was a civil suit for libel by L. B. Sullivan, the police commissioner of Montgomery, Alabama, against the *New York Times* for an advertisement that contained some false statements of facts about the action of police during a civil rights protest. Overturning a jury finding for Sullivan, which included punitive damages, Justice William Brennan wrote for a unanimous Court that the First Amendment provided strong safeguards for the press when public officials sued for libel.

Brennan argued, as had Madison, that the defense of truth was insufficient to protect a full exchange of ideas. Error was inevitable in the heat of public debate, and proving truth in all its particulars was difficult. "Under such a rule," wrote Brennan, "would-be critics of official conduct may be deterred from voicing their criticism, even though it is believed to be true and even though it is, in fact, true, because of doubt whether it can be proved in court or fear of the expense of having to do so. They tend to make only statements which 'steer far wider of the unlawful zone.'" Even so, Brennan and the Court were not willing to confer absolute protection for writings critical of public officials. The First Amendment protected even false defamatory statements—as long as they were made innocently. The First Amendment did not protect falsehoods made with knowledge that they were false—the intentional lie. Nor did it protect falsehoods made with a reckless disregard for whether a statement was true or not.[29]

The Court had not considered the Sedition Act of 1798 before it expired, but Brennan declared that "the attack on its validity has carried the day in the court of history." He noted that Congress had repaid the fines "on the ground that it was unconstitutional" and that Jefferson had pardoned those who were convicted.[30] Brennan declared that the controversy that roiled the nation over the Sedition Act had "first crystallized a national awareness of the central meaning of the First Amendment."[31]

What was that central meaning? Brennan declared that it was "a profound national commitment to the principle that debate on public issues should be uninhibited, robust, and wide-open, and that it may well include vehement, caustic, and sometimes unpleasantly sharp attacks on government and public officials."[32] Brennan used those words deliberately—*uninhibited, robust, wide-open, unpleasantly sharp attacks*—to emphasize that political discussion bears no resemblance to the polite language learned at finishing school. For the founding generation that had protested against the British and then argued over the Constitution, debate was coarse, rough, and unrestrained. Brennan quoted Madison's "Report of 1800," that the press had "exerted a freedom in canvassing the merits and measures of public men."[33] Indeed, Brandeis's revolutionaries "who won our independence" were a hardy lot, and established a political culture that had changed little over the years.

The long journey to *New York Times v. Sullivan* had started as far back as 1687, when the Reverend John Wise had been jailed on charges of seditious libel for criticizing taxes imposed by the royal governor of Massachusetts. Nearly three centuries later, the Supreme Court celebrated robust and wide-open speech as central to the way Americans govern themselves.

NOTES

PROLOGUE: THE CHIEF JUSTICE

1. Josiah Quincy Jr., ed., *Reports of Cases Argued and Adjudged in the Superior Court of Judicature of the Province of Massachusetts Bay, Between 1761 and 1772* (Boston, 1865), 244–45; see also Leonard W. Levy, *Emergence of a Free Press* (New York: Oxford University Press, 1985), 65–68.
2. Quincy Jr., *Reports of Cases*, 309.
3. Quincy Jr., *Reports of Cases*, 274–75.
4. Levy, *Emergence*, 6
5. Levy, *Emergence*, 6.
6. William Blackstone, *Commentaries on the Laws of England*, 4:151–52, 1769, in Philip B. Kurland and Ralph Lerner, ed., *The Founders' Constitution* (Indianapolis: Liberty Fund, 1987), 5:119.
7. Patterson v. Colorado, 205 U.S. 454, 462 (1907).
8. Henry Schofield, *Essays on Constitutional Law and Other Subjects* (Boston: Chipman Law Publishing Company, 1921), 2:521–22.
9. Zechariah Chafee Jr., *Freedom of Speech* (New York: Harcourt, Brace and Howe, 1920), 23–24.
10. Leonard W. Levy, *Legacy of Suppression: Freedom of Speech and Press in Early American History* (Cambridge, MA: Harvard University Press, 1960), vii.
11. Levy, *Legacy*, 176, 87.
12. Levy, *Emergence*, xviii.
13. Antonin Scalia and Bryan A. Garner, *Reading Law: The Interpretation of Legal Texts* (St. Paul, MN: Thomson/West, 2012), 16.
14. Merrill Jensen, review of *Legacy of Suppression: Freedom of Speech and Press in Early American History*, by Leonard W. Levy, *Harvard Law Review* 75 (1961–1962): 456, 457.
15. Levy, *Emergence*, x.
16. Levy, *Emergence*, x, xii, xvi.
17. Lovell v. City of Griffin, GA, 303 U.S. 444, 452 (1938).
18. Talley v. California, 362 U.S. 60, 64, 65 (1960).
19. Richmond Newspapers v. Virginia, 448 U.S. 555, 569, 572 (1980).
20. Whitney v. California, 274 U.S. 357, 375 (1927) (Brandeis, concurring).
21. Akhil Reed Amar, "30th Annual Sullivan Lecture: How America's Constitution Affirmed Freedom of Speech Even Before the First Amendment," *Cap. U.L. Rev.* 38 (Spring 2010): 503, 513.
22. For example, see Tinker v. Des Moines Independent Community School District, 393 U.S. 503 (1969); and Texas v. Johnson, 491 U.S. 397 (1989).

23. Eugene Volokh, "Symbolic Expression and the Original Meaning of the First Amendment," *Geo. L. J.* 97 (2008–2009): 1057–59.

24. *Johnson,* 491 U.S. 397 (1989), U.S. v. Eichman, 496 U.S. 310 (1990).

25. Volokh, "Symbolic Expression."

26. Levy, *Emergence,* 188–89.

27. Jack N. Rakove, *Original Meanings: Politics and Ideas in the Making of the Constitution* (New York: Alfred A. Knopf, 1997), 6.

28. Alexis de Tocqueville, *Democracy in America,* ed. Eduardo Nolla, trans. James T. Schleifer (Indianapolis: Liberty Fund, 2010), 1:cviii–cix.

29. John Adams to Thomas Jefferson, August 14, 1815, in *The Adams-Jefferson Letters: The Complete Correspondence Between Thomas Jefferson & Abigail & John Adams,* ed. Lester J. Cappon (Chapel Hill: University of North Carolina Press, 1959), 455.

CHAPTER 1: THE MINISTER

1. For descriptions of the town meetings in Ipswich and of Wise's role in the protest, see George Allan Cook, *John Wise: Early American Democrat* (New York: King's Crown Press, 1952), 45–50; *Edward Randolph; Including His Letters and Official Papers from the New England, Middle, and Southern Colonies in America. . . . 1676–1703* (Boston: Prince Society, 1899), 4:171–177; Joseph B. Felt, *History of Ipswich, Essex, and Hamilton* (Cambridge, MA: Charles Folsom, 1834), 123–126; and John M. Palmer, *The Revolution in New England Justified and the People there Vindicated from the Aspersions Cast upon them* (Boston, 1691), 12–16.

2. Felt, *History of Ipswich,* 125.

3. *Randolph; Including His Letters,* 176; Felt, *History of Ipswich,* 48; Cook, *John Wise,* 49.

4. Felt, *History of Ipswich,* 258–60; Cook, *John Wise,* 3–4, 6, 14, 24.

5. Cook, *John Wise,* 34, 41.

6. Felt, *History of Ipswich,* 120.

7. Felt, *History of Ipswich,* 24, 38, 95, 108; "First Period Buildings of Eastern Massachusetts," National Register of Historic Places Registration Form, United States Department of the Interior, National Park Service, 1990.

8. Cook, *John Wise,* 43.

9. Larry D. Eldridge, "Before Zenger: Truth and Seditious Speech in Colonial America, 1607–1700," *American Journal of Legal History* 39, no. 3 (July 1995), 347.

10. Larry D. Eldridge, *A Distant Heritage: The Growth of Free Speech in Early America* (New York: New York University Press, 1994), 54.

11. Eldridge, *Distant Heritage,* 3.

12. Eldridge, "Before Zenger," 338–39.

13. Eldridge, "Before Zenger," 344.

14. Leonard W. Levy, *Emergence of a Free Press* (Oxford: Oxford University Press, 1985), 17–18; Harold L. Nelson, "Seditious Libel in Colonial America," *American Journal of Legal History* 3, no. 2 (April 1959): 163–64; Michael E. Stevens, "Legislative Privilege in Post-Revolutionary South Carolina," *William and Mary Quarterly* 46, no. 1 (January 1989): 71–92.

15. Eldridge, *Distant Heritage,* 44.

16. Eldridge, *Distant Heritage,* 46.

17. Eldridge, *Distant Heritage,* 92–93.

18. Eldridge, *Distant Heritage,* 95.

19. Eldridge, *Distant Heritage,* 27–28.

20. Eldridge, *Distant Heritage,* 95.

21. Eldridge, *Distant Heritage,* 43–44.

22. Eldridge, *Distant Heritage,* 91–92.

23. Eldridge, *Distant Heritage,* 16.

24. Thomas Franklin Waters, *Ipswich in the Massachusetts Bay Colony* (Ipswich, MA: Ipswich Historical Society, 1905), 238.

25. Cook, *John Wise*, 49–54.

26. *Randolph; Including His Letters*, 175.

27. Cook, *John Wise*, 51, 55.

28. *Randolph; Including His Letters*, 180–82; Cook, *John Wise*, 56–57.

29. Cook, *John Wise*, 57.

30. Cook, *John Wise*, 57–59.

31. Clinton L. Rossiter, "John Wise: Colonial Democrat," *New England Quarterly* 22, no. 1 (March 1949): 8.

32. Charles W. Upham, *Salem Witchcraft; with An Account of Salem Village and A History of Opinions on Witchcraft and Kindred Subjects* (Boston: Wiggin and Lunt, 1867), 2:304–7; Paul Boyer and Stephen Nissenbaum, *Salem Possessed: The Social Origins of Witchcraft* (Cambridge, MA: Harvard University Press, 1974), 200–202.

33. Cook, *John Wise*, 85–86, 102, 104, 105–27.

34. John Wise, *The Churches' Quarrel Espoused: Or, A Reply in Satire* (1710) in John Wise, *A Vindication of the Government of New England Churches* (Boston: Congregational Board of Publication, 1860), 135–36; Cook, *John Wise*, 105–27.

35. Wise, *The Churches' Quarrel Espoused*, 136.

36. Wise, *The Churches' Quarrel Espoused*, 141, 209.

37. Cook, *John Wise*, 125.

38. Rossiter, "John Wise," 13.

39. John Wise, *A Vindication of the Government of New England Churches* (Boston: 1717), 47; Rossiter, "John Wise," 14, 19, 20, 22.

40. Cook, *John Wise*, 150.

41. *The High Church Mask pull'd off* (London: A. Baldwin, 1770), 15–16.

42. *A Vindication of the Last Parliament in four Dialogues Between Sir Simon and Sir Peter* (London, 1711), 210.

43. Rossiter, "John Wise," 30.

CHAPTER 2: THE ADVOCATE

1. T. B. Howell, *A Complete Collection of State Trials, 1726–1743* (London: 1813), 17:721–722.

2. Howell, *Complete Collection of State Trials*, 17:722.

3. *Boston Weekly News-Letter*, 17 August 1732.

4. Edwin G. Burrows and Mike Wallace, *Gotham: A History of New York City to 1898* (Oxford: Oxford University Press, 1999), 63, 109–10.

5. Burrows and Wallace, *Gotham*, 144.

6. Burrows and Wallace, *Gotham*, 119–20.

7. Burrows and Wallace, *Gotham*, 125, 144.

8. Burrows and Wallace, *Gotham*, 150.

9. Vincent Buranelli, *The Trial of Peter Zenger* (New York: New York University Press, 1957), 8.

10. Buranelli, *The Trial*, 9–10.

11. Gail Jarrow, *The Printer's Trial: The Case of John Peter Zenger and the Fight for a Free Press* (Honesdale, PA: Calkins Creek Books, 2006), 17; Livingston Rutherfurd, *John Peter Zenger: His Press, His Trial and a Bibliography of Zenger Imprints* (New York: Dodd, Mead & Company, 1904), 8.

12. Rutherfurd, *John Peter Zenger*, 8–9; Buranelli, *The Trial*, 11–12; Joseph H. Smith and Leo Hershkowitz, "Courts of Equity in the Province of New York: The Cosby Controversy, 1732–1736," *American Journal of Legal History* 16, no. 1 (January 1972), 18. The Smith-Hershkowitz article contains an extended discussion of the Cosby salary dispute.

13. Rutherfurd, *John Peter Zenger*, 10; Stanley Nider Katz, ed., *A Brief Narrative of the Case and Trial of John Peter Zenger, Printer of the New York Weekly Journal* (Cambridge, MA: Harvard University Press, 1963), 3.

14. Whitfield J. Bell Jr., *Patriot-Improvers: Biographical Sketches of Members of the American Philosophical Society 1743–1768* (Philadelphia: American Philosophical Society, 1997),

1:87; William Cosby to the Duke of Newcastle, 18 December 1732, in *Documents Relative to the Colonial History of the State of New-York,* vol. 5, ed. E. B. O'Callaghan (Albany: Weed, Parsons and Company, 1855), 5:940.

15. Buranelli, *The Trial,* 5–8, 11; Rutherfurd, *John Peter Zenger,* 10–12; Smith and Hershkowitz, "The Cosby Controversy," 21; Eben Moglen, "Considering 'Zenger': Partisan Politics and the Legal Profession in Provincial New York," *Columbia Law Review* 94, no. 5 (June 1994): 1505.

16. Smith and Hershkowitz, "The Cosby Controversy," 24–31; Rutherfurd, *John Peter Zenger,* 14–20; William Smith Jr., *The History of the Province of New-York, Volume 2: A Continuation, 1732-1762,* ed. Michael Kammen (Cambridge, MA: Harvard University Press, 1972), 6–7.

17. William Cosby to the Duke of Newcastle, 3 May 1733, in *Documents Relative to the Colonial History of the State of New-York,* 5:942–50.

18. Rutherfurd, *John Peter Zenger,* 14–15; Smith and Hershkowitz, "The Cosby Controversy," 28.

19. Buranelli, *The Trial,* 14–15.

20. Lewis Morris to the Lords of Trade, 27 August 1733 and postscript of 1 September 1733, in *Documents Relative to the Colonial History of the State of New-York,* 5:951–55.

21. Katz, *A Brief Narrative,* 4–5.

22. Buranelli, *The Trial,* 16–19.

23. *New York Gazette,* 7 January 1734.

24. Burrows and Wallace, *Gotham,* 108–9, 124.

25. Leonard W. Levy, *Emergence of a Free Press* (New York: Oxford University Press, 1985), 9.

26. Levy, *Emergence,* 6.

27. Levy, *Emergence.*

28. Levy, *Emergence.*

29. Paul Starr, *The Creation of the Media: Political Origins of Modern Communications* (New York: Perseus Books, 2004), 32–36.

30. Sir Edward Coke, *The Selected Writings and Speeches of Sir Edward Coke,* ed. Steve Sheppard (Indianapolis: Liberty Fund, 2003), vol. 1, Chapter [125 a], "The Case *de Libellis Famosis,*" http://oll.libertyfund.org/title/911/106331, accessed June 8, 2013; Levy, *Emergence,* 7.

31. Levy, *Emergence,* 7.

32. William Waller Hening, *The Statutes at Large Being A Collection of All the Laws of Virginia from the First Legislature in the Year 1619* (New York: R. & W. & G. Bartow, 1823), 2:511, 517.

33. *Proceedings of the Massachusetts Historical Society,* 2nd ser., 8 (1892–1894): 273.

34. *Publick Occurrences Both Forreign and Domestick,* 25 September 1690; see also National Humanities Center, http://nationalhumanitiescenter.org/pds/amerbegin/power/text5/PublickOccurrences.pdf.

35. *Virginia Gazette,* 6 August 1736, excerpt, *Virginia Historical Register and Literary Companion,* ed. William Maxwell (Richmond: MacFarlane & Fergusson, 1853), 6:20–23.

36. Katz, *A Brief Narrative,* 8.

37. James Alexander to Robert Hunter, 1733, in Rutherfurd, *John Peter Zenger,* 28–29.

38. *New York Weekly Journal,* 5 October 1733; Moglen, "Considering 'Zenger,'" 1507.

39. *New York Weekly Journal,* 21 January 1734.

40. *New York Weekly Journal,* 28 January 1734.

41. Alison Olson, "The Zenger Case Revisited: Satire, Sedition and Political Debate in Eighteenth Century America," *Early American Literature* 35, no. 3 (2000): 226.

42. Jonathan Swift, "The Importance of the Guardian Considered," *The Prose Works of Jonathan Swift* (London: Henry Washbourne, 1841), 1:391.

43. *New York Weekly Journal,* 10 December 1733.

44. *New York Weekly Journal,* 24 December 1733.

45. *New York Weekly Journal,* 26 November 1733.

46. Levy, *Emergence*, 109–18.

47. *New York Weekly Journal*, 18 February 1733.

48. *New York Weekly Journal*, 25 February 1733.

49. James Madison, "Report on the Virginia Resolutions," January 1800, in *James Madison: Writings*, ed. Jack N. Rakove (New York: Library of America Literary Classics of the United States, 1999), 647.

50. Rutherfurd, *John Peter Zenger*, 33–34.

51. William Cosby to the Lords of Trade, 19 June 1734, in *Documents Relative to the Colonial History of the State of New-York*, vol. 6, 4-7

52. Jerry Silverman, *New York Sings: 400 Years of the Empire State in Song* (Albany, NY: Excelsior Editions, 2009), 16–17.

53. Rutherfurd, *John Peter Zenger*, 39–40; Smith Jr., *History of the Province of New-York*, 2:14–15.

54. Rutherfurd, *John Peter Zenger*, 40–43; Smith Jr., *History of the Province of New-York*, 2:15.

55. Howell, *State Trials*, 17:681–82; Rutherfurd, *John Peter Zenger*, 46–47.

56. Howell, *State Trials*, 17:682.

57. Howell, *State Trials*, 17:682–83.

58. Jarrow, *The Printer's Trial*, 61–62.

59. Howell, *State Trials*, 17:683–87.

60. Moglen, "Considering 'Zenger,'" 1518.

61. For a discussion of Andrew Hamilton's early career, see Foster C. Nix, "Andrew Hamilton's Early Years in the American Colonies," *William and Mary Quarterly*, 3rd ser., 21, no. 3 (July 1964): 390–407.

62. William Lowell Putnam, *John Peter Zenger and the Fundamental Freedom* (Jefferson, NC: McFarland & Company, 1997), 70–71.

63. For a discussion of the role of the jury in seditious libel trials like Zenger's, see Frederick Schauer, "The Role of the People in First Amendment Theory," *California Law Review* 74, no. 3 (May 1986): 762–64.

64. Howell, *State Trials*, 17:691.

65. Howell, *State Trials*, 17:693–94.

66. Howell, *State Trials*, 17:696.

67. Howell, *State Trials*.

68. Howell, *State Trials*, 17:698–99.

69. Howell, *State Trials*, 17:703–4.

70. Howell, *State Trials*, 17:705–6.

71. Howell, *State Trials*, 17:706–7.

72. Howell, *State Trials*, 17:708.

73. Howell, *State Trials*, 17:721–22.

74. Howell, *State Trials*, 17:722–23.

75. Howell, *State Trials*.

76. Putnam, *John Peter Zenger and the Fundamental Freedom*, 119.

77. Levy, *Emergence*, 44–45; Leonard W. Levy, "Did the Zenger Case Really Matter? Freedom of the Press in Colonial New York," *William and Mary Quarterly*, 3rd ser., 17, no. 1 (January 1960): 38–39.

78. Levy, *Emergence*, 17–18; Harold L. Nelson, "Seditious Libel in Colonial America," *American Journal of Legal History* 3, no. 2 (April 1959): 163–64; Michael E. Stevens, "Legislative Privilege in Post-Revolutionary South Carolina," *William and Mary Quarterly* 46, no. 1 (January 1989): 71–92.

CHAPTER 3: THE EDITORS

1. For background on Benjamin Edes, I relied on Rollo G. Silver, "Benjamin Edes, Trumpeter of Sedition," *Papers of the Bibliographical Society of America* 47 (1953): 248–68.

2. Leonard W. Levy, *Emergence of a Free Press* (New York: Oxford University Press, 1985), 30–32.
3. Silver, "Benjamin Edes," 251–52.
4. Francis Bernard to the Board of Trade, 15 August 1765, in *Papers of Francis Bernard: Governor of Colonial Massachusetts, 1760–1769,* ed. Colin Nicolson (Boston: Colonial Society of Massachusetts, 2012), 2:301.
5. *Boston Evening-Post,* 19 September 1774.
6. *Boston Evening-Post,* 19 September 1774.
7. Francis Bernard to Henry Seymour Conway, 28 February 1766, in *Papers of Francis Bernard,* 3:99.
8. Thomas Hutchinson to Thomas Pownall, 8 March 1766, in Edmund S. Morgan, *Prologue to Revolution: Sources and Documents on the Stamp Act Crisis, 1764–1766* (Chapel Hill: University of North Carolina Press, 1959), 122–26.
9. William H. Ukers, *All About Coffee* (New York: Tea and Coffee Trade Journal Company, 1922), 53–54, 74; Jurgen Habermas, *The Structural Transformation of the Public Sphere: An Inquiry into a Category of Bourgeois Society,* trans. Thomas Burger with the assistance of Frederick Lawrence (Cambridge, MA: MIT Press, 1989), 32–33.
10. Ukers, *All About Coffee,* 73; Tom Standage, *Writing on the Wall: Social Media in the First 2,000 Years* (New York: Bloomsbury, 2013), 104–23.
11. *Diary and Correspondence of Samuel Pepys, F.R.S.,* (Philadelphia: J. B. Lippincott, 1855), 1:7, 9.
12. Thomas Babington Macaulay, *The History of England from the Accession of James II* (Philadelphia: J. B. Lippincott, 1875), 1:286–88.
13. *An Historical and Chronological Deduction of the Origin of Commerce, from the Earliest Accounts, containing An History of the Great Commercial Interests of the British Empire . . .* (London: Logographic Press, 1787), 2:531.
14. Habermas, *Structural Transformation,* 27–33.
15. Habermas, *Structural Transformation,* 42.
16. John Adams, "A Dissertation on the Canon and Feudal Law," in *The Works of John Adams, Second President of the United States* (Boston: Charles C. Little and James Brown, 1851), 3:450. Also, the essay was published in four parts in the *Boston Gazette* in August 1765.
17. Adams, "A Dissertation," 3:451.
18. Adams, "A Dissertation," 3:456, 457.
19. Clyde Augustus Duniway, *The Development of Freedom of the Press in Massachusetts* (Cambridge, MA: Harvard University Press, 1906), 22, 29, 30, 32, 38, 39.
20. Duniway, *Development of Freedom,* 41, 46–50, 68–69; *Publick Occurrences Both Forreign and Domestick,* 25 September 1690; see also National Humanities Center, http://nationalhumanitiescenter.org/pds/amerbegin/power/text5/PublickOccurrences.pdf.
21. Duniway, *Development of Freedom,* 78; Jeffrey L. Pasley, *The Tyranny of Printers: Newspaper Politics in the Early American Republic* (Charlottesville: University of Virginia Press, 2001), 30.
22. Duniway, *Development of Freedom,* 91, 94–96, 99–102.
23. David W. Conroy, *In Public Houses: Drink & the Revolution of Authority in Colonial Massachusetts* (Chapel Hill: University of North Carolina Press, 1995), 143, 153.
24. Conroy, *In Public Houses,* 178.
25. Conroy, *In Public Houses,* 256–58.
26. Conroy, *In Public Houses,* 276.
27. *Rivington's New York Gazetteer,* 9 March 1775.
28. For discussion of the Boston Caucus and various political clubs, I relied on G. B. Warden, "The Caucus and Democracy in Colonial Boston," *New England Quarterly* 43, no. 1 (March 1970): 19–45; and Alan Day and Katherine Day, "Another Look at the Boston 'Caucus,'" *Journal of American Studies* 5, no. 1 (April 1971): 19–42.

29. Warden, "The Caucus and Democracy in Colonial Boston," 19–21; Day and Day, "Another Look at the Boston 'Caucus,'" 19–25.

30. John Adams, diary entry, February 1763, *Diary and Autobiography of John Adams*, ed. L. H. Butterfield (Cambridge, MA: Harvard University Press, 1961), 1:238.

31. For discussion of the town meeting, I drew from a number of sources, including David Syrett, "Town-Meeting Politics in Massachusetts, 1776–1786," *William and Mary Quarterly*, 3rd ser., 21, no. 3 (July 1964): 352–66; Benjamin W. Labaree, "New England Town Meeting," *American Archivist* 25, no. 2 (April 1962): 165–72. For voting in Massachusetts, see Robert E. Brown, "Democracy in Colonial Massachusetts," *New England Quarterly* 25, no. 3 (September 1952): 291–313; Albert Edward McKinley, *The Suffrage Franchise in the Thirteen English Colonies in America* (Philadelphia, 1905), 353–57; J. R. Pole, "Suffrage and Representation in Massachusetts: A Statistical Note," *William and Mary Quarterly*, 3rd ser., 14, no. 4 (October 1957): 560–92; Alexander Keyssar, *The Right to Vote: The Contested History of Democracy in the United States* (New York: Basic Books, 2000), 3–21; Marchette Chute, *The First Liberty: A History of the Right to Vote in America, 1619–1850* (New York: E. P. Dutton, 1969).

32. Labaree, "New England Town Meeting," 168.

33. Brown, "Democracy in Colonial Massachusetts," 300–301.

34. *New York Gazette*, 8 November 1756, reprinted in *Boston Evening Post*, 22 November 1756.

35. Edmund S. Morgan and Helen M. Morgan, *The Stamp Act Crisis: Prologue to Revolution* (Chapel Hill: University of North Carolina Press, 1962), 6, 21–22.

36. Morgan and Morgan, *Stamp Act Crisis*, 24–25.

37. Morgan and Morgan, *Stamp Act Crisis*, 30–32.

38. Morgan and Morgan, *Stamp Act Crisis*, 72–74; Russell Bourne, *Cradle of Violence: How Boston's Waterfront Mobs Ignited the American Revolution* (Hoboken, NJ: John Wiley & Sons, 2006), 95–98.

39. Lynne Oats and Pauline Sadler, "Accounting for the Stamp Act Crisis," *Accounting Historians Journal* 35, no. 2 (December 2008): 117–22.

40. Oats and Sadler, "Accounting for the Stamp Act Crisis," 124.

41. Benjamin Franklin to David Hall, 14 February 1765, in *The Writings of Benjamin Franklin, Collected and Edited with a Life and Introduction by Albert Henry Smyth, 1760–1766* (New York: Macmillan, 1906), 4:363–64.

42. Background on Benjamin Edes is taken from Silver, "Benjamin Edes, Trumpeter of Sedition," 248–68.

43. Jeffrey L. Pasley, *The Tyranny of Printers: Newspaper Politics in the Early American Republic* (Charlottesville: University of Virginia Press, 2001), 33, 401–3.

44. Arthur M. Schlesinger, *Prelude to Independence: The Newspaper War on Britain, 1764–1776* (New York: Alfred A. Knopf, 1958), 303–4.

45. Schlesinger, *Prelude to Independence,* 52–55.

46. Schlesinger, *Prelude to Independence,* 58–61; Pasley, *Tyranny of Printers,* 31–32.

47. *Papers of Francis Bernard,* 2:2; Morgan and Morgan, *Stamp Act Crisis,* 8–10.

48. Morgan and Morgan, *Stamp Act Crisis,* 218.

49. Bernard Bailyn, *Pamphlets of the American Revolution: 1750–1765* (Cambridge, MA: Harvard University Press, 1965), 410–13; Morgan and Morgan, *Stamp Act Crisis,* 219.

50. John Adams to William Tudor, 29 March 1817, in *The Works of John Adams,* 10:248.

51. James Otis, *The Rights of the British Colonies Asserted and Proved* (Boston: J. Almon, 1764), 82.

52. Bailyn, *Pamphlets,* 415, 447, 454.

53. Bailyn, *Pamphlets,* 604; Morgan and Morgan, *Stamp Act Crisis,* 81.

54. Samuel Seabury, *A View of the Controversy Between Great-Britain and her Colonies* (New York: James Rivington, 1774), 10.

55. Morgan and Morgan, *Stamp Act Crisis,* 35–40.

56. Merrill Jensen, *The Founding of a Nation: A History of the American Revolution, 1763–1776* (New York: Oxford University Press, 1968), 254.
57. Colin Nicolson, *The 'Infamas Govener': Francis Bernard and the Origins of the American Revolution* (Boston: Northeastern University Press, 201), 11–13, 144.
58. Morgan and Morgan, *Stamp Act Crisis,* 127–28.
59. Henry Bass to Samuel P. Savage, 19 December 1765, in *Proceedings of the Massachusetts Historical Society, October, 1910–June, 1911* (Boston: Massachusetts Historical Society, 1911), 44:688–89.
60. John Adams, diary entry, 3 September 1769, *Diary and Autobiography of John Adams,* 1:342–43.
61. *Boston Gazette,* 16 September 1765.
62. *Boston Gazette,* 2 December 1765.
63. *Boston Gazette,* 2 December 1765.
64. *Boston Evening-Post,* 4 November 1765.
65. *Boston Gazette,* 23 September 1765.
66. *Newport Mercury,* 30 September 1765.
67. Lieutenant-Governor Colden to Secretary Conway, 23 September 1765, in *Documents Relative to the Colonial History of the State of New-York,* ed. By E. B. O'Callaghan (Albany: Weed, Parsons, 1856), 7:759.
68. *Boston Gazette,* 13 May 1765.
69. *Boston Evening-Post,* 13 May 1765.
70. Francis Bernard to Thomas Pownall, 20 July 1765, in *Papers of Francis Bernard,* 2:295–96.
71. For my discussion of the Virginia Resolves, I relied on Morgan and Morgan, *Stamp Act Crisis,* 92–121; and Jensen, *Founding of a Nation,* 100–105.
72. "Jefferson's Recollections of Patrick Henry," *Pennsylvania Magazine of History* 34, no. 4 (1910): 389, 400; Francis Bernard to Thomas Pownall, 20 July 1765, in *Papers of Francis Bernard,* 2:296, note 3.
73. Morgan and Morgan, *Stamp Act Crisis,* 102.
74. *Newport Mercury,* 24 June 1765.
75. *Boston Gazette,* 1 July 1765.
76. *Virginia Gazette,* 30 August 1765; article also published in *Maryland Gazette,* 3 October 1765.
77. Francis Bernard to John Pownall, 20 July 1765, in *Papers of Francis Bernard,* 2:295–96.
78. Morgan and Morgan, *Stamp Act Crisis,* 102–3.
79. *Boston Gazette,* 8 July 1765.
80. Morgan and Morgan, *Stamp Act Crisis,* 107–21.
81. *Boston Gazette,* 4 November 1765.
82. Schlesinger, *Prelude to Independence,* 73–74; Francis Bernard to the Board of Trade, 17 October 1765, in *Papers of Francis Bernard,* 2:377–80.
83. Cadwallader Colden to Henry Seymour Conway, 12 October 1765, in Albert Matthews, "The Snake Devices, 1754–1776, and the *Constitutional Courant,* 1765," *Publications of the Colonial Society of Massachusetts,* Transactions, 1906–1907 (Boston: Colonial Society of Massachusetts, 1910), 11:436.
84. Matthews, "Snake Devices," 422–32.
85. *Pennsylvania Gazette,* 9 May 1754.
86. *Massachusetts Spy,* 7 July 1774.
87. Lester C. Olson, *Benjamin Franklin's Vision of American Community: A Study in Rhetorical Iconology* (Columbia: University of South Carolina Press, 2004), 27–76.
88. Edwin Wolf II, "Benjamin Franklin's Stamp Act Cartoon," *Proceedings of the American Philosophical Society* 99, no. 6 (December 15, 1955): 388–96.
89. Benjamin Franklin to Jane Mecom, 1 March 1766, in *The Papers of Benjamin Franklin,* ed. Leonard W. Labaree et al. (New Haven, CT: Yale University Press, 1969), 13:187–89.
90. Olson, *Benjamin Franklin's Vision,* 77–111.
91. Morgan and Morgan, *Stamp Act Crisis,* 164.

92. Michael Kraus, *Intercolonial Aspects of American Culture on the Eve of the Revolution, with Special Reference to the Northern Towns* (New York: Columbia University Press, 1928), 91–105.

93. Morgan and Morgan, *Stamp Act Crisis*, 195; Kraus, *Intercolonial Aspects of American Culture*, 91–105.

94. *Boston Gazette,* 7 October 1765.

95. Morgan and Morgan, *Stamp Act Crisis,* 165–86.

96. For an excellent review of the reaction of colonial newspapers to the starting date of the Stamp Act, see Arthur M. Schlesinger, "The Colonial Newspapers and the Stamp Act," *New England Quarterly* 8, no. 1 (March 1935): 74–80.

97. *Boston Gazette,* 4 November 1765; Schlesinger, "Colonial Newspapers," 74.

98. Schlesinger, "Colonial Newspapers," 77.

99. *New-Hampshire Gazette,* 31 October 1765.

100. Francis Bernard to Henry Seymour Conway, 28 February 1766, in *Papers of Francis Bernard,* 3:99.

101. Josiah Quincy Jr., ed., *Reports of Cases Argued and Adjudged in the Superior Court of Judicature of the Province of Massachusetts Bay, Between 1761 and 1772* (Boston, 1865), 237.

102. Quincy Jr., ed., *Reports of Cases Argued and Adjudged,* 244–45; see also Levy, *Emergence,* 65–68; *Boston Gazette,* 27 April 1767.

103. *Boston Gazette,* 29 February 1768.

104. Quincy Jr., ed., *Reports of Cases Argued and Adjudged,* 265–68.

105. Quincy Jr., ed., *Reports of Cases Argued and Adjudged,* 270.

106. Francis Bernard to Earl of Shelburne, 12 March 1768, in *Legal Papers of John Adams,* ed. L. Kinvin Wroth and Hiller B. Zobel (Cambridge, MA: Harvard University Press, 1965), 1:206–7, note 30.

107. *Boston Gazette,* 21 March 1768.

108. Quincy Jr., ed., *Reports of Cases Argued and Adjudged,* 272–73.

109. Quincy Jr., ed., *Reports of Cases Argued and Adjudged,* 274–75.

110. *Boston Gazette,* 14 March 1768.

111. Francis Bernard to the Earl of Hillsborough, 25 January 1769, and Bernard to John Pownall, 25 March 1769, *The Papers of Francis Bernard, Governor of Colonial Massachusetts, 1760–69,* vol. 5: 1768–1769, ed. Colin Nicolson (Boston: Colonial Society of Massachusetts, 2015), 5:173, 237.

112. Quincy Jr., ed., *Reports of Cases Argued and Adjudged,* 305.

113. Quincy Jr., ed., *Reports of Cases Argued and Adjudged,* 309.

CHAPTER 4: THE SHOEMAKER

1. I relied on descriptions of the demonstrations of 14 August 1765 from sources, including *Boston Gazette,* 19 August 1765; Francis Bernard to the Board of Trade, 15 August 1765, in *Papers of Francis Bernard: Governor of Colonial Massachusetts 1760–1769,* ed. Colin Nicolson (Boston: Colonial Society of Massachusetts, 2012), 2:301–5; John Avery to John Collins, 19 August 1765, in *Extracts from the Itineraries and Other Miscellanies of Ezra Stiles, D.D., LL.D., 1755–1794 with a Selection of His Correspondence,* ed. Franklin Bowditch Dexter (New Haven, CT: Yale University Press, 1916); *Massachusetts Gazette and Boston News-Letter,* 22 August 1765.

2. *Boston Gazette,* 16 September 1765.

3. George P. Anderson, "Ebenezer Mackintosh: Stamp Act Rioter and Patriot," *Colonial Society of Massachusetts Publications* 26 (1927): 15–64.

4. I relied on descriptions of colonial Boston from a number of sources including: *Commonwealth History of Massachusetts,* vols. 1 and 2, ed. Albert Bushnell Hart (New York: Russell & Russell, 1966); Robin Carver, *History of Boston* (Boston: Lilly, Wait, Colman, and Holden, 1834); Mary Caroline Crawford, *Old Boston in Colonial Days; or, St. Botolph's Town* (Boston: Page Company, 1922); Thomas H. O'Connor, *The Hub: Boston*

Past and Present (Boston: Northeastern University Press, 2001); and J. H. Benton Jr., *Early Census Making in Massachusetts 1643–1765, with a Reproduction of the Lost Census of 1765* (Boston: Charles E. Goodspeed, 1905), 72–73.

5. Nathaniel B. Shurtleff, *A Topographical and Historical Description of Boston* (Boston: City Council of Boston, 1871), 68.

6. Anderson, "Ebenezer Mackintosh," 16, 22–25.

7. Peter Shaw, *American Patriots and the Rituals of Revolution* (Cambridge, MA: Harvard University Press, 1981), 15–18, 69–70.

8. *Boston News-Letter,* 8 November 1764; Anderson, "Ebenezer Mackintosh," 26.

9. Francis Bernard to John Pownall, 26 November 1765, in *The Papers of Francis Bernard,* 2:422–24.

10. Anderson, "Ebenezer Mackintosh," 26–27.

11. Thomas Hutchinson to Thomas Pownall, 8 March 1766, quoted in Edmund S. Morgan, *Prologue to Revolution: Sources and Documents on the Stamp Act Crisis, 1764–1766* (Chapel Hill: University of North Carolina Press, 1959), 125.

12. Gordon S. Wood, "The Democratization of Mind in the American Revolution," in *The Moral Foundations of the American Republic,* 2nd ed., ed. Robert H. Horwitz (Charlottesville: University Press of Virginia, 1979), 106–7.

13. Lynne Oats and Pauline Sadler, "Accounting for the Stamp Act Crisis," *Accounting Historians Journal* 35, no. 2 (December 2008): 120.

14. Anderson, "Ebenezer Mackintosh," 30; David Hackett Fischer, *Liberty and Freedom* (Oxford: Oxford University Press, 2005), 21.

15. Anderson, "Ebenezer Mackintosh," 30.

16. *Boston Gazette,* 19 August 1765.

17. *Boston Gazette,* 19 August 1765.

18. Francis Bernard to the Board of Trade, 15 August 1765, in *Papers of Francis Bernard,* 2:301–5.

19. John Avery to John Collins, 19 August 1765, in Dexter, *Extracts from the Itineraries.*

20. *Massachusetts Gazette and Boston News-Letter,* 22 August 1765.

21. *Boston Gazette,* 19 August 1765.

22. *Boston Gazette,* 16 September 1765.

23. "A Discourse at the Dedication of the Tree of Liberty," in *The American Republic: Primary Sources,* ed. Bruce Frohnen (Indianapolis: Liberty Fund, 2002), http://oll.libertyfund.org/title/669/206135, accessed December 6, 2013.

24. Frohnen, *The American Republic: Primary Sources,* ; Fischer, *Liberty and Freedom,* 19–36; and Arthur M. Schlesinger, "Liberty Tree: A Genealogy," *New England Quarterly* 25, no. 4 (December 1952): 435–58.

25. Sir Edward Coke, "The Case de *Libellis Famosis,*" in *The Selected Writings and Speeches of Sir Edward Coke,* ed. Steve Sheppard (Indianapolis: Liberty Fund, 2003), 1:147, accessed April 8, 2013, http://oll.libertyfund.org/title/911/106331.

26. William Blackstone, *Commentaries on the Laws of England,* 4:150–53, 1769, in Philip B. Kurland and Ralph Lerner, ed., *The Founders' Constitution* (Indianapolis: Liberty Fund, 1987), 5: 119.

27. Eugene Volokh, "Symbolic Expression and the Original Meaning of the First Amendment," *Georgetown Law Journal* 97 (2009): 1057–84.

28. *Newport Mercury,* 21 April 1766.

29. Fischer, *Liberty and Freedom,* 23; Schlesinger, "Liberty Tree," 441–42.

30. John Adams, diary entry, May 4, 1766, *Diary and Autobiography of John Adams,* ed. L. H. Butterfield (Cambridge, MA: Belknap Press of Harvard University Press, 1961), 1:311–12.

31. Fischer, *Liberty and Freedom,* 24.

32. Gage to Lt. Col. William Dalrymple, 8 January 1770, quoted in Fischer, *Liberty and Freedom,* 45.

33. For sources on the 14 August 1765 demonstration, see note 1.

34. Francis Bernard to the Board of Trade, 15 August 1765, in *Papers of Francis Bernard*, 2:301–2.
35. Francis Bernard to the Board of Trade, 15 August 1765, in *Papers of Francis Bernard*, 2:301–7.
36. Francis Bernard to the Board of Trade, 15 August 1765, in *Papers of Francis Bernard*, 2:301–7.
37. Francis Bernard, Proclamation Concerning the Stamp Act Riot of 14 August 1765, issued 15 August 1765, in *Papers of Francis Bernard*, 2:334–35.
38. Francis Bernard to the Board of Trade, 22 August 1765, in *Papers of Francis Bernard*, 2:316–17.
39. Edmund S. Morgan and Helen M. Morgan, *Stamp Act Crisis: Prologue to Revolution* (Chapel Hill, NC: University of North Carolina Press, 1962), 132–35.
40. Thomas Hutchinson to Richard Jackson, 30 August 1765, in Morgan, *Prologue to Revolution*, 108–9; Thomas Hutchinson, *The History of the Colony and Province of Massachusetts-Bay*, ed. Lawrence Shaw Mayo (Cambridge, MA: Harvard University Press, 1936), 90–91; Morgan and Morgan, *Stamp Act Crisis*, 132–35.
41. Francis Bernard to Thomas Gage, 27 August 1765, in *Papers of Francis Bernard*, 2:323–24.
42. Morgan and Morgan, *Stamp Act Crisis*, 134–35.
43. Francis Bernard, Proclamation Concerning the Stamp Act Riot of 26 August 1765, issued 28 August 1765, *Papers of Francis Bernard*, 2:335–36.
44. Francis Bernard to Lord Colvill, 27 August 1765, in *Papers of Francis Bernard*, 2: 325–26.
45. Hutchinson to Richard Jackson, 30 August 1765, in Morgan, *Prologue to Revolution*, 108–9.
46. *Boston Gazette*, 2 September 1765.
47. *Boston Gazette*, 2 December 1765.
48. Francis Bernard to Henry Seymour Conway, 28 September 1765, in *Papers of Francis Bernard*, 2:367–69; Morgan and Morgan, *Stamp Act Crisis*, 135.
49. *Boston Gazette*, 16 September 1765.
50. Anderson, "Ebenezer Mackintosh," 29–30.
51. Jonathan Mayhew, *A Discourse Concerning Unlimited Submission and Nonresistance to the Higher Powers*, 1750, in Bernard Bailyn, ed. *Pamphlets of the American Revolution: 1750-1765* (Cambridge, MA: Harvard University Press, 1965), 228.
52. John Adams to Thomas Jefferson, 18 July 1818, in *The Adams-Jefferson Letters: The Complete Correspondence Between Thomas Jefferson & Abigail & John Adams*, ed. Lester J. Cappon (Chapel Hill: University of North Carolina Press, 1959), 527.
53. Francis Bernard to the Board of Trade, 22 August 1765, in *Papers of Francis Bernard*, 2:315–17.
54. Bernard Bailyn, *Faces of Revolution: Personalities and Themes in the Struggle for American Independence* (New York: Random House, 1992), 127–32.
55. Jonathan Mayhew to Richard Clarke, 3 September 1765, in *The New-England Historical and Genealogical Register*, vol. 46 (Boston: New-England Historic Genealogical Society, 1892), 15–20.
56. See, for example, Francis Bernard to John Pownall, 1 November 1765, and Bernard to Richard Jackson, 7 November 1765, in *Papers of Francis Bernard*, 2:395–401, 404–7.
57. Morgan and Morgan, *Stamp Act Crisis*, 137–38.
58. *Boston Gazette*, 4 November 1765.
59. Francis Bernard to John Pownall, 1 November, 1765, in *Papers of Francis Bernard*, 2:395–401.
60. *Boston Evening Post*, 4 November 1765; Francis Bernard to John Pownall, 1 November 1765, in *Papers of Francis Bernard*, 2:395–401.
61. *Boston Gazette*, 11 November 1765.
62. Descriptions of the Pope's Day demonstration are taken from the *Boston Gazette*, 11 November 1765; *Boston Evening-Post*, 11 November 1765; and Francis Bernard to John

Pownall, 26 November 1765, in *Papers of Francis Bernard*, 2:422–26; Anderson, "Ebenezer Mackintosh," 42.

63. *Boston Gazette*, 18 November 1765; Francis Bernard to John Pownall, 26 November 1765, in *Papers of Francis Bernard*, 2:422–26, 424n7.

64. The events of December 16–17 are described in Andrew Oliver's own words in several letters to Francis Bernard, 17 December 1765, and 19 December 1765, in *Papers of Francis Bernard*, 2:434–41. I also relied on descriptions in the *Boston Gazette*, 16 December and 23 December 1765; Anderson, "Ebenezer Mackintosh," 43; Morgan and Morgan, *Stamp Act Crisis*, 143–45; and James Truslow Adams, *Revolutionary New England: The History of New England in Three Volumes* (Boston: Little, Brown, 1927), 2:334.

65. Henry Bass to Samuel P. Savage, 19 December 1765, in Massachusetts Historical Society, *Proceedings* 44 (1911): 688–89.

66. Andrew Oliver to Francis Bernard, 19 December 1765, in *Papers of Francis Bernard*, 2:441.

67. Lynne Oats and Pauline Sadler, "Accounting for the Stamp Act Crisis," *Accounting Historians Journal* 35, no. 2 (December 2008): 120.

68. *Newport Mercury*, 2 September 1765 and 21 October 1765; William Almy to Elisha Story, 29 August 1765, in *Proceedings of the Massachusetts Historical Society*, 3rd ser., 55 (October 1921–June 1922): 234–36.

69. *Newport Mercury*, 2 September 1765.

70. *Providence Gazette*, 24 August 1765.

71. *Massachusetts Gazette and Boston News-Letter*, 12 September 1765.

72. James McEvers to Barlow Trecothick, August 1765, in Morgan and Morgan, *Stamp Act Crisis*, 158.

73. James McEwers to Lt. Gov. Colden, in *Documents Relative to the Colonial History of the State of New-York*, ed. E. B. O'Callaghan (Albany: Weed, Parsons, 1856), 761.

74. Morgan and Morgan, *Stamp Act Crisis*, 159.

75. *Boston Gazette*, 16 December 1765; Morgan and Morgan, *Stamp Act Crisis*, 160.

76. Morgan and Morgan, *Stamp Act Crisis*, 161.

77. Morgan and Morgan, *Stamp Act Crisis*, 161–63; Philip Davidson, *Propaganda and the American Revolution, 1763–1783* (Chapel Hill: University of North Carolina Press, 1941) 176; W. Roy Smith, *South Carolina as a Royal Province, 1719–1776* (New York: Macmillan, 1903), 351–53.

78. Henry Laurens, *The Papers of Henry Laurens, September 1, 1765–July 31, 1768*, ed. George C. Rogers Jr. et al. (Columbia: University of South Carolina Press, 1976), 5:29.

79. Morgan and Morgan, *Stamp Act Crisis*, 163.

80. The protest of 20 February 1766 is described in the *Boston Gazette*, 24 February 1766.

81. Colin Nicolson, *The "Infamas Govener": Francis Bernard and the Origins of the American Revolution* (Boston: Northeastern University Press, 2001), 143–45.

82. Francis Bernard to the Earl of Halifax, 7 September 1765, in *Papers of Francis Bernard*, 2:351–54.

83. Francis Bernard to Henry Seymour Conway, 28 September 1765, in *Papers of Francis Bernard*, 2:367–72.

84. Francis Bernard to the Board of Trade, 30 November 1765, in *Papers of Francis Bernard*, 2:426–30.

85. Francis Bernard to John Pownall, 1 November 1765; and Francis Bernard to Richard Jackson, 7 November 1765, in *Papers of Francis Bernard*, 2:395–403, 404–7.

86. Francis Bernard to the Board of Trade, 30 November 1765, in *Papers of Francis Bernard*, 2:426–30.

87. Repeal of the Stamp Act is detailed in Morgan and Morgan, *Stamp Act Crisis*, 271–92.

88. *Georgia Gazette*, 4 June 1766.

89. "Great Britain: Parliament—The Declaratory Act," March 18, 1766, in Avalon Project: Documents in Law, History and Diplomacy, Yale Law School, http://avalon.law.yale.edu/18th_century/declaratory_act_1766.asp.

90. *Boston Gazette*, 19 May 1766.
91. *Boston Gazette*, 26 May 1766.
92. *Boston Gazette*, 26 May 1766.
93. Jonathan Mayhew, *The Snare Broken: A Thanksgiving Discourse Preached at the Desire of the West Church in Boston, Friday, May 23, 1766 Occasioned by the Repeal of the Stamp Act* (Boston, 1766), 8.
94. Mayhew, *The Snare Broken*, 6, 36, 4, 6, 18, 36.
95. Mayhew, *The Snare Broken*, 36.
96. Adams, *Diary and Autobiography*, 1:312–13.
97. Adams, *Diary and Autobiography*, 1:263–65.

CHAPTER 5: THE MERCHANT

1. *New York Journal or the General Advertiser*, 22 March 1770.
2. *New York Gazette and Weekly Mercury*, 30 April 1770.
3. *New York Journal or the General Advertiser*, 29 March 1770.
4. Details about McDougall's early life are available in William L. MacDougall, *American Revolutionary: A Biography of General Alexander McDougall* (Westport, CT: Greenwood Press, 1977), 3–21; Roger J. Champagne, *Alexander McDougall and the American Revolution in New York* (Schenectady: New York State Bicentennial Commission and Union College Press, 1975), 5–10; Richard M. Ketchum, *Divided Loyalties: How the American Revolution Came to New York* (New York: Henry Holt, 2002), 218–19; and Patricia Bonomi, *A Factious People: Politics and Society in Colonial New York* (New York: Columbia University Press, 1971), 267–68.
5. "A List of the Names, Ages, and Descriptions of the Men belonging to the Sloop Tyger," commissioning papers, 26 November 1757, McDougall files, New York Historical Society.
6. *New York Gazette or Weekly Post-Boy*, 3 October 1757.
7. *New York Mercury*, 17 October 1757; MacDougall, *American Revolutionary*, 12–13.
8. MacDougall, *American Revolutionary*, 13–15.
9. MacDougall, *American Revolutionary*, 19–21; Champagne, *Alexander McDougall*, 8–10.
10. Alexander McDougall, *Waste Book,* June 1767, McDougall files, New York Historical Society.
11. Champagne, *Alexander McDougall*, 8–10.
12. MacDougall, *American Revolutionary*, 20.
13. MacDougall, *American Revolutionary*, 15.
14. Joseph S. Tiedemann, *Reluctant Revolutionaries: New York City and the Road to Independence, 1763–1776* (Ithaca, NY: Cornell University Press, 1997), 34–36, 133–37, 141–64; MacDougall, *American Revolutionary*, 18–19; Champagne, *Alexander McDougall*, 14–18.
15. James McEvers to Barlow Trecothick, August 1765, in Edmund S. Morgan and Helen M. Morgan, *The Stamp Act Crisis: Prologue to Revolution* (Chapel Hill: University of North Carolina Press, 1959), 158, 206.
16. "Declaration of Rights and Grievances," First Congress of the American Colonies, 19 October 1765; Morgan and Morgan, *Stamp Act Crisis*, 111.
17. Robert R. Livingston to General Monckton, 8 November 1765, in *Collections of the Massachusetts Historical Society*, 4th ser., vol. 10 (Boston, 1871), 567; Morgan and Morgan, *Stamp Act Crisis*, 274.
18. Morgan and Morgan, *Stamp Act Crisis*, 274.
19. Details about the 1 November 1765 protests in New York are available in a number of sources: Robert R. Livingston to General Monckton, 8 November 1765, in *Collections of the Massachusetts Historical Society*, 561–562; *New York Mercury*, 7 November 1765; Pauline Maier, *From Resistance to Revolution: Colonial Radicals and the Development of American Opposition to Britain, 1765–1776* (New York: W. W. Norton, 1991), 67–69.

20. Robert R. Livingston to General Monckton, 8 November 1765, in *Collections of the Massachusetts Historical Society,* 561.

21. *New York Gazette and Weekly Mercury,* 7 November 1765; Morgan and Morgan, *Stamp Act Crisis,* 206–7.

22. Thomas Gage to Secretary Conway, 21 December 1765, in *The Correspondence of General Thomas Gage with the Secretaries of State, 1763–1775,* ed. Clarence E. Carter (New Haven, 1931), 1:79; Morgan and Morgan, *Stamp Act Crisis,* 192.

23. Champagne, *Alexander McDougal,* 13–15.

24. *New York Journal,* 1 March 1770.

25. Champagne, *Alexander McDougall,* 16–17.

26. Champagne, *Alexander McDougall,* 17–20; Tiedemann, *Reluctant Revolutionaries,* 141–42.

27. Frank Moore, *Diary of the American Revolution from Newspapers and Original Documents* (New York: Charles Scribner, 1860), 1:55–56; George Henry Payne, *History of Journalism in the United States* (New York: D. Appleton, 1920), 87–88.

28. Mason I. Lowance Jr. and Georgia B. Bumgardner, eds., *Massachusetts Broadsides of the American Revolution* (Amherst: University of Massachusetts Press, 1976), ix–xi, 1–3.

29. Beaumont Hotham to Portland, 10 May 1763, in John Brewer, *Party Ideology and Popular Politics at the Accession of George III* (Cambridge: Cambridge University Press, 1976), 152.

30. John Wilkes, "A Letter to a Noble Member of the Club in Albemarle Street" (W. Nicoll, 1764), 2–3.

31. Noble E. Cunningham Jr., "Early Political Handbills in the United States," *William and Mary Quarterly,* 3rd ser., 14, no. 1 (January 1957): 70–73; Worthington Chauncey Ford, "Broadsides, Ballads Printed in Massachusetts, 1639–1800," *Collections of the Massachusetts Historical Society* 75 (1922); Lowance and Bumgardner, *Massachusetts Broadsides of the American Revolution,* ix–xi, 1–3; "Declaring Independence: Drafting the Documents," Library of Congress Exhibitions, http://www.loc.gov/exhibits/declara/declara4.html.

32. "Benjamin Franklin in His Own Words," American Treasures of the Library of Congress, Special Presentations, http://www.loc.gov/exhibits/treasures/franklin-cause.html.

33. Alexander McDougall, "To the Betrayed Inhabitants of the City and Colony of New York," broadside, New York, 16 December 1769.

34. McDougall, "To the Betrayed Inhabitants."

35. *New York Gazette and Weekly Mercury,* 25 December 1769; *New York Gazette and Weekly Post-Boy,* 1 January 1770; Tiedemann, *Reluctant Revolutionaries,* 145.

36. "Notes and Comments: The Constitutional Right to Anonymity: Free Speech, Disclosure and the Devil," *Yale Law Journal* 70, no. 7 (June 1961): 1084–85; "A Note on Certain of Hamilton's Pseudonyms," *William and Mary Quarterly,* 3rd ser., 12, no. 2 (April 1955): 282.

37. Philip Davidson, *Propaganda and the American Revolution, 1763–1783* (Chapel Hill: University of North Carolina Press, 1941), 5.

38. *New York Journal,* 4 August 1774.

39. Michael Patrick Marden, "Concealed Authorship on the Eve of the Revolution: Pseudonymity and the American Periodical Public Sphere, 1766–1776, appendix, 107–138 (master's thesis, University of Missouri–Columbia, 2009).

40. Roger B. Berry, "John Adams: Two Further Contributions to the Boston Gazette, 1766–1768," *New England Quarterly* 31, no. 1 (March 1958): 91.

41. *Journal of the Votes and Proceedings of the General Assembly of the Colony of New-York From 1766 to 1776 Inclusive* (Albany, NY: J. Buel, 1820), 42.

42. A Proclamation by the Honourable Cadwallader Colden, New York, 20 December 1769, Library of Congress, http://memory.loc.gov/cgi-bin/ampage?collId=rbpe&fileName=rb

pe10/rbpe103/10302800/rbpe10302800.db&recNum=0&itemLink=D?rbpebib:2:./te
mp/~ammem_194T::&linkText=0.

43. The dispute over the Liberty Pole is discussed in "The Liberty Pole on the Commons," *New York Historical Society Quarterly Bulletin* 3, no. 4 (January 1920).

44. For descriptions of Manhattan, I relied on Tiedemann, *Reluctant Revolutionaries,* 16–21.

45. "Liberty Pole on the Commons," 114–15.

46. Maier, *From Resistance to Revolution,* 6–7, 9–12, 20.

47. "Liberty Pole on the Commons," 127.

48. John Montresor, "Journals of Capt. John Montresor," in *The Montresor Journals,* ed. G. D. Scull (New York: New York Historical Society, 1882), 382.

49. "Liberty Pole on the Commons," 110–12, 127.

50. *New York Gazette and Weekly Post-Boy,* 22 January 1770; "Liberty Pole on the Commons," 115–19.

51. *New York Journal,* 1 March 1770.

52. *New York Journal,* 1 March 1770; *"Liberty Pole on the Commons,"* 116–121.

53. "Liberty Pole on the Commons," 121–126; *New York Journal,* 8 February 1770; *New York Gazette and Weekly Mercury,* 5 February 1770, 12 February 1770.

54. The description of events surrounding McDougall's arrest is taken from his account, "To the Freeholders and Inhabitants of the Colony of New York, and to all the Friends of Liberty in North America," *New York Journal,* 15 February 1770; See also *New York Gazette or Weekly Post–Boy,* 12 February 1770; Champagne, *Alexander McDougall,* 28; Tiedemann, *Reluctant Revolutionaries,* 150.

55. Lieutenant-Governor Colden to the Lords of Trade, 8 July 1763, in *Documents Relative to the Colonial History of the State of New York* (Albany, NY: Weed, Parsons, 1856), 7:527–29, note 1; biography of Daniel Horsmanden, Historical Society of the New York Courts, http://www.nycourts.gov/history/legal-history-new-york/legal-history-eras-01/history-era-01-horsmanden.html.

56. Edward Hagerman Hall, *The Old Martyrs' Prison, New York* (New York: American Scenic and Historic Preservation Society, 1902).

57. *New York Gazette and Weekly Mercury,* 27 July 1772.

58. *New York Journal,* 15 February 1770; *Boston Gazette,* 26 February 1770.

59. Details about John Wilkes come from Maier, *From Resistance to Revolution,* 161–69; Pauline Maier, "John Wilkes and American Disillusionment with Britain," *William and Mary Quarterly,* 3rd ser., 20, no. 3 (July 1963): 374–85; Leonard Levy, *Emergence of a Free Press* (New York: Oxford University Press, 1985), 145–47; Jack Lynch, "Wilkes, Liberty, and Number 45," *Colonial Williamsburg Journal* (Summer 2003).

60. Committee of the Boston Sons of Liberty to John Wilkes, 6 June 1768, *Papers of John Adams,* September 1755–October 1773, ed. Robert J. Taylor (Cambridge, MA: Harvard University Press, 1977), 1:214–216.

61. *New York Gazette and Weekly Mercury,* 25 December 1769, 1 January 1770, 15 January 1770.

62. *New York Gazette and Weekly Mercury,* 13 June 1768.

63. *New York Gazette and Weekly Mercury,* 30 July 1770.

64. *New York Gazette and Weekly Mercury,* 15 August 1768.

65. *New York Gazette and Weekly Mercury,* 5 September 1768.

66. *Boston Gazette,* 16 October 1769.

67. *New York Gazette and Weekly Mercury,* 29 May 1769, 18 December 1769.

68. Edward McCrady, *The History of South Carolina Under the Royal Government, 1719–1779* (New York: Macmillan, 1899), 604–605.

69. Cadwallader Colden to Lord Hillsborough, 21 February 1770, in Thomas Jones, *History of New York During the Revolutionary War* (New York: New York Historical Society, 1879), 1:431–32.

70. *New York Journal,* 29 March 1770.

71. *New York Gazette or Weekly Post-Boy,* 19 February 1770.
72. *New York Gazette or Weekly Post-Boy,* 5 March 1770.
73. *New York Journal,* 15 February 1770.
74. *New York Journal,* 15 February 1770.
75. *New York Journal,* 29 March 1770.
76. Maier, *From Resistance to Revolution,* 169–170.
77. *New York Gazette or Weekly Post-Boy,* 2 April 1770.
78. *New York Gazette or Weekly Post-Boy,* 2 April 1770.
79. See, for example, *New York Journal,* 29 March 1770, 12 April 1770; *New York Gazette and Weekly Mercury,* 30 April 1770.
80. *New York Gazette and Weekly Mercury,* 26 March 1770; Tiedemann, *Reluctant Revolutionaries,* 151.
81. *New York Journal,* 5 April 1770.
82. *New York Journal,* 16 February 1770, 29 March 1770.
83. *New York Journal,* 3 May 1770, 10 May 1770.
84. "The Dougliad," series begun in the *New York Gazette and Weekly Mercury* on 4 April 1770.
85. *New York Gazette and Weekly Mercury,* 21 May 1770.
86. *New York Journal,* 15 March 1770.
87. *New York Journal,* 15 March 1770.
88. *New York Gazette and Weekly Mercury,* 23 April 1770.
89. *New York Gazette and Weekly Mercury,* 23 April 1770.
90. *A Letter from Candor, to the Public Advertiser,* 2nd ed. (London: J. Almon, 1764), 11, 14.
91. Father of Candor, *A Letter Concerning Libels, Warrants, The Seisure of Papers . . .* 7th ed. (London: J. Almon, 1771), 48; Levy, *Emergence,* 147–152.
92. Father of Candor, *Concerning Libels,* 16–17, 46–47.
93. Father of Candor, *Concerning Libels,* 161.
94. Father of Candor, *Concerning Libels,* 48.
95. *New York Gazette or Weekly Post-Boy,* 7 May 1770.
96. Father of Candor, *A Letter Concerning Libels,* 49.
97. Josiah Quincy Jr., ed., *Reports of Cases Argued and Adjudged in the Superior Court of Judicature of the Province of Massachusetts Bay, Between 1761 and 1772* (Boston, 1865), 309.
98. Tiedemann, *Reluctant Revolutionaries,* 152; *New York Gazette or Weekly Post-Boy,* 7 May 1770.
99. Tiedemann, *Reluctant Revolutionaries,* 152.
100. *New York Gazette or Weekly Post-Boy,* 7 May 1770; Tiedemann, *Reluctant Revolutionaries,* 152; Champagne, *Alexander McDougall,* 34.
101. Levy, *Emergence,* 79.
102. Levy, *Emergence,* 79–80.
103. Leonard W. Levy, "Did the Zenger Case Really Matter? Freedom of the Press in Colonial New York," *William and Mary Quarterly,* 3rd ser., 17, no. 1 (January 1960): 38–43; Levy, *Emergence,* 17–18; Harold L. Nelson, "Seditious Libel in Colonial America," *American Journal of Legal History* 3, no. 2 (April 1959): 163–64; Michael E. Stevens, "Legislative Privilege in Post-Revolutionary South Carolina," *William and Mary Quarterly* 46, no. 1 (January 1989): 71–92.
104. For details about McDougall's appearance before the Assembly, I have relied on the official record and McDougall's own account: *Journal of the Votes and Proceedings of the General Assembly of the Colony of New-York From 1766 to 1776 Inclusive* (Albany: J. Buel, 1820), 6–8; *New York Journal,* 20 December 1770, 24 January 1771, and 31 January 1771; *New York Gazette or Weekly Post-Boy,* 24 December 1770; Tiedemann, *Reluctant Revolutionaries,* 168.
105. *New York Journal,* 31 January 1771.
106. Champagne, *Alexander McDougall,* 43.

CHAPTER 6: THE SILVERSMITH

1. Details about the confrontation on the evening of March 5 were taken from Hiller B. Zobel, *The Boston Massacre* (New York: W. W. Norton, 1970), 180–205; Neil L. York, *The Boston Massacre: A History with Documents* (New York: Routledge, 2010), 26; Esther Forbes, *Paul Revere and the World He Lived In* (Boston: Houghton Mifflin, 1942), 147–51.

2. *Paul Revere,* Jonathan Singleton Copley, Museum of Fine Arts, Boston, http://www.mfa .org/collections/object/paul-revere-32401.

3. David Hackett Fischer, *Paul Revere's Ride* (New York: Oxford University Press, 1994), 6; Forbes, *Paul Revere,* 3–8, 10, 13.

4. Fischer, *Paul Revere's Ride,* 8–14; Forbes, *Paul Revere,* 21–22, 27–29.

5. Fischer, *Paul Revere's Ride,* 14–19.

6. Forbes, *Paul Revere,* 113–15.

7. Forbes, *Paul Revere,* 116–19.

8. Clarence S. Brigham, *Paul Revere's Engravings* (Worcester, MA: American Antiquarian Society, 1954), 44–45.

9. Brigham, *Paul Revere's Engravings,* 129–30.

10. Brigham, *Paul Revere's Engravings,* 44.

11. Brigham, *Paul Revere's Engravings,* 47–48.

12. Richard L. Bushman, "Caricature and Satire in Old and New England Before the American Revolution," *Proceedings of the Massachusetts Historical Society,* 3rd ser., 88 (1976): 19–21; Isabel Simeral Johnson, "Cartoons," *Public Opinion Quarterly* 1, no. 3 (July 1937): 21–22.

13. Charles Press, "The Georgian Political Print and Democratic Institutions," *Comparative Studies in Society and History* 19, no. 2 (April 1977): 218.

14. Clare Walcot, "Hogarth's *The South Sea Scheme* and the Topography of Speculative Finance," *Oxford Art Journal* 35, no. 3 (2012): 413–16; *The South Sea Scheme,* National Portrait Gallery, http://www.npg.org.uk/collections/search/portrait/mw113127/The-South -Sea-Scheme.

15. Douglass Adair, "The Stamp Act in Contemporary English Cartoons," *William and Mary Quarterly,* 3rd ser., 10, no. 1 (October 1953): 538–42; E. P. Richardson, "Stamp Act Cartoons in the Colonies," *Pennsylvania Magazine of History and Biography* 96, no. 3 (July 1972): 277–83.

16. Bushman, "Caricature and Satire," 22–23.

17. *Pennsylvania Gazette,* 9 May 1754; Lester C. Olson, *Benjamin Franklin's Vision of American Community: A Study in Rhetorical Iconology* (Columbia: University of South Carolina Press, 2004), 77–111.

18. Joseph Harrison to Charles Watson-Wentworth, second Marquis of Rockingham, 17 June 1768, in D. H. Watson, "Joseph Harrison and the Liberty Incident," *William and Mary Quarterly,* 3rd ser., 20, no. 4 (October 1963): 585–595; York, *The Boston Massacre,* 14; Richard Archer, *As If an Enemy's Country: The British Occupation of Boston and the Origins of Revolution* (New York: Oxford University Press, 2010), 85–89.

19. Wallace Brown and Henry Hulton, "An Englishman Views the American Revolution: The Letters of Henry Hulton, 1769–1776," *Huntington Library Quarterly* 36, no. 1 (November 1972): 3–4.

20. Archer, *As If an Enemy's Country,* 99–107.

21. Archer, *As If an Enemy's Country,* 99–103.

22. *Boston Evening-Post,* 3 October 1768, 12 December 1768.

23. *Boston Evening-Post,* 3 October 1768; *Boston Chronicle,* 29 September 1768, 3 October 1768.

24. Thomas Gage to Council, 28 October 1768, in *Boston Evening-Post,* 31 October 1768.

25. "The Sam Adams Regiments in the Town of Boston," *Atlantic Monthly* 10 August 1862 (Boston: Ticknor and Fields, 1862), 181.

26. Archer, *As If an Enemy's Country*, xvi.

27. Archer, *As If an Enemy's Country*, 127–33.

28. Jesse Lemisch, "Jack Tar in the Streets: Merchant Seamen in the Politics of Revolutionary America," *William and Mary Quarterly*, 3rd ser., 25, no. 3 (July 1968): 400.

29. The publishing effort is described, and the articles reprinted, in Oliver Morton Dickerson, *Boston Under Military Rule 1768–1769 as Revealed in a Journal of the Times* (Boston: Mount Vernon Press, 1936); Zobel, *Boston Massacre*, 109–10.

30. Francis Bernard to Lord Hillsborough, 25 February 1769, in *The Papers of Francis Bernard, Governor of Colonial Massachusetts, 1760–69*, vol. 5: 1768–1769, ed. Colin Nicolson (Boston: Colonial Society of Massachusetts, 2015), 5:216.

31. Archer, *As If an Enemy's Country*, 141–42.

32. *Boston Gazette*, 7 August 1769.

33. Archer, *As If an Enemy's Country*, 142–43.

34. Zobel, *Boston Massacre*, 54–55, 173–78.

35. Thomas Hutchinson, *The History of the Province of Massachusetts Bay from 1749 to 1774* (London: John Murray, 1828), 270; *Boston Gazette*, 26 February 1770, 5 March 1770.

36. John Adams, diary entry, 5 March 1770, Founders Online, National Archives, http://founders.archives.gov/documents/Adams/01-03-02-0016-0016.

37. Adams, diary entry, Founders Online.

38. *Report of the Record Commissioners of the City of Boston, Containing the Boston Town Records, 1770 Through 1777* (Boston: Rockwell and Churchill, 1887), 1, 4.

39. *Report of the Record Commissioners of the City of Boston*, 3; Zobel, *Boston Massacre*, 206–10.

40. Zobel, *Boston Massacre*, 219–21.

41. *Report of the Record Commissioners of the City of Boston*, 10.

42. *A Short Narrative of the Horrid Massacre in Boston Perpetrated in the Evening of the Fifth Day of March, 1770 by Soldiers of the 29th Regiment . . .* (Boston: Edes and Gill, 1770), 7–8.

43. Thomas Hutchinson, *History of the Province of Massachusetts Bay from 1749 to 1774* (London: John Murray, 1828), 277.

44. *Report of the Record Commissioners of the City of Boston*, 13–18.

45. William Dalrymple to Thomas Gage, 12 March 1770, in *Proceedings of the American Antiquarian Society* 47 (October 1937): 281–82.

46. William Dalrymple to Thomas Gage, 19 March 1770, in *Proceedings of the American Antiquarian Society* 47: 288–89.

47. *Boston Gazette*, 2 April 1770.

48. Brigham, *Paul Revere's Engravings*, 51.

49. *Boston Gazette*, 12 March 1770; Thomas Gage to William Dalrymple, 17 June 1770; Gage to Dalrymple, 26 March 1770, in *Proceedings of the American Antiquarian Society* 47:310–11, 292–93.

50. Publications of the Colonial Society of Massachusetts, Transactions, (Boston: Colonial Society of Massachusetts, 1905), 7:2–21.

51. William Dalrymple to Thomas Gage, 27 March 1770; and Thomas Hutchinson to Thomas Gage, 18 March 1770, in *Proceedings of the American Antiquarian Society* 47: 294–95, 286–87.

52. *Boston Gazette*, 12 March 1770.

53. *Boston Gazette*, 19 March 1770.

54. *Providence Gazette*, 17 March 1770; *Connecticut Courant*, 19 March 1770; *Massachusetts Gazette and Boston Weekly News-Letter*, 15 March 1770; *New Hampshire Gazette*, 23 March 1770; *Boston Gazette*, 2 April 1770; *Boston Evening-Post*, 2 April 1770; Kurt William Ritter, "Rhetoric and Ritual in the American Revolution: The Boston Massacre Commemorations, 1771–1783" (PhD diss., Indiana University, 1974), 41–46.

55. *New York Journal*, 15 March 1770, 29 March 1770, 5 April 1770, 12 April 1770; *Pennsylvania Chronicle*, 26 March 1770; *Pennsylvania Gazette*, 22 March 1770; Arthur M.

Schlesinger, *Prelude to Independence: The Newspaper War on Britain 1764–1776* (New York: Alfred A. Knopf, 1958), 117; Ritter, "Rhetoric and Ritual," 43–44.

56. Schlesinger, *Prelude to Independence,* 126.

57. *Georgia Gazette,* 11 April 1770, 25 April 1770; Ritter, "Rhetoric and Ritual," 41–46.

58. Forbes, *Paul Revere,* 152–53.

59. Forbes, *Paul Revere,* 153–54; Zobel, *Boston Massacre,* 198–99; Louise Phelps Kellogg, "The Paul Revere Print of the Boston Massacre," *Wisconsin Magazine of History* 1, no. 4 (June 1918): 381–82.

60. Henry Pelham to Paul Revere, 29 March 1770, in *Proceedings of the Massachusetts Historical Society,* 2nd ser., 8 (1894): 227; Brigham, *Paul Revere's Engravings,* 41–43.

61. Brigham, *Paul Revere's Engravings,* 41–45; Kellogg, "The Paul Revere Print of the Boston Massacre," 381–35; Zobel, *Boston Massacre,* 211.

62. Brigham, *Paul Revere's Engravings,* 46, 51–53.

63. Mason I. Lowance Jr. and Georgia B. Bumgardner, *Massachusetts Broadsides of the American Revolution* (Amherst: University of Massachusetts Press, 1976), 28–29.

64. "A Verse Occasioned by the late horrid Massacre in *King-Street*"; "On the Death of Five young Men who was Murthered, March 5th 1770 By the 29th Regiment," Library of Congress, http://hdl.loc.gov/loc.rbc/rbpe.03700300; "A Particular Account of the Most Barbarous and horrid massacre Committed in King-Street, *Boston,* on Monday, *March* 5, by the Soldiery Quartered in Said Town," broadside, Boston, 1770; Ritter, "Rhetoric and Ritual," 40–41.

65. Trial of William Wemms et al., Superior Court of Judicature, Boston, November 29, 1770 (Boston and London: T. Evans, 1770), 77.

66. *Boston Gazette,* 16 October 1769, 16 April 1770; Brigham, *Paul Revere's Engravings,* 59.

67. Brigham, *Paul Revere's Engravings,* 58–64; "The Illustrated Inventory of Paul Revere's Works at the American Antiquarian Society," Revere Collection Box 2, http://www.americanantiquarian.org/Inventories/Revere/b2.htm; Catharina Slautterback, "*A View of Part of the Town of Boston,*" Boston Athenaeum, http://www.bostonathenaeum.org/view-part-town-boston.

68. James R. Gilmore, "Nathaniel Emmons and Mather Byles," *New England Magazine,* New Series, 16, Old Series, 22 (March 1897 and August 1897); J. L. Bell, "Mather Byles, Sr., and 'Three Thousand Tyrants,' *Boston 1775* (blog), March 11, 2007, http://boston1775.blogspot.com/2007/03/mather-byles-sr-and-three-thousand.html.

69. John Lathrop, "Innocent Blood Crying to God from the Streets of Boston" (London, 1770), 5–7, 12.

70. Edward M. Griffin, *Old Brick: Charles Chauncy of Boston, 1705–1787* (Minneapolis: University of Minnesota Press, 1980), 15, 24.

71. Griffin, *Old Brick,* 147–149

72. *Boston Gazette,* 4 June 1770; *Boston Evening–Post,* 18 June, 1770.

73. Peter Oliver, *Peter Oliver's Origin & Progress of the American Rebellion: A Tory View,* ed. Douglass Adair and John A. Schutz (San Marino, CA: Huntington Library, 1961), 91–92.

74. Oliver, *Peter Oliver's Origin & Progress of the American Rebellion,* 91.

75. Zobel, *Boston Massacre,* 265, 294; Diary, 5 March 1773, *The Works of John Adams, Second President of the United States* (Boston: Charles C. Little and James Brown, 1850), 2:317.

76. *Boston Gazette,* 21 January 1771.

77. Diary, 5 March 1773, in *Works of John Adams,* 317–18.

78. Thomas Gage to Thomas Preston, 26 March 1770, in *Proceedings of the American Antiquarian Society* 47:291–92.

79. Thomas Gage to William Dalrymple, 19 March 1770, in *Proceedings of the American Antiquarian Society* 47:289–90.

80. "The City of Boston's Account of their Conduct to Capt. Preston, after the Massacre of March the 5th," *Publications of the Colonial Society of Massachusetts: Transactions* (Boston: Colonial Society of Massachusetts, 1905), 7:15.

81. *Pennsylvania Gazette,* 6 September 1770.

CHAPTER 7: THE FARMER

1. Thomas Jefferson, 1776–1818, Weather Record, *The Thomas Jefferson Papers*, 7th ser., Miscellaneous Bound Volumes, Library of Congress American Memory, http://hdl.loc.gov/loc.mss/mtj.mtjbib026574, accessed July 26, 2014.
2. Pauline Maier, *American Scripture: Making the Declaration of Independence* (New York: Alfred A. Knopf, 1997), 44–45.
3. Russell F. Weigley, ed., *Philadelphia: A 300-Year History* (New York: W. W. Norton, 1982), 128.
4. John Adams to Archibald Bulloch, 1 July 1776, in *Letters of Delegates to Congress*, ed. Paul H. Smith et al. (Washington, DC: Library of Congress, 1976–2000), 4:345.
5. *Journals of the American Congress from 1774 to 1788*, 8 July 1775 (Washington, DC: Way and Gideon, 1823) 1:391–392; John Dickinson and J. H. Powell, "Notes and Documents," *Pennsylvania Magazine of History and Biography* 65, no. 4 (October 1941): 461.
6. John Dickinson, "Arguments Against the Independence of These Colonies, in Congress," 1 July 1776, in Dickinson and Powell, "Notes and Documents," 468.
7. Milton E. Flower, *John Dickinson: Conservative Revolutionary* (Charlottesville: University Press of Virginia, 1983), 1–12; William Murchison, *The Cost of Liberty: The Life of John Dickinson* (Wilmington, DE: Intercollegiate Studies Institute, 2013), 7–10.
8. John Dickinson to Mary Cadwalader Dickinson, 8 March 1754 and 15 August 1754, in H. Trevor Colbourn and Richard Peters, "A Pennsylvania Farmer at the Court of King George: John Dickinson's London Letters, 1754–1756," *Pennsylvania Magazine of History and Geography* 86, no. 3 (July 1962): 261–64, 279–81.
9. Colbourn and Peters, "A Pennsylvania Farmer," 246–48.
10. John Dickinson to Samuel Dickinson, 19 February 1755, in Colbourn, "A Pennsylvania Farmer at the Court of King George: John Dickinson's London Letters, 1754–1756," *Pennsylvania Magazine of History and Geography* 86, no. 4 (October 1962) 425–27.
11. John Dickinson to Samuel Dickinson, 21 January 1755, in Colbourn, "A Pennsylvania Farmer," 86, no. 4, 420–22.
12. Flower, *John Dickinson*, 22–23, 28–30.
13. John Dickinson to George Read, 1 October 1762, in *Life and Correspondence of George Read* (Philadelphia: J. B. Lippincott, 1870), 16–18.
14. Homer L. Calkin, "Pamphlets and Public Opinion During the American Revolution," *Pennsylvania Magazine of History and Biography* 64, no. 1 (January 1940): 23.
15. Calkin, "Pamphlets and Public Opinion," 32–33.
16. Joad Raymond, *Pamphlets and Pamphleteering in Early Modern Britain* (Cambridge: Cambridge University Press, 2003), 8.
17. "Marprelate Controversy," *Encyclopædia Britannica Online*, http://www.britannica.com/EBchecked/topic/366058/Marprelate-Controversy, accessed July 10, 2014.
18. Raymond, *Pamphlets and Pamphleteering*, 10, 331–41, 367–68.
19. Bernard Bailyn, ed., *Pamphlets of the American Revolution: 1750–1765* (Cambridge, MA: Harvard University Press, 1965), 11.
20. Bailyn, *Pamphlets*, 21, 23–24, 27–30.
21. Bailyn, *Pamphlets*, 447.
22. Edmund S. Morgan and Helen M. Morgan, *The Stamp Act Crisis: Prologue to Revolution* (Chapel Hill: University of North Carolina Press, 1962), 107–21.
23. John Dickinson to James Otis Jr., 5 December 1767, in *Warren-Adams Letters, Being chiefly a correspondence among John Adams, Samuel Adams, and James Warren, 1743–1777* (Massachusetts Historical Society, 1917), 1:3–4.
24. For an interesting discussion of Dickinson's strategy, see Carl F. Kaestle, "The Public Reaction to John Dickinson's Farmer's Letters," *Proceedings of the American Antiquarian Society* 78 (1969): 338–42.
25. Forrest McDonald, ed., *Empire and Nation: Letters from a Farmer in Pennsylvania (John Dickinson); Letters from the Federal Farmer (Richard Henry Lee)* (Englewood Cliffs, NJ: Prentice-Hall, 1962), 3.

26. I drew from Stephen H. Browne's excellent analysis of the pastoral voice in the Farmer's *Letters*. See Stephen H. Browne, "The Pastoral Voice in John Dickinson's 'First Letter from a Farmer in Pennsylvania,'" *Quarterly Journal of Speech* 76, no. 1 (1990): 46–57.

27. For this discussion of sovereignty, I am indebted to Bernard Bailyn, *The Ideological Origins of the American Revolution* (Cambridge, MA: Harvard University Press, 1967), 198–229, also available in Bailyn, *Pamphlets*, 115–38; Gordon S. Wood, *The Creation of the American Republic 1776–1787* (Chapel Hill: University of North Carolina Press, 1998), 344–89; and Andrew C. McLaughlin, "The Background of American Federalism," *American Political Science Review* 12, no. 2 (May 1918).

28. William Blackstone, *Commentaries on the Laws of England* (Philadelphia: J. B. Lippincott, 1893), 1:48.

29. *Letters from a Farmer in Pennsylvania*, Letter 5, in McDonald, *Empire and Nation*, 26, 28.

30. *Letters from a Farmer in Pennsylvania*, Letter 9, in McDonald, *Empire and Nation*, 50.

31. William Franklin to Lord Hillsborough, 23 November 1768, in *New Jersey in the American Revolution, 1763–1783: A Documentary History,* ed. Larry R. Gerlach (New Jersey Historical Commission, 1975), http://www.njstatelib.org/slic_files/imported/NJ_Information/Digital_Collections/NJInTheAmericanRevolution1763-1783/2.5.pdf, accessed July 20, 2014.

32. Leland J. Bellot, *William Knox: The Life & Thought of an Eighteenth-Century Imperialist* (Austin: University of Texas Press, 1977), 97–98.

33. Wood, *Creation of the American Republic*, 345.

34. John McPherson Jr. to William Patterson, 11 March 1768, in John Macpherson Jr., "Extracts from the Letters of John Macpherson, Jr. to William Patterson, 1766–1773," *Pennsylvania Magazine of History and Biography* 23, no. 1 (1899): 53–54.

35. Governor Francis Bernard to Lord Barrington, 28 January 1768, in *The Barrington–Bernard Correspondence and Illustrative Matter, 1760–1770,* ed. Edward Channing and Archibald Cary Coolidge (Cambridge, MA: Harvard University Press, 1912), 135.

36. Benjamin Franklin to William Franklin, 13 March 1768, in *The Writings of Benjamin Franklin,* ed. Albert Henry Smyth, vol. 5 1767–1772 (New York: Macmillan, 1906), 5:113–114; *Boston Gazette,* 21 December 1767.

37. *Pennsylvania Chronicle,* 16 May 1768.

38. Kaestle, "The Public Reaction to John Dickinson's Farmer's Letters," 325–29, 352–59.

39. *Boston Gazette,* 21 March 1768.

40. *New-London Gazette,* 29 April 1768.

41. *Massachusetts Gazette and Boston News-Letter,* 24 March 1768; *Boston Gazette,* 4 April 1768; *Boston News-Letter,* 25 August 1768; *Boston Evening-Post,* 26 September 1768.

42. *Pennsylvania Gazette,* 1 September 1768.

43. *New York Gazette and Weekly Mercury,* 5 September 1768.

44. *Pennsylvania Chronicle,* 29 August 1768.

45. *Pennsylvania Chronicle,* 22 August 1768.

46. *Boston Evening-Post,* 15 May 1768.

47. *Boston Evening-Post,* 13 February 1768.

48. *Boston Evening-Post,* 5 June 1768.

49. John Dickinson to James Otis Jr., 4 July 1768, in *The Writings of John Dickinson,* ed. Paul Leicester Ford, vol. 1, Political Writings 1764–1774 (Philadelphia: Historical Society of Pennsylvania, 1895), 1:421.

50. *Boston Gazette,* 18 July 1768; Ford, *Writings of John Dickinson,* 1:421–22.

51. *Boston Gazette,* 18 July 1768.

52. Evelyn Kendrick Wells, *The Ballad Tree: A Study of British and American Ballads, Their Folklore, Verse, and Music* (New York: Roland Press, 1950), 211–14.

53. *Manual of the Corporation of the City of New-York, 1862* (New York: Edmund Jones, 1862), 703–4; *The Memorial History of the City of New-York From Its First Settlement to the Year 1892,* ed. James Grant Wilson (New York: New York History Company, 1892), 2:237–38.

54. Clyde Augustus Duniway, *The Development of Freedom of the Press in Massachusetts* (New York: Longmans, Green, 1906), 115.

55. Frank Moore, *Songs and Ballads of the American Revolution* (New York: D. Appleton, 1856), 48–50.

56. Ford, *Writings of John Dickinson,* 1:421–22.

57. Monday, 14 August 1769, *Founding Families: Digital Editions of the Papers of the Winthrops and the Adamses,* ed. C. James Taylor (Boston: Massachusetts Historical Society, 2007).

58. Moore, *Songs and Ballads,* 95–96.

59. *Boston Evening-Post,* 22 August 1768.

60. *Boston Gazette,* 26 September 1768.

61. *Boston Evening-Post,* 3 October 1768.

62. Weigley, *Philadelphia: A 300-Year History,* 109–54; David McCullough, *John Adams* (New York: Simon & Schuster, 2001), 79–81; Craig Nelson, *Thomas Paine: Enlightenment, Revolution, and the Birth of Modern Nations* (New York: Viking, 2006), 53–54; John William Wallace, *An Old Philadelphian, Colonel William Bradford, The Patriot Printer of 1776: Sketches of His Life* (Philadelphia: Sherman & Company, 1884), 47–54, 95–101; Robert Earle Graham, "The Taverns of Colonial Philadelphia," *Transactions of the American Philosophical Society,* n.s., 43, no. 1 (1953): 321; Flower, *John Dickinson,* 112.

63. John Adams, diary entry, 31 August 1774, *Diary and Autobiography of John Adams,* ed. L. H. Butterfield (Cambridge, MA: Harvard University Press, 1961), 2:117–18.

64. John Adams, diary entry, 12 September 1774, *Diary and Autobiography of John Adams,* 2:132–33.

65. John Adams, diary entry, 24 September 1774, *Diary and Autobiography of John Adams,* 2:137.

66. John Adams, diary entry, 3 October 1774, *Diary and Autobiography of John Adams,* 2:146–47.

67. William Murchison, *The Cost of Liberty: The Life of John Dickinson* (Wilmington, DE: Intercollegiate Studies Institute, 2013), 63–65; Flower, *John Dickinson,* 72–75.

68. Samuel Adams to John Dickinson, 27 March 1773, in Charles J. Stillé, *The Life and Times of John Dickinson 1732–1808* (Philadelphia: J. B. Lippincott, 1891), 102–3.

69. John Dickinson, "A Letter from the Country, To a Gentleman in Philadelphia," 27 November 1773, in *The Writings of John Dickinson,* 1:455–63.

70. John Dickinson, "An Essay on the Constitutional Power of Great Britain Over the Colonies in America," 1774, *Pennsylvania Archives,* 2nd ser., 3 (1875): 565.

71. John Dickinson to George Logan, 15 September 1804, in Stillé, *Life and Times of John Dickinson,* 143–48.

72. John Adams, diary entry, 24 October 1774, *Diary and Autobiography of John Adams,* 2:156–57.

73. James Warren to John Adams, 15 January 1775, in *Warren-Adams Letters,* 35–36.

74. *Boston Gazette,* 21 March 1774; John Adams to James Warren, 22 December 1773, 9 April 1774, in Founders Online, National Archives, http://founders.archives.gov/documents/Adams/06-02-02-0002 and http://founders.archives.gov/documents/Adams/06-02-02-0009 (ver. 2014-05-09), source: "The Adams Papers," *Papers of John Adams,* vol. 2, *December 1773_–_April 1775,* ed. Robert J. Taylor (Cambridge, MA: Harvard University Press, 1977), 82–84.

75. *Boston Gazette,* 23 January 1775; Nancy Rubin Stuart, *The Muse of the Revolution: The Secret Pen of Mercy Otis Warren and the Founding of a Nation* (Boston: Beacon Press, 2008), 48–49, 51–52, 67–70.

76. Mercy Warren to John Adams, 30 January 1775, in *Warren-Adams Letters,* 1:36–39.

77. John Adams to Mercy Warren, 15 March 1775, in *Warren-Adams Letters,* 1:42–44.

78. Alexander Cowie, "John Trumbull as Revolutionist," *American Literature* 3, no. 3 (November 1931): 290–293; Lennox Grey, "John Adams and John Trumbull in the 'Boston Cycle,'" *New England Quarterly* 4, no 3 (July 1931): 510–11.

79. Bruce Ingham Granger, "Hudibras in the American Revolution," *American Literature* 27, no. 4 (January 1956): 499–503.

80. Leonard W. Levy, *Emergence of a Free Press* (New York: Oxford University Press, 1985), 71.

81. Dwight L. Teeter, "'King' Sears, the Mob, and Freedom of the Press in New York, 1765–76," *Journalism Quarterly* (fall 1964): 539–544.

82. I. N. Phelps Stokes, *The Iconography of Manhattan Island* (New York: Robert H. Dodd, 1922), 4:885, 888.

83. Stokes, *Iconography*, 4:891.

84. Stokes, *Iconography*, 4:905–6.

85. "The Letters of Novanglus," editorial note, *Papers of John Adams*, vol. 2, Massachusetts Historical Society Digital Editions: Adams Papers, http://www.masshist.org/publications/apde/portia.php?&id=PJA02dg5, accessed July 27, 2014.

86. John Dickinson to Arthur Lee, 29 April 1775, in *Life of Arthur Lee*, ed. Richard Henry Lee (Boston: Wells and Lilly, 1829), 2:307–11.

87. *Diary and Autobiography of John Adams*, ed. L. H. Butterfield (Cambridge, MA: Harvard University Press, 1961), 3:314.

88. Maier, *American Scripture*, 19–20; Julian T. Boyd, "The Disputed Authorship of the Declaration on the Causes and Necessity of Taking Up Arms, 1775," *Pennsylvania Magazine of History and Biography* 74, no. 1 (January 1950): 51–73; "A Declaration by the Representatives of the United Colonies . . . Setting Forth the Causes and Necessity of Their Taking Up Arms," Avalon Project, Yale Law School, http://avalon.law.yale.edu/18th_century/arms.asp.

89. *The Works of Thomas Jefferson*, Federal ed., ed. Paul Leicester Ford (New York and London: G. P. Putnam's Sons, 1904–5), 1:17–19, in Online Library of Liberty, Liberty Fund, http://oll.libertyfund.org/titles/800.

90. The Olive Branch Petition, 8 July 1775, *Journals of the American Congress from 1774 to 1788* (Washington, DC: Way and Gideon, 1823), 1:104–6.

91. Butterfield, *Diary and Autobiography of John Adams*, 3:320–21.

92. Ford, *Works of Thomas Jefferson*, 1:17–19.

93. Butterfield, *Diary and Autobiography of John Adams*, 3:318.

94. John Adams to Abigail Adams, 23 July 1775, in Taylor, *Founding Families*.

95. John Adams to James Warren, 24 July 1775, in *The Adams Papers Digital Edition*, ed. C. James Taylor (Charlottesville: University of Virginia Press, Rotunda, 2008–2015), original source: *Papers of John Adams*, vol. 3, May 1775–January 1776; John Adams to Abigail Adams, 24 July 1775, in *Adams Papers Digital Edition*, original source: *Adams Family Correspondence*, vol. 1, December 1761–May 1776; *Massachusetts Gazette and Boston Weekly News-Letter*, 17 August 1775.

96. John Adams to James Warren, 24 July 1775, in *Adams Papers Digital Edition*, fn. 6.

97. John Adams, diary entry, 16 September 1775, in *Diary and Autobiography of John Adams*, 2:173–75.

98. Samuel Adams to James Warren, 12 December 1776, in *Warren-Adams Letters*, 1:279–81.

99. King George III, "A Proclamation for Suppressing Rebellion and Sedition," 23 August 1775; King's Speech to Both Houses, 26 October 1775, *American Archives*, ed. Peter Force (Washington, DC: 1833–1846), 6:1–2, at American Archives: Documents of the American Revolution, 1774–1776, http://lincoln.lib.niu.edu/cgi-bin/amarch/getdoc.pl?/var/lib/philologic/databases/amarch/.15918.

100. Christopher Hitchens, *Thomas Paine's Rights of Man: A Biography* (London: Atlantic Books, 2006), 19–29; Craig Nelson, *Thomas Paine: Enlightenment, Revolution, and the Birth of Modern Nations* (New York: Viking, 2006), 52–100.

101. Frank Smith, "New Light on Thomas Paine's First Year in America, 1775," *American Literature* 1, no. 4 (January 1930): 347–71.

102. Thomas Paine, "African Slavery in America," *Writings of Thomas Paine*, ed. Moncure Daniel Conway (New York: G. P. Putnam's Sons, 1906), 1:4-9

103. Benjamin Rush, *The Autobiography of Benjamin Rush: His "Travels Through Life" Together with his Commonplace Book for 1789–1813* (Westport, CT: Greenwood Press, 1948), 113–14.

104. Eric Foner, *Tom Paine and Revolutionary America* (New York: Oxford University Press, 2005), 79.

105. Foner, *Tom Paine*, 75. For an excellent discussion of Paine and the public sphere, see xvi, 71–87.

106. *Pennsylvania Packet and General Advertiser,* 31 December 1778; *Writings of Thomas Paine,* 1:409.

107. For a study that compares the language used in *Common Sense* to fourteen other pamphlets of the time, see Lee Sigelman, Colin Martindale, and Dean McKenzie, "The Common Style of Common Sense," *Computers and the Humanities* 30 (1997): 373–79.

108. Edmund Randolph, "Essay on the Revolutionary History of Virginia 1774–1782," *Virginia Magazine of History and Biography* 43, no. 4 (October 1935): 306.

109. Many authors analyze *Common Sense* in depth. See, for example, Foner, *Tom Paine*, 71–87; Hitchens, *Thomas Paine's Rights of Man*, 31–37; Harvey J. Kaye, *Thomas Paine and the Promise of America* (New York: Hill and Wang, 2005), 42–50; and David Freeman Hawke, *Paine* (New York: Harper & Row, 1974), 41–46.

110. *Common Sense,* in *Thomas Paine: Collected Writings,* ed. Eric Foner (New York: Library of America, 1995), 15–17, 28, 34, 52.

111. Randolph, "Essay on the Revolutionary History of Virginia," 306.

112. James Chalmers, *Plain Truth: Addressed to the Inhabitants of America Containing Remarks on a late Pamphlet, Intitled Common Sense* (Philadelphia, 1776).

113. "To John Adams from Hugh Hughes, 31 March 1776," Founders Online, National Archives, http://founders.archives.gov/documents/Adams/06-04-02-0030 (ver. 2014-05-09), source: *The Adams Papers,* Papers of John Adams, vol. 4, *February–August 1776,* ed. Robert J. Taylor (Cambridge, MA: Harvard University Press, 1979), 98–101; "A Crack-Brained Zealot for Democracy," *National Humanities Center Toolbox, Making the Revolution: America, 1763–1791,* http://americainclass.org/sources/makingrevolution /rebellion/text7/inglisdeceiverunmasked.pdf, accessed July 14, 2014.

114. For descriptions of the work of the Continental Congress from 7 June through 4 July 1776, I relied on *Journals of the American Congress,* July 1–2, 391–93; Maier, *American Scripture,* 41–46; Flower, *John Dickinson,* 153–67; Murchison, *Cost of Liberty,* 149; Stillé, *Life and Times,* 196–97.

115. "Resolution introduced in the Continental Congress by Richard Henry Lee (Virginia) proposing a Declaration of Independence, June 7, 1776," http://avalon.law.yale. edu/18th_century/lee.asp, accessed July 23, 2014.

116. John Dickinson to Thomas Cushing, 11 December 1774, in Smith, *Letters of Delegates to Congress,* 1:264.

117. John Dickinson, "Arguments Against the Independence," in Dickinson and Powell, "Notes and Documents," 478–80.

118. John Adams, diary entry, 1 July 1776, *Diary and Autobiography of John Adams,* 3:396.

119. Charles Thomson to John Dickinson, 16 August 1776, in Stillé, *Life and Times of John Dickinson,* 209–11.

120. John Adams to Abigail Adams, 23 June 1775, in *Adams Family Correspondence,* ed. L. H. Butterfield, Wendell D. Garrett, and Marjorie Sprague (Cambridge, MA: Harvard University Press, 1963), 1:226–27.

121. John Adams to Abigail Adams, 3 July 1776, in *Adams Family Correspondence,* 2:29–33.

122. John Adams to Thomas Jefferson, 12 November 1813, in *The Adams-Jefferson Letters: The Complete Correspondence Between Thomas Jefferson & Abigail & John Adams,* ed. Lester J. Cappon (Chapel Hill: University of North Carolina Press, 1987), 392–94.

CHAPTER 8: THE PLANTER

1. Primary sources on ratification of the Constitution are collected in the multivolume set *The Documentary History of the Ratification of the Constitution,* ed. John P. Kaminski,

Gaspare J. Saladino, et al. (Charlottesville: University of Virginia Press, 2009), hereafter *DHRC*. Two excellent historical accounts on which I relied are Pauline Maier, *Ratification: The People Debate the Constitution, 1787–1788* (New York: Simon & Schuster, 2010); and Jürgen Heideking, *The Constitution Before the Judgment Seat: The Prehistory and Ratification of the American Constitution, 1787–1791*, ed. John P. Kaminski and Richard Leffler (Charlottesville: University of Virginia Press, 2012).

2. *Independent Gazetteer,* 2 October 1787, in *DHRC,* 8:15–16, fn. 2.

3. George Washington to Patrick Henry, 24 September 1787, in *DHRC,* 8:15–16.

4. James Madison to George Washington, 18 October 1787, in *DHRC,* 8:77.

5. Patrick Henry to George Washington, 19 October 1787, in *DHRC,* 8:79.

6. George Washington to James Madison, 5 February 1788, in *DHRC,* 8:279–280.

7. James Madison to Thomas Jefferson, 9 December 1787, in *DHRC,* 8:227.

8. For an extended discussion of the significance of the vigorous ratification debate to the meaning that the founding generation attached to the freedom of speech and press, see Akhil Reed Amar, "30th Annual Sullivan Lecture: How America's Constitution Affirmed Freedom of Speech Before the First Amendment," 38 *Cap U.L. Rev.*503, (2010).

9. For a discussion of public opinion and the ratification, see Heideking, *Constitution Before the Judgment Seat,* 53–61.

10. James Madison to Thomas Jefferson, 6 June 1787, in *DHRC,* 13:84.

11. Archibald Stuart to John Breckinridge, 21 October 1787, in *DHRC,* 8:89.

12. *DHRC,* 22:1768.

13. Francis Hopkinson to Thomas Jefferson, 17 July 1788, in *DHRC,* 18:270.

14. Jeffrey L. Pasley, *The Tyranny of Printers: Newspaper Politics in the Early American Republic* (Charlottesville: University of Virginia Press, 2001), 33.

15. *DHRC,* 13:xvii–xviii.

16. *DHRC,* 2:62–64.

17. James Madison to Edmund Randolph, 21 October 1787, in *DHRC,* 13:429–30.

18. *DHRC,* 13:xviii.

19. *DHRC,* 19:137–43.

20. *DHRC,* 21:1264–75; John Montgomery to James Wilson, 2 March 1788, in *DHRC,* 2:701–2; Pierce Butler to Elbridge Gerry, 3 March 1788, in *DHRC,* 16:300, note 4.

21. *DHRC,* 13:xviii.

22. *Albany Gazette,* 15 November, 1787, in *DHRC,* 14:117–19.

23. *New York Daily Advertiser,* 11 December 1787, in *DHRC,* 14:118, note 1.

24. Thomas S. Kidd, *Patrick Henry: First Among Patriots* (New York: Basic Books, 2011), 9–11; William Wirt, *The Life of Patrick Henry,* 4th ed. (New York: M'Elrath & Bangs, 1831), 22.

25. Kidd, *Patrick Henry,* 14–15; Wirt, *Life of Patrick Henry,* 25–29.

26. Kidd, *Patrick Henry,* 1, 17–19; Wirt, *Life of Patrick Henry,* 30–33.

27. Wirt, *Life of Patrick Henry,* 32–33.

28. Kidd, *Patrick Henry,* 22–25; Wirt, *Life of Patrick Henry,* 36.

29. Kidd, *Patrick Henry,* 27–28; Jon Kukla, "Patrick Henry (1736–1799)," *Encyclopedia Virginia*, Virginia Foundation for the Humanities, http://www.EncyclopediaVirginia.org/Henry_Patrick_1736–1799.

30. Edmund S. Morgan and Helen M. Morgan, *The Stamp Act Crisis: Prologue to Revolution* (Chapel Hill: University of North Carolina Press, 1962), 92–121; and Merrill Jensen, *The Founding of a Nation: A History of the American Revolution 1763–1776* (New York: Oxford University Press, 1968), 100–105.

31. John Adams to Thomas Jefferson, 12 November 1813, in *The Adams-Jefferson Letters: The Complete Correspondence Between Thomas Jefferson & Abigail & John Adams,* ed. Lester J. Cappon (Chapel Hill: University of North Carolina Press, 1959), 392.

32. William Lee Miller, *The First Liberty: America's Foundation in Religious Freedom* (Washington, DC: Georgetown University Press, 2003), 71–72.

33. John P. Kaminski, *The Great Virginia Triumvirate: George Washington, Thomas Jefferson, & James Madison in the Eyes of Their Contemporaries* (Charlottesville: University of Virginia Press, 2010), 154.

34. Kaminski, *Virginia Triumvirate,* 154.

35. James Madison to William Bradford, 1 July 1774, in Founders Online, National Archives, http://founders.archives.gov/documents/Madison/01-01-02-0032 (last update: 2014-12-01), source: *The Papers of James Madison, vol. 1, 16 March 1751_-_16 December 1779,* ed. William T. Hutchinson and William M. E. Rachal (Chicago: University of Chicago Press, 1962), 114–17.

36. James Madison to William Bradford, 24 January 1774, in *Madison: Writings,* ed. Jack N. Rakove (New York: Library of America, 1999), 5–6.

37. Madison to Bradford, 24 January 1774, in *Madison: Writings;* Miller, *First Liberty,* 5–7.

38. Miller, *First Liberty,* 5–7.

39. Garry Wills, *James Madison* (New York: Henry Holt, 2002), 17–18.

40. "Notes on Ancient and Modern Confederacies, [April–June?] 1786," Founders Online, National Archives, http://founders.archives.gov/documents/Madison/01-09-02-0001 (last update: 2014-12-01), original source: *The Papers of James Madison, 9 April 1786_-_24 May 1787 and supplement 1781–1784,* ed. Robert A. Rutland and William M. E. Rachal (Chicago: University of Chicago Press, 1975), 9:3–23; "Vices of the Political System of the United States, April 1787," Founders Online, National Archives, http://founders.archives.gov/documents/Madison/01-09-02-0187 (last update: 2014-12-01), original source: *Papers of James Madison,* 9:345–58.

41. James Madison to Thomas Jefferson, 24 October 1787, in *Madison: Writings,* 146.

42. Edmund Randolph to Patrick Henry, 6 December 1786, and Henry to Randolph, 13 February 1787, in William Wirt Henry, *Patrick Henry: Life, Correspondence and Speeches* (Harrisonburg, VA: Sprinkle Publications, 1993), 2:310–11.

43. Madison to Edmund Randolph, 25 March 1787, in William Wirt Henry, *Patrick Henry: Life,* 2:312–13.

44. Leonard W. Levy, *Emergence of a Free Press* (New York: Oxford University Press, 1985), 183.

45. *Journals of the Continental Congress, 1774-1789,* January 2, 1776 (Washington, DC: Government Printing Office 1906), 4:18, 20; Claude Halstead Van Tyne, *The Loyalists in the American Revolution* (New York: Macmillan, 1902), 198–202, 327–29; William Walter Hening, ed., *The Statutes at Large, Being a Collection of All the Laws of Virginia, 1619–1792* (Richmond, 1809–23), 9:170–71; Levy, *Emergence,* 177–79.

46. Levy, *Emergence,* 188–89.

47. Levy, *Emergence,* 183–89; Leonard W. Levy, *Origins of the Bill of Rights* (New Haven, CT: Yale University Press, 1999), 120.

48. Levy, *Emergence,* 163–65.

49. *Massachusetts Spy,* 5 December 1771; Levy, *Origins,* 162.

50. James Burgh, *Political Disquisitions,* 3:246–52, in *The Founders' Constitution,* ed. Philip B. Kurland and Ralph Lerner (Indianapolis: Liberty Fund, 1987), 5:120–21.

51. Levy, *Emergence,* 167–68; Jeremy Bentham, *A Fragment on Government,* ed. Ross Harrison and H. L. A. Hart (Cambridge: Cambridge University Press, 1988), 97–98.

52. *Freeman's Journal,* 26 September 1787; *Independent Gazetteer,* 28 September 1787; *Independent Gazetteer,* 29 September 1787; in *DHRC,* 2:146–49.

53. *DHRC,* 13:xviii.

54. Heideking, *Constitution Before the Judgment Seat:,* 84–85; also, see *DHRC,* 13:xvii–xx.

55. *DHRC,* 13:293–94; *DHRC,* 15:7–13.

56. *DHRC,* 13:326–37.

57. *DHRC,* 13:255–57, 411–21; James Madison to Edmund Randolph, 21 October 1787, in *DHRC,* 13:429–30.

58. *DHRC,* 15:156.

59. James Madison to George Washington, 18 November 1787, *DHRC*, 8:167.
60. James Madison to Thomas Jefferson, 9 December 1787, *DHRC*, 8:226–28.
61. *DHRC*, 8:260.
62. *DHRC*, 8:260–75.
63. James Madison to Edmund Randolph, 10 January 1788, *DHRC*, 8:288–91.
64. *DHRC*, 8:40–41.
65. *DHRC*, 8:40–42; George Mason to George Washington, 7 October 1787, *DHRC*, 8:43.
66. *DHRC*, 13:339–340.
67. Thomas Jefferson to James Madison, 20 December 1787, *DHRC*, 8:250–51.
68. Heideking, *Constitution Before the Judgment Seat*, 102, 101, 94–104.
69. Heideking, *Constitution*, 95.
70. Heideking, *Constitution*, 102.
71. *DHRC*, 8:110.
72. Edward Carrington to James Madison, 10 February 1788, in *DHRC*, 8:359.
73. Edward Carrington to Henry Knox, 10 February 1788, in *DHRC*, 9:606.
74. John Blair Smith to James Madison, 12 June 1788, in *DHRC*, 9:607–8.
75. *DHRC*, 9:595–96.
76. Edmund Randolph to James Madison, 3 January 1788, in *DHRC*, 9:598.
77. James Gordon Jr., to James Madison, 18 February 1788, in *DHRC*, 9:600.
78. James Madison Sr., to James Madison, 30 January 1788, in *DHRC*, 9:599.
79. James Madison to Eliza House Trist, 25 March 1788, in *DHRC*, 9:603.
80. Hannah Tracy Emery to Mary Carter, 17 February 1788, in *Supplements to the Documentary History of the Ratification of the Constitution*, vols. 4–7—*Massachusetts*, Document 730, microfiche.
81. *Massachusetts Gazette*, 23 May 1788.
82. Heideking, *Constitution Before the Judgment Seat*, 347–49; *Massachusetts Gazette*, 23 May 1788.
83. *Massachusetts Gazette*, 23 May 1788.
84. Heideking, *Constitution Before the Judgment Seat*, 504n33.
85. Mary Newton Stanard, *Richmond: Its People and Its Story* (Philadelphia: J. B. Lippincott, 1923), 37, 49–52.
86. James Duncanson to James Maury, 7 June and 13 June 1788, in *DHRC*, 10:1583–84.
87. Henry Jackson to Henry Knox, 20 January 1788, in *DHRC*, 7:1536–37.
88. Ezra Stiles, diary entry, 3 January 1788, in *DHRC*, 3:523.
89. *DHRC*, 8:525–29; Maier, *Ratification*, 256–57.
90. *DHRC*, 8:xix–xxi.
91. Richard Henry Lee to George Mason, 7 May 1788, in *DHRC*, IX:784.
92. *DHRC*, 9:929.
93. *DHRC*, 9:929–31.
94. *DHRC*, 9:931–36.
95. *DHRC*, 9:936–40.
96. James Madison to George Washington, 4 June 1788, in *DHRC*, 10:1574.
97. *Massachusetts Centinel*, 25 June 1788, in *DHRC*, 10:1684.
98. For a discussion of oratory early in American history, see Sandra M. Gustafson, *Eloquence Is Power: Oratory & Performance in Early America* (Chapel Hill: University of North Carolina Press, 2000).
99. John Adams, Draft of a Letter to Richard Cranch, October–December 1758, Founders Online, National Archives, http://founders.archives.gov/documents/Adams/02-01-02-0010-0001-0003.
100. Thomas Jefferson and William Wirt, "Jefferson's Recollections of Patrick Henry," *Pennsylvania Magazine of History and Biography* 34, no. 4 (1910): 387, 409.
101. Merrill D. Peterson, *Thomas Jefferson and the New Nation: A Biography* (London: Oxford University Press, 1970), 20.

102. Hugh Blair Grigsby, *The History of the Virginia Federal Convention of 1788* (Richmond: Virginia Historical Society, 1890), 1:119.
103. James Breckinridge to John Breckinridge, 13 June 1788, in *DHRC*, 10:1621.
104. *DHRC*, 9:951–52.
105. *DHRC*, 9:963–64.
106. *DHRC*, 9:1036–37, 1042.
107. *DHRC*, 9:989.
108. *DHRC*, 9:990.
109. *DHRC*, 9:992.
110. *DHRC*, 9:1028–32.
111. *DHRC*, 9:1031.
112. William Grayson to John Lamb, 9 June 1788, in *DHRC*, 9:816; James Madison to Rufus King, 13 June 1788, in *DHRC*, 10:1619.
113. *DHRC*, 9:811–13.
114. *Pennsylvania Herald*, 26 May 1788, quoted in *DHRC*, 16:540–41.
115. *DHRC*, 10:1709.
116. Edward Carrington to James Madison, 10 February 1788, in *DHRC*, 8:359.
117. John Adams to Abigail Adams, 17 or 18 January 1777, in *Founding Families: Digital Editions of the Papers of the Winthrops and the Adamses*, ed. C. James Taylor (Boston: Massachusetts Historical Society, 2015), http://www.masshist.org/publications/apde2/view?id=ADMS-04-02-02-0103.
118. *The Adams Papers: Adams Family Correspondence*, March 1797–April 1798, ed. Sara Martin et al. (Cambridge, MA: Harvard University Press, 2015) 12:117.
119. *DHRC*, 16:540–42; *DHRC*, 20: 582–84; and *DHRC*, 8:517–18.
120. George Washington to John Jay, 18 July 1788, in *DHRC*, 16:595.
121. *DHRC*, 10:1673.
122. Gaspare J. Saladino, "The Federalist Express," in *New York and the Union*, ed. Stephen L. Schechter and Richard B. Bernstein (Albany: New York State Commission on the Bicentennial of the United States Constitution, 1990), 327–29.
123. *DHRC*, 18:33.
124. James Madison to Alexander Hamilton, 9 June 1788, in *DHRC*, 10:1589.
125. James Madison to Alexander Hamilton, 16 June 1788, in *DHRC*, 10:1630.
126. Patrick Henry to John Lamb, 9 June 1788, *DHRC*, 9:817.
127. *DHRC*, 10:1335, fn. 2; 10:1337, fn. 29.
128. *DHRC*, 13:196–97.
129. Levy, *Emergence*, 221; *DHRC*, 1:337–39.
130. *DHRC*, 10:1326.
131. *DHRC*, 10:1328, 1331-32.
132. *DHRC*, 10:1345, 1352.
133. James Madison to Rufus King, 18 June 1788, in *DHRC*, 10:1637.
134. *DHRC*, 10:1473–74; Maier, *Ratification*, 294.
135. *DHRC*, 10:1474, 1476–77.
136. *DHRC*, 10:1479, 1485–87, 1500.
137. *DHRC*, 10:1503.
138. *DHRC*, 10:1506.
139. *DHRC*, 10:1512.
140. *New York Daily Advertiser*, 3 July 1788, in *DHRC*, 10:1698–99.
141. *DHRC*, 10:1537–42.
142. *DHRC*, 10:1541, 1551–53.
143. Richard Henry Lee to John Lamb, 27 June 1788, in *DHRC*, 18:58.
144. *DHRC*, 8:xix–xxi; 13:xl–xlii.
145. *DHRC*, 21:1210–11.
146. Various accounts of the event are in *DHRC*, 21:1264–75.
147. *DHRC*, 22:1669–75.

CHAPTER 9: THE FRAMER

1. Adrienne Koch and Harry Ammon, "The Virginia and Kentucky Resolutions: An Episode in Jefferson's and Madison's Defense of Civil Liberties," *William and Mary Quarterly*, 3rd ser., 5, no. 2 (April 1948): 145–76; Ralph Ketchum, *James Madison: A Biography* (New York: Macmillan, 1971), 394.
2. Ketchum, *James Madison*, 394.
3. John P. Kaminski, *The Great Virginia Triumvirate: George Washington, Thomas Jefferson, & James Madison in the Eyes of Their Contemporaries* (Charlottesville: University of Virginia Press, 2010), 153–54; Richard Brookhiser, *James Madison* (New York: Basic Books, 2011), 15–16; Matthew G. Hyland, *Montpelier and the Madisons: House, Home and American Heritage* (Charleston, SC: History Press, 2007), 11–26; *James Madison's Montpelier: Home of the Father of the Constitution*, ed. Evelyn Bence (Orange, VA: Montpelier Foundation, 2008), 8–10; Bryan Clark Green, Ann L. Miller, with Conover Hunt, *Building a President's House: The Construction of James Madison's Montpelier* (Orange, VA: Montpelier Foundation, 2007), 2–5.
4. "Notes on Ancient and Modern Confederacies," [April–June?] 1786," Founders Online, National Archives, http://founders.archives.gov/documents/Madison/01-09-02-0001 (last update: 2015-9-29), source: *The Papers of James Madison, 9 April 1786_–_24 May 1787 and supplement 1781–1784*, ed. Robert A. Rutland and William M. E. Rachal (Chicago: University of Chicago Press, 1975), 9:3–23.
5. James Madison to Margaret B. Smith, September 1830, in *The Writings of James Madison*, ed. Gaillard Hunt (New York: G.P. Putnam's Sons, 1910), 9:405; Andrew Burstein and Nancy Isenberg, *Madison and Jefferson* (New York: Random House, 2010), 56–67; *James Madison: Writings*, ed. Jack N. Rakove (New York: Library of America, 1999), 894–95.
6. Margaret Bayard Smith to Susan B. Smith, March 1809, in *The First Forty Years of Washington Society*, ed. Gaillard Hunt (New York: Frederick Ungar, 1906), 63.
7. Thomas Jefferson to Elizabeth Wayles Eppes, 3 October 1782, in *The Papers of Thomas Jefferson, 21 May 1781–1 March 1784*, ed. Julian P. Boyd et al. (Princeton, NJ: Princeton University Press, 1952), 6:198.
8. Thomas Jefferson to James Madison, 14 April 1783, in *Papers of Thomas Jefferson*, 6:262; Madison to Jefferson, 22 April 1783, *Papers of Thomas Jefferson*, 6:262.
9. James Madison to Thomas Jefferson, 11 August 1783, in *Papers of Thomas Jefferson*, 6:333; Jefferson to Madison, 31 August 1783, *Papers of Thomas Jefferson*, 6:335–36; Richard Beeman, *Plain, Honest Men: The Making of the American Constitution* (New York: Random House, 2009), 24–25.
10. Thomas Jefferson to James Madison, 20 February 1784, in *Papers of Thomas Jefferson*, 6:550; Madison to Jefferson, 16 March 1784, *Papers of Thomas Jefferson*, 7:37.
11. Thomas Jefferson to James Madison, 20 February 1784, in *Papers of Thomas Jefferson*, 6:550; Madison to Jefferson, 16 March 1784, *Papers of Thomas Jefferson*, 7:39.
12. James Madison to Thomas Jefferson, 25 December 1797, *Papers of Thomas Jefferson*, 29:591; Jefferson to Madison, 3 January 1798, *Papers of Thomas Jefferson*, 30:9.
13. Thomas Jefferson to James Madison, 17 November 1798, in *Papers of Thomas Jefferson*, 30:579–80.
14. James Madison to Thomas Jefferson, 11 December 1798, in *Papers of Thomas Jefferson*, 30:603.
15. Thomas Jefferson to James Madison, 8 January 1797, in *Papers of Thomas Jefferson*, 29:255.
16. James Madison to Thomas Jefferson, 12 March 1798, in *Papers of Thomas Jefferson*, 30:175.
17. Neil H. Cogan, *The Complete Bill of Rights: The Drafts, Debates, Sources, and Origins*, 2nd ed. (New York: Oxford University Press, 2015), 165.

18. Cogan, *Complete Bill of Rights* 163.
19. James Madison to Thomas Jefferson, 17 October 1788, in *James Madison: Writings*, 420.
20. Thomas Jefferson to James Madison, 15 March 1789, in *Papers of Thomas Jefferson*, 14:659–60.
21. Gaillard Hunt, *The Life of James Madison* (New York: Doubleday, Page, 1902), 162–65; Richard Labunski, *James Madison and the Struggle for the Bill of Rights* (Oxford: Oxford University Press, 2006), 134–36, 139–40, 148–52.
22. James Madison to Thomas Mann Randolph, 13 January 1789, in Founders Online, National Archives, http://founders.archives.gov/documents/Madison/01-11-02-0304 (last update: September 29, 2015), source: *The Papers of James Madison, 7 March 1788-1 March 1789*, ed. Robert A. Rutland and Charles F. Hobson (Charlottesville: University Press of Virginia, 1977), 11:415–41.
23. Labunski, *James Madison and the Struggle for the Bill of Rights*, 162–66, 174.
24. Speech of James Madison, June 8, 1789, *Annals of Congress*, 1st Cong., 1st Sess., 449, 451, 456, 457.
25. James Madison to Richard Peters, 19 August 1789, in *James Madison: Writings*, 471.
26. Speech of James Madison, August 17, 1789, *Annals of Congress*, 1st Cong., 1st Sess., 783–84; Leonard W. Levy, *Emergence of a Free Press (New York: Oxford University Press, 1985)*, 262.
27. Levy, *Emergence*, 257–66.
28. Thomas Jefferson to Edward Carrington, 16 January 1787, in Cogan, *Complete Bill of Rights*, 178.
29. Thomas Jefferson to James Madison, 31 July 1788, in *Papers of Thomas Jefferson*, 13:442; Jefferson to Madison, 28 August 1789, *Papers of Thomas Jefferson*, 15:367.
30. *The Documentary History of the Ratification of the Constitution*, ed. John P. Kaminski, Gaspare J. Saladino et al. (Charlottesville: University of Virginia Press, 2009), 2:455.
31. David A. Anderson, "The Origins of the Press Clause," *UCLA L. Rev.* 30 (February 1983): 455, 476, 480; Levy, *Emergence*, 257–63.
32. Anderson, "Origins of the Press Clause," 483–86; Levy, *Emergence*, 262–67.
33. Levy, *Emergence*, 198–201.
34. Gordon S. Wood, *The Creation of the American Republic, 1776–1787* (Chapel Hill: University of North Carolina Press, 1969), 282–283; David M. Rabban, "The Ahistorical Historian: Leonard Levy on Freedom of Expression in Early American History," review of *Emergence of a Free Press*, by Leonard Levy, *Stanford Law Review* 37, no. 3 (February 1985): 828–829.
35. "Continental Congress to the Inhabitants of the Province of Quebec," 26 October 1774, in *The Founders' Constitution*, ed. Philip B. Kurland and Ralph Lerner (Indianapolis: Liberty Fund, 1987), 442
36. *Independent Gazetteer*, 14 December 1782.
37. *Independent Gazetteer*, 9 November 1782; Levy, *Emergence*, 208–9.
38. Cogan, *Complete Bill of Rights*, 173.
39. Cogan, *Complete Bill of Rights*, 167.
40. Hortensius, *An Essay on the Liberty of the Press* (Richmond, 1803), 25.
41. Hunt, *Writings of James Madison*, 5:380–381.
42. See Burt Neuborne, *Madison's Music: On Reading the First Amendment* (New York: New Press, 2015), 17–20.
43. Speech of James Madison, 15 August 1789, *Annals of Congress*, 1st Cong., 1st Sess., 766.
44. Speech of James Madison, 27 November 1794, *Annals of Congress*, 3rd Cong., 2nd Sess., 934.
45. Ron Chernow, *Washington: A Life* (New York: Penguin, 2010), 671.
46. Chernow, *Washington*, 677, 680.
47. Thomas Jefferson to James Madison, 7 July 1793, in *Papers of Thomas Jefferson*, 26: 444.

48. Alexander Hamilton and James Madison, *The Pacificus-Helvidius Debates of 1793–1794: Toward the Completion of the American Founding,* ed. Morton J. Frisch (Indianapolis: Liberty Fund, 2007), http://oll.libertyfund.org/titles/1910, accessed February 26, 2015.

49. Chernow, *Washington,* 671, 686; Brookhiser, *James Madison,* 101–2.

50. *The Argus, or Greenleaf's New Daily Advertiser,* 26 December 1795.

51. Joseph J. Ellis, *His Excellency: George Washington* (New York: Alfred A. Knopf, 2006), 227–29.

52. Ellis, *His Excellency,* 231.

53. George Washington to Thomas Jefferson, 6 July 1796, in *Papers of Thomas Jefferson,* 29:142.

54. John C. Miller, *Crisis in Freedom: The Alien and Sedition Acts* (Boston: Little, Brown, 1951), 4.

55. Miller, *Crisis in Freedom,* 4–5.

56. *The Works of Alexander Hamilton,* Federal ed., ed. Henry Cabot Lodge (New York: G. P. Putnam's Sons, 1904), 6:301.

57. Miller, *Crisis in Freedom,* 4–7.

58. *Works of Alexander Hamilton,* 6:302.

59. Miller, *Crisis in Freedom,* 6.

60. Miller, *Crisis in Freedom,* 11–12.

61. Miller, *Crisis in Freedom,* 40–43.

62. *Works of Alexander Hamilton,* 6:318–19.

63. Miller, *Crisis in Freedom,* 26–29.

64. Miller, *Crisis in Freedom,* 211, 214, 216.

65. Miller, *Crisis in Freedom,* 55.

66. *Columbian Centinel,* 29 December 1798.

67. Thomas Jefferson to John Taylor, 4 June 1798, in *Papers of Thomas Jefferson,* 30:389.

68. John Adams to Tristam Dalton, 19 January 1797, in *The Magazine of American History* (New York: Historical Publication Co., 1883), 9:470.

69. John Adams, "To the Mayor, Aldermen, and Citizens of the City of Philadelphia," April 1798, in *The Works of John Adams* (Boston: Little, Brown, 1854), 9:182.

70. John Adams, "To the Inhabitants of the Town of Braintree, Massachusetts," in *Works of John Adams,* 9:197.

71. Abigail Adams to Mary Cranch, 26 April 1798 and 26 May 1798, in *New Letters of Abigail Adams 1788–1801,* ed. Stewart Mitchell (Boston: Houghton Mifflin, 1947), 165, 179. See also David McCullough, *John Adams* (New York: Simon & Schuster, 2001), 506–507.

72. James Madison to Thomas Jefferson, 20 May 1798, *Papers of Thomas Jefferson,* 30:359.

73. Thomas Jefferson to James Madison, 7 June 1798, in *Papers of Thomas Jefferson,* 30:393.

74. Henry Tazewell to James Madison, 28 June 1798, in *Papers of James Madison,* ed. David B. Mattern, J. C. A. Stagg, Jeanne K. Cross, and Susan Holbrook Perdue (Charlottesville: University Press of Virginia, 1991), 17:159.

75. "The Alien Act—An Act Respecting Alien Enemies," Avalon Project, Yale Law School, http://avalon.law.yale.edu/18th_century/alien.asp, accessed March 12, 2015; "The Sedition Act—An Act in Addition to the Act, Entitled 'An Act for the Punishment of Certain Crimes Against the United States," Avalon Project, Yale Law School, http://avalon.law.yale.edu/18th_century/sedact.asp, accessed March 12 2015.

76. Phillip I. Blumberg, *Repressive Jurisprudence in the Early American Republic: The First Amendment and the Legacy of English Law* (Cambridge: Cambridge University Press, 2010), 85–86.

77. Speech of Robert Goodloe Harper, 5 July 1798, in *Annals of Congress,* 5th Cong., 2nd Sess., 2102.

78. Speech of Harrison Otis, 10 July 1798, in *Annals of Congress,* 5th Cong., 2nd Sess., 2148, 2150.

79. Speech of Albert Gallatin, 5 July 1798, in *Annals of Congress,* 5th Cong., 2nd Sess., 2110.

80.	Speech of John Nicholas, 10 July 1798, in *Annals of Congress*, 5th Cong., 2nd Sess., 2144.

81.	Speech of Albert Gallatin, 10 July 1798, in *Annals of Congress*, 5th Cong., 2nd Sess., 2158–2160.

82.	Speech of Albert Gallatin, 10 July 1798, in *Annals of Congress*, 5th Cong., 2nd Sess., 2162.

83.	Speech of Albert Gallatin, 5 July 1798, in *Annals of Congress*, 5th Cong., 2nd Sess., 2110.

84.	Speech of Albert Gallatin, 10 July 1798, in *Annals of Congress*, 5th Cong., 2nd Sess, 2162.

85.	Speech of Albert Gallatin, 10 July 1798, in *Annals of Congress*, 2162.

86.	Speech of Albert Gallatin, 10 July 1798, in *Annals of Congress*, 2141.

87.	For my account of Madison's and Jefferson's secret work in opposition to the Alien and Sedition Acts, including the Virginia and Kentucky Resolutions, I relied on the excellent scholarship of Koch and Ammon, "Virginia and Kentucky Resolutions," 145–76; and *Papers of Thomas Jefferson*, 30:529–35.

88.	Thomas Jefferson to Thomas Mann Randolph, 9 May 1798, and Jefferson to James Madison, 26 April 1798, in *Papers of Thomas Jefferson*, 30:341, 300.

89.	Barbara B. Oberg, "A New Republican Order, Letter by Letter," *Journal of the Early Republic* 25, no. 1 (Spring 2005): 7–9.

90.	Thomas Jefferson to James Monroe, 23 January 1799, in *Papers of Thomas Jefferson*, 30:636.

91.	Wilson Cary Nicholas to Thomas Jefferson, 4 October 1798, in *Papers of Thomas Jefferson*, 30:556.

92.	Thomas Jefferson to Wilson Cary Nicholas, 5 October 1798, in *Papers of Thomas Jefferson*, 30:557; Koch and Ammon, "Virginia and Kentucky Resolutions," 155–56.

93.	Koch and Ammon, "Virginia and Kentucky Resolutions," 156–58; *Papers of Thomas Jefferson*, 30:529–56.

94.	Thomas Jefferson to James Madison, 17 November 1798, in *Papers of Thomas Jefferson*, 30:580.

95.	Koch and Ammon, "Virginia and Kentucky Resolutions," 160–61; *Madison: Writings*, 589–91.

96.	Thomas Jefferson to Wilson Cary Nicholas, 29 November 1798, in *Papers of Thomas Jefferson*, 30:590; Koch and Ammon, "Virginia and Kentucky Resolutions," 158–60; Madison, *Madison: Writings*, 589–91.

97.	Joseph McGraw, "'To Secure These Rights': Virginia Republicans on the Strategies of Political Opposition, 1788–1800," *Virginia Magazine of History and Biography* 91, no. 1 (January 1983): 62–63; Frank Maloy Anderson, "Contemporary Opinion of the Virginia and Kentucky Resolutions I," *American Historical Review* 5, no. 1 (October 1899): 46; Thomas Jefferson to Edmund Pendleton, 14 February 1799, in *Papers of Thomas Jefferson*, 31:36–37.

98.	Jeffrey L. Pasley, *The Tyranny of Printers: Newspaper Politics in the Early American Republic* (Charlottesville: University of Virginia Press, 2001), 105–7.

99.	Richard N. Rosenfeld, *American Aurora: A Democratic-Republican Returns. The Suppressed History of Our Nation's Beginnings and the Heroic Newspaper That Tried to Report It* (New York: St. Martin's Press, 1997), 44. For a discussion of Cobbett, see Eric Burns, *Infamous Scribblers: The Founding Fathers and the Rowdy Beginnings of American Journalism* (New York: Public Affairs, 2006), 338–50.

100.	*American*, 18 May 1799; Pasley, *Tyranny of Printers*, 161–62.

101.	Thomas Jefferson to James Madison, 5 February 1799, in *Papers of Thomas Jefferson*, 31:10.

102.	Pasley, *Tyranny of Printers*, 405, 407–9; Miller, *Crisis in Freedom*, 222–23.

103.	*Aurora*, 28 August 1798; Pasley, *Tyranny of Printers*, 129–30.

104.	Thomas Jefferson to James Monroe, 19 October 1823, in *The Works of Thomas Jefferson*, ed. Paul Leicester Ford (New York: G.P. Putnam's Sons, 1905), 12:316.

105.	Thomas Jefferson to Thomas Mann Randolph, 9 May 1798 and note, in *Papers of Thomas Jefferson*, 30:341–42; Eugene Volokh, "Symbolic Expression and the Original Meaning of the First Amendment," *Georgetown Law Journal* 97 (2009): 1061.

106. John Adams to Abigail Adams, 28 April 1777, in *Familiar Letters of John Adams and His Wife Abigail Adams During the Revolution*, ed. Charles Francis Adams (New York: Hurd and Houghton, 1876), 267–68.

107. *Porcupine's Gazette,* 15 August 1798; *Massachusetts Mercury,* 19 June 1798.

108. *Aurora,* 18 July 1798.

109. *Independent Chronicle,* 3 December to 6 December 1798; *Bee,* 12 December 1798; *Gazette of the United States,* 17 December 1798.

110. Abigail Adams to Mary Cranch, 11 December 1799, in *New Letters of Abigail Adams 1788–1801,* 221.

111. Geoffrey R. Stone, *Perilous Times: Free Speech in Wartime* (New York: W. W. Norton, 2004), 46.

112. I drew from several excellent accounts of the prosecution of David Brown: James Morton Smith, "The Federalist 'Saints' versus 'The Devil of Sedition': The Liberty Pole Cases of Dedham, Massachusetts," 1798–1799, *New England Quarterly* 28, no. 2 (June 1955): 198–215; Frank Maloy Anderson, "The Enforcement of the Alien and Sedition Laws," *Annual Report of the American Historical Association for the Year 1912* (Washington, DC: American Historical Association, 1914), 122–25.

113. *Columbian Centinel* (Boston), 7 November 1798.

114. Stone, *Perilous Times,* 58.

115. Blumberg, *Repressive Jurisprudence,* 101–2; Stone, *Perilous Times,* 48, 63.

116. Blumberg, *Repressive Jurisprudence,* 102–5; Thomas Jefferson to James Madison, 3 November 1798, in *Papers of Thomas Jefferson,* 30:576.

117. Blumberg, *Repressive Jurisprudence,* 126; Miller, *Crisis in Freedom,* 136–37.

118. Blumberg, *Repressive Jurisprudence,* 125–31.

119. Blumberg, *Repressive Jurisprudence,* 77–79.

120. Frank Maloy Anderson, "Contemporary Opinion of the Virginia and Kentucky Resolutions," *American Historical Review* 5, no. 2 (December 1899): 241; Miller, *Crisis in Freedom,* 177.

121. Frank Maloy Anderson, "Contemporary Opinion of the Virginia and Kentucky Resolutions I," *American Historical Review* 5, no. 1 (October 1899): 45–61.

122. Anderson, "Contemporary Opinion," 235.

123. Thomas Jefferson to James Madison, 23 August 1799, in *Papers of Thomas Jefferson,* 31:173–74; Koch and Ammon, "Virginia and Kentucky Resolutions," 165–67.

124. Koch and Ammon, "Virginia and Kentucky Resolutions," 165–70; Thomas Jefferson to Wilson Cary Nicholas, 5 September 1799, in *Papers of Thomas Jefferson,* 31:178–79.

125. James Madison to Thomas Jefferson, 29 December 1799, in *Papers of Thomas Jefferson,* 31:278.

126. Speech of John Nicholas, *Annals of Congress,* 5th Cong., 3rd Sess., 25 February 1799, 3003–14.

127. *Madison: Writings,* 612.

128. *Madison: Writings,* 645–46.

129. *Madison: Writings,* 652, 655.

130. *Madison: Writings,* 648–50.

131. *Madison: Writings,* 654.

132. *Madison: Writings,* 647.

133. *Madison: Writings,* 647.

134. *Madison: Writings,* 647–48.

135. *Madison: Writings,* 647.

136. For a comprehensive account of freedom of expression during wartime, see Geoffrey R. Stone, *Perilous Times: Free Speech in Wartime, From the Sedition Act of 1798 to the War on Terrorism* (New York: W. W. Norton, 2004).

137. Anderson, "Origins of the Press Clause," 455, 516–19.

138. *Papers of Thomas Jefferson,* 33:134–35.

139. *Papers of Thomas Jefferson,* 33:148–52.

140. Miller, *Crisis in Freedom*, 227.
141. Abigail Adams to Thomas Jefferson, 1 July 1804; Jefferson to Abigail Adams, 22 July 1804, in *Adams-Jefferson Letters*, 273, 275.
142. *Boston Patriot*, 7 June 1809.

AFTERWORD

1. Thomas Jefferson to Levi Lincoln, 24 March 1802, in *The Papers of Thomas Jefferson*, ed. Barbara B. Oberg (Princeton, NJ: Princeton University Press, 2010), 37:119.
2. Dumas Malone, *Jefferson the President: First Term, 1801–1805* (Charlottesville: University of Virginia Press, 1970), 4:208–18.
3. *Jefferson: Writings*, ed. Merrill D. Peterson (New York: Library of America, 1984), 521.
4. Thomas Jefferson to Abigail Adams, 11 September 1804, in *The Adams-Jefferson Letters: The Complete Correspondence Between Thomas Jefferson & Abigail & John Adams*, ed. Lester J. Cappon (Chapel Hill: University of North Carolina Press, 1959), 279.
5. Second Inaugural Address, March 4, 1805, *Jefferson: Writings*, 521.
6. Phillip I. Blumberg, *Repressive Jurisprudence in the Early American Republic: The First Amendment and the Legacy of English Law* (Cambridge: Cambridge University Press, 2010), 149–50.
7. Blumberg, *Repressive Jurisprudence*, 204–9.
8. Thomas McKean to Thomas Jefferson, 7 February 1803, in *Papers of Thomas Jefferson*, 39:473; Jefferson to McKean, 19 February 1803, *Papers of Thomas Jefferson*, 39:553; Blumberg, *Repressive Jurisprudence*, 151, 185, 192–94.
9. Blumberg, *Repressive Jurisprudence*, 151, 156–166.
10. *James Madison: Writings*, ed. Jack N. Rakove (New York: Library of America, 1999), 651.
11. See generally Leonard W. Levy, *Jefferson and Civil Liberties: The Darker Side* (Chicago: Ivan R. Dee, 1989).
12. Thomas Jefferson to John Norvell, 11 June 1807, in *Memoirs, Correspondence, and Private Papers of Thomas Jefferson*, ed. Thomas Jefferson Randolph (London: Henry Colburn and Richard Bentley, 1829), 4:82–83.
13. Thomas Jefferson to Walter Jones, 2 January 1814, in Founders Online, National Archives, http://founders.archives.gov/documents/Jefferson/03-07-02-0052 (last update: 2015-03-20), source: *The Papers of Thomas Jefferson*, Retirement Series, vol. 7, *28 November 1813 to 30 September 1814*, ed. J. Jefferson Looney (Princeton, NJ: Princeton University Press, 2010), 100–104.
14. *Boston Patriot*, 7 June 1809.
15. John Adams to Thomas Jefferson, 24 August 1815, in *Adams-Jefferson Letters*, 455.
16. Thomas Jefferson to Monsieur A. Coray, 31 October 1823, in *The Writings of Thomas Jefferson*, ed. H. A. Washington (Washington, DC: Taylor & Maury, 1854), 7:323–24.
17. *Madison: Writings*, 647.
18. Gitlow v. New York, 268 U.S. 652 at 666 (1925).
19. Patterson v. Colorado, 205 U.S. 454 at 462 (1907).
20. Schenck v. United States, 249 U.S. 47 (1919).
21. For an excellent discussion of Holmes's change in his views of freedom of speech, see Thomas Healy, *The Great Dissent: How Oliver Wendell Holmes Changed His Mind—and Changed the History of Free Speech in America* (New York: Metropolitan Books, 2013).
22. Abrams v. United States, 250 U.S. 616 at 630 (1919) (Holmes, J., dissenting).
23. *Abrams*, 250 U.S. at 628, 630 (1919) (Holmes, J., dissenting).
24. *Abrams*, 250 U.S. at 630 (Holmes, J., dissenting).
25. For a discussion of Justice Brandeis's concurring opinion, see Vincent Blasi, "The First Amendment and the Ideal of Civic Courage: The Brandeis Opinion in Whitney v. California," *Wm. & Mary L. Rev.* 29 (summer 1988): 653.
26. Blasi, "Civic Courage," 671–72.
27. Whitney v. California, 274 U.S. 357 at 375–77 (1927) (Brandeis, J., concurring).

28. *Whitney,* 274 U.S. at 375–77 (Brandeis, J., concurring).
29. New York Times v. Sullivan, 376 U.S. 254 at 279–80.
30. *New York Times,* 376 U.S. at 276.
31. *New York Times,* 376 U.S. at 273.
32. *New York Times,* 376 U.S. at 270.
33. *New York Times,* 376 U.S. at 275.

INDEX